SHAW 24

The Annual of Bernard Shaw Studies

Volume Twenty-Four

DIONYSIAN SHAW

Edited by

Michel W. Pharand

The Pennsylvania State University Press
University Park, Pennsylvania

ISBN 0-271-02519-0 ISSN 0741-5842
Copyright © 2004 The Pennsylvania State University
All rights reserved
Printed in the United States of America

It is the policy of The Pennsylvania State University Press to use acid-free paper for the first printing of all clothbound books. Publications on uncoated stock satisfy the minimum requirements of American National Standard for Information Sciences—Permanence of Paper for Printed Library Materials. ANSI Z39.48–1992.

Note to contributors and subscribers. *SHAW*'s perspective is Bernard Shaw and his milieu—its personalities, works, relevance to his age and ours. As "his life, work, and friends"—the subtitle to a biography of G.B.S.—indicates, it is impossible to study the life, thought, and work of a major literary figure in a vacuum. Issues and people, economics, politics, religion, theater, and literature and journalism—the entirety of the two half-centuries the life of G.B.S. spanned was his assumed province. *SHAW*, published annually, welcomes articles that either explicitly or implicitly add to or alter our understanding of Shaw and his milieu. Address all manuscript contributions (in 3 copies with, if possible, an additional copy on disk) to Gale K. Larson, *SHAW* Editor, Department of English, California State University, Northridge, CA 91330. Subscription correspondence should be addressed to *SHAW*, Penn State University Press, Suite C, 820 North University Drive, University Park, PA 16802. Unsolicited manuscripts are welcomed but will be returned only if return postage is provided. In matters of style *SHAW* recommends the *MLA Style Sheet* and advises referring to recent volumes of the *SHAW*. Please indicate the format and program used on the disk copy.

CONTENTS

NOTICES

Request for Manuscripts: Future *SHAW* Volumes

The *SHAW* editorial board seeks article-length manuscripts for coming volumes. ***SHAW 25***, while a general volume, will be devoted primarily to selected papers presented at the Sarasota Shaw Conference, 17–21 March 2004; it will also include other papers approved prior to the conference. ***SHAW 26*** will be a special issue focusing on new critical—for example, postmodern and postcolonial—approaches to Shaw and his works. Mary-Ann K. Crawford and Heidi Holder will be the guest editors for that issue. Manuscript submissions for *SHAW 26* should be sent to MaryAnn K. Crawford, 1111 S. Lincoln Road, Mt. Pleasant, MI. 48858. The deadline for submissions is early 2005. Direct inquiries to crawf1ma@cmich.edu.

SHAW 27 will be a general volume open to articles on any subject related to the life, times, and works of G. Bernard Shaw. ***SHAW 28*** will be another special issue. Its theme will be "Shaw and War," with Lagretta Lenker as guest editor. Contributors to *SHAW 27* and *SHAW 28* should submit manuscripts by early 2006 and 2007 to Gale K. Larson, *SHAW* Editor, Department of English, California State University, Northridge, CA 91330-8248. Inquiries should be directed to glarson@csun.edu.

All contributors should submit manuscripts in three copies and on disk and follow the MLA Style Sheet format (referring to recent *SHAW* volumes is advisable). Please indicate the format and program used on the disk copy and include postage for return of material.

Request for Manuscripts: The University of Florida Bernard Shaw Series

The University Press of Florida is pleased to offer the Florida Bernard Shaw Series. Under the editorship of R. F. Dietrich of the University of

South Florida, the Shaw Series seeks book-length manuscripts on any sub-ject relating to the life, career, and times of G. Bernard Shaw. The work of younger scholars or scholars with new critical paradigms will be especially welcome. Direct inquiries or manuscripts to Professor Dietrich, English Department, University of South Florida, Tampa, FL 33620, to Acquisi-tions Editor Susan Fernandez, University Press of Florida, 15 NW 15th St., Gainesville, FL 32611-2079, to the Shaw Series website http://www.upf .com/se-shaw.shtml, or to the Bernard Shaw Society Web site: http:// chuma.cas.usf.edu/~dietrich/shawsociety.html

42nd Annual Shaw Festival 2004 Season, Niagara-on-the-Lake 8 April–November 27 2004

The Shaw Festival will feature two plays by Bernard Shaw: *Pygmalion* (8 April to 27 November) and *Man and Superman* (26 June to 9 October). The playbill also includes *The Importance of Being Earnest* (Oscar Wilde), *Three Men on a Horse* (John Cecil Holm and George Abbott), *Pal Joey* (music by Richard Rodgers, lyrics by Lorenz Hart, book by John O'Hara), *Ah, Wilderness!* (Eugene O'Neill), *Rutherford and Son* (Githa Sowerby), *Waiting for the Parade* (John Murrell), *The Tinker's Wedding* (J. M. Synge), *Nothing Sacred* (George F. Walker), *Harlequinade* (Terrence Rattigan), *Floyd Collins* (music and lyrics by Adam Guettel, book by Tina Landau).

For further information, write to Shaw Festival, Post Office Box 774, Niagara-on-the-Lake, Ontario, Canada, L0S 1J0; or call 1-800-511-SHAW [7429] or 905-468-2153; website: www.shawfest.sympathico.ca

International Shaw Society

The International Shaw Society has begun its life by hosting a Shaw con-ference, "GBS by the Bay," at the University of South Florida's Sarasota campus, 17–21 March 2004, and a Shaw Symposium at the Shaw Festival in Ontario, 23–25 July 2004. Planning is under way for a regular schedule of conferences and symposia at sites around the world relevant to Shaw Studies, notice of which will occur on the ISS Web site at http://chuma.cas .usf.edu/~dietrich/iss.htm. Notice will also be found there of travel grants and the like. ISS president Richard F. Dietrich, Professor Emeritus at the University of South Florida, reports that membership is building fast in this exciting new venture, and those interested in becoming members should fill out and mail in the form found at http://chuma.cas.usf.edu/ ~dietrich/iss-membership-form.htm.

Michel W. Pharand

INTRODUCTION: DIONYSIAN SHAW

Nothing is rarer in nature than a man who, on accepting a new idea, proceeds to overhaul his old ideas and see how many of them must be scrapped to make logical room for the newcomer.

—Bernard Shaw, in *The Irish Statesman* (15 September 1923)

Although the above epigraph could stand as a motto for all of Shaw's writings—letters and speeches, reviews and articles, prefaces and plays—it is especially pertinent to the topic of this volume. Self-appointed iconoclast and gadfly, Shaw devoted his life to exhorting the world to overhaul its old ideas about love and sex, romance and sentimentality, marriage and divorce, prostitution and venereal disease, asceticism and adultery, obscenity and censorship, birth control and sexual education. "It has now become axiomatic," writes Bruce R. Smith in "Premodern Sexualities," that "sexuality . . . is a function of ideology, a social construction that varies according to time and place. Different cultures at different moments in history construct sexuality differently."[1] Shaw's cultures— Victorian, fin-de-siècle, Edwardian, and Modern—were usually resistant to his attempts at a sexual overhaul. And with reason: the messenger could be abrasive, the message was often shocking.

That message, simply put, was the need for the honest and realistic expression, on stage and in life, of what Shaw termed "sexual emotion." One must underscore the crucial importance of this idea for Shaw. In his 1909 preface to a volume of Eugène Brieux's plays in English—one of them translated by Charlotte Shaw—he affirmed that "sex is a necessary and healthy instinct; and its nurture and education is one of the most important uses of all art; and, for the present at all events, the chief use of the theatre."[2] A few years later, in a letter published on 8 November 1913 in *The Times*, Shaw answered the Bishop of Kensington, who had complained two days earlier about the "atmosphere of immorality and the suggestion of vice" of a recent show (which he had not seen) at the Palace

Theatre: "Now a Bishop who goes into a theatre and declares that the performances there must not suggest sexual emotion is in the position of a playwright going into a church and declaring that the services there must not suggest religious emotion. The suggestion, gratification, and education of sexual emotion is one of the main uses and glories of the theatre."[3] Shaw reiterated the idea with equal panache in his 1929 address to the third International Congress of the World League for Sexual Reform: "I am an expert in sex appeal. What I mean is that I am a playwright. I am connected with the theatre. The theatre is continually occupied with sex appeal. . . . One very important function of the theatre in society is to educate the audience in matters of sex."[4] In all of these pronouncements, not unexpectedly, arch-realist G.B.S. is concerned with the notion of education, or rather reeducation: with making "logical room" for the new idea that the theater should not shy away from "sexual emotion."

Of course by now, the case for Shavian "sex appeal" has been argued often—but primarily by Shaviophiles. Bernard Dukore has shown that "Shaw's plays contain more sexuality than is generally credited," and that "sensuality, red corpuscles, or 'lower centres' [Shaw's term] permeate Shavian drama."[5] Jacques Barzun believes that in all of the plays up to *Heartbreak House,* "it is sexuality that is at work, with or without the glow of romance," and that plays such as *Widowers' Houses, Mrs Warren's Profession,* and *The Philanderer* "are suffused with eroticism."[6] And Louis Crompton refutes the charge that Shaw writes "sexless drama" by asserting that "no playwright has dramatized the naked power of the sex impulse more directly or with more respect."[7]

With these endorsements in mind, how do we explain Shaw's ongoing reputation with the public at large as the high priest of dramatic dryness? And, according to Shaw, not only the general public, as he pointed out in 1907, exasperated at being misconstrued as an asexual idea-monger: "I am almost ruined by the persistence with which the critics declare that I am a bloodless, passionless intellectual machine."[8] And when we do find a red-blooded, passionate G.B.S.-in-L.U.V., he is drawn in caricature: starry-eyed Shaw penning love letters—on a bed with frilly pillows and teddy bears—on the cover of a book of quotations entitled *A Curmudgeon's Garden of Love* (1989). Now this might lead the common reader to assume that Shaw was an Über-Curmudgeon in matters of the heart—and of the boudoir. Yet look at some of these sobering (but apparently curmudgeonly) quips: "We are not taught to think decently on sex subjects, and consequently we have no language for them except indecent language"; "We throw the whole drudgery of creation on one sex, and then imply that no female of any delicacy would initiate any effort in that direction."[9] This is precisely the kind of über-realism that made Shaw such an Eminent (anti-)Victorian.

There are a number of reasons for the general public's obliviousness to Shavian sex appeal. First of all, today's audiences are shocked or scandalized by very little, inured as they have become to everything from physical violence and verbal profanity to sexual themes and full nudity on the stage. Second, much of the eroticism and sex-play in Shaw's works are lost in translation, so to speak: on the stage, the "sexual emotion" is frequently embedded in (and at times diluted by) language, while on the page, the erotic or sexual nuances in an actor's tone of voice or body language are absent. Third, Shaw consciously fashioned and constantly publicized his ascetic persona, his public image as a man whose lifestyle eschewed the "lower centers" in favor of higher, cerebral ones: no alcohol, no meat, no sex. It is little wonder, therefore, that in the public imagination, the name "Bernard Shaw" still conjures up "too many words" or "too much self-denial."

It is high time, therefore, to make the pendulum swing from Ascetic Shaw, that workaholic intellectual teetotaler and vegetarian of a well-known celibate marriage—a late one, mind you, and not entirely celibate—to what I will call Dionysian Shaw: a man possessed by the notion that all progress stems from the erotic impulse (more on that topic shortly).

Shaw as a latter-day Dionysus? No far-fetched fable he. That feisty, subversive deity from Asia Minor, newly arrived in Greece, at odds with established authority and seeking to convert others to his personal religion, prefigures our newly exiled Dubliner in England and his dogged attempts at toppling false idols—from Parisian "well-made" plays to London's commercial prostitution industry. In addition, just as Dionysus held sway over the Bacchae (the female worshipers whom he entranced, literally, into slavish devotion), Shaw too had his women admirers—many of them.

And quite a few did more than admire. Although neither a rake nor a libertine, Shaw had numerous attachments and flirtations—some epistolary, others of varying degrees of intimacy—beginning in his late twenties and continuing into his seventies, many of them well documented. A partial list of Shaw's *liaisons*—a few bordering on *dangereuses*—would include (alphabetically) Janet Achurch, Eleanor Marx Aveling, Annie Besant, Mrs. Patrick Campbell, Florence Farr, Alice Lockett, May Morris, Edith Nesbit, Bertha Newcombe, Jenny Patterson, Ellen Terry, and Molly Tompkins. And Shaw, ever the arch-realist, was careful not to confound the erotic or romantic impulse with long-term companionship. As he famously explained to his biographer Frank Harris in a letter of 24 June 1930 (reprinted in this volume), "I found sex hopeless as a basis for permanent relations, and never dreamt of marriage in connection with it."[10] Hence, among other reasons, his celibate marriage.

On the other hand, while marital domesticity excluded sex, Shaw viewed the erotic impulse, at least in theory, as a means of transcending reality itself: "I liked sexual intercourse," he told Harris, "because of its amazing power of producing a celestial flood of emotion and exaltation of existence which, however momentary, gave me a sample of what may one day be the normal state of being for mankind in intellectual ecstasy."[11] In the 1949 published version of Shaw's letter, "sexual intercourse" became "sexual experience," and the last part was altered to read "the normal condition of conscious intellectual activity."[12] This theoretical mental orgasm, fanciful as it is, forms the logical nexus of both the Ascetic and Dionysian sides of Shaw's psyche.

Jacques Barzun claims that sexuality is at work in most of Shaw's plays. But what *kind* of sexuality, and just how does it work? Shaw's hypothetical *frisson intellectuel* finds its way into *Man and Superman* (complete by 1902), where the transmutation of physical into mental energy—leading to "intellectual ecstasy"—informs Shaw's well-known theory of Creative Evolution. In the "Don Juan in Hell" scene—where hell is the self-gratification of the voluptuary (pure pleasure) and heaven the struggle of the artist-philosopher toward higher consciousness (pure thought)—Don Juan, one of literature's archetypal playboys, subverts our expectations by leaving the trivial pursuit of romance for the transcendent business of intellectual work. Juan, who erstwhile thrived on the erotic impulse, is now the mouthpiece for Shaw's evolutionist credo and an apologist of the Life Force. "I tell you that as long as I can conceive something better than myself I cannot be easy unless I am striving to bring it into existence or clearing the way for it. That is the law of my life. That is the working within me of Life's incessant aspiration to higher organization, wider, deeper, intenser self-consciousness, and clearer self-understanding."[13]

But these lofty metaphysical goals are impossible to attain without a female principle. In *Man and Superman,* the agents of the Life Force are Doña Ana and her earthly counterpart, Ann Whitefield, and the force that draws Jack Tanner to Ann and Juan to Ana is clearly sexual: when Doña Ana cries out, "A father! a father for the Superman!" she beckons an impregnator, not a husband. As Shaw told Harris, "the relation between the parties in copulation is not a personal relation. It can be irresistibly desired and rapturously executed between persons who could not endure one another for a day in any other relation."[14] The Life Force may serve a metaphysical end, but its nature is primarily instinctual and its catalyst sexual. Sex, via its helpmate, love, is only a means to an end: to engender a Superman.

From the foregoing, the function of what Shaw calls "sexual emotion" seems clear enough. But how does it work? Shaw offers an explanation in *You Never Can Tell* (1895–96), where he treats the erotic impulse in a less abstract and philosophical manner than he would six years later in "Don

Juan in Hell." When Gloria asks her suitor, the appropriately named Valentine, for a "scientific explanation of those fancies that cross us occasionally," he replies: "It's a curiously helpless sensation: isn't it? As if Nature . . . were suddenly lifting her great hand to take us . . . by the scruffs of our little necks, and use us, in spite of ourselves, for her own purposes, in her own way." When Valentine asks her if she sees what she has "set to work" in his imagination, Gloria replies, "I hope you are not going to be so foolish—so vulgar—as to say love." To which Valentine replies: "No, no, no, no, no. Not love: we know better than that. Let's call it chemistry." Gloria replies, *"contemptuously"*: "Nonsense!"[15]

Nonsense? A century later, we too know better than that, and today's Valentine would have responded: "Let's call it pheromones." Whatever the name, Shaw's message is simple: our "fancies" are nothing more than Nature working to perfect the species. J. L. Wisenthal sums up the process eloquently: "We must liberate sex so that it can fulfill its natural heavenly function as a servant of the Life Force."[16]

Two weeks before the première of "Don Juan in Hell," Shaw delivered a lay sermon, entitled "The New Theology," in which he spoke of the Life Force as "struggling through us to become an actual organized existence, enjoying what to many of us is the greatest conceivable ecstasy, the ecstasy of a brain."[17] We have come a long way from "sexual emotion" to "intellectual ecstasy" and "the ecstasy of a brain"—or have we? Is it not simply a matter of transposing sexual emotion onto a cerebral plane—and beyond? In 1913, the Bishop of Everywhere replied to the Bishop of Kensington by asserting the convergence of our erotic and spiritual natures: "There is a voluptuous side to religious ecstasy and a religious side to voluptuous ecstasy," wrote Shaw, claiming that one is no less sacred than the other, and concluding that there is a "divine grace which grows in the soil of our sex instincts when they are not deliberately perverted and poisoned."[18] Many of Shaw's works can be read both as an assertion of an erotico-spiritual convergence and as a warning against perverting and poisoning our sex instincts.

Moreover, Shaw's erotico-intellectual convergence, his great hope for future "intellectual ecstasy," was prescient, according to Dr. Geoffrey Miller's *The Mating Mind* (2000), his treatise on sexual selection and the evolution of human intellect. The idea has emerged of late among evolutionary psychologists and psychoneuroendocrinologists that intelligence exists as a beneficial by-product of the sexual selection of mates who have more evolved brains. The theory is that historically humans have instinctively chosen mates based on better brains, leading to even better brains with each generation—an idea that would have delighted Shaw. When he spoke of "the ecstasy of a brain," Shaw was seeing far into the future to a point where the true nature of desire is revealed not as a primitive scent trail for immunological compatibility, but as a trail further expanded in our reckoning to include the importance of the mind in how we have emerged as a species and—of crucial importance to Shaw—how we yet stand to evolve. Shaw was literally seeing, as he put it himself, as far as thought can reach.[19]

Only H. L. Mencken, a bona fide Über-Curmudgeon, and Shaw are allotted their own sections in *A Curmudgeon's Garden of Love:* "Mencken on Marriage" and "Shaw's Garden of Love." Surely a brave soul willing to comb the acres of Shavian word-forest would be able to gather enough pronouncements for "Shaw's Garden of Sex"? A brief sampler:

Shaw on dramatic censorship (1907): "Now it is futile to plead that the stage is not the proper place for the representation and discussion of illegal operations, incest and venereal disease. If the stage is the proper place for the exhibition and discussion of seduction, adultery, promiscuity and prostitution, it must be thrown open to all the consequences of these things, or it will demoralize the nation."[20]

Shaw on sexual education (1944): "Instruction in sex is as important as instruction in food; yet not only are our adolescents not taught the physiology of sex, but never warned that the strongest sexual attraction may exist between persons so incompatible in tastes and capacities that they could not endure living together for a week much less a lifetime. . . . They are not even warned against venereal disease, and, when they contract it, can only raise the old cry, 'Why was I not told?'"[21]

Shaw on homosexuality (1928): "My own experience of life has led me—as a matter of necessary practice—to treat sexual life as outside the scope of the judgments we have to pass on one another for social, political, and business purposes. . . . I should say that a dishonored cheque is a safer index to character for worldly purposes than inversion."[22]

Shaw on marriage (1908): "The Reformation left marriage where it was: a curious mixture of commercial sex slavery, early Christian sex abhorrence, and later Christian sex sanctification."[23]

Shaw on divorce (1908): "There is no magic in marriage. If there were, married couples would never desire to separate. But they do. And when they do, it is simple slavery to compel them to remain together. . . . Divorce, in fact, is not the destruction of marriage, but the first condition of its maintenance."[24]

Shaw on the language of love (1903): "The moment a woman applies to a man a word that fits a child, it is all over: she is in love with him."[25]

Shaw on sex in literature (1925): "A pornographic novelist is one who exploits the sexual instinct as a prostitute does. A legitimate sex novel elucidates it or brings out its poetry, tragedy, or comedy."[26]

Shaw on the sex in his plays (1928): "When I began, [William] Archer complained that my plays were reeking with sex. Now that I am ending you complain that I am an anchorite. Women have never complained of me either way. *They* know that I know what I am talking about."[27]

Shaw on the inconsistency of the sex instinct (1916): "We become mad in pursuit of sex: we become equally mad in the persecution of that pursuit. Unless we gratify our desire the race is lost: unless we restrain it we destroy ourselves."[28]

Seventy-six-year-old Shaw on anatomy: "Have you noticed the projection [of my ears] at the base of my skull? Catherine the Great had the same. I'm told it means excessive sexual development."[29]

And so on—and on, and on. The word-forest is vast and dense, as befits a long life devoted to shocking people into overhauling their old ideas. But now Shaw's own life and work are being overhauled, and when the topic is sex, the findings range from amusing to absurd. A 1964 article in the *British Journal of Medical Psychology*—by that winning combination, a professor of Psychiatry and a professor of English—concludes: "It is probable, therefore, that Shaw was impotent, a latent homosexual, and that his relish of teasing and hurting women was the expression of a pre-oedipal oral-sadistic and especially anal fixation."[30] In 1982, Arnold Silver claimed that the sheer length of *Man and Superman* "allows [Shaw] to turn his secret defeat as a lover into a public victory as a writer, answering the threat to his masculinity by erecting [!] his biggest single dramatic structure to date, seeking almost to humiliate the men in his audience by his brilliance and to make the woman half fantasize whether such a formidable man as this dramatist might not father for them a Superman."[31] In 1983, Arthur Ganz deconstructed a scene in *Widowers' Houses*, between Blanche Sartorius and her parlormaid, to suggest "a long-standing sado-masochistic relationship with overtones of barely repressed lesbianism."[32] By 1996, Sally Peters had found enough evidence, detailed in her book *Bernard Shaw: The Ascent of the Superman,* to claim that Shaw "accepted responsibility for the genius and homosexuality that he believed to be his twin inheritance."[33] And in his 2002–3 revival of *Mrs Warren's Profession* at the Strand Theatre in London, director Sir Peter Hall cast Praed as an outright homosexual.[34]

Would Shaw have been amused? Not bloody likely. "I was not impotent," he told the prurient Frank Harris in 1930, "I was not sterile; I was not homosexual," adding in the 1949 published version: "Sexual experience seemed a natural appetite, and its satisfaction a completion of human experience necessary for fully qualified authorship."[35] What is likely, however, is that interpretations of Shaw's life and works will continue to push the envelope. Hopefully the essays in this special volume of *SHAW* will provide challenging, if not controversial, perspectives on Shaw's Dionysian side. At the very least, they bear witness to Shaw's perennial interest in the erotic impulse and to the importance of that impulse in his personal, ideological, and creative pursuits.

Patricia M. Carter's interview with Peter Tompkins reveals the true nature of Shaw's long romance with Molly Tompkins. Dan H. Laurence offers a glimpse into the Victorian underworld that was the backdrop to Kitty Warren's profession, while L. W. Conolly traces the Lord Chamberlain's persistent efforts—eventually overcome—to keep Kitty off the English stage. Margery M. Morgan elucidates the attempts by Shaw and some of his contemporaries to reform social perceptions of so-called "abnormal" sexual behavior. Bernard F. Dukore demonstrates how directors and actors might enrich our understanding of *Major Barbara* by a more realistic treatment of the play's erotic aspects ("the lower centers") on stage. Continuing the Freudian theme developed in previous issues of *SHAW*, Rodelle Weintraub unveils the symbolic subtext of *Man and Superman*. Peter Gahan explores the textual and sexual transgression of *Jitta's Atonement*. And on a more platonic note—enter Apollonian Shaw—Stanley Weintraub examines Shaw's relationship with the unconventional artist Kathleen Scott; Karma Wiltonen analyses Saint Joan as a New Woman resisting the Victorian sex-gender system; and Harold Pagliaro explores the occurrences of "truncated love" in *Candida* and *Heartbreak House*.

Finally, we reprint Shaw's famous letter of 24 June 1930 to his *soi-disant* biographer, Frank Harris, in which he summarizes, in a manner both explicit and allusive, his own sexual history, and where he expounds with habitual verve on romance, sex, women, and marriage. Bernard Shaw, as always, gets the last word.

Notes

1. Bruce R. Smith, "Premodern Sexualities," *PMLA* 115, no. 3 (2000): 320.

2. Shaw, "Brieux: A Preface," in *Bernard Shaw: The Drama Observed. Volume III: 1897–1911*, ed. Bernard F. Dukore (University Park: Penn State University Press, 1993), p. 1219.

3. Shaw, letter in *The Times* (8 November 1913), in *Bernard Shaw: Agitations, Letters to the Press, 1875–1950*, ed. Dan H. Laurence and James Rambeau (New York: Frederick Ungar, 1985), p. 154. The controversy closed down the production and sent its star, actress Gaby Deslys, back to France. For details, see Allan Chappelow, *Shaw—"The Chucker-Out"* (London: George Allen & Unwin, 1969), pp. 61–77.

4. Quoted in *Platform and Pulpit*, ed. Dan H. Laurence (New York: Hill & Wang, 1961), p. 201.

5. Bernard F. Dukore, "G.B.S. and S.E.X.: Sexuality and Sexual Equality," *Essays in Theatre* 6, no. 2 (May 1988): 86–87.

6. Jacques Barzun, "Eros, Priapos, and Shaw," in *The Play and Its Critic: Essays of Eric Bentley*, ed. Michael Bertin (New York: University Press of America, 1986), pp. 70–71.

7. Louis Crompton, *Shaw the Dramatist* (Lincoln: University of Nebraska Press, 1969), pp. 88–89.

8. Shaw, letter in *Pall Mall Gazette* (2 December 1907), in *Bernard Shaw: Agitations*, p. 111.

9. Quoted in *A Curmudgeon's Garden of Love*, ed. Jon Winokur (New York: NAL, 1989), pp. 164 and 196.

10. Shaw, letter to Frank Harris, 24 June 1930, in *Bernard Shaw: Collected Letters IV, 1926–1950*, ed. Dan. H. Laurence (New York: Viking, 1988), p. 192. Henceforth "letter to Harris."

11. Shaw, letter to Harris, p. 192.

12. Shaw, *Sixteen Self Sketches* (New York: Dodd, Mead, 1949), p. 115.

13. Shaw, *Man and Superman*, in *Bernard Shaw: Collected Plays with Their Prefaces*, editorial supervisor Dan H. Laurence (7 volumes, 1970–74), vol. 2 (New York: Dodd, Mead, 1975), pp. 679–80.

14. Shaw, letter to Harris, p. 190.

15. Shaw, *You Never Can Tell*, in *Bernard Shaw: Collected Plays with Their Prefaces*, vol. 1, p. 737.

16. J. L. Wisenthal, *The Marriage of Contraries: Bernard Shaw's Middle Plays* (Cambridge, Mass.: Harvard University Press, 1974), p. 54.

17. Shaw, "The New Theology," in *The Portable Shaw*, ed. Stanley Weintraub (Harmondsworth: Penguin, 1983), p. 314.

18. Shaw, letter in *The Times* (8 November 1913), in *Bernard Shaw: Agitations*, p. 154. Shaw refers to himself as "a sort of unofficial Bishop of Everywhere" in the Afterword to *The Adventures of the Black Girl in Her Search for God* (New York: Dodd, Mead, 1933), p. 63.

19. See Geoffrey F. Miller, *The Mating Mind: How Sexual Choice Shaped the Evolution of Human Nature* (New York: Doubleday/Heinemann, 2000). I am grateful to my wife, Ginger, for these insights and observations.

20. Shaw, letter in *The Nation* (16 November 1907), in *Bernard Shaw: Agitations*, p. 100.

21. Shaw, *Everybody's Political What's What?* (London: Constable, 1944), p. 176.

22. Shaw, letter to the very reverend Albert Victor Baillie, 24 November 1928, in *Bernard Shaw: Collected Letters IV, 1926–1950*, ed. Dan H. Laurence (New York: Viking, 1988), p. 119.

23. Shaw, Preface to *Getting Married*, in *Bernard Shaw: Collected Plays with Their Prefaces*, vol. 3, p. 535. According to Louis Crompton, "[E. Belfort] Bax's ideas on marriage had a direct influence on *Getting Married*, especially his [1908] essay *The Legal Subjection of Men*." Bax believed that "birth control, homosexuality, and divorce should be treated, not in terms of traditional taboos or Comtian moral idealism, but simply from the point of view of good social policy" (*Shaw the Dramatist*, p. 237, n. 4). One should also keep in mind that Bax is the author of *Fraud and Feminism* (1913).

24. Shaw, Preface to *Getting Married*, pp. 519–20 and 522.

25. Shaw, letter to Siegfried Trebitsch, 7 January 1903, in *Bernard Shaw's Letters to Siegfried Trebitsch*, ed. Samuel A. Weiss (Stanford: Stanford University Press, 1986), p. 33.

26. Shaw, *Table-Talk of G.B.S.* (London: Chapman and Hall, 1925), p. 125.

27. Shaw, letter to St. John Ervine, 12 March 1928, in *Collected Letters IV, 1926–1950*, p. 97 (Shaw's emphasis).

28. Shaw, "Inconsistency of the Sex Instinct," in the Preface to *Androcles and the Lion*, in *The Complete Prefaces*, vol. 2, ed. Dan H. Laurence and Daniel J. Leary (Allen Lane, The Penguin Press, 1995), p. 216. See the indexes of all three volumes for further references.

29. Shaw in conversation with artist Dame Laura Knight, during a portrait sitting; quoted in *Bernard Shaw on the London Art Scene, 1886–1950*, ed. Stanley Weintraub (University Park: Penn State University Press, 1989), p. 40.

30. Lisbeth J. Sachs and Bernard H. Stern, "Bernard Shaw and His Women," *British Journal of Medical Psychology* 37 (1964): 349.

31. Arthur Sliver, *Bernard Shaw: The Darker Side* (Stanford: Stanford University Press, 1982), p. 175.

32. Arthur Ganz, *George Bernard Shaw* (New York: Grove, 1983), p. 86.

33. Sally Peters, *Bernard Shaw: The Ascent of the Superman* (New Haven: Yale University Press), p. 259.

34. My thanks to L. W. Conolly for this information. See his essay in this issue.

35. Shaw, *Sixteen Self Sketches,* p. 113. On Shaw's use of "sterile" and Michael Holroyd's contention that Jenny Patterson, Shaw's first sexual partner, miscarried Shaw's child in mid-1886, see Fred D. Crawford, "Review Essay," *Victorian Review* (Spring 1989): 10–11.

Patricia M. Carter

"UNTIL IT WAS HISTORICAL": A LETTER AND AN INTERVIEW

There can hardly be any surprise in the revelation of Bernard Shaw's sexual intimacy with Molly Tompkins. After all, Charles A. Berst built the case for such a revelation with a masterful analysis in his 1986 article (in *SHAW* 5, 81–114), "Passion at Lake Maggiore: Shaw, Molly Tompkins, and Italy, 1921–1950." Although the particulars of that sexual intimacy have thus far been preserved by Peter Tompkins in the privacy of his personal archives, he has now agreed to the publication in full of Shaw's 4 December 1944 letter, a document previously published without three crucial sentences.

Peter Tompkins (b. 1919), OSS hero, noted writer, war correspondent, film director, ecologist, and environmentalist, knighted by the President of Italy in 1998, is the only child of Molly (1898–1960) and Laurence (1897–1972) Tompkins. He discussed with me his reasons for censoring the important letter—published as such in *To a Young Actress: The Letters of Bernard Shaw to Molly Tompkins* (1960)—during a long videotaped interview at his farm in Shepherdstown, West Virginia, in January 1999. He believed the candor of that letter might have hurt his father, still alive at the time of the publication of *To a Young Actress*. Now, more than forty years later, there is no need to protect his father's sensibilities. When asked if his father knew of the depth of Molly's feeling for Shaw, Peter replied, "Oh, I'm sure he did, but I don't think he necessarily wanted to. As they say, a husband is usually the last to know. I thought I'd wait until it was historical, and no longer upsetting to anybody."

According to Berst, Molly and Italy thus amount to a significant chapter in Shaw's life, one "casting a tantalizing light on his old age" (*SHAW* 5, 82) since Shaw was in his sixties in the late 1920s. Shaw was eighty-eight years old in 1944, when he wrote so honestly to Molly on 4 December, more than twenty years beyond their first meeting and at least sixteen years beyond their affair. But there seems no reason to question Shaw's memory, especially in light of the information in the books Peter Tompkins has written about his mother and Shaw. Berst himself drew some of his conclusions from both *To a Young Actress* (1960) and *Shaw and Molly Tompkins: In Their Own Words* (1961), the latter written (from Molly's reports) and edited by Peter Tompkins. Michael Holroyd also used these volumes, as well as personal correspondence with their author, to write about the relationship between Shaw and Molly.

As Berst points out, however, Shaw's other biographers—Archibald Henderson, Frank Harris, Hesketh Pearson, William Irvine, and St. John Ervine—make no mention of Molly Tompkins (*SHAW 5*, 82). The reason is simple: before the publication of *Shaw and Molly Tompkins,* there was no source of information about their relationship. Of course, by the time he was researching his three-volume biography, Holroyd had access to that book and was able to write about Molly Tompkins as a significant person in Shaw's life. Now, in order to make the record of their relationship even more accurate, Peter Tompkins would like to see the 4 December 1944 letter published in full, in an authoritative journal, so that it may become part of Shavian history.

Although that letter does confirm the physical union between Molly Tompkins and Bernard Shaw, it does not answer all the questions surrounding their relationship. Shaw was not forthcoming about the length or depth of their affair, nor did he admit to it in writing until after the death of his wife, Charlotte. His stance was perhaps not significantly different from that of other powerful or famous men of his time, or of any time, whose affairs were or are accepted, but usually not made public until much later, if at all. But was their affair entirely private? Who else might have known? Those friends in or near the Lake Maggiore region are likely to have known, or at least suspected. What written record do we have from those neighbors on the lake? And of what real import was or is the affair? Perhaps the very desire for secrecy is a measure of the intensity—if not the importance and significance to Shaw—of the relationship. Although Shaw did write in candor to Molly about the affair, did he ever write to anyone else about it? Was it kept secret not only from Charlotte and (perhaps) from Laurence Tompkins, but also from everyone? Can we dismiss it as too familiar to be interesting—that of a powerful, older man with an ambitious young woman more than willing to serve his needs? That Molly was unfaithful to her husband and had lovers is known. But is there some aspect of Shaw's attitude toward his own sexuality in evidence here, in the long-withheld secret of his love for Molly, a passion that spanned nearly thirty years and concluded only with his death in 1950?

Do not Shaw's very words—"Did any of your numerous Sunday husbands, of whom I was certainly the most eminent, really fail to respect Laurence's conjugal rights as we did. I hope he never suspected me of 'betraying' him. Yet no consummated love affair ever gave me greater pleasure"—written in 1944 and published here for the first time, lend themselves to various interpretations? And given Shaw's acknowledged genius for drama and his profundity of thought, how much interest should we take in his sexual attitudes? Will we deepen our understanding of that genius in learning more about the nature of his feelings during the affair?

Certainly rereading the letters in *To a Young Actress* helps to answer some of these questions. After the first years of affectionate teasing and advice, there is hardly a letter without some mention of Laurence and Peter. Until the summer of 1926, there is only one mention of Laurence, and then he appears regularly. Peter is called "baby" earlier in that year, in a letter of 27 January, and is mentioned intermittently from that time onward. What change occurred to make Shaw more conscious of Molly's husband and son? A letter of 12 January 1927 suggests that Molly will have some good memories to counter those of her recent trip to Athens, Georgia. Shaw refers specifically to the "shelter at Ayot," in all probability an allusion to a sexual encounter—perhaps their first, as Molly later reported to her son. Precisely when the physical affair began remains uncertain, but the change in Shaw's letters, that is, the inclusion of Laurence and Peter in many of them, suggests a change in the relationship, a more intimate, less patronizing attitude toward his "Mollimia." And although Shaw kept the physical nature of his relationship with Molly a secret, he never tried to isolate her from her husband or her son. The familial affection evidenced in his letters seems to support Peter Tompkins's idea that there was a certain feeling of tenderness among Shaw, Molly, and Laurence.

Now that we are aware of the true, consummated nature of the affair, one must also note that it was more than a mere secret sexual union. It was a relationship that developed and evolved, one in which Molly, whom Shaw always perceived as more than a naïve, self-educated beauty, in a real sense became a life companion. In 1945, following Shaw's vehement refusal of her request to visit him at Ayot, Molly articulated what their relationship had meant to her and why she wanted to see him: "I wanted a short visit with somebody I could be as free as air with. . . . Somebody that you loved and who in spite of themselves loved you. And with the solid background of that love behind you (and me) there would be no awkward snags because one or the other of us wanted (or thought they did) something the other didn't have to give" (quoted in *SHAW 5*, 111–12).

Today, thanks to Peter Tompkins and the restoration of those telling lines from Shaw's 1944 letter, we can linger again—this time without surmise or speculation—over "that love" and the secret romance of the Italian summers of Molly Tompkins and Bernard Shaw.

An Interview with Peter Tompkins

CARTER: I'd like you to talk a bit about your mother, in a general way, or specific way, whichever you please. Let my questions come from what you say.

TOMPKINS: She was a strange creature. The problem with being that beautiful is that . . . it has its downside, you go up and down. Of course, to me it was great to walk down the street with her, because everybody looked at her and admired her. And everybody loved her, so that I sort of basked a bit in that radiance.

CARTER: Your earliest memories of her are that she attracted attention.

TOMPKINS: Oh yes. She was really stunningly beautiful.

CARTER: From the pictures she was, I can see that.

TOMPKINS: But, the thing about the pictures is, they don't tell it all. Anytime a camera came near her, pop, she went right out of her body and just left the dead body there. It was when she was animated that she was beautiful . . . it was her animation, really, that attracted. And if she got into a mood, her looks changed completely, and could she be moody.

CARTER: The other important person in your life, for my purposes, was George Bernard Shaw. You know, Shaw was born more than 140 years ago, and there aren't many people left who knew him. John Wardrop worked for him. I believe he's still in Washington.[1] Not very many people, though, unless they were very, very young when they knew him, which you were. You had a relationship of twenty-eight or thirty years with him, at least, because you were two years old when you first met him. I don't suppose you remember anything about that.

TOMPKINS: I was three. I remember him coming to the house, very definite.

CARTER: In London?

TOMPKINS: In London, yes . . . two things about the memory. One is that he sided with me against my mother, and that was a big help. It was extraordinary at that age to have somebody side with you. And the other thing I remember: I climbed up onto his lap and his tweeds were itchy . . . on my legs . . . I had shorts on, bare legs, and I'll never forget the scratchiness of his tweeds. But his taking my side was memorable.

CARTER: Why do you suppose that was?

TOMPKINS: Because I asked him to tell me a story. And he said, "I told your mother all the stories I know. You tell me one." So I said, "I have a pigeon." And my mother said, "No, you don't," because I had a wooden pigeon. I said, "Yes, I do, I have a real pigeon." And she said, "No, no, that's a story." And Shaw said "Molly," in a gentle admonishing tone, "don't accuse a child of lying. You never know." So I got off his lap and I went upstairs. A pigeon had flown in my window with a broken wing, or with a hurt wing. So I brought it down, and I said, "Here's the pigeon," and I went back onto his lap. He stroked it and said, "You see Molly?"

CARTER: That's remarkable. We know very little about his feeling toward children.

TOMPKINS: He was very sweet.

CARTER: Well, he didn't want any children.

TOMPKINS: Yes, he did.

CARTER: Ostensibly they chose . . .

TOMPKINS: He very badly wanted a child.

CARTER: Ah! How do you know that?

TOMPKINS: Because I know the conversation. I know the circumstances, and it got aborted, so he was miserable.

CARTER: Tell me about that.

TOMPKINS: All in due course. As a result, he really took care of me, all the way to adulthood. Paid for my education.

CARTER: I have heard that.

TOMPKINS: He was constantly interested in my welfare and whereabouts, and what I was doing, constantly saying, tell Peter to do this, tell Peter not to do that.

CARTER: So in some sense you were his son.

TOMPKINS: In a spiritual sense; the other one, the aborted one, would have been his son.

CARTER: He and his wife did not have children.

TOMPKINS: I don't think they ever consummated the marriage.

CARTER: No, but they chose . . .

TOMPKINS: Everybody says they didn't, but who's to know? Yet I don't think so, because I think Charlotte really didn't want any part of it.

CARTER: Do you remember meeting her?

TOMPKINS: Oh sure, they came . . . they came every day to the island, to swim, and would stay for supper.

CARTER: That was the summer of '27 and '28, yes. But not in London. Did you ever see Charlotte in London, when Shaw had first met your mother, in the early '20s?

TOMPKINS: I'm trying to remember, perhaps at my mother's *vernissage* [gallery preview], but I don't remember seeing her. It was a very funny

180

AYOT. ST LAWRENCE , WELWYN, HERTS.   4,WHITEHALL COURT, LONDON, S.W.1.
STATION: WHEATHAMPSTEAD,L.& N.E.R. 2¼ MILES.   4th December 1944.
TELEGRAMS: BERNARD SHAW, CODICOTE.
TELEPHONE: CODICOTE 18.

My dear Molly
          I see you are settled at the same address﹏﹏ as that of two ﹏﹏
years ago, which I took to be a temporary one. Had I known, I should
have written.
          I am a vecchio, nearly eightyeight and a half. I am also a widower.
Charlotte died on the 12th September 1943. I was not in the least ﹏﹏﹏﹏
grieved ; for she was only a year younger than I ﹏﹏ ; and it was ﹏﹏﹏﹏﹏
time for her to go; but I was very deeply moved. Her four years illness
thretened to have a dreadful end ; but a miracle intervened : she ﹏﹏﹏﹏
suddenly became younger than I had ﹏ever seen her, and incredibly beatiful, and had thirty hours of ecstatic happiness before she ceased to
 breathe. It was an unspeakable relief. The hundreds of letters I got
commiserating on my sorrow were all wrong. My health improved so much
that I realized that if she had lived another year she would have killed
us all, though we were not conscious of the strain while we were under
it. I have had some offers of marriage since, as ﹏﹏﹏ I am rather a ﹏﹏
catch now, having only a few years at most to live (quite probably a
few days) and my widow would be well provided for, though the terrific
war taxation and the death duties on Charlotte's property have left me
far poorer than people think.
          But I have had enough of marriage, and am quite happy alone, as I
inherit from my mother a great capacity for solitude in my own company.
          Tell Pete that to hoard money, or waste it, or neglect to invest ﹏
it in socially useful enterprises, or at least lend it to the State,
is a crime of which no Socialist, and certainly no Shavian, should be
guilty.
          You do not tell me what Pete has been doing or where he has been ﹏
all this time. Nor do you say a word about Lawrence's work. He should
be recognized by this time as a very cosiderable scupltor. By the way, I
hope you two have had the good sense to marry again : that silly divoree
will make no end of trouble later on unless it is got rid of.
Do you keep your good looks still ? I can still write a bit, with

Fig. 1. Letter from Bernard Shaw to Molly Tompkins, 4 December 1944, as
published by Peter Tompkins with passage edited out. Courtesy Peter Tompkins
(Copyright Peter Tompkins).

181

many blots and blunders (the book has _at least_ thirty howlers in it) ;
and I can produce a stage effect of being sound in wind and limb, though
a trifle deafish ; but really I am not very majestic ruin.
    All your Italian friends must be starving now that we have "libe-
rated them. Albert and Madelon, now no longer man and wife, are well
out of it. Cecil Lewis has married again, this time apparently quite
comfortably. He has managed to hold on to his villa on the Maggiore,
but is too busy in the Air Force to go back there yet.
    What is Pete's branch of military service. A spell of discipline
in corporative service is probably good for him after his anarchical
bringing-up. _Or has he been a war correspondent all the time ? How old is he now?_
    Let me have a line occasionally. We can write more freely now that
Charlotte can never read our letters. As I have more letters in a
week than I can deal with in a month dont mind if my answers are belated.
Take care they dont get out of your hands. Journalists regard letters by
me as their natural prey.
    Goodnight. I can now go to bed as late as I please.

G. Bernard Shaw

never I could bring myself to write a line that would hurt her; but now I can write anything.

IYOT. GT LAWRENCE, WELWYN, HERTS.
STATION: WHEATHAMPSTEAD, L.&N.E.R. 2¼ MILES.
TELEGRAMS: BERNARD SHAW, CODICOTE.
TELEPHONE: CODICOTE 18.

4,WHITEHALL COURT, LONDON, S.W.1.

4th December 1944.

My dear Molly

I see you are settled at the same address ~~that~~ as that of two ~~that~~ years ago, which I took to be a temporary one. Had I known, I should have written.

I am a vecchio, nearly eightyeight and a half. I am also a widower. Charlotte died on the 12th September 1943. I was not in the least ~~worried~~ grieved ; for she was only a year younger than I ~~am~~ ; and it w s ~~useless~~ time for her to go; but I was very deeply moved. Her four years illness thretened to have a dreadful end ; but a miracle intervened : she ~~suddenly~~ suddenly became younger than I had ~~never~~ seen her, and incredibly beatiful, and had thirty hours oi ecstatic happiness before she ceased to breathe. It was an unspeakable relief. The hundreds of letters I got commiserating on my sorrow were all wrong. My health improved so much that I realized that if she had lived another year she would have killed us all, though we were not conscious of the strain while we were under it. I have had some offers of marriage since, as ~~though~~ I am rather a ~~good~~ catch now, having only a few years at most to live (quite probably a few days) and my widow would be well provided for, though the terrific war taxation and the death duties on Charlotte's property have left me far poorer than people think.

But I have had enough of marriage, and am quite happy alone, as I inherit from my mother a great capacity for solitude in my own company.

Tell Pete that to hoard money, or waste it, or neglect to invest it in socially useful enterprises, or at least lend it to the State, is a crime of which no Socialist, and certainly no Shavian, should be guilty.

You do not tell me what Pete has been doing or where he has been all this time. Nor do you say a word about Lawrence's work. He should be recognized by this time as a very cosiderable scupltor. By the way, I hope you two have had the good sense to marry again : that silly divorce will make no end of trouble later on unless it is got rid of. Did any of your numerous Sunday husbands, of whom I was certainly the most eminent, really fail to respect Lawrence's conjugal rights as we did. I hope he never suspected me betraying" him. *Yet no unconsummated love affair ever gave me greater pleasure.*

Do you keep your good looks still ? I can still write a bit, with

many blots and blunders (the book has ~~almost~~ _at least_ thirty howlers in it) ;
and I can produce a stage effect of being sound in wind and limb, thoug
a trifle deafish ; but really a not very majestic ruin.
  All your Italian friends must be starving now that we have "liberated them. Albert and Madelon, now no longer man and wife, are well
out of it. Cecil Lewis has married again, this time apparently quite
comfortably. He has managed to hold on to his villa on the Maggiore,
but is too busy in the Air Force to go back there yet.
  What is Pete's branch of military service. A spell of discipline
in corporative service is probably good for him after his anarchical
bringing-up. _Or has he been a war correspondent all the time? How old is he now?_
  Let me have a line occasionally. We can write more freely now that
Charlotte can never read our letters. As I have more letters in a
week than I can deal with in a month dont mind if my answers are belate
Take care they dont get out of your hands. Journalists regard letters b:
me as their natural prey.
  Goodnight. I can now go to bed as late as I please.

                                        G. Bernard Shaw

never I could bring myself to write a line that would hurt her; but now I can write anything.

Fig. 3. Molly Tompkins with her Roman Hunter "Bigio." Courtesy Peter Tompkins (Copyright Peter Tompkins).

Fig. 4. Molly Tompkins with her son, Peter, on Lake Maggiore. Courtesy Peter Tompkins (Copyright Peter Tompkins).

Fig. 5. Shaw with Molly and Laurence Tompkins at a Fabian summer school, 1922. Courtesy Peter Tompkins (Copyright Peter Tompkins).

Fig. 6. Laurence Tompkins and Shaw on the Isolino. Courtesy Peter Tompkins (Copyright Peter Tompkins).

Fig. 7. Molly Tompkins as she appeared in London in 1924 in a play by Leon M. Lion, *Lord o' Creation,* at the Savoy a week before Shaw's *Saint Joan* opened at the New Theatre with Sybil Thorndike. Courtesy Peter Tompkins (Copyright Peter Tompkins).

scene, because Shaw had done everything he could with Messrs. Brown and Phillips, who were the gallery owners, to prevent the show, because he hadn't yet seen her paintings. He had only seen a few photos of her show in Milan. He hadn't seen the beauty of her palette.

CARTER: That was in her art show, in 1929, pictures brought from Italy, right?

TOMPKINS: At the Leicester Gallery, thirty-five large canvases. When they were taking them out of the packing cases, Shaw went down on his hands and knees and exclaimed, "Look Charlotte, she *can* paint, this is great." Then they got out one of the Adam and Eve, and Messrs. Brown and Phillips said, "Oh, we can't exhibit those." The reason they were shocked was because my mother would have her Adam and the Eve pose together naked; when Adam got a little excited my mother just painted what she saw. And Shaw said, "You must show them. Her nudes are much too important." But they said no, because when D. H. Lawrence's drawings were exhibited, it closed down the gallery, they were so sexually explicit.[2] Then my mother remembered that when Titian was an old man he would go down at night and paint over his day's canvas, and his students knew that he was going to ruin a great painting. So they substituted olive oil for his siccative. That way the paint wouldn't harden and the next day they could use olive oil to wipe it out again. To show her nudes, my mother painted fig leaves or a branch over Adam's offending anatomy, so she could later remove the paint.

CARTER: They were exhibited that way.

TOMPKINS: Yes, and when the critics were invited, I was allowed to come up from school and heard my mother say to Shaw, "Now you be quiet. You talk all the time. This is my day." His face fell a bit, and he cheered up again, saying, "Is it all right if I talk, but I talk only about you," which he did. When the press came he went from painting to painting, and stopped at the one called "The Road to Baveno." To him, who stayed at Stresa, it was the road to Baveno. To my mother, who stayed in Baveno, it was the road to Stresa. In any case, it was where, I think, they first made love; certainly one of the places they made love.

CARTER: Do you know where that picture is now?

TOMPKINS: Somebody bought it.

CARTER: It was . . . Shaw bought it first, I think.

TOMPKINS: No, Shaw bought the one of the island. I don't know whether he bought the other. He should have!

CARTER: So he approved of your mother as a painter.

TOMPKINS: She was a big success. All the critics were very good. They said her unusually developed color sense rivaled Van Gogh. Only the *Daily Herald* mentioned the nudity of Adam, saying, "When women paint the nude, they go in for it more thoroughly than men."

CARTER: Getting back to Shaw's first ideas for her . . .

TOMPKINS: At first, he didn't believe in her painting, and wrote her letters . . . two page long letters saying, "I did not tell you to stop painting. I told you to work away at it for ten years." It was the same sort of advice he gave her about acting.

CARTER: Did you ever see your mother on the stage?

TOMPKINS: Oh yes.

CARTER: And what was your impression of her ability as an actress?

TOMPKINS: There was no way at that time for me to judge . . . I was five years old.

CARTER: But you do remember seeing her on the stage.

TOMPKINS: Oh yes.

CARTER: *Shaw and Molly Tompkins,* which you have written, describes her disappointments with the theater, and I think says that people, maybe Shaw, but more people than Shaw, wanted her to do comedy, and it wasn't in her to do comedy.

TOMPKINS: No, she was strictly a tragedian.

CARTER: That's an interesting aspect of her, though. She really was a profound nature, wasn't she?

TOMPKINS: Absolutely. All she wanted to do was play Lady Macbeth.

CARTER: Did she ever play Lady Macbeth?

TOMPKINS: No, unfortunately . . . she got this job as leading lady in Plymouth, in a repertory theater, where she had to play endless Restoration comedies such as *She Stoops to Conqueror* and *School for Scandal.* And in these, because of the Plymouth audience, she was supposed to be gay and twitter and laugh and go about, and she couldn't do it. It wasn't in her nature.

CARTER: She didn't have ingénue looks, either. She had better looks than that. Wouldn't you say? Did Hollywood ever have any interest in her?

TOMPKINS: No, in those days . . . after Plymouth she went on the stage in London, where she played, for instance, in Oscar Wilde's *A Woman of No Importance.* That was a role that suited her. She was fine. Shaw came to see her in one of these roles, when she was in one theater, and he was doing *Methuselah* in another theater. He came from rehearsal to see her, and then when the reviews came out in *The Times,* my mother got a good review, and Shaw got a pan.

CARTER: A terrible review.

TOMPKINS: Which is ridiculous.

CARTER: We've been talking about her time in London, which is the time Shaw first knew your mother, but then there was a whole other period, in which they were together, and those were the summers in Italy. Could you tell me about that, from your memory and your knowledge of them.

TOMPKINS: He and Charlotte would stay at the Hotel Regina in Stresa, which was across the lake from us. And every morning about ten, they would come over in this big old motorboat, and swim or go on picnics, or go over to Albert Coates's to swim; he had a house across the lake, the other way.[3] And then they'd usually stay for dinner. It's in that period, also, that my mother and Shaw would go off in the car, to look at the endless Sacri Monti, or Stations of the Cross, which are very pretty in Lombardy. And what with one thing and another, they would stop and make love. My mother has described these scenes to me, so I know about them: but if you read the letters carefully, you'll find he mentions all the places that they made love. And it's amusing, because in one of them he wrote: "You will have the Cerro passage at noon, and even the shelter at Ayot to steal into your sleep from the past. You will then wake up puzzled but pleased, and say but what on earth was the name of that old man?"

CARTER: Your mother talked to you freely about Shaw when you were grown . . .

TOMPKINS: Even when I was young, even when I was in my teens, I knew more or less what her love life was like, because she had separated from my father. And they both always treated me like a grown-up, in sexual matters in particular. In my father's studio I was always privy to watching the naked models, and at the island people swam naked, sex was openly discussed in front of me, with all the emotional jealousies and ins and outs, you know, it just happened all around me.

CARTER: So it was not hard for you to think that your mother and Shaw were involved, and were having . . .

TOMPKINS: No, people don't understand. Shaw makes a deliberate distinction between marriage and sexuality. And because of his belief in the Life Force, he wanted a child with my mother, and he joked with her just as he had with Mrs. Patrick Campbell, who said, "Joey, wouldn't it be great, to have a child," and he retorted, "What if it has your brains and my looks?" My mother knew the story perfectly well. His idea was to create a superman wherever possible, out of beautiful women and intelligent men. His ideas of eugenics at the time were a part of it. When [Michael] Holroyd called me up and asked me, "how do you explain this extraordinary love affair between your mother and Shaw that lasted thirty years," I said, "It's obviously a past life association." They obviously recognized each other immediately, because their relationship in this life stuck all the way to the end. I mean, his last letter, in his ninety-fourth year, finally says, "You must cast me off like a laddered stocking and get another correspondent." Then, he added, "Don't think however that I am forgetting you." And in 1949 the last postcard he sent her showed him standing at the gate of Shaw's Corner, inscribed, "The Old Man at his gate / As he was in fortyeight / And is still at ninety three / Awaiting news of thee, Molly Bawn." Otherwise, he wrote to her all the time in between. He had this notion of being a Sunday husband, that a woman needed, in order to keep her matrimonial sex life alive, a Sunday husband, maybe husbands. Just as Ibsen changed the world's look at women, Shaw's was even more advanced in his way. Love and marriage are two quite different things, and my mother loved my father all her life. He was the man in her life. But Shaw was another and very important part of her life. And she used to say, "Why isn't there room for both? I'm not taking anything away from my husband, because I have this other association." And if you think about it, it's puzzling: as you relive life to life, what do you do when you remeet one, two, three, or four old friends, former lovers—what do you do? Are you going to stop loving someone you've loved? Is there not room? I mean, do you stop loving your second or your third child because you love your first? It's absurd. You love all your children. So why can't you love all your lovers?

CARTER: Well, I think Shaw would be applauding you for saying all of that.

TOMPKINS: It is I who am applauding him.

CARTER: Did your mother feel that she had known Shaw before?

TOMPKINS: I don't think my mother thought in those terms. You must realize that past lives really came into style in the '60s and '70s. I think L. Ron Hubbard revived the notion with his regressions, with his multiple regressions into past lives.[4] But I remember that Shaw wrote to my mother at one point when she was in Rome, "Rome is a magical place. When I was there I knew I had been there in a former existence." So there are many things about Shaw that are odd. Certainly when he gets into religion, he's often on two sides of the same question . . . and he can be against both sides. He shifts. But his mind is always open. For instance, he doesn't believe that Joan's voices could be real. He gives Joan the line that God speaks to her through her imagination.

CARTER: That's not what Joan believes.

TOMPKINS: No, nor what I believe. She was burned because she actually saw the nature spirits which had to be exorcized by the local priest.
[. . .]

CARTER: Tell me what your mother thought about Shaw's mind. Was she taken with his theories and his bravery intellectually?

TOMPKINS: So taken that they [my parents] came all the way over from America to find him, "to put him on the map!" Because in Georgia, where they lived, he was virtually unknown. In that Bible Belt atmosphere, he was relegated to a mountebank or a terror.

CARTER: And a bit pro-German from his writings, probably.

TOMPKINS: My parents were seized with what he had to say socially about medicine in *The Doctor's Dilemma,* and they thought that here was a man who is struggling to improve the world and nobody's listening to him.

CARTER: Were your parents from intellectual backgrounds? Were they university families, or what? . . . How do you account for that interest in Shaw?

TOMPKINS: My grandfather, who was a judge, courted my grandmother in Latin, and he had a vast library. In those days, there wasn't any television, so they read, and they read the classics. That was the southern way of life. My father was always more the artist, without being an academic, whereas his brother, my uncle, was at Yale, and he had an extraordinary talent. He could recite chapters from *Finnegans Wake* from memory. I was absolutely stunned. And he could recite endless Shakespeare. The tragedy of my uncle was that metaphysics didn't exist for him.

CARTER: This was not your mother's bent, though, this kind of interest in what age she was in, or which philosophers might have the truth for her. It seems to me that she was more hedonistic than that. Is that a bad word to use with her? *Hedonistic?*

TOMPKINS: I don't see how you can be a hedonist and a tragedian. What you have to realize is that the reason Shaw loved being with them was that he could be not the G.B.S. on the pedestal, obliged to constantly spout out his witticisms. He could just *be,* and they would say to him, "Shut up, B. You don't know what you're talking about. Have you read Huxley? . . . not Julian Huxley, but Aldous Huxley." They could talk and he could be free. He didn't have to wear his mask all the time. And, of course, he was obviously much taken with my mother, and she was much taken with him. And there's nothing nicer for a man than to have some young woman really taken with him, some really beautiful, sexy, younger woman. I mean, he was seventy and she was thirty.

CARTER: Did she write to him?

TOMPKINS: Every day, virtually. And that's the tragedy, that the letters are lost.

CARTER: How are they lost?

TOMPKINS: Well, maybe . . . you see, in the one . . . in the letter right after Charlotte died, he said, "I never wanted to write a word when Charlotte was alive, because I didn't want it to hurt her. Now we can say . . . now I can write anything I like." And that's when he said that of his consummated love affairs my mother gave him the greatest pleasure. Though he read many of my mother's letters to Charlotte, he obviously censored some, and in the end may have burnt them all. Or his secretary may have burnt them after he died, possibly suffering from Prossy's complaint.[5]

CARTER: They weren't left after his death anywhere else?

TOMPKINS: Five or six of them, the last ones, when she threatened to come live with him, turned up in the British Museum. And that's when he misunderstood her. There's a very good letter, because she's very fiery. She said, "What the hell do you mean by misunderstanding? I didn't want to marry you . . . I just wanted to come take care of you."[6] And I don't have those letters, but somebody found them. And they're in the British Museum.

CARTER: But very few.

TOMPKINS: About five or six.

CARTER: And his letters to her, which were a hundred, 130 at least, or so you say in *To a Young Actress.*

TOMPKINS: Yes, well, everything I could find I put in that book, except for the ones stolen by Miss Little, who tried to blackmail him,[7] and the December 1944 one that describes in detail their sexual relationship. I didn't publish that one.[8] In his letters to my mother, he said, "You should be a writer, that's your job." He wanted her to write his life, because, he says, "you know me better than anyone." And obviously, he must have talked to her at great length, as they wandered around together.

CARTER: Those letters you collected for *To a Young Actress,* those are now at a university, aren't they?

TOMPKINS: Yes, I think in Texas.[9]

CARTER: And you have copies of them?

TOMPKINS: Yes, I have copies. Almost all of them are in *To a Young Actress,* which I insisted with the publisher we reproduce as is, in facsimile, so that you can see his tiny writing and his corrections, and you can see the postcards. The only thing that annoys me is that when the letters were taken from me I had saved all the envelopes, because it's very important to get the dates correct. You can't tell where she was, except from the envelope.

CARTER: So you kept some of the letters out of that collection.

TOMPKINS: My father was still alive.

CARTER: Your father didn't know about the depth of this feeling?

TOMPKINS: Oh, I'm sure he did, but I don't think he necessarily wanted to.[10] As they say, the husband is usually the last to know. I thought I'd wait until it was historical, and no longer emotionally upsetting to anybody.

CARTER: Neither you, in *Shaw and Molly Tompkins,* nor Holroyd in the biography. . . . You both skirt around.

TOMPKINS: I was very deliberate. . . . I knew perfectly well where, when, and how. And there's one scene that I re-created in a film script I wrote, but that is still to be shot, which takes place at Ayot St. Lawrence in the shelter.[11]

CARTER: Yes.

TOMPKINS: When he showed her his work place with its desk and its cot, that is one place when he jumped on her. And I can hear my mother saying, "Now I know why Mrs. Patrick Campbell said, 'If you feed him a beefsteak, no woman in England would be safe.'" He was obviously very passionate, and the people who maintain that he was sexless haven't a clue. There must be eight hundred books written by professors about him and his plays without any idea of how he really was.

CARTER: That's why it's important to talk to you.

TOMPKINS: Well, my knowledge of him is very limited and much of it secondhand, except that I realized that it was because he didn't have to be the great G.B.S., that he could be free and laugh with them, that he was happy.

CARTER: He could be a private person.

TOMPKINS: As a house present, he brought a Victrola to the island. So we were always playing music for the joy of it. I can still see him as he gesticulated, pretending to direct the music. And it surprised me when I went back to the island a few years ago. This time, there was Beethoven roaring out of my father's room. It was Toscanini who had taken over the island, and he was listening to his own records of his own conducting.[12] His daughter very kindly took me around, back to my childhood haunts.

CARTER: Toscanini had rented the island?

TOMPKINS: Yes, but it was all very different and severe, not carefree. Even the gardener was upset. He was distressed because he said, "The Maestro never goes out into the garden. He wears a black suit, and black umbrella and he never goes into the garden," one of the most beautiful gardens in Italy.

CARTER: Well, I'd like you to tell me more about your mother and Shaw.

TOMPKINS: Shaw says, if you ask about him, "My biography is in my works. Just read my plays and read my prefaces, and then you'll know who I am." My mother was naturally very interested in his relations with other women. And obviously he must have told her a lot, details that weren't passed on to me, so they're lost. Interesting, because my mother obviously would have been a bit jealous, even though they were all in the past. I mean, he's seventy years old. I remember we went to see Gordon Craig in Rapallo with Max Beerbohm because my mother wanted to see what a son of Ellen Terry would be like.[13] And she was disappointed.

CARTER: Would you say that your mother may have been Shaw's last great love?

TOMPKINS: Oh, I think so, yes. I think possibly the greatest, certainly the last, and the most enduring. His affair with Mrs. Patrick Campbell didn't last very long. She went off with someone else . . . this lasted longer.

CARTER: She married George Cornwallis-West. But Shaw wrote to her, to Mrs. Patrick Campbell, over a period of thirty years, until 1939. About the same number of years that he wrote to your mother.

TOMPKINS: I don't know about the others, except what's written in the history books.

CARTER: You said that Michael Holroyd contacted you. That was one of my questions, because the report in the Holroyd biography is your book paraphrased.

TOMPKINS: He just took it from my book.

CARTER: And then apparently had no other sources.

TOMPKINS: No. When he called me, he just said, "How do you explain this love affair?" And as I said, they must have known each other, maybe several lifetimes. The minute you recognize somebody, it's instantaneous.

CARTER: That's astounding, that he had never seen this young woman before; she appeared on his doorstep in London, and he invited her in for tea.

TOMPKINS: Yes, but you've got to realize that when a girl that pretty accosts you, and she's well dressed, and she's *soignée* [well groomed], and she's very, very beautiful, and she's very young, and she's obviously madly in love with you, what do you do? He said, "Come on up." Now whether she was in love . . . maybe not so much with the man as in love with GBS, who was going to be the salvation of the planet. Yet, the rapport must have been very, very fast.

CARTER: You're saying she did love him?

TOMPKINS: By the time he took them—my father and my mother—to Godalming to one of the Fabian Summer Schools, she seemed to be less in love with him. And he said to her: "According to Rochefoucault, the old and the young should not speak of love."[14] Then it matured. He tried to keep a distance as long as he could. But I don't think she wanted any distance.

CARTER: It isn't a story just about an older man and a beautiful young woman, though, because he was the artist that he was, because he's a major figure in world literature, really, not just English literature. And

I wonder if your father . . . what was your father's opinion of him, or your father's feeling . . .

TOMPKINS: Oh, it was a ménage à trois in a sense that all three loved each other. He and my father would go daily to swim at the automobile club, and they would talk, talk, talk. In his studio, my father was making *bozzeti* [sketches] for the facade of a theater, to represent Shaw's Creative Evolution.[15] And so they would discuss constantly. And then when he took them to Stratford, to the Shakespeare Festival, and my mother and father went punting, and when they came back, they found him on the shore of the Avon looking very pleased with himself. And he said, "I've just started a new play." And they said, "Well, what is it?" And he said, "St. Joan." And they said, "Why St. Joan?" And he laughed and said, "To save her from Drinkwater."[16]

[. . .]

CARTER: Did your mother appear in any of his plays as a character?

TOMPKINS: No, because at the RADA, at the Royal Academy of Dramatic Art in London, where she was studying, they kept making her play Eliza in *Pygmalion*. And she kept stamping her foot and saying, "But Eliza isn't funny." In fact, when she played it, he was up in the balcony, kneeling down, so she wouldn't see him, because he was afraid she'd throw a floodlight at him, for laughing at his own jokes. She didn't find it funny at all. Neither did Mrs. Patrick Campbell, who made such a success of it.

CARTER: Is Molly Tompkins portrayed in any of Shaw's drama?

TOMPKINS: There are references here and there, but, you know, I haven't read everything I should have.

CARTER: That's a hard job to do with Shaw.

TOMPKINS: Oh, it's endless.

CARTER: Could we go back for a moment to Italy and the summer of '28 and "The Road to Baveno" and the child that wasn't born? Could you talk a bit more about that?

TOMPKINS: About what?

CARTER: The child that was not born to your mother.

TOMPKINS: There's a very funny scene to illustrate that. They were in the delta of the Toce, which is the river that runs into the lake. And they had been making love when the Guardia di Finanza [customs official], or border police, turned up, who obviously had been watching the whole scene. They coughed discreetly and said, "You're not allowed to be here. It's a military place." And maybe a couple of weeks later she knows that she's pregnant. And he [Shaw] is convinced—if you count the days—that it is his child. Yet she doesn't want to have any more children. So he gives her the Life Force argument: that she should have children all the time. But she's adamant, and goes to Milan and has it aborted. And when she comes back, and they're putting her in the boat to take her back to the island, she describes Shaw standing over her, with the life gone out of him, gray-faced with his arms folded, looking down at her, saying, "Molly, Molly." So she said to my father, "he makes me feel as if I committed murder." Which in point of fact she had.

CARTER: So you've never had brothers or sisters.

TOMPKINS: No. It would have been fun to have a Shavian brother, or maybe a Shavian sister would have been even greater.

CARTER: So after Shaw retired to his old age, and didn't see your mother, they still wrote to one another.

TOMPKINS: He saw her again in England in the '29s or '30s, and they parted very amicably with Charlotte, because it was all over by then, physically.

CARTER: Is this when the art exhibit was in London?

TOMPKINS: At first my mother couldn't stand Charlotte . . . she was jealous and she considered her a prig and a prude and a bore. Then she softened. There's a biography of Charlotte that I haven't read, that I would like to read, to understand her better.[17] Because she was a very dim figure in my memory.

CARTER: Your mother and Shaw didn't talk on the telephone in later years, or have any contact?

TOMPKINS: Both of them hated the telephone, and the telephone wasn't the way it is nowadays, not in those days. You couldn't hear very well, and it was a bore. But they talked on the phone obviously. My mother must have written a thousand letters to him. She wrote to him, voluminously and in detail, and the extraordinary thing is that when she wrote to him or wrote to me, it was beautiful. But if she tried to write for publication, it was a disaster. She became self-conscious. Some portal closed down, and it wasn't good. When I went off to the war and asked her to write for me, to describe the whole twenty years between the two wars and the whole association with Shaw, I came back from the war and found a trunk full of this absolutely glorious material. With it, I could have really answered your questions much better, because she wrote in great detail, in a lucid and entertaining style.

CARTER: And where are those?

TOMPKINS: She burnt it all because she went back to live with my father . . .[18]

CARTER: Did they remarry?

TOMPKINS: Whether they remarried or not, they lived together. They had a house in Georgia, and he had his studio in New York, so he came and went. But they had a life together again.

CARTER: When is the last time you saw Shaw?

TOMPKINS: Must have been in the '30s. He avoided coming to see me at school because I think he didn't want to make a show of it. It would have been, you know, very grand, and he quite sensibly stayed out. He just paid the bills and saw that I was getting on all right. Then I went back to America.

CARTER: Was he happy when you went to Harvard?

TOMPKINS: Yes, . . . because he kept saying I should be brought up as an American in America, although my English public schooling would not have done me any harm. In fact, it saved me during the war, when I had to deal with inane military types. An English public-school training does give you the feeling of superiority. They could be colonels or generals, but they didn't affect me. It's extraordinary what it does to instill a sense of who you are, and what you can get away with.

CARTER: Really.

TOMPKINS: I mean, that's its purpose.

CARTER: Yes, of course.

TOMPKINS: That's its purpose, and it works.

CARTER: You went to two English public schools.

TOMPKINS: No, I went to a prep school, which is where you go to prepare yourself for public school, and then I went to Stowe.

CARTER: And Fernden?

TOMPKINS: Fernden is a prep school.

TOMPKINS: During the war Shaw wanted to follow what I was doing, but it was very difficult because even my parents didn't know. It was all hush-hush in the OSS and all not communicable.[19] Then he wanted to know about my children, and my new wife and so on.

CARTER: So he wrote to you, or [was it] to your mother?

TOMPKINS: No, he wrote to my mother, keeping track of me. He wrote to me once or twice about this, that, or the other. But mostly he kept an avuncular view of it. I don't think there could have been much intercourse between us: A twenty-year-old boy and an eighty-year-old genius? What could we have talked about?

CARTER: Ideas, probably.

TOMPKINS: I wasn't up to it yet. I didn't discover the metaphysical world 'till I came back from the war, in '46. And he was almost dead.

CARTER: Yes, he's dead in '50. Your mother lived until 1960, but probably didn't see him for the last twenty-five years of her life.

TOMPKINS: No.

CARTER: And your father lived how long?

TOMPKINS: My father lived until he was in his seventies. But you see, people don't understand the relationship between my father and Shaw, in the sense that though a ménage à trois, he probably was not aware of when they consummated their love. Also, he wanted to work, and he was very happy if somebody would take my mother off his hands. Until she learned to paint, she was a disaster. When she was acting, that occupied her. But afterwards, because they had enough money, she had nothing to do. He was very happy for Shaw to afford him some freedom, because all he wanted was to go to his studio and work. That was his life. And somebody had to take care of my mother while he worked.

CARTER: In 1944, in the midst of the war, Shaw wrote to your mother, "You do not tell me what Pete has been doing or where he has been all this time. Nor do you say a word about Laurence's work. He should be recognized by this time as a very considerable sculptor."

TOMPKINS: You see that the fondness was there. The fondness, the tenderness, among the three of them, was what counted. It's a pity the more than fifty letters Shaw wrote to my father were lost. They would have shown the degree of intimacy between them.

Notes

1. According to Dan H. Laurence, "John Wardrop (b. 1919), a young Scottish journalist, whose ardor for Shaw verged on idolatry, injected himself into the dramatist's life in 1939, commencing a bizarre relationship between an impetuous, immature, hypersensitive but deeply sincere youth and an irrepressibly mischievous, frequently curmudgeonly old man that continued until, in the last year of Shaw's life, Wardrop emigrated to America." See headnote to Shaw's letter of 3 September 1942 to Wardrop in Dan H. Laurence, ed., *Bernard Shaw: Collected Letters, 1926–1950* (New York: Viking, 1988), pp. 636–37.

2. When an exhibition of D. H. Lawrence's paintings was held at the Warren Gallery in London in 1929, Scotland Yard confiscated thirteen of them on the grounds of obscenity.

3. Shaw was good friends with teacher, composer, and conductor Albert Coates (1882–1953).

4. L. Ron Hubbard (1911–86) wrote *Dianetics: The Modern Science of Mental Health* (1950), the basic text of the Church of Scientology, which he founded.

5. Shaw's secretary was Blanche Patch. In *Candida*, Candida tells her husband, the Reverend James Morell, that the women who come to hear him preach are—like his secretary Proserpine ('Prossy')—in love with him, a syndrome she calls "Prossy's complaint."

6. Charles A. Berst quotes at length from Molly's "fiery" November 1945 letter in his "Passion at Lake Maggiore: Shaw, Molly Tompkins, and Italy, 1921–1950," in *SHAW: The Annual of Bernard Shaw Studies 5*, ed. Rodelle Weintraub (University Park: Penn State University Press, 1985), pp. 111–12.

7. See *SHAW* 5, p. 86 and p. 113, n. 5. According to Shaw, Molly's housekeeper-secretary Mollie Little asked him "with extraordinary persistence for sums of money in three figures."

8. Tompkins did "publish that one"—in bowdlerized facsimile—in *To a Young Actress: The Letters of Bernard Shaw to Molly Tompkins* (New York: Clarkson N. Potter, 1960), pp. 180–81.

9. The Harry Ransom Humanities Research Center at the University of Texas at Austin has only two letters from Shaw to Molly: one in shorthand dated 27 January 1931, the other undated. Peter Tompkins estimates that his mother wrote "close to a thousand" letters to Shaw (*To a Young Actress*, p. 6).

10. According to *Shaw and Molly Tompkins* (New York: Clarkson N. Potter, 1961), when

Laurence asked Molly if she loved Shaw, she replied: "Of course. You know I do" (160). Quoted by Berst in *SHAW* 5, p. 99.

11. The "shelter" is the revolving writing hut located at the bottom of the garden at Shaw's Corner, in Ayot St. Lawrence. Along with a telephone and typewriter, it was also equipped with a small bed.

12. Arturo Toscanini (1867–1957), arguably the most renowned conductor of his age.

13. Stage designer Edward Gordon Craig (1872–1966) settled in Italy in 1906. Writer and caricaturist Max Beerbohm (1872–1956), who succeeded Shaw as drama critic of *The Saturday Review,* moved to Rapallo in 1910.

14. François, duc de La Rochefoucauld (1613–80), whose *Réflexions, ou sentences et maximes morales* (1665) offer an often sardonic view of human nature.

15. The Tompkinses had moved to London with the intention of establishing a Shavian Theater, in which Molly would perform in Shaw's plays and for which Laurence would be scene designer.

16. Biographer, poet, and minor dramatist John Drinkwater (1882–1937), first manager of the Birmingham Repertory Theatre.

17. Janet Dunbar's *Mrs. G.B.S.: A Portrait* (London: Harrap; New York: Harper and Row, 1963).

18. Laurence had divorced Molly in 1936.

19. During World War II, the OSS (Office of Strategic Services), forerunner and parent organization of the CIA (Central Intelligence Agency), supplied espionage services through its Special Operations (SO) and Secret Intelligence (SI) branches.

Dan H. Laurence

VICTORIANS UNVEILED: SOME THOUGHTS ON *MRS WARREN'S PROFESSION*

According to the critic William Archer,[1] the great distinguishing mark of the Victorian Anglo-Saxon was his ability to be shocked. And shock was the prime weapon in Bernard Shaw's arsenal of rhetorical munitions.

The play *Mrs Warren's Profession,* as the drama critic Clive Barnes remarked some years ago, is Shaw at his best, "with his prejudices bared and his hatred rampant."[2] It is a frontal attack on a smug, greedy society of prostitutes, not merely of whores who provide sexual gratification for a fee, but industrialists, politicians, clergy, press, country squires—all reaping benefits from the working prostitute without sharing the labor, and earning knighthoods, baronies, and social prominence in the process. Some are active investor-partners; others cash in surreptitiously, or accept the profit without regard for the source. Harlotry, long recognized as the oldest profession, has throughout recorded time been encouraged, fostered, demanded by a profit-motivated economic system.

And still is. When as recently as 1967 the city council of New York removed licensing requirements for massage parlors, many landlords in Midtown and on the East Side leased their property to whoremasters in the face of rising vacancy rates and foreclosures in a weak economy. By 1976 there were almost a hundred parlors in the area of Times Square alone. In a frustrated attempt to rid the city of a plethora of white slavers, the mayor's staff surreptitiously distributed to the press a list of respectable institutions and corporations that, through building rents, were gar-

First delivered under the title *Victorians Unmasked; or, Will the Real Prostitutes Please Stand Up,* at the annual seminar of the Shaw Festival, Niagara-on-the-Lake, Ontario, 14 August 1997. Revised and expanded as a plenary address in the conference *Shaw's Brave New World* at Marquette University, Milwaukee, 19 April 2001. Further revised for present publication.

nering enormous profit from the prostitution rings that leased the properties. The list disclosed a number of highly embarrassed central pillars, ostensibly including clerical dioceses and universities.[3]

Shaw, who resided for a dozen years in central London, just north of Soho, was accustomed to being accosted by prostitutes in the street as they plied their trade. Moreover, from his extensive daily perusal of newspapers in the British Museum and from his committee involvements in the St. Pancras Vestry and, later, the Borough Council, he was thoroughly familiar with the vastness of prostitution as an international venture for profit, like any other form of commerce, enormously lucrative to the great city estates in London as well as to the Church of England through rents of houses in which it was practiced. In 1857, the medical journal *The Lancet* estimated that one house in every sixty in London was a brothel, and one female in every sixteen (of all ages) was a whore.[4] On this basis there would have been more than 6,000 brothels in London and about 80,000 prostitutes.

Prostitution flourished as well in London's music-halls, notoriously in the Empire, Leicester Square, a whoremarket patronized by young blades and military cadets, where girls, who (if experienced) could earn no more for factory and shop labor than the eighteen shillings a week set by the London County Council (with novices lucky to earn more than five shillings), could earn twenty to thirty pounds a week operating from the Empire's lounges: over a thousand pounds a year. When the authorities shuttered the Empire in 1894 until the management agreed to eliminate the wet bars by erection of canvas barriers, indignant young patrons of the bars attacked the barriers, ripping down the canvas. Leading the assault was a twenty-year-old Sandhurst cadet, who celebrated the victory with a loud exhortation: "You have seen us tear down these barricades tonight. See that you pull down those who are responsible for them at the coming election!" The cadet, who six years later made his maiden speech in parliament, was the Honorable Winston Churchill.[5]

The press, too, capitalized on prostitution. In New York in October 1905, when *Mrs Warren's Profession* achieved a single performance before being unceremoniously padlocked by the police, the most flagrantly abusive newspaper among those calling for the suppression of the play was the *New York Herald*, which, in a front-page review,[6] scourged it as "Morally rotten . . . and degenerate." The only way one could expurgate it, the editor harangued, was "to cut the whole play out. You cannot have a clean pig sty. The play is an insult to decency." The irony here is that a major feature of this newspaper was a Personals column, profitably running each morning to about half a dozen pages, identified by most New Yorkers as the *Whores' Daily Guide and Compendium*, with gaudy advertisements for "massage parlors" run by "chic Parisian ladies with cozy suite[s]," seeking the company of "jolly sports" for their houses of assignation.[7] A year later the federal postal authorities demanded the *Herald* "cease and desist," slapping the paper with a substantial fine.

Kitty Warren's decision to join with her sister Liz in capitalizing on prostitution grew from the painful experience of a young half-sister, one of the two "respectable ones" of the family, who died of lead poisoning after toiling in a white-lead factory twelve hours a day for nine shillings a week. Other workers like this youngster developed phosphorous poisoning in the Bryant & May match factory while earning five shillings a week, succumbing finally to a deterioration of cranial bones, known as "fossy jaw"; or from tuberculosis contracted in a sweater's den while laboring miserably for twopence an hour. In 1855 and 1856 (the latter the year of Shaw's birth), the House of Commons was offered a bill to regulate the labor in bleaching factories where preteen girls worked eighteen to twenty hours a day in a temperature mounting to 130 degrees.[8] The House rejected the bill. In 1860 Lord Brougham (former Lord Chamberlain) informed the House of Lords that in these same factories youngsters of seven or eight were worked for as many as four consecutive days and nights without sleep. Again no action was taken.[9]

Prostitution, Shaw reiterated in *Everybody's Political What's What?*, was "an economic phenomenon produced by an underpayment of honest women so degrading, and an overpayment of whores so luxurious, that a poor woman of any attractiveness actually owed it to her self-respect to sell herself in the streets rather than toil miserably in a sweater's den sixteen hours a day for twopence an hour."[10] "No normal woman," he stressed earlier, in the 1930 preface to *Mrs Warren's Profession*, "would be a professional prostitute if she could better herself by being respectable, nor marry for money if she could afford to marry for love."[11]

Moreover, the luxurious superpayment of whores was related directly to the Victorian social code of behavior created and dictated by the male of the species to serve his domestic and social convenience and to gratify his desire, abetted by laws that gave him total control of his wife's person— and her fortune. The prosperous Victorian male sought to marry not a woman but an upholstered angel whom he could set on a pedestal. His ideal was a female of delicacy and gentility, who would create a genial, comfortable, and uncomplicated home for him; but a being of frigidity and inaccessibility, cohabiting with him only for the purpose of impregnation. The determined philoprogenitiveness of those who could afford to cultivate large families (like the Barretts of Wimpole Street) became known as the Cult of the Double Bed."[12]

Queen Victoria, with nine offspring, barely made the team. The average was thirteen or fourteen. Lady Durham, who expired at thirty-five after birthing thirteen children in seventeen years, was a typical sacrifice to Victorian fecundity.[13] For the wife there was no more sex than the Double Bed cult provided. Until as late as World War I, medical opinion in Britain persisted in viewing the genteel woman as devoid of sexual appetite. As the celebrated gynecologist Dr. William Acton proclaimed, any woman who achieved orgasm in intercourse with her husband was a whore.[14]

For the husband, however, there was a second cult, "The Cult of the Double Life." And not even a *secret* life, for it was widely known. Dr. John Chapman, distinguished editor of the *Westminster Review,* for one, domiciled his attractive mistress in the same house as his spouse; the writer George Eliot shared the home of her lover George Henry Lewes with his wife, Agnes. In Hyde Park's Rotten Row, as in Paris's Bois de Boulogne, Victorian gentlemen enjoyed the fresh air by driving in expensive carriages with the celebrated courtesans for whom they had purchased the vehicles. Hundreds of husbands nightly poured into the classy bordellos that had sprung up all over central London, from Mayfair to Bloomsbury, each presided over by a notorious "soiled dove" like the ravishing madam, Cora Pearl, while the wife, the epitome of "perfection," sat quietly at home, a model housekeeper and mother, gracing her husband's table, and providing evidence of a frightening distortion of natural desires and inclinations.

Amid middle-class males, a harlot or mistress was, on economic grounds, often preferred to a wife. *The Lancet* (again in 1857) informed readers that "with the increase of . . . luxurious civilization, there is a diminution of marriage, except in the patrician class," noting that a progressive decrease between 1796 and 1845 approximated ten percent. "It is thought impossible," the article went on, "in a large class of society now to marry unless you have a thousand to fifteen hundred pounds a year."[15] The average workingman's wage was at this time under a pound a week—or one-twentieth of what society deemed necessary for a wedlock status. This, even for professional men, shopkeepers, and skilled workers, resulted in late and ultraprudent marriages—and the resort to whores for gratification. Restraints on marriage among young men of the middle class, wrote a correspondent to *The Times* (1857), were "the real cause of our social corruption."[16] Thousands of young men, he lamented, live in sin. And "the mischief is on the increase with our increasing worship of money," which was good news for such capitalists as Mrs. Warren and Crofts.

In *Mrs Warren's Profession,* Shaw's indictment is leveled not at prostitutes but at the social system. It was crucial to Shaw that the play contain no conscious miscreant on whom audiences could pin blame and thus absolve themselves of complicity, for Shaw's fundamental message was that ALL members of society are blameworthy and must, accordingly, suffer their consciences to be stricken before leaving the playhouse. Like Vivie in Act

III, the audience must "feel among the damned already." To Shaw, complicity of all members of society in the social crime was inescapable.

Further, there were degrees of guilt. Crofts is more guilty than Kitty, for he, by investing in her, is reaping benefits without the slightest effort. He is, as Vivie calls him, "a capitalist bully," exploiting Mrs. Warren. Shaw, however, neither defends nor condemns Kitty. Though Victorian morality demanded in the theater that a prostitute either be a villain or be virtuous at heart and merely weak-willed, thus sentimentalizing her, Shaw presents Mrs. Warren as neither: she is created solely to reveal an end-product of society's guilt. And that guilt grows out of society's greed for the material.

There is, it must be interjected here, a counterbalance, of course, to Kitty's success story, in the thousands of young women who escaped the bleaching factories only to burn out and expire of disease, addiction, and, eventually, of starvation—alone and miserable. As this did not relate to Shaw's agenda and was not relevant to the direction the play was taking, he left it unmentioned.

It was Ibsen who inspired Shaw, and Shaw who inspired Granville Barker, to capitalize in their plays on the materialistic instinct, which becomes the driving force of the most dramatic argument as it grapples with moral imperative. And, parenthetically, after nearly a century, in Britain at least, the political drama that Shaw and Barker espoused has re-emerged victoriously in plays like David Hare's *The Secret Rapture* and Caryl Churchill's *Serious Money*—and occasionally in America as well, as in the witty comedy of the late Jerry Sterners, *Other People's Money*.

The theme of *Mrs Warren's Profession* is almost identical with that of Shaw's first and fellow "unpleasant play," *Widowers' Houses*. In the earlier work Harry Trench, like Vivie Warren after him, passes through a spiritual crisis of revelation. When he learns that Sartorius, father of his beloved Blanche, is the worst kind of slum landlord, he piously refuses to touch the filthy lucre that Sartorius would have settled on Blanche, and thereby upsets the marriage arrangements, until Sartorius startlingly reveals Trench's own complicity in the social crime, from the seven hundred pounds a year he receives upon a usurious interest rate on slum property. "Do you mean to say," asks Trench, "that I am just as bad as you are?" "If, when you say you are just as bad as I am," replies Sartorius, "you mean that you are just as powerless to alter the state of society, then you are unfortunately quite right." Trench acquiesces, finally, joining ranks with the voluptuaries. Vivie Warren, contrastingly, firmly rejects her mother's corrupt earnings, hardening herself against the infected system to which her conventional parent adheres.

Of interest, though unnoted, Trench and Vivie derive from a common literary source. Just as Shaw drew on characters in *Little Dorrit* for *Widowers' Houses*, he appropriated from one of his favorite Dickens novels the catastrophic revelation to Philip Pirrip (better known as Pip) that he has lost his "great expectations." Pip, we recall, upon discovering that the source of his good fortune is the escaped convict Magwitch, rejects further endowment, snobbishly shrinking from his benefactor with loathing, much as Frank Gardner in *Mrs Warren's Profession*, who has been prepared to prostitute himself by marriage to Kitty Warren's daughter, withdraws when he learns the source of her wealth because "I can't bring myself to touch the old woman's money now."

Vivie and Pip are alike in many ways, sharing a lack of culture and of religious or aesthetic sensibility to fall back on. Pip is, as Vivie defines herself to Praed, "an arrogant barbarian." At the end, their world is a melancholy and desolate place—a world of expectation curtailed—more cruelly for Pip, who is jilted by his adored Estella and never marries, than for Vivie, for whom Frank's abrupt exit fits comfortably in her plans, which were decided upon before the rise of the Act I curtain and before her discussion with her mother. Still, there can only be loneliness and isolation in the individuation that Vivie insists on, "permanently single" and "permanently unromantic."

Many viewers or readers of *Mrs Warren's Profession*, unable to distinguish between disenchantment and disillusion, are left dissatisfied with Vivie's decision, for to them it appears to be a negation of life. But Shaw never concerns himself with this. He is satisfied to take a pragmatic view of women's search for self-identity, and as a dramatic psychiatrist he is rarely concerned with *what* people do, but rather with *why* they do it. His concentration remains focused on motivation.

Equally frustrating for his audience is the way Shaw introduces an element he will then not explore or put to dramatic use. A good example of this is the issue of consanguinity, which in the play creates questionable relationships between Vivie and Frank, Crofts and Vivie, and Mrs. Warren and Frank (the latter couple indulging at the opening of Act II in playful flirtation), and Sam Gardner and Kitty. Why, the critics ask, does Shaw introduce the subject of incest into the play if he is not going to develop it as a theme? Because apparently he is not interested, as Shelley and Ibsen were, in the dramatic possibilities of the subject, which might in any event lead him into extraneous tangents. The presence of incest, as Shaw slips it in, is just sufficient to remind the audience that incest is a natural consequence of an iniquitous system tolerated by a profit-minded society. Promiscuous sexual intercourse must inevitably result in the raising of insoluble questions of consanguinity, which, apparently, was all Shaw thought it necessary to do.

More important, Shaw in his play had created his first significant woman, Vivie Warren, defying Victorian pretensions, strong, determined, and apart, as all Shaw's great women will be, through Saint Joan and the millionairess Epifania. From the first, Vivie has had to deal with life on her own. Boarded at schools most of the year and, between terms, lodged by foster families concerned only for income, occasionally receiving fleeting visits from a woman who allegedly is her mother, Vivie has had to survive by her own inner drive and by an ability to make her own decisions, untainted by familial ties. Only once does she expose herself as vulnerable, when Kitty wins her admiration and sympathy. Ironically, Vivie is saved from disaster because Kitty, who has rebelled against Victorian inequities and insensitiveness and has survived by adopting instinctively the Victorian capitalist morality of doing what pays best, loses her daughter by falling prey to the debilitating disease of conventionality, which disenchants and alienates Vivie. One might make a case for the individualist Vivie as the theater's earliest existentialist.

When Shaw described *Mrs Warren's Profession* as an "unpleasant" play, he was doing so in the Victorian acceptance of the adjective, not just as something nasty, or distasteful, like swigging a draft of ipecac, but something unspeakable, something not to be discussed in polite society or in the presence of one's wife. In that respect Shaw's play is akin to Shakespeare's *Measure for Measure*, pervaded by a terrifying world of grotesques, representing aristocracy, commerce, church, and art, all of them caught up in their hypocrisies, greed, lust, perverted sense of values, and superficialities—a world whose conventions demand unearned and undeserved parental respect and obedience by children whose profit-motivated philosophy debauches the sacrament of marriage into mere sex relations for money and a conviction that one can commit almost any depravity so long as one doesn't "fly openly," as Crofts puts it, "in the face of society." Its platitudes by Frank of "love's young dream," and by Praed as "the beauty and romance of life," reveal a pitiful dependence on illusion, a condition invariably deplored in Shaw's work, and one that very few of us face up to unflinchingly. Not until the death of the Elderly Gentleman in Part IV of *Back to Methuselah* will we encounter such unwavering resolve and moral force in Shaw's work as we find it in Vivie's decision (whatever our personal feelings), and her final moment in the play is certainly painfully Pinteresque.

Mrs Warren's Profession no longer shocks an audience, though it can make it, as Shaw hoped, "thoroughly uncomfortable," despite there not being a single word uttered that could put a strain on our sensibilities. Considering the amazing increase of frank expression in his own time, Shaw wondered what it would be like in another fifty years. As he wrote to Frank Harris in 1931, in urging him not to emulate the tendency toward obscene speech in the books of James Joyce and the plays of Eugene O'Neill, "[E]ven George Moore does not imagine that force in literature is attained by calling a spade a f——g shovel."[17]

Most important, *Mrs Warren's Profession* a century after its initial appearance has not dated in ethical consideration, and still has the power to overwhelm us with its forceful dialogue. Shaw, in fact, remains unique in the English language in his skill of creating a play without visible action, in which the dialogue becomes the action in the cut and thrust of vocal rapiers and the mental wrestling of the Greek agon, as he creates with a fine-drawn sense a series of individual temperaments in conflict, blended in brilliantly orchestrated voices.

Happily, *Mrs Warren's Profession* survives as one of Shaw's most frequently produced plays: not bad at all for the work of a man charged by his contemporaries in the 1890s with incapacity to write creatively for the theater.

Notes

1. In his article, "America and 'Mrs. Warren,'" *Morning Leader,* London (4 November 1905), 4:6. Source supplied by Thomas Postlewait.

2. "*Mrs. Warren's Profession* Is at the Beaumont," *New York Times,* 20 February 1976, 15:1–4.

3. Kenneth T. Jackson, ed., *Encyclopedia of New York City* (New Haven: Yale University Press, 1995), p. 948. Gratitude to Jacques Barzun for his generous assistance.

4. Cyril Pearl, *The Girl with the Swansdown Seat* (Indianapolis: Bobbs-Merrill, 1955), p. 36.

5. Cited by Winston Churchill in *My Early Life: A Roving Commission* (New York: Scribner, 1930), p. 57.

6. "The Limit of Stage Indecency" (31 October 1905), pp. 1:6, 5:6.

7. Richard O'Connor, *O. Henry: The Legendary Life of William S. Porter* (Garden City, N.Y.: Doubleday, 1970), p. 170.

8. See Hansard Parliamentary Debates: House of Commons (25 July 1855 and Debate in vol. 139), pp. 1354–69; also 1362B.

9. Pearl, *The Girl with the Swansdown Seat,* p. 52.

10. Bernard Shaw, *Everybody's Political What's What?* Standard Edition, (London: Constable, 1944), p. 196.

11. Bernard Shaw, *Plays Unpleasant* (London: Constable, 1930), p. 151. (*Collected Edition,* vol. 7.)

12. Pearl, *The Girl with the Swansdown Seat,* p. 88.

13. Ibid., 89.

14. Dr. William Acton, *The Functions and Disorders of the Reproductive Organs* (Philadelphia: Blakiston, 1857), pagination undetermined. See also Judith R. Walkourtz, *Prostitution and Victorian Society* (Cambridge: Cambridge University Press, 1930), p. 45.

15. Pearl, *The Girl with the Swansdown Seat,* p. 87.

16. The correspondence appeared under the pseudonym Theophrastus. The portion of the letter reproduced here apparently was cited in *The Lancet* and quoted in Pearl.

17. Shaw to Frank Harris, ALS (21 April 1931), in *Bernard Shaw: Collected Letters IV, 1926–1950* (London: Max Reinhardt, 1988), pp. 235–36.

L. W. Conolly

MRS WARREN'S PROFESSION AND THE LORD CHAMBERLAIN

Prominently projected onto the drop-curtain for Sir Peter Hall's sexually charged (but not sexually explicit) 2002 revival of Shaw's *Mrs Warren's Profession* at the Strand Theatre in London's West End were two short statements: "Written in 1893. Banned until 1925." Eye-catching? Thought-provoking? Yes, indeed. But true? Alas, not really—or at least not the truth, the whole truth, and nothing but the truth. It would be folly, of course, to claim to know the whole truth about anything (let alone expect to see it displayed on a drop-curtain, or even revealed in the pages of *SHAW*), but through a review of key primary sources (including many unpublished documents) I hope at least in this article to add a little to current knowledge and understanding of the complex history of Shaw's (and his allies') struggles to overcome the Lord Chamberlain's refusal to license his notorious play in the years between the first request in 1898 and the first licensed performance in England at the Prince of Wales Theatre, Birmingham, on 27 July 1925.[1] It's really a far more interesting (and much longer!) story than the Strand's drop-curtain theater historian would have us believe—a story, on the one hand, of obduracy, obtuseness, and, ultimately, pragmatism; and, on the other, of persistence, naïvety, ingenuity, and determination.

I gratefully acknowledge the editorial skills and Shavian expertise of Michel Pharand in detecting errors and inconsistencies in the first submission of this essay. Thanks are also due the following institutions for facilitating access to their collections and for granting permission for quoting from and/or reproducing manuscript material: the Harry Ransom Humanities Research Center, the University of Texas at Austin; the Houghton Library, Harvard University; the Bernard F. Burgunder Collection, Carl A. Kroch Library, Cornell University; the British Library; the Dan H. Laurence Collection, L. W. Conolly Theatre Archives, University of Guelph Library.

The Independent Theatre, 1895

The drop-curtain's dating of Shaw's writing of *Mrs Warren's Profession* is accurate. He began it on Sunday, 20 August 1893, on a train journey home after a visit to Charles Charrington and his wife, Janet Achurch. Ten days later he had finished the first act. He worked further on the play through September, reading parts of it to Achurch (his choice for the first Vivie Warren, Charrington was to be Crofts) and other friends as he made progress. More train rides, a walk in the Mall, an afternoon on Primrose Hill— these and other occasions and locations afforded opportunities for further progress. He finished Act III—and read it to the Charringtons—on 24 October, and completed the play on 2 November before attending a performance of Berlioz's *Faust* at the Albert Hall (Weintraub II, 963–82, passim).[2]

In November and December 1893, Shaw read parts of the new play to other friends—William Archer, the Webbs—by which time J. T. Grein, founder of the Independent Theatre Society, had got to hear of it. Grein had produced *Widowers' Houses* in December 1892, and now inquired about *Mrs Warren's Profession*. Shaw outlined the play to Grein—describing Mrs Warren as "a woman of bad character, proprietress of two *maisons tolérées* in Brussels, and of similar establishments in other continental cities"—but cautioned him that "I do not think there is the least chance of the play being licensed" (12 December 1893; Laurence I, 413). Shaw hoped that Grein would be willing to mount a private production of the play, thereby evading the Lord Chamberlain's authority (as Grein had in March 1891 with Ibsen's highly controversial *Ghosts*), and in the meantime continued to read the play to his circle of friends. He read *Mrs Warren's Profession* to Grein on 13 February 1895 (Weintraub II, 1065), but Grein, while sympathetic to a Norwegian play about venereal disease, disappointed Shaw by rejecting his play because of its subject matter.[3] There was no prospect either of a public performance, Shaw not even having thought it worthwhile submitting the play to the Lord Chamberlain for licensing (Laurence I, 470). Shaw hadn't entirely given up hope of a production, however, telling R. Golding Bright in November 1895 that he had proposed the role of Mrs Warren (who is "much worse than a prostitute," she is "an organism of prostitution") to Mrs. Theodore Wright (wife of a Fabian colleague), who had appeared in Grein's production of *Ghosts*. A week later (on 11 November 1895), in another letter to Golding Bright, Shaw seemed reasonably optimistic that there would be an Independent Theatre production of *Mrs Warren's Profession*, with or without the Lord Chamberlain's approval, but he was again disappointed. He conceded to

Bright in a letter of 10 June 1896 that "[t]here is no question of its immediate or remote production" (Laurence I, 632).

So nearly three years after Shaw's having completed it, *Mrs Warren's
Profession* remained unproduced and unpublished. There is "no likeli-
hood," Shaw wrote to Dublin friend Edward McNulty on 10 May 1897,
of this "immoral" play being licensed for performance, but now he was
determined to publish it. And therein lay another problem.

The Dublin Initiative, 1897

In his letter to McNulty, Shaw explained the "idiotic chaos" of copyright
and performance law, whereby if a play was published before it was performed the playwright lost "rights of representation" (i.e., the play was up
for grabs by anyone who cared to produce it—without approval from or
payment to the playwright). Since, given its subject matter, the chances of
anyone wanting to, or being allowed to, produce *Mrs Warren's Profession*
were negligible, one might wonder what Shaw was worried about, but—
astutely—he was taking a longer-term view and wanted to ensure that his
rights were protected in the event that the censorship system (or the prejudices governing it) in England were to change, or if producers abroad
took an interest in the play (as proved to be the case). Theaters in Ireland
not being subject to the Lord Chamberlain's control—but a public performance in that country nonetheless establishing "performance rights"—
Shaw came up with the notion of arranging a Dublin production for just
that purpose. He outlined his scheme to McNulty:

> If necessary I should announce Hamlet, with "to be preceded, at
> such & such an hour, by 'Mrs W's Profession,'" as if it were an old
> farce. You understand the sort of performance. A few people gabble
> through the play, reading the parts. There is no scenery, only a
> raising & dropping of the curtain. The hour selected is the most
> unlikely one possible. No announcement is made except that half
> an hour before the play begins a very modest poster is stuck on the
> door in view of the passer-by, with "Admission: One Guinea" at the
> foot of it. One person (a confederate, of course) comes in and pays
> the guinea, of which a box office return is solemnly made. Legally,
> this constitutes a public performance & saves the stage rights as
> effectively as if the play had been produced with full honours at the
> Lyceum. (Laurence I, 758)

It was an ingenious plan, similar to the one that Shaw (as he pointed out to McNulty) had recently used in London to protect his performance rights of *The Devil's Disciple* (at the Bijou Theatre on 17 April 1897). All Shaw asked of McNulty was that he "do this trick" for him, "or get it done, or, if it can't be done, find out the why and wherefore for me." More easily said than done: find a theater (one of those "obscure little theatres in Dublin at which amateurs perform," Shaw suggested); search for a cast ready to "gabble" for a couple of hours (without pay?); identify an accomplice to come up with a guinea, and so on. McNulty, it seems, was having none of it, for the performance never took place, and there is no evidence that McNulty made any effort to help Shaw out.

From Prostitute to Shoplifter

It was now nearly four years since Shaw had finished *Mrs Warren's Profession,* and he still didn't have any prospect of a production. But he remained determined to publish it, telling Ellen Terry on 24 May 1897 that he was preparing it ("the best of them all, which you haven't seen") for the printer (Laurence I, 767), and keeping her informed over the next few weeks of progress on revisions. On 5 August 1897 he received a nearly complete set of proofs, and two days later he sent her a complete set with a request that she "look through" the play (Laurence I, 793–94). At the same time, he was devising a strategy to get the play, or a version of it, performed in London to protect his stage rights. The plan, as he explained in a letter to Janet Achurch on 19 August 1897 (Laurence I, 795–97), was to submit the play for licensing in the usual way to George Redford, the Examiner of Plays, who read scripts on behalf of the Lord Chamberlain. (Redford had been appointed Examiner in March 1895.) If Redford, as anticipated, refused to recommend the play for licensing, Shaw had two plans ready. The first was to ask Redford to "blue pencil" those parts of the play he objected to and license the rest. Shaw was prepared to produce a censored version of the play as sufficient legal protection against any attempt to mount a pirated version. If Redford refused to go along with the blue-pencil approach, as proved to be the case, Shaw had another plan ready. This was to censor the play himself by turning Mrs. Warren into a "washerwoman or a pickpocket or whatever will enable [Redford] to license enough of the text to protect me."

It was not until March 1898 that Shaw received the printed proof copies of *Mrs Warren's Profession* needed for his plan. The copies were uncut, unfolded, and unbound, so Shaw invited wife-to-be, Charlotte Payne-Towns-

hend, round to his home in Fitzroy Square to spend an evening of
unconventional courtship "cutting & folding and stapling into brown
paper covers" not just *Mrs Warren's Profession,* but also two other (less controversial) plays being readied for performances—*You Never Can Tell* and
The Philanderer. Ms. Payne-Townshend was requested to bring her own
staples: size 5/8 of an inch, "50, if you have them" (4 March 1898; Laurence II, 11). One of these stapled copies of *Mrs Warren's Profession* was
forwarded to the manager of the Victoria Hall, Bayswater (also known as
the Bijou Theatre), site of the proposed performance, for submission to
Redford for licensing. Now in the Lord Chamberlain's Papers (LCP, List
1, Box 1) in the British Library, the copy contains a short comment (in
ink) by Shaw on the title page: "This play is designed to give an extremely
disagreeable, but much needed, shock to the conscience of the public in a
matter of deep social importance." Prompted, no doubt, by Shaw's forthright declaration, it didn't take Redford very long to read the play and
respond to the license application. On 11 March he wrote back to the
theater to say that he was "unable to recommend" that a license be
granted. He enclosed with the letter a receipt for the two-guinea reading
fee required with all submissions.[4] (see Figure 1.)

Shaw was ready for the rejection.[5] The first part of his counter-attack,
the "blue pencil" plan, was launched on 12 March. He wrote to Redford
(Laurence II, 13–14), in convivial style, suggesting that they both had a
problem and that a cooperative approach would be mutually beneficial.
Shaw's problem was clear: he wanted to publish *Mrs Warren's Profession,* but
publication before performance would risk "forfeiture of my stage rights."
Redford's problem, Shaw ventured to suggest, was that if *Mrs Warren's
Profession* remained unlicensed and unperformed, some unscrupulous
producer might choose to put the play on somewhere "outside your jurisdiction" unrestrained by controls that Shaw would exercise if he held performance rights. Why not, then, simply delete those sections that the Lord
Chamberlain might deem objectionable (Shaw helped, of course, by iden-
tifying them) and license the rest for performance? True, a "pirate" could
purloin the unlicensed (and unperformed) parts, but they would be mean-
ingless in performance without the rest of the play—over which Shaw
would have control. It was a neat proposal, and, as Shaw knew, it was
routine practice for the Examiner to delete objectionable passages. But
Redford wouldn't cooperate. In his reply to Shaw (14 March, quoted in
Laurence II, 14), Redford didn't bother to point out that what went on
outside the Lord Chamberlain's jurisdiction was not the Lord Chamberlain's business (or responsibility), but he did curtly tell Shaw that "it is not
for me to attempt any 'dramatic expurgation' with the blue pencil, as you
appear to suggest. It is for you to submit, or cause to be submitted, a

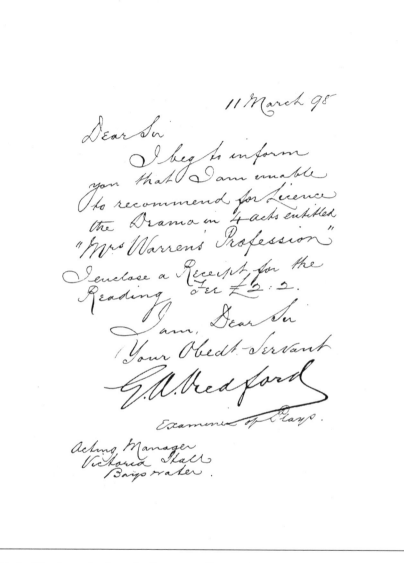

Fig. 1. The first rejection of a license application for *Mrs Warren's Profession*, 11 March 1898. By permission of the Houghton Library, Harvard University (bMS Eng 954 [26]).

licensable play, and if you do this I will endeavour to forget that I ever read the original."

It wasn't a knockout punch, but Redford certainly won that round. "Thirst for his blood" was Shaw's self-assessment to Charlotte of his attitude to Redford the day he received the letter (14 March 1898; Laurence II, 15). After returning home that same evening from a St. Pancras Ratepayers' Association meeting, Shaw got to work on his backup plan. He described it to Charlotte: "before going to bed make a new version of 'Mrs Warren,' omitting the second act & making Mrs W a pickpocket who trains young girls to steal." He mailed it before going to bed, "with a cheque for £2.2.0 [the two-guinea fee for the Examiner to read the new script] & my curse" (14 March 1898; Laurence II, 15).

Redford probably received the new version (British Library, Add MS 53654) on 15 March (a Tuesday). It took him until the Saturday to read and respond. This time everything was fine. Redford's official letter (Harvard University, Houghton, bMS Eng 954 [27]), dated 19 March 1898, informed the Victoria Hall manager that *Mrs Warren's Profession*, "a Drama [in] 3 Acts," had been read "and passed for Licence" and "may be produced." When the letter was forwarded to Shaw, he added a note in the top left-hand corner: "This refers to the mutilated copy, with the 2nd Act omitted & Mrs. Warren converted into a female Fagin." The entry for the play in the Lord Chamberlain's files is dated 1 April 1898. It records the official licensing date as 30 March 1898, a note clarifying that "[t]his Official License for Representation applies only to an Expurgated Version of the Drama entitled 'Mrs. Warren's Profession' *in three acts*" (British Library, Add MS 53708, fol. 126; Figure 2).

The Female Fagin, 1898

In the "blue pencil" proposal rejected by Redford, Shaw suggested that Redford should license Act I of *Mrs Warren's Profession* "with the exception of the duologue between Praed and Crofts," reject Act II entirely ("leaving Mrs W's profession unspecified"), license the third act "down to the beginning of the scene between Crofts and Vivie," and license the last act "from the entry of Praed onward" (Laurence I, 13).

Shaw's own censored version—the three-act "female Fagin" version he quickly constructed after the Ratepayers' Association meeting on 14 March—essentially follows this scheme. After Mrs Warren joins Vivie in the cottage (*Bodley Head* 284), leaving Crofts and Praed alone in the garden, Shaw adds a stage direction—"*Crofts accompanying her. Praed is follow-*

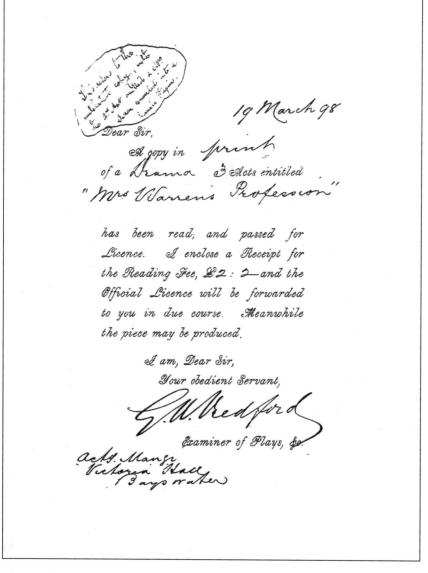

Fig. 2. Licensing approval, 19 March 1898, for the copyright performance of *Mrs Warren's Profession*, 30 March 1898. Shaw's note reads: "This refers to the mutilated copy, with the 2nd Act omitted & Mrs. Warren converted into a female Fagin." By permission of the Houghton Library, Harvard University (bMS Eng 954 [27]).

ing slowly when he is hailed by a young gentleman who has just appeared on the common & is making for the gate. He is a pleasant, pretty"—and links this with the direction that brings Frank on stage some eighty lines later. The intervening conversation between Crofts and Praed about the identity of Vivie's father is cut.[6] The second act is entirely omitted, eliminating Mrs. Warren's kissing of Frank, the issue of Vivie and Frank being related, Vivie's demands to know the name of her father, and Mrs. Warren's account to Vivie of her (Mrs. Warren's) upbringing and her entry with her sister into the business of "pleasing men." The third act (now the second) has cuts of about six pages, including much of the conversation between Frank and Vivie in which Frank warns Vivie that her mother is "a bad lot, a very bad lot" (*Bodley Head* 323–24), the long and important scene between Crofts and Vivie in which Crofts reveals that Mrs. Warren is still in business with a chain of "private hotels" across Europe and that many upper levels of British society benefit from businesses such as Mrs. Warren's (*Bodley Head* 327–32), and the dramatic moment when Crofts introduces Frank to Vivie as his half-sister (*Bodley Head* 333). Shaw deleted Crofts's "Allow me, Mister Frank, to introduce you to your half-sister, the eldest daughter of the Reverend Samuel Gardner. Miss Vivie: your half-brother. Good morning." He replaced it with the somewhat less compelling "This young lady's mother was convicted five times of shoplifting before she took to her present trade of training young girls to the profession of larceny." Act IV (now Act III) has a series of short cuts. The early part of the conversation between Frank and Vivie (*Bodley Head* 337–39) in which Frank countenances a romantic relationship with Vivie even in the face of their likely blood relationship is removed, as is the section in which Vivie lets Praed in on the full truth about her mother's profession (*Bodley Head* 343–45), though she cannot bring herself to speak the "two infamous words" that describe it. This section of about sixty lines is replaced by the following:

VIVIE. Oh, do you think Mr Praed does not know about my mother? [*Turning on Praed*] You had better have told me that morning, Mr Praed. I know now that my mother is a convicted thief.

PRAED. But she has repented, and atoned for that slip of her youth and poverty.

VIVIE. You are mistaken. She no longer steals; but she teaches others to steal.

PRAED. Great Heaven! And you have the courage to tell us this.

The dialogue then jumps to Vivie's "Thank you. You can always depend on me for two things: not to cry and not to faint" (*Bodley Head* 345). The remaining cuts in Act IV relate mainly to removing Vivie's Aunt Lizzie from the text, her presence having become redundant with the deletion of her mentoring role from Act II.

This mangled and mutilated three-act version of *Mrs Warren's Profession*—"as gratuitous an offence against good manners as any dramatist was ever guilty of"[7]—was duly given a single (and rudimentary) reading (with *The Philanderer*) at the Victoria Hall on Wednesday, 30 March 1898, with Annie Horniman as Vivie, Mrs. Dewar as Mrs. Warren, Brimley Johnson as Praed, H. M. Paget as Crofts, Percy Addleshaw as Frank Gardner, and David Dewar as the Reverend Gardner.[8] Happily, few were there to witness it, but it served its purpose of establishing Shaw's legal performance rights for the play. Just over two weeks later, on 19 April 1898, *Mrs Warren's Profession* was published in volume 1 of *Plays: Pleasant and Unpleasant* by Grant Richards in London and Herbert S. Stone in Chicago and New York.[9]

The Stage Society, 1902

More than four years after completing *Mrs Warren's Profession,* Shaw at least had the satisfaction of seeing the play in print, and of having taken all the steps he possibly could to protect his performance rights. There still seemed little prospect, however, of a production of the full unexpurgated text. And then came along the Stage Society, successor to J. T. Grein's Independent Theatre Society, which closed down in December 1898. Like the Independent Theatre Society, the Stage Society was dedicated to mounting private productions—beyond the jurisdiction of the Lord Chamberlain—of controversial and noncommercial plays from the British and European repertoire. And the Stage Society's founder, Frederick Whelen, like Grein, had a predilection for Shaw, signaled by the Society's opening production, the première of the licensed *You Never Can Tell* at the Royalty Theatre on 26 November 1899. Unlike Grein, however, Whelen also wanted to produce the unlicensed *Mrs Warren's Profession,* but he met with resistance from—of all people—Shaw himself. The problem was that since the Stage Society (like the Independent Theatre Society) did not have its own theater, it had to rent whatever facility was both suitable and available, which usually meant performing on Sunday evenings when public theaters, by law, were dark. Shaw feared that the management of any theater that allowed a private Sunday evening performance of *Mrs Warren's Profession* would be in double jeopardy: on the one hand for flouting the Sunday performance law, on the other for aiding and abetting circumvention of the Lord Chamberlain's ban on *Mrs Warren's Profession.* On both counts, any management would be perfectly within its rights, but since the operating licenses of public theaters (as well as plays) were also under the jurisdiction of the Lord Chamberlain, such cooperation with the Stage Society might expose the manager, as Shaw put it in a letter to R. Golding Bright, "to the intimidation of the Censor, and his absolutely autocratic power—to ruin any West End manager who offends him, without reason given or remedy available" (30 November 1901; Laurence II, 243). And so Shaw—magnanimously—"urged the Society to let it alone," recommending *The Philanderer* instead. "But the Society," Shaw told Golding Bright, "objected to the morals and tone of the Philanderer, and overbore me as to Mrs Warren. They would have it; and the cast would have it; and, in short, I had to withdraw my prudent objections in some disgrace, which served me right" (30 November 1901; Laurence II, 242).

The whimsicality of some aspects of Shaw's report to Golding Bright shouldn't be allowed to disguise the fact that finding a theater for *Mrs Warren's Profession* did prove to be a serious problem. Shaw reported to Mrs. Campbell on 22 November 1901 that he was in "hideous straits" about finding a theater: "We had it all arranged beautifully—Fanny Brough for Mrs Warren—when the theatre was withdrawn lest the Reader of Plays [George Redford] should revenge himself by suspending its license" (Laurence II, 214), and only after several theaters had turned down the Society's request (Laurence II, 240) was the small New Lyric Club secured for performances on 5 and 6 January 1902.

Directed by Shaw himself, the cast consisted of Fanny Brough as Mrs. Warren (who had initially turned down the part because of the play's subject matter), Madge McIntosh as Vivie, Julius Knight as Praed, Charles Goodhart as Crofts, Cosmo Stuart as the Reverend Gardner, and Harley Granville Barker as Frank Gardner. *The Times* (7 January 1902) gave the production a lengthy review, but expressed hardly any concern about the subject matter, taking Shaw to task instead for writing "a series of explanations" rather than a play. But J. T. Grein was there as well (at the January 5th matinée) for the *Sunday Special,* and he made it clear that his reasons for rejecting the play for the Independent Society hadn't changed one bit. "It was," Grein told his readers, "an exceedingly uncomfortable afternoon. For there was a majority of women to listen to that which could only be understood by a minority of men." The play "was not fit for women's ears"; its representation "was unnecessary and painful"; the problem it raises "is neither vital nor important"; "the play causes only pain and bewilderment" (Grein 293–95). The *St James Gazette* went further, considering the "tendency" of *Mrs Warren's Profession* to be "wholly evil" (quoted by Shaw, *Bodley Head* 255).

Grein and his colleagues at least expressed their distress—or, in some cases, disappointment at the lack of titillation—publicly. Others shielded themselves in anonymity. On 17 March 1902, Shaw received in the post a printed "Prospectus of the Pornographic Play Society (Limited)," announcing that "[t]he recent success of the suppressed Play called 'MRS. WARREN'S PROFESSION' encourages the Committee of the P.P. Society to follow it up by a series of performances suitable to the taste of supersensuous audiences." The Society promised a play based on the "sensational details" of a recent court case featuring "the services of all the young ladies engaged in the original case," followed by a play based on "the Life and Adventures of the late lamented Author [of] 'Lady Windermere's Fan.'" "It will deal with the foibles of Sodom and Gomorrah, and with certain 'piquant' practices of our 'modern Babylon' without an intimate knowledge of which, the education of 'Young England' cannot be regarded as complete."[10] An intriguing, but, alas, unfulfilled promise.

New Haven and New York, 1905

The years immediately following the Stage Society production of *Mrs Warren's Profession* were hectic and rewarding for Shaw, as his theatrical and political reputation grew apace in England and abroad. Occupied with many other matters, a public production of *Mrs Warren's Profession* was not among Shaw's priorities, at least not in England. He did, however, encourage and license Arnold Daly in America to produce (and direct) the first public performance of the play, which took place at the Hyperion Theatre, New Haven, on 27 October 1905. The original agreement with Daly[11] stipulated that Fanny Brough must play the role of Mrs. Warren (as she had in the Stage Society production), but in the event it was played by Mary Shaw, champion of Ibsen's plays in the United States, with Daly as Frank Gardner. Further clauses in Shaw's contract with Daly required Daly to use "the whole dialogue" of the play as published in *Plays: Pleasant and Unpleasant* and "as far as may be practicable" to "apprise the public of the fact that the Play is suitable for representation before serious adult audiences only." The caution was justified (though Daly seems not to have taken it seriously). Theatrical freedom of expression in the United States was not impeded by arbitrary and archaic censorship systems such as that practiced in England, but the guardians of American public morality, both official and self-appointed, had their own effective means of keeping objectionable plays such as *Mrs Warren's Profession* off the stage.

The New Haven production attracted massive publicity, most of it hostile, and after one performance the theater was closed by order of Mayor John P. Studley, who (while admitting that he hadn't read or seen the play) judged *Mrs Warren's Profession* to be "grossly indecent and not fit for public representation" (*New York Times,* 29 October 1905). Undaunted—but apprehensive—Daly took the play to New York, where it opened at the Garrick Theatre on 30 October 1905, again to hostile advance publicity. Opposition led by Anthony Comstock and the Society for the Suppression of Vice stopped the play in its tracks after one performance, even though Daly (never mind Shaw's instructions and sensibilities) had allowed New York Police Commissioner William McAdoo to go through the prompt script and cut every line he thought offensive. Daly gave strict instructions to the cast to follow McAdoo's expurgated text, and McAdoo was at the performance, script in hand, to make sure they did (though he apparently slept through part of the evening). Even so, McAdoo reported the next day to New York Mayor McClellan that the play was "revolting, indecent, and nauseating where it was not boring" (*New York Times,* 1 November 1905). This time Daly didn't have time to leave town. Along with the owner, manager, and members of the cast, he was charged with disorderly conduct, while the house manager, Samuel W. Gumpertz, was charged with committing a public nuisance. In the subsequent trial held in the New York Court of Special Sessions on 6 July 1906, the charges were dismissed, the court, much to Shaw's delight and satisfaction, determining that "instead of exciting impure imagination in the mind of the spectator, that which is really excited is disgust; that the unlovely, the repellant, the disgusting in the play, are merely accessories to the main purpose of the drama, which is an attack on certain social conditions relating to the employment of women, which the dramatist believes, as do many others with him, should be reformed."[12]

Mrs Warren's Profession also had a rough ride elsewhere in North America. It managed more performances (three) at the Walker Theatre in Winnipeg (where it opened in a Rose Coghlan touring production on 30 April 1907) than in New Haven or New York, but a local critic still condemned it as "a beatification of evil living, a sermon on the advantages of vice, and the story of a woman whom to term a courtesan would be a compliment" (*Manitoba Free Press,* 1 May 1907). Mary Shaw's way of dealing with opposition to the play when she toured it through the Midwest and on to the West Coast of the United States in the spring and summer of 1907 was to meet with local groups and prominent citizens in each community and change the text (without, of course, Shaw's knowledge, let alone permission) to accommodate their concerns.

However, the international acceptance of *Mrs Warren's Profession* as a powerful and important contemporary play was rapidly developing. There were productions throughout North America and Europe—Berlin, Stockholm, Budapest, Madrid, Munich, Paris—in 1907 and 1908.[13] And while some elements of the British press scoffed at the American treatment of *Mrs Warren's Profession* (e.g., the *Manchester Guardian* leader on 2 November 1905), the fact was that in the first decade of the twentieth century England was perhaps the only country in the world where public performances of *Mrs Warren's Profession* were banned.

The Manchester Application, 1907

The next effort to change this state of affairs was made by Ben Iden Payne. After involvement early in his career with Frank Benson's Shakespearean productions, Payne joined Annie Horniman in 1907 as general manager of her Manchester Repertory Company. It was in this capacity that Payne, with Shaw's approval, approached the Examiner of Plays (still George Redford) to request that he reconsider his earlier (1898) decision not to license *Mrs Warren's Profession*. Payne submitted his request on 29 July 1907 (Laurence II, 707). The response was immediate. Without bothering to read the play again, Redford returned Payne's letter to him, adding a curt note: "Surely you must be aware that the Licence for Representation of this piece was refused some years ago." Payne informed Shaw. Shaw replied to Payne on 4 August 1907, criticizing Redford for committing "one of his characteristic indiscretions," by which Shaw meant not only the discourteous informality of Redford's response to Payne, but also, as he explained in later correspondence with Payne, Redford's ignoring the changed circumstances since his first refusal of a license—i.e., the elapse of some years and a public trial (the New York 1906 trial) that had "resulted in a judicial decision that the play was not improper and might even lead to desirable reforms" (12 September 1909; Laurence II, 867). Shaw also enclosed with his 4 August 1907 letter to Payne a lengthy draft response for Payne to send to Redford, with instructions as well to Payne to "keep a copy carefully, with all the rest of the correspondence" (Laurence II, 707).

The draft drew Redford's attention to the international acceptance of *Mrs Warren's Profession*, to the New York court decision, to the dramatic and social importance of the play ("one of his masterpieces, not only as a play but as a dramatic sermon aimed at a crying social evil"—a generous self-compliment from Shaw), to other instances where the Lord Chamberlain had reversed his decisions, and to the reasonable elapse of time since the first application for a license. Strong arguments all—but to no avail. There was no need for Shaw's instruction to Payne to keep "the rest of the correspondence." There wasn't any—though one assumes that Redford, conscientious bureaucrat that he was, at least sent Payne an official rejection (and returned the reading fee that Payne had sent him).

The Pioneer Players, 1912

Five years passed before there was more activity with the still unlicensed *Mrs Warren's Profession*,[14] though there was plenty of activity from those, including, of course, Shaw, who were opposed to the censorship system. Two of Shaw's plays, *The Shewing-up of Blanco Posnet* and *Press Cuttings*, were denied licenses in 1909, and Shaw was an eager and prominent witness before the parliamentary Joint Select Committee established that year, in response to pressure from Shaw and others, to review the stage censorship law. The committee produced a substantial report in November 1909 with several recommendations to reform—but not abolish—the censorship, but the government took no action. (See Laurence II, 747–50, for a summary of Shaw's involvement in anti-censorship activities at this time.)

As regards *Mrs Warren's Profession,* another private performance was now arranged, again, as with the 1902 Stage Society production, bypassing the need for licensing by the Lord Chamberlain. The producer and director this time was Edith Craig, daughter of Ellen Terry and sister of Edward Gordon Craig. Edy Craig had a good Shavian heritage, having played Proserpine Garnett in both the first public (Independent Theatre, Aberdeen, 30 July 1897) and London (Stage Society, Strand Theatre, 1 July 1900) productions of *Candida,* and Mrs. Bridgenorth in the première of *Getting Married* at the Haymarket in June 1908 (replacing Mary Rorke after her one appearance at a matinée on 12 May). Also a talented costume designer, Edy Craig linked her theatrical career to her political interests through organizations such as the Actresses' Franchise League (which had, in part, a women's suffrage agenda) and the Pioneer Players, a group she formed in 1911 specifically to focus on women's issues. The Pioneer Players normally presented an annual series of five plays, usually with just a single Sunday matinée performance of each play, and always in a borrowed (small) theater. The company ran until 1921, mounting some 150 plays, and earning, among many others, the respect of Shaw. The company's "singleness of artistic direction, and unflagging activity," he said, "did more for the theatrical vanguard than any of the other coterie theatres."[15] Shaw was on the company's advisory committee, and Charlotte Shaw was on the board of directors, so it is not surprising that a Shaw play was selected for the first season. The choice of *Mrs Warren's Profession* was, however, controversial within the company, prompting the resignation of some board members (Fisher 49), but the production itself was a success.

Craig secured the King's Hall in Covent Garden for the production and decided that the play would generate sufficient interest to merit two performances. *Mrs Warren's Profession* opened on Sunday, 16 June 1912 (evening), and was repeated on Tuesday, 18 June (matinée), with a strong cast headed by Gertrude Kingston (for whom Shaw wrote *Great Catherine* in 1913) as Mrs. Warren. The production was widely advertised, but since it was a private production tickets could be obtained only from members of the Pioneer Players. Shaw attended the Tuesday matinée, and the London press was well represented at both performances. The reviews were decidedly more positive—and far less hysterical—than those for the Stage Society production. The house was "spell-bound" (*London Weekly Budget,* 23 June 1912) by a play of "ruthless courage and sincerity" (*Athenaeum,* 25 June 1912). This "daring and scintillating work" (*Vanity Fair,* 19 June 1912) was "excellently staged" (*Labour Leader,* 20 June 1912), though the short rehearsal period and the makeshift production facilities allegedly left a few rough edges. (See Fisher, 49–54, for a more detailed summary of the reviews.)

The production necessarily directed attention again to the Lord Chamberlain's ban on public performances of the play. The *Manchester Guardian* (17 June 1912) argued that most "sensible people" now recognize *Mrs Warren's Profession* as a "reasoned and eloquent plea for looking at things as they are." "The play is clear-sighted, it is logically convincing, it is witty, and the author's view which it expresses rings true with a broad humanity and sympathy." Why, then, the ban by the "senseless censor" (*Era,* 22 June 1912)? "And how our children and grandchildren will laugh at us, when they have digested their inevitable contempt" (the *Star,* 17 June 1912).

The Glasgow Playgoers League Club, 1913

In 1913, Japan joined those countries that had enjoyed professional productions of *Mrs Warren's Profession* (Conolly and Pearson 99), but the general public in England was still denied the opportunity. The number of people around the world who had by this time seen *Mrs Warren's Profession* probably numbered in the tens of thousands; in England, the number was barely a few hundred (at the Stage Society and Pioneer Players productions), limited to Londoners or those who had the time and money to get to London.

Credit for the first British production of *Mrs Warren's Profession* outside

London goes to Alfred Wareing, founder (in 1909) of the Glasgow Repertory Theatre. Wareing lacked the theatrical celebrity of Edith Craig, but he was equally—perhaps more—determined to get *Mrs Warren* on stage. And whereas Edy Craig had Shaw's backing and the Lord Chamberlain's dispassion, Wareing seems to have had no contact at all with Shaw and found himself subject to inquiries in the House of Commons and the attention of legal investigation at the highest level.

On Tuesday, 18 March 1913, a question was asked in the House of Commons by MacCallum Scott, a Scottish Member of Parliament. Had the attention of the Lord Advocate (the senior government law officer for Scotland), Scott wondered, "been called to the advertisement of the production at the Royalty Theatre, Glasgow, of a play which has been prohibited by the censor?" And, if so, does he propose to "take any action either to give effect to the censorship or to remove it altogether in Scotland?"[16] Scott may or may not have known that Wareing had already informed a government law official in Glasgow of his intention to form "The Glasgow Playgoer's League" to "enable Glasgow playgoers to witness George Bernard Shaw's play 'Mrs Warren's Profession' and any other censored play that may be produced under Mr Wareing's management." The official, the Procurator Fiscal (i.e., the public prosecutor), duly informed the government's Crown Agent in Edinburgh, advising him in a letter on 13 March 1913 that Wareing intended to produce *Mrs Warren's Profession* at the Royalty Theatre in Glasgow "in about a month," and that it was Wareing's view that he was only doing what was being done in London "under similar arrangements without interference" (presumably a reference to the Pioneer Players' production of *Mrs Warren's Profession* the previous year). The Procurator Fiscal concluded, quite rightly, that Wareing's proposal "looks very much like the scheme of an association to evade the Act" (the legislation that empowered the Lord Chamberlain's censorship).

Scott's question in the House of Commons five days later prompted a flurry of legal activity. Wareing had achieved impeccable social credentials for the League—the president was the Lord Provost of Edinburgh, and there were three professors and a cleric among the vice presidents—but this didn't stop the Scottish legal establishment going on full alert in reaction to Scott's inquiry. The Lord Advocate's legal secretary wrote to the Crown Agent in Edinburgh on 19 March 1913 informing him that the Lord Advocate had advised Scott that he was "considering whether legal proceedings should be taken" against the League. There had been consultation with the Lord Chamberlain and with the Home Office about policy on private performances of banned plays, and the Lord Advocate had learned that "wherever the admission to the performance is limited to the members of a club there is no contravention of the provisions of the statute." However, such a club must not be "purely illusory" and must have "some form of proposal or nomination and election of members." The Lord Advocate thought it advisable that the Procurator Fiscal "communicate with Mr Wareing privately" to clarify the requirements of the law and to ensure that he take "the very small steps" necessary to avoid any infringement—in which case "Mr Wareing need fear no interference."

The Procurator Fiscal duly met with Wareing (twice) and then reported to the Crown Agent on 29 October 1913 that Wareing and officers of the (by now established) Glasgow Playgoers League had agreed to form the Glasgow Playgoers League Club, the objects of which "shall be to support the REPERTORY THEATRE movement in general and to organise private performances of such censored plays as may be considered worthy of production." Membership in the club was by application, and the executive committee could accept or reject applications or, "on a good or sufficient reason being shown," expel members. Since members of the Glasgow Playgoers League automatically became members of the Glasgow Playgoers League Club, and since the officers of each organization were the same people, there were clearly some legal niceties afoot to add to this bizarre series of events and characters that could well have provided the plot for a Gilbert and Sullivan opera. And all that Wareing wanted to do was produce a play that was now in the standard repertoire of theater companies around the world.

But the law was deferred to, and the Lord Advocate pronounced his contentment in a memorandum of 3 April 1913: "I am satisfied that no breach of the law will be committed if the censored play is performed for the members of the club and their guests. Having seen Mr Wareing I assured him that no proceedings would be taken."

Mrs Warren's Profession opened at the Royalty Theatre, Glasgow, under the auspices of the Glasgow Playgoers League Club, on Thursday, 10 April 1913, with two additional performances on Saturday, 12 April (matinée), and Tuesday, 15 April (advertised in the *Glasgow News,* 7 and 11 April 1913), with Ruth Mackay as Mrs. Warren and Helen Brown as Vivie. The theater was crowded on opening night, management, "familiar with every move in the game," according to the reviewer for the *Glasgow News,* having "cleverly boomed" the occasion, implying (an intriguing possibility) that the "question in Parliament" had been set up by Wareing. Neither the booming nor the play impressed the reviewer. He sensed that "someone was out for blood," Redford's blood, he thought, in which case Redford (who had, in fact, retired in 1911) "is to be congratulated" for emerging from the evening with "infinitely more credit" than Shaw:

> *Mrs Warren's Profession* is a play that deserved the Censor's disapproval, and there is no need to labour the point. To those who saw it produced last night much of it appealed, it could scarcely fail to,

for it is admirably well done in its way. But we do not like its way, and for the simple reason that while granting a full measure of sympathy to Mrs Warren, the prostitute, we decline to accept the defence of Mrs Warren, the procuress; it is a defence put up after the admission of guilt, the defence of a woman still engaged in a trade unspeakable, a defence absolutely nauseating. But we are not going to weave a network of argument. We know that Mr Shaw shows virtue triumphant, and that his sneers are not levelled against that. What we object to is that the procuress should be heard in public. Her case is for closed doors.

The Dublin Repertory Theatre, 1914

Redford couldn't have put it better himself. He was still keeping English theater doors closed to *Mrs Warren,* but they continued to open elsewhere. It was now Ireland's turn.[17] Shaw had tried (and failed) in 1897 to arrange a copyright performance of *Mrs Warren's Profession* in Dublin (see above), but it would have been a hasty and shabby affair at best, arranged only to protect Shaw's legal interests. Any company in Ireland planning to produce a play banned in England had to be alert to the possibility of political pressure from Dublin Castle, seat of the Lord Lieutenant, the British government's authority in the not-yet-independent Ireland. Such pressure, including a threat to close the theater, had been brought to bear when the Abbey Theatre produced Shaw's *The Shewing-up of Blanco Posnet* in August 1909, its production in England having been prevented by the Lord Chamberlain (on Redford's recommendation) because of the play's alleged blasphemy (see Laurence II, 856). And now another Dublin company, the Dublin Repertory Theatre, showed its disdain for the Lord Chamberlain by choosing to produce *Mrs Warren's Profession.*

The production was announced in the *Irish Independent* on 10 November 1914. It was to be performed for five nights at the Little Theatre, 40 Sackville Street, Dublin, opening on 16 November. There was swift reaction from Dublin Castle. The *Irish Times* reported on 14 November 1914 that the Attorney-General "had warned the Dublin Repertory Theatre that, if they put their play on the stage in an unpatented theatre, they incur a penalty of £300 for each performance." The article explained that the intervention had nothing to do with "anything in the play itself"; it was simply that the Little Theatre was not a properly licensed venue for theatrical productions. The same article also pointed out, however, that previous productions in the same venue had not excited any interest from the

Castle. The Dublin Repertory Theatre ignored the Castle, and *Mrs Warren's Profession* opened as scheduled on 16 November. It was advertised as being performed "for the First Time in Public"—which was true if one ignored the world beyond the United Kingdom—and the play's notoriety, now augmented by government threats against the producers, ensured great interest in opening night. The public, said the *Irish Independent* (17 November 1914) "looked forward to a shindy." The *Irish Times* (17 November 1914), put it more prosaically: ticket holders "understood that the play had been banned, and they naturally expected that the forces of the Crown would bar their access to the theatre." Castle authorities, however, wisely backed off from any such confrontation, and everything, the *Irish Times* reported (17 November 1914), "was plain sailing." It was also "very dull and very commonplace" sailing according to the *Irish Independent* critic, and the "frequent and hearty applause" was for the cast, not the play. "It was a pity to see two such clever actresses as Miss Flora MacDonald and Miss Una O'Connor wasting their talents on the ungrateful parts of mother and daughter, respectively" (17 November 1914). But Shaw's contribution was warmly acknowledged by the *Irish Times:* "the author captivates the audience by the brilliancy of dialogue and by sly thrusts at hypocritical folk who hold up their hands in horror at the mere mention of unsavoury things" (17 November 1914).

The remaining four performances in Dublin took place uneventfully, which only served to emphasize the absurdity of the continuing ban in England.

The Plymouth Venture, 1916

The next effort to secure the Lord Chamberlain's license for a public performance of *Mrs Warren's Profession* in England came from George S. King, co-lessee and co-manager of the Plymouth Repertory Theatre. George Redford had retired from the position of Examiner of Plays at the end of 1911, and when King made his pitch on 4 October 1916 there were two Examiners in office, Ernest Bendall and George Street. King's case for a reconsideration of the ban was based on his (naive, as it turned out) sense that "a more enlightened censorship" seemed to be in place, and (more interestingly) that since *Mrs Warren's Profession* is "essentially a play for women, to whom it conveys a great moral lesson," and since "with the bulk of our manhood on war service, the theatre is largely patronised by women," it is appropriate time to reverse the ban.[18] One wonders what King took to be the "great moral lesson" of the play, but in any event he never got the chance to reveal it. In a memo to Douglas Dawson, Comptroller of the Lord Chamberlain's Office, Bendall quickly dismissed King's argument, saying that it gave him no reason to reconsider earlier adverse decisions about the play. Street concurred, but at least advanced a few reasons for his decision. "The author" (he meant Shaw), he appreciated, "is entirely in earnest"; and "no doubt the theme [of *Mrs Warren's Profession*] is important and can be rightly discussed in the press." But not in the theater—"except before an audience well knowing what it is to expect and of a special kind, as is the Stage Society." That was good enough for Dawson. He wrote immediately to King to say that he was "desired by the Lord Chamberlain to inform you that he regrets he cannot see his way to alter his decision not to license the Play *Mrs Warren's Profession* for public performance on the stage." The two-guinea reading fee sent by King was returned, and on 6 October King wrote back to Dawson to acknowledge receipt of the returned fee and to note "with great regret" the Lord Chamberlain's decision. King also sent a copy of Dawson's letter to Shaw, who made a brief handwritten comment on it (undated): "On this I wrote a long private letter to Lord Sandhurst (asking him not to answer it) pointing out that the correct course was to re-read the play and accept the fee as otherwise the original opinion could never be revised, and suggesting that he should make a regulation to that effect."[19]

Shaw's six-page letter (8 October) to Lord Sandhurst, who served as Lord Chamberlain from 1912 to 1921, essentially made the point that if the Lord Chamberlain's Examiners of Plays declined to reread a play that had previously been denied a license, then there was no chance that the play would ever be licensed at all, which was, as Shaw put it, "governing the stage by the Dead Hand." Shaw recommended, quite reasonably, that Sandhurst should implement a regulation that "plays may be sent in for reconsideration after a certain interval on payment of a fresh reading fee."[20] There was no need, Shaw said, for Sandhurst to reply to the letter, but there was a response anyway (19 October 1916), based on advice received from Bendall (memo of 12 October), in which Sandhurst ignored Shaw's arguments and said simply that "the reason why the reading fee was returned was because both my present Examiners of Plays had read the play. I was thoroughly well acquainted with it and I did not require it to be read again before giving a decision."

Clearly fed up by now with such obfuscation, Shaw wrote back (20 October) to say that *Mrs Warren's Profession* "should be read carefully through every year by your whole staff," for which Shaw would be happy to pay an annual reader's fee. By the end of the letter, however, Shaw's frustration was even clearer: "as the older I grow the more inclined I am to believe that all plays whatsoever should be prohibited, I have nothing more to say, and am unaffectedly apologetic for having said so much." Sandhurst's handwritten note at the top of the letter reads "[t]his letter not ackn[d] as I look on it as closing the correspondence."[21] And that was that for Plymouth. By now Shaw was surely wondering if the "Dead Hand" of George Redford had a permanent grip on *Mrs Warren's Profession*.

Edwin T. Heys, 1917

It took just over two weeks for the Lord Chamberlain's Office to see off Plymouth's George King (and Shaw's follow-up). Mrs Warren's next champion was far more persistent and insistent. Like King, he hailed from the provinces. Edwin T. Heys ran his own production company in Manchester, though he had had managerial experience in London and he maintained an office there. It was from Manchester, however, that Heys wrote to the Lord Chamberlain (still Sandhurst) on 9 June 1917, "with the approval of the author," and enclosing a copy of *Mrs Warren's Profession* and the reading fee, to inform Sandhurst of his intention to produce the play "at a London West End Theatre." "I shall be glad," Heys politely concluded, "to receive your formal sanction in due course."[22] The "due course" lasted six months, and Sandhurst remained resolute in his denial of a license, but not without first having to withstand considerable pressure from numerous Shavian allies, many from unexpected quarters.

Heys quickly got the initial response. It came on 11 June 1917 from the chief clerk in the Lord Chamberlain's Office. The Lord Chamberlain, the chief clerk told Heys, "thinks that perhaps you are not aware that he has refused to issue a license for this play, and as lately as last Autumn [the Plymouth application] the matter was again reconsidered, but he was unable to change his views." Heys's check for the reading fee and his copy of *Mrs Warren's Profession* were returned to him.

That seemed to end the matter until Heys got things moving again in September, but in the meantime, perhaps quite unrelated to Heys's efforts, the Lord Chamberlain received an interesting letter (3 August [1917]) from a Fred Jarman in Exeter. Mr. Jarman told Lord Sandhurst that he had been asked "by some people interested in social problems to see you with a view to getting the ban against the performance of Mr Shaw's play 'Mrs Warren's Profession' removed." Jarman argued that the play "deals with a great social evil & should prove a strong instrument to its reform." Plays such as Eugène Brieux's *Damaged Goods* and Ibsen's *Ghosts* have been licensed and are "educating the public," so it is time,

Jarman said, to reconsider the ban on *Mrs Warren's Profession*, "which also aims at making the world a cleaner place to live in." Jarman sought an interview with the Lord Chamberlain to discuss the matter, but he was rebuffed in a letter of 7 August 1917: "it is hardly worthwhile putting you to the trouble of coming up to London" since the Lord Chamberlain "sees no reason to change his views" about the play.

Jarman may well have been acting independently of Heys (or Shaw), but the cases of *Ghosts* and *Damaged Goods*, as we shall see, were important to Heys (and Shaw) as well.[23] *Ghosts* had finally been licensed in 1914, more than twenty years after its English première in a private Independent Theatre Society production in 1891, and Brieux's *Damaged Goods*, another play that deals with the fact and consequences of venereal disease, was licensed early in 1917, mainly because it was viewed by officialdom as a warning to soldiers on leave in London about the dangers of syphilis (de Jongh 53–55).

Heys returned to the fray in earnest in September 1917. It was easy enough for the Lord Chamberlain to reject license applications from individual theater managers, so perhaps what was needed was a collective approach. With Shaw's active support, Heys took steps to organize a petition. On 12 September 1917, from his London office on Leicester Street in the West End, Heys distributed two thousand copies[24] of a package of material that included a request for support to remove the ban on *Mrs Warren's Profession*, a long letter from Shaw, a brief appreciation of the plays of Brieux by novelist Hall Caine, and the petition itself:

> We, the undersigned, are of the opinion that the ban hitherto placed upon the performance of George Bernard Shaw's play 'MRS. WARREN'S PROFESSION' should now be withdrawn, and the play licensed for production in this country. We make this request on the grounds that:—
> 1. The problem with which the play so effectively deals is now recognised to be one of extreme gravity.
> 2. The stage is being more and more utilised as a much-needed educational factor in connection with this subject.
> 3. 'MRS. WARREN'S PROFESSION' is a dramatic work of acknowledged excellence by one of our foremost British dramatists, and we would respectfully urge that facilities for its production should be accorded in the same way as has been done with other plays of similar tendency by foreign authors.
> 4. We believe there is a widespread desire amongst British playgoers to witness this play on the British stage. The play has been already performed many times in America and other countries.

The letter that Shaw wrote in support of the petition is a powerful statement about the "special persecution" of *Mrs Warren's Profession*. (The ellipses are Shaw's.)

Dear Mr. Heys,

My play entitled 'MRS. WARREN'S PROFESSION' was written more than twenty years ago. It was refused a license by the Lord Chamberlain, and has never been publicly performed in Great Britain, though, as you know, it has been repeatedly performed in the United States and Canada, as well as on the Continent. All attempts to induce the Lord Chamberlain to reconsider his decision have failed. . . . I greatly doubt whether it will ever be licensed in this country, because it has against it the huge commercial interests in prostitution, which are not exposed by the plays of Brieux, or by the many other plays which deal with sexual vice in a frankly pornographic manner, and are licensed without demur.

It is noteworthy in this connection that the play was prosecuted in America; and though the Courts finally vindicated its morality and dismissed the charge, yet in one town, where the municipal government was in the hands of the brothel trade, the Company was driven out by a threat of prosecution at common law for an offence against morals.[25]

The reason for this special persecution of a play obviously much more innocent than the majority of those which are tolerated without question is that whereas these latter act as aphrodisiacs and actually stimulate the trade in women, my play makes it extremely repulsive, not in a sensational way—for all the sensational ways advertise what they pretend to condemn—but by simply exposing the venality of the transaction to which the prostitute is a party. To experienced men of the world it seems impossible that a young soldier should be taken in by the endearments of the prostitute. But the prostitute would not use those endearments if she did not know their value; in fact she does not use them with the people who neither desire nor believe in them. In my young days, when prostitutes accosted me, I became familiar not only with the mask of affection, but with the cynical frankness with which it is dropped when it is no use. If a young man has any decent feeling left in him—and most of the prostitute's younger clients have plenty of it—he is more repelled by the idea of being entertained for money alone by a secretly disgusted woman than by all the sermons that can be preached to him about his own purity and duty. I think a really good performance of 'MRS. WARREN'S PROFESSION' would keep its audience out of the hands of the women of the street for a fortnight at least. And that is precisely why it encounters an opposition unknown in the case of plays which stimulate the sex illusion to such an extent that the prostitute reaps a richer harvest from them than the actors.

I have been asked why I omitted from 'MRS. WARREN'S PROFESSION' the contingency of venereal disease, the agitation against which has forced the Lord Chamberlain to license the admirable play by Brieux entitled 'Damaged Goods.' My reason was that venereal disease is not an essential part of prostitution. A knowledge of that danger, far from deterring men from resorting to prostitutes, will simply enable both the prostitute and her client to take effective precaution against it. Metchnikoff made the means of preventing infection widely known; and long before he experimented, the hygiene of sexual intercourse was familiar enough to many prostitutes.[26] In fact the better instructed a man is in this matter, the better he knows that seduction is more dangerous than prostitution in this respect. Therefore all plays which aim merely at awakening the public to the danger of venereal disease—a very important and praiseworthy object—can have no ultimate effect on prostitution but to make it safer and more popular.

My play avoids these side issues. It strikes straight at prostitution by exposing its sordid economics. And it exposes also the inevitable result of promiscuous sexual intercourse in raising insoluble questions of consanguinity. How badly the play was needed was shown by the hysterical unpreparedness of the public for the White Slave agitation, and the useless and savage legislation which followed,[27] and which had the effect of making Mrs. Warren complete mistress of the situation by ridding her of male competitors. Had 'MRS. WARREN'S PROFESSION' been allowed to take its proper place on the stage when I wrote it, that blunder and all those hysterics might have been averted. But the Lord Chamberlain's Office would not allow Sir George Crofts's business to be exposed; and I doubt if it will ever do so. It will allow the prostitute and the procuress and the brothel to supply the sensations of a hundred melodramas; but it will always ward off the one touch at which the attraction of these things withers like the garden of Klingsor.[28]

I am no less convinced than I was in 1895 of the need for such a play as 'MRS. WARREN'S PROFESSION'. . . .

If England clings to the belief that her harlots are doing for love what they have been driven by poverty to do for money, let her cling to it; and much good may it do her.

I should let you have the play with pleasure if it were available.

As it is, you must find some piece that will not threaten the profits of Euston and Marylebone Roads.

Yours faithfully,
G. BERNARD SHAW

By early October, Heys judged that he had enough support to submit the petition to the Lord Chamberlain. He wrote on 9 October 1917, again requesting that a license be issued for *Mrs Warren's Profession*. Included this time was "a representative list of names of prominent and influential men and women who have signed the petition in favor of that course." It was an impressive list of politicians (including thirty-six MPs), actors, producers, playwrights, writers, senior military personnel, academics, and medical practitioners. The 180 signatories included Wells, Chesterton, Galsworthy, Barrie, Martin Harvey, Brieux, William Poel, Ellen Terry, Gilbert Murray, Masefield, Sidney Webb, and even William Archer (who had initially supported the suppression of the play[29]). Among the women signatories was Millicent Garratt Fawcett, president of the National Union of Women's Suffrage Societies. Twenty-seven medical officers from Accrington to Yeovil also signed, as did a bishop (the Right Reverend Lord Bishop of Lincoln).

There were, to be sure, some who made it clear that they thought the petition ill-judged. One request was returned to Heys with the scribbled comment "Surely we do *not* [double underlining] want this sort of stuff in our theatres at such a period of earnest anxiety & stress [i.e., the war]." Critic and essayist (and with Archer, co-translator of Ibsen) Edmund Gosse wrote directly and forcefully to Sandhurst on 15 October 1917:

My dear Sandhurst,

I had not heard—but I am not surprised to hear—that you are to be pressed to licence "Mrs. Warren's Profession". My own belief is that the best cure for it would be to let people see for themselves what an empty, ugly, essentially untrue and uninteresting affair it is. I take it to be the least amusing and the least skilful (or one of the least) of all Shaw's plays.

The Censorship is in this difficulty, that no one, not even the Bishop of London, c^ld say that it is *immoral*. It is just its preposterous morality which makes it so offensive. It is like a priggish old clergyman preaching "to men only" in a night-shelter.

I cannot help thinking that you might determine on the bold step of saying to the petitioners, "Very well, then—there *is* your 'Mrs Warren's Profession'! Take the dull and dirty thing and make the most you can of it!" The result, I firmly believe, would be an ignominious fiasco for the play, and it would withdraw to appear no more.

The difficulty seems to me to rest in the fact that you cannot by any stretch of terms call the nasty production *immoral*. It is as cold and uninviting as ditch-water or a tract. It is, in fact, a *tract* and a very tiresome one.

Now it seems to me very irksome to think of the Lord Chamberlain, on his high throne, stooping to crush a *tract* between his thumb-nail and the floor. It is too small, and the value of the object not worth it.

But I am sure you will act with wisdom. You have been by far the best Censor of Plays this country has ever had, & I think we may continue to trust you. But beware of the temptation of making a martyr of a flea.

Sincerely y[rs]
Edmund Gosse

Sandhurst was getting other unsolicited advice, though not so bitingly expressed. The secretary of the Catholic Federation of the Archdiocese of Westminster sent a "strong protest" against the possible licensing of *Mrs Warren's Profession* on 1 October 1917, and also generously volunteered to help with censoring "plays of this description." And Sandhurst had at his disposal as well, of course, his own Examiner of Plays, whose advice was resolute. It was perfectly reasonable, Ernest Bendall wrote in a memo on 21 September 1917, to license a play such as *Damaged Goods,* "disagreeable" though it is, because of its "possible usefulness for propaganda." *Mrs Warren's Profession* was a different matter altogether: its "offensiveness" has no propaganda value "as it merely deals with prostitution as a trade to be followed as an alternative to less well-paid labour. It teaches . . . no valuable lesson: and the offensiveness of its subject and treatment still prevents its being recommended for license." Just to make sure, Bendall read the play again, but the rereading didn't cause him to change his mind (memorandum, 8 October 1917). An advisory board (established in 1909) was also available to give advice to the Lord Chamberlain on sensitive or difficult licensing cases. Sandhurst consulted the board in October 1917 about *Mrs Warren's Profession.* The only voice against maintaining the ban was that of Sir Walter Raleigh, professor of English at Oxford, who defended Shaw—in a backhanded kind of way—as "an established institution" who "has ceased to be irresponsible."

Sandhurst, then, was not short of advice. It was time for a decision. He summarized his views in a handwritten memorandum to the advisory board. He shrugged off Shaw's letter (the one with the petition) as "singu-

larly weak for so able a man." The subject matter of *Mrs Warren's Profession*
he judged "unsavoury to the last degree," and the play "presents nothing
to ameliorate affairs." And although it had been widely performed in the
United States, he was aware that some Americans "strongly condemned
it." As regards the signatures supporting the petition, he had also received
"collective and individual protests against the licence."

The outcome was clear. The chief clerk wrote to Heys on 30 October
1917 to advise him that the Lord Chamberlain, "after re-reading the play
and fully considering the accompanying documents . . . is unable to revise
former decisions." The license application was again denied.

But Heys was not giving up just yet. On 31 October, Heys mailed another letter to the chief clerk with an additional twenty-two names for the
petition, including two more bishops and four more medical officers.
There is no record of a response to this letter, but a month later (30 November 1917) Heys made one more effort. There were no further names
this time, just a summary of the support he had received: three bishops;
twelve "important" army officers; thirty-seven medical officers and physi-
cians; forty-four privy councillors and MPs; "most of the leading men and
women in the Theatrical profession;" "practically *every living author of note*"
[Heys's emphasis]; and "many other distinguished men and women." Furthermore, the petition had been "presented" (presumably to the Lord
Chamberlain—though Heys's meaning here is not entirely clear) by none
other than J. T. Grein, "probably the most distinguished critic in England," and, of course, like William Archer, one of the fiercest opponents
of *Mrs Warren's Profession* when Shaw was first trying to get the play produced (though, sensibly, Heys did not point this out to Sandhurst). Heys
once again reminded Sandhurst of the important subject matter of the
play, of the licensing of other controversial plays, of the increasing importance of women in the labor force, of the frequent performances of the
play in North America and Europe, of his "scrupulously careful" avoid-
ance of attacking "the censorship as such," and of his significant experience as a manager and producer. Then, sounding close to the end of his
tether, Heys tried one last strategy: "I am prepared to enter into any reasonable guarantee for [a] clean and sincere production, and would be willing to devote all and any profits derived from the performance of 'MRS.
WARREN'S PROFESSION' in London to any charitable purpose you may
denominate." Heys concluded his letter by requesting a meeting with
Sandhurst "so that I may answer any questions you may feel disposed to
ask, and attempt to remove the unfavourable impression which you appear to have received."

That final comment was something of an understatement, but Heys got
the meeting he requested. It took place in the Lord Chamberlain's Office
in St. James's Palace on 12 December 1917. Sandhurst made a handwrit-

ten note about the meeting: "I had a talk with Mr Heys & said that I could not licence Mrs W's Profession & declared the matter over."

Conspiracy?

It was beginning to look like a conspiracy. Shaw had hinted darkly in his letter that accompanied Heys's petition that "the huge commercial interests in prostitution" would forever prevent a production of *Mrs Warren's Profession* in England. The idea of collusion between the Lord Chamberlain's Office and the barons of prostitution (i.e., the George Crofts of England) seems far-fetched, but consider the persuasive case made by Shaw in his preface to the 1902 edition of the play:

> The profits of Mrs Warren's profession are shared not only by Mrs Warren and Sir George Crofts, but by the landlords of their houses, the newspapers which advertize them, the restaurants which cater for them, and, in short, all the trades to which they are good customers, not to mention the public officials and representatives whom they silence by complicity, corruption, or blackmail. Add to these the employers who profit by cheap female labor, and the shareholders whose dividends depend on it (you find such people everywhere, even on the judicial bench and in the highest places in Church and State) and you get a large and powerful class with a strong pecuniary incentive to protect Mrs Warren's profession, and a correspondingly strong incentive to conceal, from their own consciences no less than from the world, the real sources of their gain. (*Bodley Head* 262–63)

In the aftermath of the Heys affair, Beatrice Webb also suspected that there were factors involved in the suppression of *Mrs Warren's Profession* that went beyond the play itself. On 19 March 1918, she wrote to Lord Haldane, the prominent Liberal statesman (former Secretary of State for War and former Lord Chancellor), who knew Shaw well. Mrs. Webb had more names of medical officers opposed to the ban that she wanted Haldane to pass on to Sandhurst ("You will see that the principal women doctors are among them, and some of the most eminent of the municipal medical men"), but she also brought to Haldane's attention the feeling among "many of the Labour people [who are] interested in intellectual questions and moral reform . . . that the Lord Chamberlain is prejudiced against Bernard Shaw on account of his 'other opinions.'" Mrs. Webb professed not to believe that this was the case, but she did wonder why the "queer morality which is promulgated by the ordinary conventional Tory dramatist is permitted to be freely expressed" while "G.B.S.'s puritanism is suppressed."[30]

Shaw's "other opinions" no doubt included, in Mrs. Webb's mind, his controversial views on the First World War and on Ireland, though neither she nor Haldane (when he wrote to Sandhurst about *Mrs Warren's Profession*) went into any detail about this. Haldane's intervention was, in fact, half-hearted. He wrote to Sandhurst immediately he received Mrs. Webb's letter (both are dated 19 March 1918), and enclosed not only the list of names she had sent him but also her letter. Haldane also indicated that "[s]everal influential members of the Labour party" (including Sidney as well as Beatrice Webb) had been to see him about the "embargo" on *Mrs Warren's Profession*. "They take pride in a different view of the doctrine in it from that which is sometimes held." The strongest admonition to Sandhurst that Haldane could muster from all of this, however, was that "[w]hat Mrs Webb writes in the enclosed is, I think, worth considering." Sandhurst's response to Haldane is not in the Lord Chamberlain's papers, but his handwritten note on Haldane's letter gives the gist of what, predictably, the reply said: "matter fully considered."[31]

Birmingham: Round One, 1921

The Public Prosecutor of Hungary damned *Mrs Warren's Profession* in the summer of 1920: "I know of no more contemptible, filthier drama than this. Why, I can't even force my lips to utter what the subject-matter of this play really is," he was reported (by the *Daily Herald*, 2 August 1920) to have said.[32] But audiences in Hungary still got to see the play. It ran successfully at the Magyar Theatre, Budapest, in 1919 and again through the 1920–21 season (Pálfy 95). There were also productions in Berlin and Vienna in the 1917–18 seasons (Weiss 182), in Japan in 1919 (Conolly and Pearson 99), and, from 1920 onward, in various theaters in Estonia, Latvia, and Lithuania (Conolly and Pearson 103). Almost everywhere, in fact, but England.

And now another provincial city made a bid for the distinction of producing the first public performance in the country of *Mrs Warren's Profession*. Bache Matthews, business manager of the Birmingham Repertory Theatre—a theater that was to figure prominently in a later stage of Shaw's career (Conolly xi–xxiv)—wrote to the Lord Chamberlain's Office (enclosing, as usual, a copy of the play and the two-guinea reading fee) on

30 June 1921, stating, optimistically, that the planned opening night for
the play was Saturday, 9 July.[33]

Perhaps part of the reason for Matthews's optimism—or was it bra-
vado?—was that there had been a change of personnel in the Lord Chamberlain's Office. Douglas Dawson, Comptroller, was still there, but there
was a new Lord Chamberlain (the Duke of Atholl succeeded Lord Sandhurst, who died in office in 1921) and, more important perhaps, Ernest
Bendall (who also died in office, in 1920) was no longer there—though
George Street, who had worked with Bendall since 1914, was; Street was
appointed the new Senior Examiner on Bendall's death. Both Bendall and
Street had been unbending in their opposition to licensing *Mrs Warren's
Profession* on previous occasions, but now there seemed to be at least some
potential for fresh thinking.

On receiving the Birmingham application, Street wrote a long internal
memorandum (2 July 1921). The first sentence was unremarkable: "This
play has been refused a licence more than once." Indeed. But Street's
next sentence must have startled his colleagues: "The refusal was entirely
justified at the time, but for reasons to be stated later I think on the whole
a licence may now be granted." For the first time in more than twenty
years, there was support in the Lord Chamberlain's Office for allowing
Mrs Warren's Profession to be publicly performed. Street's memo goes on
to outline the plot of the play, "though it is no doubt well known by the
Lord Chamberlain and the Board." And then the crucial section, worth
quoting in full because of the extraordinary change from earlier pronouncements:

> My reasons for reconsidering the refusal are: (1) The play has been
> performed more than once by private societies in England and
> publicly in other countries. It has been freely circulated in book
> form. It has been extensively discussed for years. It is in fact very
> well known to a large public. Therefore it is in a way futile to pro-
> hibit its public performance. (2) The far greater liberty in the case
> of serious plays now enjoyed by the stage might cover the present-
> ment of such a character as Mrs. Warren, done seriously and in
> good faith. An audience will no longer be shocked as it would have
> been. (3) A considerable number of people regard it as a valuable
> play on the side of morality. It may be difficult to follow this argu-
> ment, but the fact remains. Certainly the play is deeply serious in
> intention. (4) Beyond the frankness necessary to state the theme
> there is no offence in the play.

"If there should be any inconsistency in granting a licence I share it,"
Street conceded, "since I agreed with my colleague [Bendall] in not rec-

ommending a licence some years ago." However, "[a]fter very careful consideration I have changed my mind. The Lord Chamberlain will no doubt have other advice. So far as I am concerned the play is, though quite without enthusiasm, Recommended for Licence."

Street's inability to understand the "morality" of the play and his total lack of enthusiasm for enabling it to be performed are regrettable, but forgivable in this context. His memo is otherwise remarkable for its good sense and pragmatic outlook. Never had *Mrs Warren's Profession* been so close to being licensed. All that was required now was the Lord Chamberlain's assent to his official's recommendation—normally a formality. But not this time. Atholl did not even bother to consult the advisory board. His handwritten comment on the second page of Street's memo is a blunt rejection of Street's advice: "I feel I cannot reverse the decision already arrived at by my predecessors. Conditions now are different to when the play was written & it makes it almost worse to produce it now than then as facts regarding work & life & wages now are much better than when the play was written, & many people might think that the conditions then are the conditions *now* in social life."[34] That is about as bizarre and befuddled a rationale for continuing to suppress *Mrs Warren's Profession* as one could imagine, but the Duke had spoken and on 5 July 1921 the Comptroller sent out the standard "his Lordship regrets" letter to Matthews, enclosing the submitted copy of the play and the reading fee. Matthews replied on 6 July 1921, with a tart comment that "a careful reading of the play might have convinced his Lordship of the advisability of licensing a work that has undoubtedly taken a permanent place in standard English drama." Matthews also on the same day wrote to Shaw to inform him of the outcome of the license application. Shaw simply wrote on it, "File, 'Mrs Warren's Profession.'"[35]

Birmingham: Round Two, 1922

It is hard to know what prompted the Birmingham Repertory Theatre to apply for a license again only a few months after the July 1921 rejection. But apply Matthews did, this time on 25 January 1922 (enclosing, of course, a copy of the play and the two-guinea reading fee). He seemed to think that it might be possible for Street and Shaw to come to "some arrangement" about the play (one wonders if Shaw had been consulted about this), and Matthews arranged to have H. K. Ayliff (who would direct the play) visit Street to discuss the matter. The proposed date of the production was 16 March 1922. Given Street's new attitude toward licensing

Mrs Warren's Profession, it is conceivable—though barely—that he privately gave Matthews some encouragement to pursue a new application, and it does appear that he arranged a meeting between Ayliff and the Lord Chamberlain.[36]

On 28 January an official pulled out the file from Matthews's 1921 application and sent it to the Lord Chamberlain with a reminder—as if Atholl needed one—that "this play has in the past been one of the Lord Chamberlain's stumbling blocks." Atholl took a couple of weeks to get around to determining what the next steps should be, and then directed (in a memo on 19 February) that the advisory board should be consulted. The same memo, however, contains the startling comment that "My opinion is that we should pass it, though I think it is unsavoury. I think it probably does more harm to the censorship unpassed than passed." The Duke of Atholl thus became the first Lord Chamberlain (of five who had held office since the first application in 1898) to support the licensing of *Mrs Warren's Profession.* Neither he nor his Examiner of Plays thought the play had any merit—moral or artistic—but neither saw much point in continuing the ban. The way, at last, looked clear for public performances.

But there remained the advisory board. There were five board members in 1922: Lord Buckmaster, lawyer; H. H. Higgins (no relation to Henry), solicitor; Sir Walter Raleigh, Oxford don; Squire Bancroft, retired actor-manager; and Sir Douglas Dawson, Comptroller of the Lord Chamberlain's Office (ex-officio). Buckmaster had strongly supported the ban when last consulted about *Mrs Warren's Profession* (in 1917) and indicated in a memo (2 February 1922) that he still held that opinion. Solicitor Higgins, however, expressed the view (26 February 1922) that "if brothel keeping is to be assumed a suitable topic for stage treatment" (which he reluctantly supposed to be the case) and since *Damaged Goods* (a play with an "even more repulsive theme" than *Mrs Warren's Profession*) had been licensed, he saw "no reason for withholding a licence in the present case." Raleigh had long felt that the play *should* be licensed (see above, p. 72), and although Dawson's ex-officio position on the board rendered his view less influential than those of the other members, he was known to be strongly opposed. That put Buckmaster and Dawson opposed to licensing, Raleigh and Higgins in favor. The position, then, of the eighty-one-year-old Squire Bancroft, the only theater professional—though long since retired—on the advisory board, was crucial. It became clear in a letter of 27 February 1922: "I know I am old, but not, I hope, 'old-fashioned.' I cannot, however, with full acknowledgement of the march of time, recommend this play for licence."

Matthews probably never knew how close he came to getting permission to produce the first public performance in England of *Mrs Warren's Profession.* Had he been given the information, he might have thought that with the Lord Chamberlain himself, plus the Examiner of Plays and two advisory board members, in support of granting the license, his chances were pretty good. But after reviewing the file, Atholl backed down. "I think after reading the criticism herein [including Buckmaster's 1917 position] that it will not be desirable to issue the license." He said that he would consult with another senior colleague, the State Chamberlain, before sending the formal notification to Matthews, but the rejection letter was eventually sent on 14 March 1922 (and the two-guinea reading fee returned).

There was one final wrinkle to Matthews's 1922 application. An actress named Susan Richmond (a member of the Birmingham Repertory Theatre company) had been cast as Vivie. The father of one of Susan Richmond's friends was a high-ranking military and court official, Lieutenant General Sir John Hanbury-Williams, Marshal of the Diplomatic Corps at St. James's Palace. Matthews thought that Hanbury-Williams might be able to use some influence. He wrote to him on 11 March 1922 asking if Hanbury-Williams "might be so kind as to do what you can to help us." On 14 March, Hanbury-Williams forwarded Matthews's letter to Atholl, asking if Atholl could "kindly do anything to help." The letter seems first to have gone to Street, who added his own note to say it all seemed a "little absurd" to him "still to refuse a licence to a play so widely known and performed." Quite. But the rejection letter, signed by Dawson, had already been written and was probably on its way to Matthews before Atholl even saw Hanbury-Williams's request.

The London Players, 1922

The file was hardly back in the draw before another inquiry came in. This one was from Edward Stirling, co-manager (with Henry Oscar) of the London Players, a repertory company founded by Stirling and Oscar in 1921. Stirling wrote on 22 May 1922 to ask "whether any change has taken place in the Lord Chamberlain's attitude towards Mr Bernard Shaw's play MRS WARREN'S PROFESSION, as I should like to submit it for licensing." The response, also dated 22 May, was no. Stirling's initiative thus began and ended on the same day.[37]

The Everyman Theatre, 1922

1922 turned out to be a bumper year for efforts to license *Mrs Warren's Profession*. On 22 August 1922, Norman Macdermott, founder (in 1920) and director of the Everyman Theatre in Hampstead, north London,[38] wrote to the Lord Chamberlain's Office on the strange assumption that "the prejudice which previously existed" against *Mrs Warren's Profession* "no longer operates." Macdermott rehearsed some of the usual arguments against the ban—it has been widely performed in other countries ("Norway, Sweden, Denmark, Czecho-Slovakia, etc."), there is "a considerable amount of desire for the performance of the play" in London, the "urgency of the problem" addressed in the play—and added a couple of new angles: the Everyman Theatre had been requested to include the play on one of its continental tours and needed time in England to incorporate it into the repertoire before the tour, and (a veiled threat?) "it would be comparatively simple to produce it in our normal course, if a license to perform were refused."[39]

Atholl looked at the application from his home in fashionable Eaton Place, S.W.1, and sent a note back to his office on 31 August 1922 to say that he saw "no reason to alter the considered opinion of myself & my predecessors," apparently forgetting that six months earlier he had supported licensing the play. The standard refusal letter was duly sent to Macdermott by the Comptroller on 6 September 1922, returning as well the reading fee and copy of the play that Macdermott—naturally—had enclosed with the license application. Macdermott's threat to mount a private production did not materialize.

Charles Macdona, 1924

Enter Charles Macdona. Macdona, as he explained to the Lord Chamberlain (now the Earl of Cromer) in a letter on 14 August 1924, held the touring rights for Shaw's plays. He was planning a production of *Mrs Warren's Profession* in his current Paris season of Shaw, and was "anxious to include this play in my repertory when I return to England." A copy of the play and the two-guinea reading fee were, for the umpteenth time, enclosed. This time they would not have to be returned. Macdona succeeded where so many before him had failed.[40]

For this, he had two people to thank—George Street, who was still the Examiner of Plays, and, particularly, the Earl of Cromer, the new Lord Chamberlain.

Macdona's letter was handled initially by Street. He wrote his report immediately (15 August 1924), pointing out again the absurdity of banning a play, however "crude and poor," that had been performed so often abroad and (privately) in England, and "in book form is familiar to everyone interested in the stage or contemporary literature." Unlike his predecessor, Cromer acted decisively on Street's advice. This is the full text of Cromer's historic directive, dated 17 August 1924, to license *Mrs Warren's Profession:*

"MRS. WARREN'S PROFESSION."

I fully appreciate and respect the motives which prompted my predecessors in the Office of the Lord Chamberlain to refuse a Licence for this Play.

Times have however greatly changed since 1898 when this Play was first stopped by Mr. Redford. Since then, as Mr. Street points out, the Play has been frequently produced by private societies in England, where it can be procured and read throughout the country in book form.

In my opinion the facts of this Play having been performed all over Europe & America, or its suppression being harmful to Censorship may be left out of account as being beside the point.

The point really is that in these days the mentality of the average adult audience would neither be shocked or harmed by the presentation of this subject on the stage merely because it is unpleasant. This may be regretable [sic], but I think it is the case.

It would therefore be absurd to go on refusing a Licence to this Play, ignoring the march of time and the change it brings about in public opinion over facing such questions openly.

I do not propose to refer this Play to the Advisory Board any further. I gather the majority would now doubtless be disposed to support Mr. Street's opinion. Even if they did not, I have no wish to involve any of them in the responsibility of licensing this Play which must necessarily rest with me.

After the most careful consideration I am therefore prepared, though reluctantly, to licence this Play, subject to some fictitious name being substituted for that of the Duke of Beaufort which appears twice in Act II, p. 180.

A reply to this effect should be returned to Mr. Charles Macdona's application of August 14th.

CROMER

It is a pity that Cromer could not be more enthusiastic about the play, and his (and Street's) sense of the "frequency" of private productions of the play in England is askew—there had, in fact, been only two: the Stage Society in 1902 and the Pioneer Players in 1912 (both in London—

perhaps Cromer also considered Glasgow to be in England). Still, apart
from the trivial issue about the Duke of Beaufort,[41] *Mrs Warren's Profession*
was finally to be licensed.

The Edinburgh License, 1924

The Comptroller (no longer Dawson—perhaps another reason the play
was licensed so quickly this time) wrote to Macdona on 26 August 1924 to
inform him that "His Lordship is now prepared to grant a Licence" for
Mrs Warren's Profession. Macdona was told he would have to substitute a
"fictitious name" in place of the Duke of Beaufort, and he was also asked
to confirm that the play would be produced at the Regent Theatre in
London (as Macdona had indicated in his application). The license would
then be forwarded to the manager of the Regent, and all would be in place
for the English public première of the play. Macdona sent a copy of the
letter to Shaw, requesting (in a marginal note) that Shaw provide a substitute name for Beaufort.[42] Shaw did not demur at this, but then things
began to fall apart, and the opening was delayed for almost a year. What
went wrong?

Shortly after learning that the Lord Chamberlain had "most unexpectedly" licensed *Mrs Warren's Profession,* Shaw wrote to Edith Evans, who had
impressed him as Hesione in *Heartbreak House* in 1921 (Court Theatre)
and as the Serpent and the Oracle in *Back to Methuselah* in 1924 (Birmingham Repertory Theatre), encouraging her to read the play (if she
had not already) with a view to taking the role of Mrs. Warren. He said
that he had told Macdona that "there is nobody else who could do anything with it" (Laurence III, 883; [29 August 1924]). Evans declined, and
Shaw tried again on 8 September 1924: "Think again about Mrs. Warren.
It is not the mere dread of the drudgery of looking for someone else that
makes me hesitate to take No for an answer: it seems to me that you are
capable of as great a success in it as the wretched old play will hold; and
it will last all your life as one of your repertory parts" (Laurence, *Theatrics*
172).

In the meantime, Macdona had acknowledged on 1 September the letter of 26 August from the Lord Chamberlain's Office. He said that he
hoped to specify "the actual date of the first performance in the course of
a day or so." The Regent Theatre was still identified as the location for
the production.[43] At the foot of the letter in the Lord Chamberlain's files
is the handwritten notation "Licence issued." The Lord Chamberlain's
Day Books (which list all licenses issued) confirm this. Licence number

5632, for *Mrs Warren's Profession,* is listed as being issued on 1 September 1924 "on the understanding that a fictitious name be substituted for that of the Duke of Beaufort."[44]

The license that was actually issued (Figures 3a, 3b), however, was not for the Regent Theatre but for the Lyceum Theatre, Edinburgh, for a production that never took place.[45]

Having failed to secure Edith Evans for the part of Mrs. Warren, Shaw received proposals from Macdona for "everybody on earth," but turned them all down. "I can't stand *anybody* as Mrs Warren, because I can't stand the play itself, I suppose," he told Gertrude Kingston (who had played the role in the 1912 Pioneer Players production) in a postcard on 16 February 1925. This prevarication, as Shaw recognized, "staved off a production which I shirk with all my soul. I shall probably let Macdona slip in with his provincial edition at the Chelsea Palace or somewhere. Ugh!"[46] In his first invitation to Edith Evans to consider the role of Mrs. Warren, Shaw described the play as "as old fashioned as Ibsen, and much cruder." And when he attended the Pioneer Players production (with Granville Barker), Shaw "could do nothing but laugh at its technique."[47] On 26 March 1924, *Saint Joan* had opened at the New Theatre to great acclaim. "[F]ancy my feelings," he told Edith Evans, "at having this horror [*Mrs Warren's Profession*] shoved on me when I am in the very odor of sanctity after St Joan." Without Edith Evans, Shaw seems to have concluded that a production of a play written in 1893 would compare so unfavorably with his great recent success that it would be an embarrassment. He therefore blocked Macdona's plans for a major London production, and put off any production at all until the play could perhaps "slip in" one of Macdona's provincial tours.

Did Macdona know by 1 September 1924 that a production in London was a nonstarter? His signature is not on the letter that was sent to the Lord Chamberlain's Office on 1 September confirming the Regent Theatre venue. (It was signed on his behalf by someone in his Charing Cross Road office.) Was the letter sent prematurely? Was Macdona already thinking instead of a relatively low-key Edinburgh production and so quickly arranged for the license to be issued for the Lyceum Theatre? More evidence is needed to sort this out, but the huge irony remains that the license issued for *Mrs Warren's Profession* after more than a quarter of a century of suppression was for a production that did not happen.[48]

Birmingham: Round Three, 1925

The Lord Chamberlain could no longer be blamed for preventing the general public from seeing *Mrs Warren's Profession.* It was now entirely in

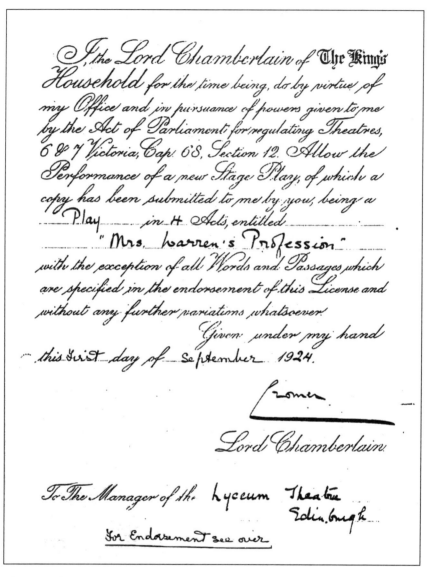

Figs. 3a and 3b. The first license issued for a public performance in Britain of *Mrs Warren's Profession*, 1 September 1924. The performance at the Lyceum Theatre, Edinburgh, never occurred. Dan H. Laurence Collection, L. W. Conolly Theatre Archives, University of Guelph.

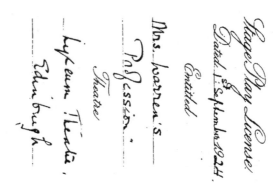

Mem. The particular attention of the Management is called to the following Regulations, which refer to all Stage Plays licensed by the Lord Chamberlain. The strict observance of these Regulations is to be considered as the condition upon which the License is signed.

Notice of the change of title of a piece to be given to the Examiner of Plays.

No profanity or impropriety of language to be permitted on the Stage.

No indecency of dress, dance, or gesture to be permitted on the Stage.

No offensive personalities or representations of living persons to be permitted on the Stage, nor anything calculated to produce riot or breach of the peace.

This Licence is issued on the understanding that a fictitious name shall be substituted in the place of that of the Duke of Beaufort.

Shaw's hands. Birmingham once again came into the picture. Following the English première of *Back to Methuselah* at the Birmingham Repertory Theatre in October 1923, Birmingham had risen in Shaw's esteem, and was to continue to do so after the Repertory Theatre's director, Barry Jackson, founded the first "Shaw Festival" at nearby Malvern in 1929 (see Conolly xxiv–xxxi). But it was not to Jackson and the Birmingham Repertory Theatre that Shaw turned, despite the efforts (supported by Shaw) made by the theater's business manager, Bache Matthews, to gain a license for *Mrs Warren's Profession* in 1921 and 1922. As Shaw explained the situation to Jackson in a letter on 28 January 1925, after Jackson had learned that Shaw had given the rights for *Mrs Warren's Profession* to Charles Macdona, Shaw felt "ridiculous" about what he described as "such a senseless caprice of pure luck" that Macdona had been successful in his license application—"binding on me because C.M.'s luck on previous occasions has been so often the other way" (Conolly 15–16). It was bad enough—from Jackson's point of view—that Macdona had the rights, and even worse that he chose to exercise them in Jackson's backyard.

Macdona announced *Mrs Warren's Profession* as part of a four-week Shaw season at the Prince of Wales Theatre, Birmingham, beginning on 20 July 1925. The other plays were *Pygmalion, Fanny's First Play, The Doctor's Dilemma, Candida, Man and Superman, You Never Can Tell, Arms and the Man,* and *Major Barbara.* Four performances of *Mrs Warren's Profession* were scheduled, opening on 27 July. The cast consisted of Florence Jackson (Mrs Warren), Valerie Richards (Vivie), Oliver Johnston (Praed), Charles Sewell (Crofts), George Bancroft (Frank), and Arthur Claremont (Reverend Gardner). The director was Esmé Percy.

Any concerns that Shaw might have had about how this "old fashioned" play would be received would have been eased by the critical reception in Birmingham. The *Birmingham Gazette* (28 July 1925) described *Mrs Warren's Profession* as "one of the finest plays in the Shavian catalogue" and "the most truly moral play ever produced on the English stage"—not excepting, the reviewer stressed, "miracle plays, morality plays, or religious propaganda plays." The reviewer for the *Birmingham Mail* (28 July 1925) was surprised by the "true to life" vividness of the characters, "which one hardly expected from an author who is so fond of hearing himself speak." And while "the play may leave a nasty taste in one's mouth," it is "undeniably gripping in construction and development." The *Birmingham Post* was similarly complimentary, praising in particular Shaw's handling of the Frank-Vivie relationship. The reviewer's reaction to Crofts's revelation of the true nature of the relationship was profound: "In a single sentence is compressed one of the most terrible experiences that can be conceived by the human imagination." "If Mr. Shaw had handled his play vulgarly or flippantly or insincerely, one could have understood why the censor had prohibited it for thirty years." According to the Birmingham reviewers, he had not and one could not. All the notices praised the cast and Esmé Percy's directing, and any moral high horses the reviewers may have owned were left safely tethered at home.

London, 1925–1926

And that, one might have thought, was that. After the successful Birmingham run, Macdona kept *Mrs Warren's Profession* in his repertoire for a season at the Regent Theatre, King's Cross (where he had wanted to mount his projected 1924 production). It opened there on 28 September 1925 and ran (in repertory) for twenty-one performances with the same cast and director as in Birmingham. The notices were mostly friendly, and the play was received (at least by the opening night audience) "with perfect equanimity" (*The Times*, 29 September 1925).

The Regent, however, was and was not a London theater, its location in King's Cross divorcing it geographically and reputationally from Shaftesbury Avenue and the West End. The play still had to face the test of a major production in the hotbed of theatrical London. And thus it was that the Lord Chamberlain, whose interest in the play would normally by now have ended, had one last kick at the can.

On 27 February 1926, the *Daily Telegraph* carried a short unsigned article that was bound to catch the attention of both Shaw and the Lord Chamberlain's Office.[49] The article refers to a production of *Mrs Warren's Profession* that was scheduled to open at the Strand Theatre (site of the 2002 revival mentioned in the opening paragraph of this essay) on 3 March 1926. It was another Macdona production, in association with Arthur Bourchier, lessee and manager of the Strand.[50] (Bourchier also appeared as Crofts.) The article then comments on the long ban on the play, and continues: "while no hint has been received that the present production will be interfered with, it is something in the nature of a challenge deliberately to insert words which have not hitherto been given the censor's approval." Bourchier is then quoted as saying that a speech by Crofts in Act III has been expanded: "It concerns the houses of ill-fame which Mr. Shaw has indicated are confined to the Continent. The original dialogue goes like this: 'We run two in Brussels, one in Berlin, one in Vienna, and two in Budapest.' To that Mr. Shaw has now added: 'Our operations in this country are rather restricted at present, but the prospects are quite healthy.'"[51] Bourchier is further quoted as saying that the censor "has no legal right to interfere. . . . I doubt very much whether he has the power

Fig. 4. Scenes from the Regent Theatre production of *Mrs Warren's Profession*, 28 September 1925. *Punch,* 7 October 1925.

to interfere in any matters outside the narrow limits of politics and religion. After all, the public is the best judge of moral turpitude, and a play that is thoroughly bad in the moral sense can never survive the acid test as applied through the box-office."

The article ruined Shaw's breakfast in his Adelphi Terrace flat that morning. Maybe Bourchier's sentiments about the censorship evoked some sympathy from him, but Bourchier was entirely wrong about the law, and his decision to challenge the censorship in connection with the London première of *Mrs Warren's Profession* was mind-bogglingly insensitive to the struggles to get the play licensed at all. And, moreover, Shaw had *not* authorized the additional dialogue for Crofts.

Sensibly, Shaw took the initiative and wrote immediately (27 February) to the Lord Chamberlain (still Cromer). He denounced the article as "pure folly, quite unauthorized by me," and assured Cromer that he would take steps to ensure that "absolutely nothing will be said on the stage . . . that has not been licensed." Cromer received the letter later that day, and promptly (still on the 27th) replied to thank Shaw and to downplay the significance of the *Telegraph* article, engineered, both Shaw and Cromer thought, by a theater press agent to generate some publicity for the production. Cromer expressed every confidence that Shaw would see to it that any "minor alterations" to the text or "additions in the stage business" that emerged in rehearsals would be submitted by Macdona to the Lord Chamberlain for approval "in time for the first performance." And, indeed, even before Cromer had finished his letter Macdona contacted his office, Cromer told Shaw, to say that "a few minor alterations" were being sent for approval. Cromer did, however, also alert Shaw to the fact that he would be attending the final rehearsal of the play on 2 March. Cromer wrote again to Shaw on 1 March to say that he had reviewed the minor alterations, and had no problem with them except where a blank epithet in a comment by Crofts about Mrs. Warren in Act III ("The old————") had been made explicit ("The old bitch").[52] Cromer expressed his preference for the original stage direction, where Crofts "swallows the epithet." Shaw promptly wrote back (1 March), assuring Cromer that Crofts would swallow rather than speak, and explained that he had not authorized the change: "I suppose the prompter, hearing Mr. Bourchier use the word (and many others) in his struggles to remember his part, wrote it into his copy." There was no further mention of Bourchier's notion that Crofts hoped to extend the continental brothel network to England. It is rather doubtful that Cromer would have approved of such a scheme.[53]

The final dress rehearsal before an invited audience (and the self-invited Lord Chamberlain) duly took place on 2 March 1926. Shaw was there as well, but it was a tense evening for him. He wrote to Bourchier the next day to thank him for his contribution, not as co-producer, but as actor:

> But for you I don't know what would have happened last night. It was a very near thing, in spite of the curtain calls. The frost was appalling until you came on. Let it be a lesson to both of us never to let any human soul into a theatre again unless he (or she) wants to come badly enough to pay for it. Tonight, with a real audience, it will be much better. The heroine will have got over her panic. . . .
>
> Many thanks for everything. The part [Crofts] looks six times its natural size in your hands; and I hope it will keep the shop open until Easter, at all events.[54]

Perhaps the frostiness of the evening was increased by the Lord Chamberlain's presence, but he had no complaints or objections to what he saw and heard that evening. Nor did the audience. At the end of the performance there was "persistent cheering." From the stage, Bourchier told the audience that "Mr Shaw was indisposed to speak," but a few moments later Shaw returned to his box, "bowed his acknowledgment to the applauding audience," and said, simply, "'Ladies and gentlemen, good-night. Come again'" (*Daily News*, 3 March 1926). And they did. *Mrs Warren's Profession* formally opened on 3 March 1926 and ran at the Strand for sixty-eight performances, freed, finally, from the grip of the Lord Chamberlain.

Notes

1. In his program notes, Hall used the example of the banning of *Mrs Warren's Profession* to remind the audience of the "sad and shameful" system under which no new plays could be performed in public theaters in England without a license issued by the Lord Chamberlain, the most senior official of the royal household. The system operated from 1737 to 1968. Plays dealing explicitly (or even implicitly or obliquely) with religion, politics, or sex were unlikely to receive a license. Not surprisingly, Shaw was both a victim and opponent of the system. The history of English stage censorship from 1737 to 1968 is documented in L. W. Conolly, *The Censorship of English Drama, 1737–1824* (San Marino: The Huntington Library, 1976); John Russell Stephens, *The Censorship of English Drama, 1824–1901* (Cambridge: Cambridge University Press, 1980); Steve Nicholson, *The Censorship of British Drama, 1900–1968, Volume 1, 1900–1932* (Exeter: University of Exeter Press, 2003); and Nicholas de Jongh, *Politics, Prudery & Perversions: The Censoring of the English Stage, 1901–1968* (London: Methuen, 2000). John Johnston's *The Lord Chamberlain's Blue Pencil* (London: Hodder & Stoughton, 1990) is a more general survey.

2. A more detailed account of the composition of *Mrs Warren's Profession* is given in Holroyd I, 291–93.

3. Grein's reaction to the subsequent Stage Society production of *Mrs Warren's Profession* in 1902 confirmed his initial reaction. In his Preface to *Plays Unpleasant,* Shaw put the blame for Grein's decision not to produce the play squarely on the Lord Chamberlain (*Bodley Head* 23), but Grein makes it clear in his review of the Stage Society production that he disapproved of the subject matter of the play—this is why, "in spite of my great admiration for Bernard Shaw, the play was not brought out by the late Independent Theatre" (Grein 293). And while Grein's wife (in her biography of Grein) says only that "the opportunity was missed" for an Independent Theatre production, Conal O'Riordan, in a foreword "censored and revised by George Bernard Shaw," says that Grein was "horrified to the soul" by the play. (Michael Orme, *J. T. Grein: The Story of a Pioneer, 1862–1935* [London: John Murray, 1936], pp. 8, 117–18.)

4. Redford's letter, though not the receipt, is in the Houghton Library, Harvard University, bMS Eng 954 (26).

5. He thought the rejection "a foregone conclusion," and had already written the preface to the play "announcing the refusal of the Censor to license it" (Shaw, *Our Theatres in the Nineties,* III, 349–50 [*Saturday Review,* 2 April 1898]).

6. All alterations and additions to the text are in Shaw's hand, in ink. Shaw's underlinings are here represented as italics.

7. Shaw, *Our Theatres in the Nineties,* III, 350.

8. From Dan H. Laurence's vertical file on *Mrs Warren's Profession,* Dan H. Laurence Collection, L. W. Conolly Theatre Archives, University of Guelph Library.

9. Dan H. Laurence, *Bernard Shaw: A Bibliography* (Oxford: Clarendon Press, 1983), I, 34.

10. A copy of the prospectus is in Dan H. Laurence's vertical file on *Mrs Warren's Profession,* Dan H. Laurence Collection, L. W. Conolly Theatre Archives, University of Guelph Library.

11. The agreement is dated 20 July 1904. A copy is held in the Harry Ransom Humanities Research Center, University of Texas at Austin (SHAW 59.10).

12. *Wilshire's Magazine,* August 1906, quoted in Laurence II, 632. See also Rhoda Nathan, "Shaw's Man in America: The Arnold Daly Scrapbooks," in Conolly and Pearson, pp. 29–41. A firsthand account of the New Haven and New York productions is given by Mary Shaw, "My 'Immoral' Play: The Story of the First American Production of *Mrs Warren's Profession,*" *McClure's Magazine,* 38 (April 1912), 684–94. Some newspaper accounts (e.g., *New York Times,* 30 October 1905) say that Daly, not McAdoo, censored the script used for the Garrick production, but Mary Shaw's account is more credible since she was directly involved in the events.

13. Some of these productions (and others) are noted in Conolly and Pearson, passim.

14. This statement may not be true. Johnston (77) refers to a 1911 license application, and in a memorandum dated 5 October 1916 Examiner of Plays Ernest Bendall mentions an application "in April 1911" (British Library, LCP CORR 1924/5632). Documentation of this application has not yet, however, come to light. Perhaps Shaw was referring to such an application when he recalled—in a letter to the Lord Chamberlain on 8 October 1916 (British Library, LCP CORR 1924/5632)—an application "made some years ago by Miss Gertrude Kingston" (who played Mrs. Warren in the unlicensed 1912 Pioneer Players production).

15. Quoted (p. 10) by Christopher St. John in a biographical note in Eleanor Arnold, *Edy: Recollections of Edith Craig* (London: Muller, 1949).

16. Documentation and correspondence relating to the Glasgow Playgoers League Club production of *Mrs Warren's Profession* are in the Lord Chamberlain's Papers, British Library (LCP CORR 1924/5632).

17. There is strong evidence, however, that there was an earlier effort in 1914 to produce

the play in England. In the memorandum cited in note 14, Bendall also refers to his "adverse Recommendation of 20th July, 1914." Johnston (77) mentions, but does not elaborate upon, a 1914 application, and no further evidence has yet been located.

18. Cf. Shaw's view that "*Mrs Warren's Profession* is a play for women . . . written for women . . . and has been performed and produced mainly through the determination of women" (*Bodley Head* 253). Documentation and correspondence relating to the Plymouth Repertory Theatre license application are in the Lord Chamberlain's Papers, British Library (LCP CORR 1924/5632).

19. This letter is at the Harry Ransom Humanities Research Center, University of Texas at Austin. A copy is in Dan H. Laurence's vertical file on *Mrs Warren's Profession,* Dan H. Laurence Collection, L. W. Conolly Theatre Archives, University of Guelph Library.

20. The letter is published in Dan H. Laurence, ed., *Bernard Shaw Theatrics* (Toronto: University of Toronto Press, 1995), pp. 127–31.

21. This letter (though not Sandhurst's note) is also published in Laurence, *Theatrics,* pp. 131–33.

22. Documentation and correspondence relating to Heys's application are in the Lord Chamberlain's Papers, British Library (LCP CORR 1924/5632).

23. Shaw's interest in Brieux was made clear when he wrote the preface for *Three Plays by Brieux* (London: Fifield, 1911).

24. The figure is from Dan H. Laurence, *Bernard Shaw: A Bibliography* (Oxford: Clarendon Press, 1983), I, 134.

25. This is probably a reference to the play's reception in Kansas City, where, according to Shaw, "the municipality, finding itself restrained by the courts from preventing the performance, fell back on a local bye-law against indecency. It summoned the actress who impersonated Mrs Warren to the police court, and offered her and her colleagues the alternative of leaving the city or being prosecuted under this bye-law" (*Bodley Head* 263).

26. Ilya Metchnikoff (1845–1916), Russian biologist, won the Nobel Prize for Medicine in 1908 for his work on immunology. He also experimented with calomel as a means of preventing and treating syphilis.

27. A reference to the controversial White Slave Traffic Act of 1912.

28. In Wagner's last opera, *Parsifal* (1882), the pagan Klingsor's castle and garden crumble and wither.

29. Archer thought it the "wildest and stupidest nonsense" to call the play immoral, but "[i]t is manifest that the play did not edify, but genuinely scandalised the public"—sufficient grounds, in Archer's view, to suppress it (*Morning Leader,* 4 November 1905).

30. Lord Chamberlain's Papers, British Library (LCP CORR 1924/5632).

31. Ibid.

32. Courtesy Dan H. Laurence's vertical file on *Mrs Warren's Profession,* Dan H. Laurence Collection, L. W. Conolly Theatre Archives, University of Guelph Library.

33. Documentation and correspondence relating to the 1921 Birmingham application are in the Lord Chamberlain's Papers, British Library (LCP CORR 1924/5632).

34. There is a problem regarding the dating of Atholl's note. Street's memo, on which the note is written, is clearly dated (typewritten) 2 July 1921 and obviously pertains to the license application submitted on 30 June 1921 by Bache Matthews. But Atholl's note is dated, in his handwriting, 14/3/22—14 March 1922—a date that pertains to a subsequent license application from the Birmingham Repertory Theatre. It is possible that the first part of Atholl's note—"I feel I cannot reverse the decision already arrived at by my predecessors"—was written, but not dated, in response to the 1921 application, while the rest of the note was added, and dated, when the earlier file was being reviewed for the 1922 application. In any event, the result was the same: Atholl personally vetoed both applications.

35. Harry Ransom Humanities Research Center, University of Texas at Austin (SHAW 48.2).

36. Documentation and correspondence relating to the 1922 Birmingham application are in the Lord Chamberlain's Papers, British Library (LCP CORR 1924/5632). The evidence of a meeting between Ayliff and Atholl is in a letter (11 March 1922) from Matthews to Sir John Hanbury-Williams (LCP CORR 1924/5632): "When our Producer, Mr. H.K. Ayliff, interviewed him a few weeks ago, he was favourably inclined towards it."

37. The two short letters that constitute Stirling's initiative are in the Lord Chamberlain's Papers, British Library (LCP CORR 1924/5632).

38. Macdermott had produced (and designed) the first London public performance of the previously banned *Shewing-up of Blanco Posnet* at the Everyman on 14 March 1921.

39. Documentation and correspondence relating to Macdermott's application are in the Lord Chamberlain's Papers, British Library (LCP CORR 1924/5632).

40. Documentation and correspondence relating to Macdona's 1924 application are in the Lord Chamberlain's Papers, British Library (LCP CORR 1924/5632).

41. The name is used in a conversation between the Reverend Gardner and Frank Gardner in Act II about providing a room for Praed at the rectory. Frank explains to his clueless father that Praed is a respectable architect: "He built that place down in Monmouthshire for the Duke of Beaufort—Tintern Abbey they call it. You must have heard of it." To which the Reverend Gardner replies: "Oh, in that case, of course we shall only be too happy. I suppose he knows the Duke of Beaufort personally." (*Plays: Pleasant and Unpleasant* [London: Grant Richards, 1898], I, 180.) This was changed by Shaw to Frank's "He built that place down in Wales for the Duke. Caernarvon Castle they call it. You must have heard of it," and the Reverend Gardner's reply, "Oh, in that case, of course we shall only be too happy. I suppose he knows the Duke personally." (*Bodley Head* 295.)

42. Harry Ransom Humanities Research Center, University of Texas at Austin (SHAW 55.6).

43. Lord Chamberlain's Papers, British Library (LCP CORR 1924/5632).

44. British Library, Add MS 61956, fol. 161.

45. A copy of the license—dated 1 September 1924, and with the same condition given in the Day Book (a substitute name for the Duke of Beaufort)—is in Dan H. Laurence's vertical file on *Mrs Warren's Profession,* Dan H. Laurence Collection, L. W. Conolly Theatre Archives, University of Guelph Library.

46. King's College Library, Cambridge University. Dan Laurence's transcription of the postcard is in his vertical file on *Mrs Warren's Profession,* Dan H. Laurence Collection, L. W. Conolly Theatre Archives, University of Guelph Library.

47. Shaw's comment is in a letter to Lord Sandhurst, the Lord Chamberlain, 8 October 1916 (Lord Chamberlain's Papers, British Library, LCP CORR 1924/5632).

48. There was some confusion in the Birmingham press about an Edinburgh production. In announcing the Birmingham production of the play, the *Birmingham Gazette* (27 July 1925) referred to Macdona's previous productions in Paris and Edinburgh, and the *Birmingham Mail* (28 July 1925) also believed that "Scotland [had] the first opportunity of seeing it played in public." It is tempting to think that a Lyceum Theatre notice that appeared in the Edinburgh *Scotsman* on 18 September 1924 had something to do with *Mrs Warren's Profession:* "REGARDING THE THREATENED BOYCOTT OF THE ABOVE THEATRE, PATRONS NEED HAVE NO FEAR OF INTERFERENCE. ANY MOLESTATION WILL BE DEALT WITH IMMEDIATELY." Had the good Scots Presbyterian citizens of Edinburgh got wind of a possible production of *Mrs Warren's Profession* in their city and risen up against the Lyceum? Apparently not. The notice referred to a dispute between two actors' unions, the Actors' Association and the Stage Guild, which looked set to disrupt the appearance of John Martin Harvey's company at the Lyceum. As it happened, Shaw was in Edinburgh at this time. He saw Irving as Richard the Third at the Lyceum on 17 September, and was interviewed the following morning by the Edinburgh *Evening Dispatch.* There is no mention of *Mrs Warren's Profession* in the interview (18 September 1924).

49. The fact that a copy of the article is in the Lord Chamberlain's files is evidence of its having attracted official attention. Other documentation and correspondence about the Strand Theatre production are also in the Lord Chamberlain's files in the British Library (LCP CORR 1924/5632). Shaw's letters to the Lord Chamberlain dated 27 February 1926 and 1 March 1926 are also published in Laurence, *Theatrics,* pp. 174–76.

50. Esmé Percy directed again, but with an entirely new cast: Edyth Goodall (Mrs. Warren), Agatha Kentish (Vivie), J. Fisher White (Praed), Arthur Bourchier (Crofts), Carleton Hobbs (Frank), and Orlando Barnett (Reverend Gardner).

51. The published 1898 text of the play reads: "We've got two in Brussels, one in Berlin, one in Vienna, and two in Buda-Pesth" (*Plays: Pleasant and Unpleasant* [London: Grant Richards, 1898], I, 211.) This was later revised to: "We've got two in Brussels, one in Ostend, one in Vienna, and two in Budapest" (*Bodley Head* 329).

52. *Plays: Pleasant and Unpleasant* (London: Grant Richards, 1898), I, 211; *Bodley Head* 329 (where the blank remains). No record of the alterations is in the Lord Chamberlain's files.

53. In an editorial on 2 March 1926, "Mr Shaw & the Censor," the *Daily News* accused Shaw of "acquiescence in the decrees of the Censor." Shaw rejected the charge in the *Daily News* the next day, insisting that the Lord Chamberlain "has not gone back on his licence in any way."

54. Cornell University, Burgunder 4167/13.

Works Cited

The Bodley Head Bernard Shaw. Dan H. Laurence, Editorial Supervisor. Volume I. London: Bodley Head, 1970.

Conolly, L. W., ed. *Bernard Shaw and Barry Jackson.* Toronto: University of Toronto Press, 2002. (*Selected Correspondence of Bernard Shaw.*)

Conolly, L.W., and Ellen Pearson, eds. *Papers from the 1989 International Shaw Conference.* Guelph, Ontario: University of Guelph, 1991.

de Jongh, Nicholas. *Politics, Prudery & Perversity: The Censoring of the English Stage 1901–1968.* London: Methuen, 2000.

Fisher, James. "Edy Craig and the Pioneer Players' Production of *Mrs Warren's Profession." SHAW: The Annual of Bernard Shaw Studies 15* (University Park: Penn State University Press, 1995), pp. 37–56.

Grein, J. T. *Dramatic Criticism.* Volume III. London: Greening, 1902.

Holroyd, Michael. *Bernard Shaw.* 5 vols. London: Chatto & Windus, 1988–92.

Johnston, John. *The Lord Chamberlain's Blue Pencil.* London: Hodder & Stoughton, 1990.

Laurence, Dan H., ed. *Bernard Shaw: Collected Letters.* 4 vols. London: Reinhardt, 1965–88.

———, ed. *Bernard Shaw Theatrics.* Toronto: University of Toronto Press, 1995. (*Selected Correspondence of Bernard Shaw.*)

Pálfy, István. "George Bernard Shaw's Reception in Hungary, 1914–1939." *Hungarian Studies in English* II (1965): 93–104.

Shaw, Bernard. *Our Theatres in the Nineties.* 3 vols. London: Constable, 1932. (Standard Edition.)

Weintraub, Stanley, ed. *Bernard Shaw: The Diaries, 1885–1897.* 2 vols. University Park: Penn State University Press, 1986.

Weiss, Samuel A., ed. *Bernard Shaw's Letters to Siegfried Trebitsch.* Stanford: Stanford University Press, 1986.

Margery M. Morgan

SHAW AND THE SEX REFORMERS

Professor Alan Sinfield has taken a conversation between Frank Harris and Oscar Wilde as marking the historic moment when current notions of the aesthete and the sodomite converged and the homosexual, as a modern personality type, became visible in British society.[1] This was the occasion mentioned by Shaw in a summary note of his doings over the year 1895, following his appointment as drama critic to *The Saturday Review*, which Harris edited: "Frank Harris tried to establish a regular lunch every Monday . . . at the Café Royale. I attended them for some time. . . . Oscar Wilde came once, immediately before the Queensbury trial, with young Douglas. They left in some indignation because Harris refused to appear as a witness."[2] The implication is that Shaw was present on this occasion. If he did not actually hear Wilde tell Harris that he was guilty as charged, he cannot have been left in doubt for long. Sinfield does not question the veracity of Harris's protested belief that the "rough trade" witnesses had been bribed by Queensbury. Even if Frank was fabricating his surprise, the moment when he was forced to admit awareness would remain significant.

Behind Sinfield's study in cultural history lies Michel Foucault's argument on gender stereotyping: its psychological, cultural, and political operations. This has reinforced the earlier (if diminishing) influence of Freud and Jung in the interpretation of literary figures. Most particularly with relation to Bernard Shaw, Sally Peters's interesting biographical study has presented us with an author whose more or less repressed homosexual tendency may be seen as a driving force for his imagination.[3] I do not set out to dispute or confirm her findings (as I sometimes may), but to explore Shaw's understanding of sexuality and ways in which his attitudes may have been affected by the Wilde tragedy.

Shaw was among Wilde's supporters after the sentence of penal servitude was passed. According to Mary Hyde, he "spent a railway journey . . . to a trade-union congress drafting a petition for Wilde's release, "but not enough signatures could be procured to make it worth sending.[4] More

Adey prompted him to draft another and printed it, but it was forestalled by a letter from the Home Secretary refusing to consider such pleas.[5] When *The Academy* printed a list of forty people agreed by its staff to be suitable members for a proposed British Academy of Letters, Shaw—and, independently, H. G. Wells—wrote proposing Oscar Wilde.[6] The disgraced author sent his fellow Dubliner a copy of *The Ballad of Reading Gaol* in recognition and continuing their established habit of sending each other copies of their publications. After Wilde's release, news of his nearpenury reached the Café Royale and Shaw was among the group contributing a sum of money to help him pay immediate debts. Laurence Housman, the youngest of them, was selected to take the money to Wilde, and he eventually wrote up his account of the episode and his other encounters with Wilde in 1923, under the title of "L'Écho de Paris."[7] But Shaw was impatient with Wilde's failure to rehabilitate himself and voiced to Harris his puritan's contempt for "an unproductive drunkard and swindler" (*CL* 2, 31).

The familiar story of how a younger Shaw, unknown and unemployed, wandered London, and continued his education in the generally "progressive" societies springing up around him, has to be revisited here in order to locate some key players.[8] Edward Aveling, scientifically educated, had been an organizer of the National Secular Society with Bradlaugh and Annie Besant (prosecuted for their propaganda for birth control). Dissatisfaction with Hyndman's Social Democratic Federation led to Aveling's departure along with William Morris and their joint founding of the Socialist League. Shaw also encountered Aveling in the Shelley Society and owed to him and Eleanor Marx his first direct familiarity with Ibsen's plays. Edward Carpenter, former Cambridge Fellow, ordained as a clergyman, then drawing back from entering the Church, had been a benefactor of the S.D.F., supplying the funds for Hyndman to start publishing *Justice*. On an occasion in 1886, Shaw went to hear Carpenter lecture to the Hammersmith Socialist Society in the stable attached to Morris's London house. Afterward, he walked back to Bloomsbury with two young men who were greatly impressed by his sparkling conversation. These were Goldsworthy Lowes Dickinson and C. R. Ashbee, who was to found the Guild of Handicrafts in the East End of London in 1888 and subsequently develop it as a Utopian community at Chipping Campden in the Cotswolds. (His great friend Goldie was to remain a Cambridge academic and did much to formulate the idea and title of the League of Nations.)[9]

A medical student, Henry Havelock Ellis, who had resolved to make the study of sexuality his lifetime speciality, was Secretary to the Progressive Association and helped Percy Chubb draw up the constitution of the Fellowship of the New Life. J. L. Joynes, then a junior master at Eton College, was associated, partly by accident, with Henry George (by whom Shaw was converted to Socialism), before joining the Fellowship together with his brother-in-law, Henry Salt, co-founder and Secretary of the Humanitarian League. To accommodate the divergence of interests among its members, the New Life Fellowship very quickly split into two branches, leaving individuals free to attend meetings of both. Shaw joined the younger branch, the Fabian Society, in its second year, but exercised his option to visit the Fellowship also.[10]

In both its manifestations, this group embraced the idea that social and political reform should come from the enlightened, those of educated intelligence who detested the gross inequalities they found throughout society. Simplifying their lives, divesting themselves of the obvious privileges of wealth and class, they would work for the common good. It was a vision that united Edward Carpenter, going to live with village laborers at Millthorpe, and Beatrice and Sidney Webb, observing the discipline of plain and healthy living as part of the work ethic. The Arts and Crafts movement offered another way of bridging the gap between the manual worker and the elite artist; and the Hammersmith way of Socialism trusted to art, liberated from commercialism, and to the transformative effect of Beauty (through its creation and perception) "to make out of the chaos of egoistic passions a great power of disinterested social action."[11] It is not surprising that W. B. Yeats was a delighted visitor to the Hammersmith Socialist Society.[12] Wilde also found his way there, as well as getting to the Fabian Society in 1888, and was inspired to write "The Soul of Man under Socialism" (1891). Also in the year 1891, Bernard Shaw made his first visit to Italy on Morris's advice, with a party from the Art Workers' Guild.[13] Like the eighteenth-century Grand Tour, this was part of his aesthetic education and a necessary qualification for a man of culture, an aspirant to the governing class. Going to Bayreuth for the Wagnerian opera was part of the same program, but more thoroughly to his personal taste.

Max Nordau's sweeping attack on then-modern art (including Ibsen, Tolstoy, Wagner, and Oscar Wilde) appeared in English as *Degeneration* in 1895 and gave Shaw his chance to emerge as art's champion—but it was only in America that his riposte appeared: "A Degenerate's View of Nordau," in *Liberty* (27 July 1895), accepting the association with opposition to the simple warrior ideal of the philistines.[14] It did not appear in England until 1908, under the more anodyne title of *The Sanity of Art*. The Wilde case had had its effect in inducing caution. Even so, Shaw had gone on to associate himself with a leading *art nouveau* journal when he published "On Going to Church," which casually posits a freely bisexual deity, in the first number of *The Savoy* (December 1895, delayed until 1896) beside Havelock Ellis on Zola. If he continued to learn from Wilde's dandy style of epigram and paradox, the other had returned the compliment in adopting Shaw's invention of serious farce, in *The Importance of Being Ear-*

nest. Although he did not follow Wilde's 1882 example of lecturing on "Dress" until 1895, the purchase of his first Jaeger suit was part of Shaw's deliberate creation of a public persona in a highly visible pose (significant word!) that is comparable with Wilde's elaborate self-creation: a protective carapace for both. Sinfield makes the point that Wilde went to America in 1882 as an aesthete, still a kind of bohemian, and returned a dandy in upper-class mode. Shaw remained at the middle-class bohemian stage.

Shaw remembered Joynes taking him to see Henry Salt at Eton when the latter was still a housemaster. It was a glimpse of what he had missed in his scantily and irregularly schooled boyhood. This takes their acquaintance back sometime before Shaw's tendency to nip the hand that fed him produced the comically complaining article, "A Sunday on the Surrey Hills," published in the *Pall Mall Gazette,* 28 April 1888.[15] (He had reviewed Joynes's *Songs of a Revolutionary Epoch* a fortnight earlier.) Salt remembered the transformation worked by the Jaeger suit, and it was he who introduced Shaw to William Archer—not a contradiction of the better-known anecdote of the two sitting alongside each other in the British Museum, for introductions were still necessary. Salt and Joynes (Kate Salt's brother) had proved too independent-minded for Eton: Joynes had been dismissed and Henry soon after took a very premature retirement on a small pension. Shaw became a regular visitor to the series of cottages in the southeast of England, where the Salts pursued the simple life partly from necessity. He could be at his ease there, among "educated and thoughtful men" and a woman who loved to play Wagner on the piano, in an environment unburdened by luxury. "I was always happy at the Salts," he recalled in the last year of his life, and added, "The bond between us was that we were Shelleyans and Humanitarians."[16] He would find them at Millthorpe in Derbyshire when he went to visit Carpenter there, and at other times in London. The connection lasted to the end of their various lives. (Joynes died prematurely, and Kate predeceased her husband.) Writing at length to Archibald Henderson on 3 January 1905, Shaw gave a brief account of a household "where there was no question of Henry George and Karl Marx, but a good deal of Walt Whitman and Thoreau" (*CL* 2, 490). The talk was uninhibited, and on sexual matters the Salts would consult Havelock Ellis as well as Carpenter. Shaw himself was reading Whitman with Florence Farr (Emery) in January 1893.[17]

The Shavian questioning of gender stereotypes had been proceeding through the novels he had been writing: mainly in the prominence he gave to independent-minded and decisive women characters. These reflected the women he had been meeting who had learned to survive outside the domestic situation largely by their own efforts. (He could count his mother and his sister Lucy among them.) He had certainly broken away from Victorian fictional stereotypes, though Thackeray's Becky

Sharp and the heroines of George Meredith, greatly admired by Salt, could be cited as forerunners. The Cleveland Street scandals prompted him to attempt a public intervention on the matter of sexual practices and the law.

"Prompt" is the wrong word for the letter Shaw wrote on 26 November 1889 (*CL* 1, 230–32),[18] when Ernest Parke, deputy editor of *The Star* and proprietor of the *North London Press,* was awaiting prosecution for libel. Though he certainly supported Parke in his reporting of the Cleveland Street affair "to expose a den of debauchees,"[19] Shaw's main onslaught was directed at the Labouchere Amendment of 1885, which made sexual intercourse between males *in private* a criminal offense (for which Wilde would be prosecuted ten years later). Of course Shaw might have been preoccupied in 1885, the year when he celebrated his twenty-ninth birthday with his seduction by Mrs. Jenny Patterson and recorded the event in his diary. Perhaps he had tried writing then and failed, for in a private letter of June 1887 to W. T. Stead he described the basic economic truths about society as "even harder to tell than were those of the Criminal Law Amendment Act" (*CL* 1, 173). Perhaps discussion in the Salt circle had encouraged him to try now.

Parke's *North London Press* had followed in the wake of *Truth* in breaking the journalistic conspiracy of silence about the male brothel in Cleveland Street raided by the police. Rumors abounded over its aristocratic clients, thought to include a member of the royal family, and Parke had published two names of titled men. In writing to the editor of *Truth,* Shaw was plausibly relying on support from the first journal to break through the "superstitious terror" that had kept the other papers silent. But his reference to the privilege enjoyed by *Truth* ("fortified by your parliamentary position") indicates that it was really the proprietor he was addressing: Henry Labouchere, MP, who was responsible for the savage Amendment. It is not surprising that the letter was not published. (A similar letter to *The Star* fared no better.)[20]

The surviving text opens with an apology for broaching a subject "everybody declares unmentionable" and works around to a plea for open discussion "with sane straightforwardness and without affectation." (He would make the same point about the power of social taboo to inhibit reform with the "two words" Vivie Warren finds herself unable to speak.) "My justification shall be that we may presently be saddled with the moral responsibility for monstrously severe punishments" may suggest that he was reworking an old letter started before the Amendment was passed. This supposition is strengthened when the letter calls on "champions of individual rights" to protest jointly "against a law by which two adult men can be sentenced to twenty years penal servitude for a private act, freely consented to and desired by both, which concerns themselves alone."

This is puzzling, for the Amendment in its original form had stipulated a penalty of one year's imprisonment, increased to two years before the Act was finally passed. Twenty years is the period mentioned again in a letter Shaw managed to get published in *The Adult* in September 1898 (*CL* 2, 57–58), protesting at the prosecution of George Bedborough of the Legitimation League (working for the rights of illegitimate children). Bedborough was accused of offering obscene literature for sale, specifically a copy of Havelock Ellis's first volume (*Sexual Inversion*) in what would ultimately become a seven-volume study, *The Psychology of Sex*, the rest of which would be published in America only. The emphasis in this letter, too, falls on the ignorant and inhumane treatment meted out by law when the "morbid idiosyncrasy," with which Ellis's indispensable and authoritative book is concerned, becomes the subject of a prosecution. "My own attention was called to the subject many years ago," Shaw continues, "by the passing of a sentence of twenty years' penal servitude on a harmless elderly gentleman who had been ill-advised enough to plead guilty to a piece of folly which involved no danger whatever to society." This raises the question of whether he was referring to the same case as in his letter to *Truth* or to a pre-1885 case. For in Shaw's childhood what the earlier letter calls "our relic of Inquisition law" remained technically in force: sodomy was punishable by death, and only in 1861 was the punishment reduced to ten years or upward.

Incidentally, his use of the word "morbid" reflects late nineteenth-century reformist policy of shifting the discussion of homosexuality from the sphere of criminal jurisprudence into that of medical pathology; Ellis's "inversion", currently implying a natural tendency, or freak of nature, to be distinguished from the corruption of sexual perversion, was similarly defensive. The more striking "idiosyncrasy," a quirk of character, looks forward to the explanation of the phenomenon as a social formation to be covered by individual rights.

This letter in *The Adult* refers to the writer's own attempt to start an earlier protest in the press: "I then discovered that the fear of becoming suspected of personal reasons for desiring a change in the law in this matter, makes every Englishman an abject coward . . . professing in public . . . views which have not the slightest resemblance to those which he expresses in private conversation with educated and thoughtful men" (*CL* 2, 57). In writing to *Truth* he had referred to the different attitude in "this matter" to be found in public schools (like Eton), among "Greek philosophers, otherwise of unquestioned virtue," soldiers, sailors, convicts, and galley slaves (isolated in all-male groups), where such "attachments" may be seen to redeem men "from utter savagery."

He also mentions the silent acceptance in "good" society of both men and women whose homosexual inclinations are privately known (an in-

stance of a degree of tolerance and freedom ensured by custom, though
not by law); but he does not go so far as to ask whether the offense that
concerns him is more social than moral. The class issue does not come
into Shaw's sights here—even to be ruled out of consideration as he "re-
serves" the original intention of the Criminal Law Amendment Bill: "the
right of the children to careful protection against debauchees." That he
was not unaware of complications class difference might introduce, with
the risk of dominance and exploitation, is apparent in his casual gibe to
Henry Salt, when talking of Clarence Darrow in 1903: "a genuine noble
savage . . . unlike that ultra-civilized impostor the ex-clergyman of Millthorpe" (CL 2, 348). Recollection of the heterosexual scandal of "the
maiden tribute of modern Babylon" gives an edge to the dialogue between
Doolittle and the two gentlemen, Higgins and Pickering ("Governors
both"), over payment for Eliza in Act II of Pygmalion. Shaw himself was
never much at ease with trade unionists.

As for the public schools, they and the older universities (especially Oxford) had replaced medieval Christianity with the classics, especially
Greek, at the center of the elite system they had devised for the education
of the governing and top military-officer class. The continuing public debate about this system was constantly dogged by another, almost-smoth-
ered debate about sexuality, often conducted with reference to Athens and
Sparta.[21] In these essentially all-male enclaves, beginning to come under
threat from still imitative and very peripheral incursions from women,
the concept of "manliness," with its connotations of dominance as well as
strength, had become crucial. Shaw's self-education included wide reading
of classical literature and drama. Allusions to it crowd his own plays, and
Gilbert Murray's versions of Euripides balanced and engaged with them
through the entire Vedrenne-Barker program, which negotiated Shaw's
access to his widest and most lasting audience.

Those letters of his were good Humanitarian League activity; yet the
art of drama was not undervalued among the reformers. (It was Havelock
Ellis who had the idea for what became the long-running Mermaid series
of English plays from the Renaissance period. Ashbee worked as an amateur actor with William Poel, the influential creator of the Elizabethan
Stage Society, whom he induced to direct one of the Elizabethan plays put
on regularly by the Guild of Handicraft at Chipping Campden.) Ibsen had
shown Shaw the way to deal with problems of sex and sexuality in the
theater. Ghosts, which the Independent Theatre Society was founded to
perform, not only focused an unwilling public attention on venereal disease, but used it as a unifying symbol for an entire social system built up
over time; furthermore, the licensing of brothels on the European continent in 1870 was a fact essential to its narrative plot, as were the less time-
specific issues of male sexual indulgence (and ways in which women could

assert their power in response), incest and illegitimacy. The furor that greeted the production was a lesson in how to draw public attention by breaking taboos on thought and expression; it also indicated a revolutionary power inherent in what lay under taboo. Shaw would put the entire lesson freshly into effect in *Mrs. Warren's Profession*.

Meanwhile, in *The Philanderer* he focused, in reassuringly farcical mode, on heterosexual promiscuity. This offense against the official and traditional doctrine of monogamy was something he deplored in fellow socialists ranging from Aveling through Hubert Bland to H. G. Wells; he was half-troubled to find a similar tendency in himself. The same play touches pointedly on the question of gender identity, mocking the commonplace preference for a clear binary distinction ("womanly women" and "manly men") as already old-fashioned.[22] Alongside this Shaw introduced the figure of Sylvia, just emerging from adolescence into adulthood, her (perhaps Shakespeare-inspired) cross-dressing signifying the sexual indeterminacy from which she might emerge as a New Woman. Ibsen had again been a forerunner in *Little Eyolf*, a play Shaw much admired, where the gradually revealed character of "Big Eyolf," truly capable of a comradely marriage, is contrasted with the deliberately seductive Rita Allmers.[23]

The Shaw play most closely related to the times he spent with the Salts and their friends is *Candida*, as is now well known. (Ellis's first book, *Men and Women*, and Carpenter's prose-poem, *Towards Democracy*, were published in this period.) In the Preface he wrote for *Plays Pleasant* is an enigmatic, almost gnomic, record of his contemporary consciousness of what was at issue. He had made his second visit to Italy and wrote in terms of "pre-Raphaelitism, medieval or modern," which he had "shewn at its best in conflict with the first broken, nervous, stumbling attempts to formulate its own revolt against itself as it develops into something higher." He identifies his antagonist to the Christian Socialist with a "higher but vaguer and timider vision, . . . incoherent, mischievous, and even ridiculous unpracticalness."[24] As a nonagenarian, Shaw told Stephen Winsten that Kate Salt was a lesbian. Winsten's own account gives a slightly different impression: of a woman a romantic novelist might have described as "unawakened," who initially understood sex simply as a matter of reproductive biology—she and Henry did not want children, and so were not very interested in sex.[25] Perhaps self-defensively, she was pleased when Carpenter gave her an acceptable sexual identity by calling her an Urning. This may well have been Shaw's introduction to the term that originated with Karl Heinrich Ulrichs in 1864 and was picked up in the Westphal article of 1869–70, which for Michel Foucault marks the moment when homosexuality was identified with a *type* of humanity, involving "a kind of interior androgyny, a hermaphroditism of the soul."[26] Ulrichs represented the type as newly emergent, and the term has as much to do with a Utopian future, when the Superman-woman may descend from the sky, as he-she does in *Misalliance,* as with the physical expression of love between two people of the same sex.

The idea of the Urning hovers over *Candida,* but not in direct relation to either of the women characters; instead, it surfaces in the still-adolescent Eugene. Sinfield quotes Shaw's description of the character from the text of *Plays Pleasant* (1898): *"A strange, shy youth of eighteen, slight, effeminate, with a delicate childish voice . . . a hunted tormented expression . . . painful sensitiveness. . . . He is so uncommon as to be almost unearthly"* (*CPP* 1: 534–35). Sinfield mentions that his attention was drawn to the play, but he does not observe that the character, though said to be a young aristocrat by birth, is dressed more like a down-and-out in soiled, cast-off garments: bohemian, perhaps, though his aesthetic credentials appear in the picture he has given to Candida that expresses his imaginative idealization of womanhood.

The word "effeminate" is not present in the original holograph manuscript of 1894. There the character is described as a "poet", aged eighteen, "Intensely nervous, slight . . . delicate organization, rather wild and strange."[27] Mention of the canvas shoes has been inserted, and the "silk handkerchief for a cravat" befits a costume that has its own style. It is suggestive of a simple-lifer in the Carpenter mode. It is also a reminder of the words of little Jim Joynes's father, dismissing the boy's first troubled realization of the rift between rich and poor. He told his son that "the world can only be redeemed by its aristocracy. 'That is why Eton exists.'"[28]

But that epithet "effeminate" jumps out of the revised text, conjuring up its opposite, "manly." Sinfield believes "effeminacy" may not have connoted homosexuality in 1894. It was much more likely to have done so in 1898—and when *Candida* was performed by the Stage Society, with Granville Barker "perfect," said Shaw, as Eugene, on 1 July 1900, a production that became an instant legend. Yet Eugene is like Sylvia in *The Philanderer,* only on the verge of definition by adulthood; and one possible reading of the end of the play is that he leaves behind him effeminacy in the old sense of having had too much to do with women. It is the dependent and uxorious Morell who is the effeminate revealed.

Instances of Shaw's understanding of "manliness" abound.[29] The art of pugilism he studied with Pakenham Beatty was transferred into his writing technique. At its most unpleasant, it is a form of bullying, though he usually manages to burlesque his fury amusingly enough. He defended the "brutality" of his criticism to Archibald Henderson: "I have always had to stand out against the notion" that people "were the better instead of the worse . . . for misfortunes. *I was trained* to look in the face the fact that infirmities disable people instead of reinforcing them. . . . I have always abhorred the petty disloyalties which we call sparing one another's feelings" (my italics. *CL* 2, 483). He dramatized the attitude supremely in the character and challenge of Andrew Undershaft. Ultimately it helped him make a political trap for himself with the defense of fascist dictators. It was the Salts who suggested he should dramatize the story of Androcles and the lion, in which "effeminate" humanitarianism and strength come paradisally together.[30]

Wilde's formulation of the ideal (platonic) relationship between an older and a younger man (a surrogate son relationship) had been applauded in open court.[31] Shaw set himself to realize his own version of this. Wilde had chosen Lord Alfred Douglas, a very good-looking young aristocrat with a distinct poetic talent: a socially acceptable connection. Though Shaw might only just have noticed him, the equally good-looking and graceful Granville Barker had been making a reputation as a director of symbolist plays, as a sensitive actor who had played Richard II in William Poel's production of Shakespeare's play, and as an interesting new playwright who, like Shaw himself, had had a play presented to critical acclaim in a West End theater and had a drawer full of others in reserve. Like Shaw, he had missed public school and university, but his family background was upper class, cultured and intellectual and, in part, High Anglican of Italian descent. He was as presentable in aristocratic society as among clever bohemians. Shaw's early rhapsodies over Barker often seem like parodies of Lord Henry Wootton talking to, or of, Dorian Gray in Wilde's "aesthetic" novel. In strong contrast to the Wilde-Douglas association, Shaw and Barker would be of enormous benefit to each other's joint and separate achievements over many years.

A number of the playwrights presented by the Vedrenne-Barker management at the Court, and later at other theaters, had direct connections with Chipping Campden (Laurence Housman,[32] St. John Hankin, and John Masefield particularly). Ashbee's settlement there was founded on the idea of comradeship presented in *A Few Chapters in Workshop Reconstruction and Citizenship*, printed at his Essex House Press in 1894: "It is not new . . . the feeling that drew Jesus to John . . . or that inspired the friendships of Greece . . . in the new citizenship we shall need it again. . . . Democracy—as socially, not politically, conceived—its basis." Granville Barker went there to lecture on how not to direct Shakespeare, in the first year of the open Extension lectures Ashbee arranged for his attempt at a classless village of artist-craftsmen.[33] He spent some weeks there, later, writing *Prunella* with Laurence Housman, and again to work with Joseph Moorat on the musical accompaniment.[34] Housman himself was a frequent visitor and a great friend of Ashbee's wife, Janet, with whom he maintained a free and friendly correspondence over many years. (She also received many intimate letters from George Ives, about whose Order of Chaeronea there seems to have been a certain amount of hocus pocus: "I

hadn't the faith for it," was Laurence's ironic comment to Janet.)[35] The
Webbs took a house in the neighborhood, not too close. Millthorpe may
have been enough for Shaw, in his skepticism about artificial communities:
the only successful ones, he told Salt, had been entirely celibate. (The
Oneida Creek community, mentioned in the letter to *Truth* and in his
Preface to *Man and Superman,* amazed and impressed him by so inge-
niously combining birth control with the near-realization of Oedipal
dreams.) Yet it seems worth observing that Ashbee's *Conradin* (Essex
House Press, 1908), a "philosophic ballad" woven around the Guild, contains an illustration (by Philip Mairet) that shows an armored and
mounted woman with a commonsense modern face and hairstyle—a Joan
of Arc, no languorous Pre-Raphaelite—with a banner-carrying knight on
either flank, and behind them an endless file of cavalry. The three leading
figures are portraits of Janet Ashbee, her comrade-husband, and Guild co-
founder, Gerald Bishop (who had played the title role in the first, amateur
presentation of *The Admirable Bashville*).

    Setting up a British Society for the Study of Sexual Psychology (soon
simplified to B.S.S.P.) in 1914 was a good way of marking Edward Carpenter's seventieth birthday. In the first meeting at the house of Montague
Summers,[36] Havelock Ellis was made president; Laurence Housman was
chairman and wrote the manifesto. Carpenter was elected an honorary life
member; and George Ives read a paper on "The Graeco-Roman View of
Youth." A series of publications was started. This being England, the first
three were anonymous, and all had to be read under supervision at the
British Museum Library. The fourth publication, *The Relation of Fellow-
Feeling to Sex* (1916), was retrospectively attributed to Housman in the list
printed in the fifth: Havelock Ellis's *The Erotic Rights of Women—the Objects
of Marriage* (1917). There is nothing surprising about Shaw's membership
in this association.[37] There are no early lists, but he is recorded as a life
member in 1930. It seems likely that Montgomery Hyde was right in suggesting that former members of the Order of Chaeronea made up a substantial part of the new, more formal organization, and Montague
Summers was an extraordinarily 1890-ish figure; but Shaw was no more
likely to have been attracted to Ives's Order than he was to the Golden
Dawn.

    More covert activities of Ives and some associates had included giving
advice and help to homosexuals in danger from the police. (Ives, besides
being an anarchist and a member of the Humanitarian League, was a
prison reformer, consulted by John Galsworthy in his campaign against
solitary confinement.) With the coming of the war and the threat of conscription, some of this attention was switched to giving similar help to
conscientious objectors. Laurence Housman was certainly involved in the
second of these activities and, in 1916, resigned from his post as art critic

of the *Manchester Guardian* to avoid giving embarrassment with what some of his obituaries were to pass over as "silliness."[38] In that same year, he, with Ashbee and Lowes Dickinson, visited the United States on a lecture tour to promote the cause of a League of Nations. They went in the wake of Gilbert and Lady Mary Murray, and their concern was still citizenship, but now extending internationally. Shaw, of course, would always avoid pacifism, as did Murray (always careful to distinguish Plato and Benjamin Jowett from any taint of "decadence"). Instead, he had chosen to attack the incompetence of politicians and "junkers" in a special supplement to the *New Statesman*.

In later life, as a known progressive in sexual matters, Shaw was liable to have his support invited by campaigners. One of these had been Louis Wilkinson, to whom he replied in December 1909 with strong words of warning: cautioning pragmatism, but also distinguishing sharply between "normal" and "abnormal people" (*CL* 2, 890).[39] In joining the protest against the banning of *The Well of Loneliness* in 1928, he remained faithful to his old belief in public openness and his consistent opposition to the theatrical censorship. Writing to the Dean of Windsor on this occasion, Shaw drew his old distinction between the sexual conduct of individuals and their general character (Hesione Hushabye's explanation, "People don't have their virtues and vices in sets; they have them anyhow: all mixed up."): "I have not found that even the most absurd aberrations are necessarily associated with any general depravity of character . . . homosexuals are sometimes conspicuously highminded" (*CL* 4, 119).[40] Perhaps surprisingly, he adds, "The wisest and best inverts never tell." This was hardly a self-referential comment, but it recognizes another kind of "manliness" in an intolerant society.

Returning to the beginning of the century: Beatrice Webb had read and disliked Carpenter's *Love's Coming of Age* and passed on her negative reaction to Shaw, until he was challenged by the author to read it for himself and admitted he had been "charmed" by the book. He reported to Carpenter that he was setting to work on a new play that would express his own views on "sex, marriage and love."[41] He may be said to have done this in *Man and Superman,* where the philanderer is apotheosized as Don Juan and (in the everyday world) punished for his audacity with political impotence. The themes are less subjectively treated in *Getting Married,* which Granville Barker (off to America to discuss the starting of a form of national theater there) left him to direct at the tail end of the Vedrenne-Barker seasons. It was the kind of play Beatrice Webb thought the management should concentrate on: a discussion of important issues on which political action was possible. As the Preface states, a Government Commission on Marriage Law was currently at work.

But Shaw's mischief began with the decision to write this play in the

"Greek form" that Vedrenne-Barker audiences associated with Euripidean tragedy, "the spontaneous falling of a play of ideas into the form most suitable to it . . . the classical form," he would say in 1933,[42] fit for the late Victorian and Edwardian matter of Greece. Master of ceremonies over the fantasy is the Greengrocer, improbably in charge of the wedding breakfast.[43] Shaw introduces his Lesbia, as much of a lesbian as Kate Salt, or Annie Besant, or Florence Farr, choosing single motherhood as Ellen Terry had done. The Anglo-Catholic Father Anthony, on the other hand, has a philosopher or mystic's vocation for celibacy and a faith in the visionary power of mind to solve all problems in the fullness of time; for him the legend of a virgin birth is a prophesy: of such a world as Shaw conceives in *Back to Methuselah*, "As Far as Thought Can Reach, "or of *in vitro* fertilization in a more prosaic universe.[44] The sybilline figure here is Mrs. George of ambiguous gender (her name oxymoronic, as was Major Barbara at that time).

Shaw's theatrical practice had taught him the need to occupy the eyes of the audience fittingly, while their ears and minds were kept busily at work. So here is a parade of transvestite males: the Alderman in his gown, the Bishop in his apron, the solicitor (Father Anthony) in his cassock and biretta, the Beadle in his robes, bearing the phallic mace; and, as an enlivening variant, the General dazzlingly be-medaled in his dress uniform. Moreover, as Hirschfeld's *Berlins drittes Geschlecht* (1905), concerned with transvestism, had appeared as *Le Troisième Sexe* in 1908 and was talked about among some of his friends, it was accessible to Shaw. The clearest confirmation that *Getting Married* was on this track comes in the play Granville Barker took up when he came back into the game. It was *The Madras House* that, in its third act, fills much of the stage with what might be Shaw's Bishop's table, the male cast seated around it in full, competitive, verbal display as the dumb female models gyrate before them in their fashions. Barker's equivalent of the wedding cake is a fantastic Edwardian lady's hat; and Windlesham, the "man-milliner" (or ladies' tailor) in charge of the show, comes off not at all badly in the end.[45]

The Preface for which *Getting Married* made the occasion speaks for itself with the usual clarity and force of Shaw's prose. It turns the tables decisively on "normality" both by the range of its survey of the varieties of sexual custom and by its discussion of the pathology and criminology of marriage as commonly accepted in Britain. His proclamation of "the absolute right to sexual experience" was more revolutionary at the time than arguments against property in human beings and the limitations of monogamy. His thinking tended to be less compromised than his attitudes and behavior in everyday life, as is not uncommon. The clarity of his denial to Almroth Wright that men's and women's minds were different[46] is a match for Sinfield's assertion, "The villain of the piece is the masculine/

feminine binary structure" (vii). There can be little doubt that Shaw's power of analyzing his society's attitudes to sexuality and its confusions had been developed by contact with a movement concerned with citizenship, aiming to modify the sensibility of a whole population and mend its divisions through the power of feeling—through Humanitarianism, in fact.

Notes

1. *The Wilde Century* (London and New York: Cassell, 1994), pp. 1–2.

2. *Bernard Shaw: The Diaries,* ed. Stanley Weintraub (University Park: Penn State University Press, 1986), vol. 2, p. 1060.

3. Sally Peters, *Bernard Shaw: The Ascent of Superman* (New Haven: Yale University Press, 1996), and the epitome, "Shaw's Life: A Feminist in Spite of Himself," in *The Cambridge Companion to George Bernard Shaw* (Cambridge: Cambridge University Press, 1998), pp. 3–24.

4. Mary Hyde, *Bernard Shaw and Alfred Douglas: A Correspondence* (London: John Murray, 1982), p. xix.

5. Ibid., p. xxi.

6. See *Bernard Shaw: Collected Letters,* 4 vols., ed. Dan H. Laurence (London: Max Reinhardt, 1965–88), vol. 1, p. 821, editorial note. Henceforth abbreviated *CL* in text and notes.

7. Collected in Laurence Housman, *Back Words and Fore Words* (London: Jonathan Cape, 1945).

8. The most accessible source of information on the inter-involvements mentioned here is probably Norman and Jeanne Mackenzie, *The First Fabians* (London: Weidenfeld & Nicolson, 1977).

9. Alan Crawford, *C. R. Ashbee: Architect, Designer, and Romantic Socialist* (New Haven: Yale University Press, 1985).

10. See *Bernard Shaw: The Diaries,* vol. 1, pp. 482–83, 568, 588, etc.

11. T. J. Cobden-Sanderson, speaking at the Arts and Crafts Exhibition, 1896.

12. Fiona MacCarthy, *William Morris: A Life for Our Time* (London: Faber & Faber, 1994), pp. 522–23.

13. See Shaw's 23 September 1891 letter to Morris, written in Venice, in *CL* 1, 308–12.

14. J. G. Pocock, *The Machiavellian Moment* (Princeton: Princeton University Press, 1975), traces the larger political discourse within which our present debate on sexuality and gender is a subtheme. The following brief quotation, referring to Montesquieu, could serve as an epigraph for the present article: "it was because the ethos of the ancient cities was essentially a warrior ethos . . . that Plato and Aristotle believed the personality could and must be entirely reshaped by music" (49). The Symbolist belief that "All Art aspires to the Condition of Music" updates the idea to Shaw's day.

15. Reprinted in *Short Stories, Scraps and Shavings* (London: Constable, 1932).

16. Stephen Winsten, *Salt and His Circle* (London and New York: Hutchinson, 1951), Preface, p. 9.

17. *Bernard Shaw: The Diaries,* vol. 2, p. 898.

18. This letter has also been discussed by Sally Peters.

19. He also helped to keep the *North London Press* going by writing leading articles for it while Parke was in prison.

20. See *Bernard Shaw: The Diaries*, vol. 1, p. 562. The editorial comment, p. 563, is slightly at variance with Laurence's in *CL* 1, 230.

21. Linda Dowling, in *Hellenism and Homosexual Life in Victorian Oxford* (Ithaca: Cornell University Press, 1994), unravels the issues illuminatingly.

22. With the nineteenth century's addiction to taxonomy, Magnus Hirschfeld was distinguishing many degrees of variation between the extremes of masculine and feminine identity.

23. There is an equivalent in Hardy's *Jude the Obscure:* in Sue Bridehead's prehistory with her student comrade, whose clothes she borrowed for herself.

24. See the Preface to *Plays Pleasant* in *The Bodley Head Bernard Shaw: Collected Plays with Their Prefaces*, editorial supervisor Dan H. Laurence (London: Max Reinhardt, 7 vols., 1970–74), vol. 1, pp. 534–35. Henceforth abbreviated *CPP* in text and notes.

25. Winsten, *Salt and His Circle*, p. 71.

26. Michel Foucault, *History of Sexuality* I: *An Introduction*, trans. R. Hurley (New York: Vintage Books, 1978), p. 43. A variation on the Urning notion was the half-secret, largely Tory society of the Souls at Cambridge, in which A. J. Balfour was the central figure, referred to as Prince Arthur. See Max Egremont, *Balfour* (London: Collins, 1980). Visual testimony of its spread among artists comes in the scarcely embodied figures that populate many book illustrations by Charles Ricketts, Shaw's preferred theatrical designer. See Stephen Calloway, *Charles Ricketts, Subtle and fantastic decorator* (London: Thames & Hudson, 1979).

27. *Early Texts: Play Manuscripts in Facsimile: Candida and How He Lied to Her Husband* (New York and London: Garland, 1981), p. 4.

28. Winsten, *Salt and His Circle*, p. 33.

29. Sinfield has two chapters on "Uses of Effeminacy" and "Manly Sentiments."

30. Members of Wilfred Scawen Blunt's (Tory) Crabbet Club were expected to write poetry at night and play tennis, naked, in the morning. See Max Egremont, *The Cousins: The Friendship, Activities, and Opinions of Wilfred Scawen Blunt and George Wyndham* (London: Collins, 1977).

31. H. Montgomery Hyde, *The Trials of Oscar Wilde* (London: Hodge, 1948), p. 31, 1976); but the statement has been printed many times.

32. Katherine Lyon Mix, in "Laurence Housman and Bernard Shaw," *SHAW: The Annual of Bernard Shaw Studies* 6 (1986), pp. 81–90, has traced the direct connections between the two men. Her article says nothing of Housman's very considerable place in the *art nouveau* world, as a book designer and illustrator, and editor (with Somerset Maugham) of *The Venture*. See Rodney Engen, *Laurence Housman*, Artist and Critic series, vol. 1 (Stroud, Glos.: Catalpa Press, 1983), which also gives an interesting account of Housman's life. At the Celebratory Dinner for Vedrenne and Barker in 1907, Housman was seated among those other friends of Wilde: Robert Ross (of the Carfax Gallery, which had supplied the pictures for Dubedat's exhibition in *The Doctor's Dilemma*), More Adey, and Reggie Turner.

33. The program for 1903–4, printed at the Essex House Press (copy seen in the National Art Library, Victoria and Albert Museum), does not give an exact date for the lecture. The Ashbee Memoirs (unpublished, Victoria and Albert Library), an epitome of the forty-four volumes of journals at King's College, Cambridge, tell of a visit by Barker with Housman in December 1903, but the lecture is not mentioned there.

34. Alec Miller (a guildsman) writes about this in "C. R. Ashbee and the Guild of Handicraft" (unpublished typescript, Victoria and Albert Library).

35. Fiona MacCarthy, *The Simple Life: C. R. Ashbee in the Cotswolds* (London: Lund Humphries, 1981, 1988), p. 144, n. 5. This book is an important source of information on the personalities involved with the Guild at Chipping Campden. Felicity Ashbee, *Janet Ashbee: Love, Marriage, and the Arts & Crafts Movement* (Syracuse: Syracuse University Press, 2002), pp. 37–38, quotes Janet's account of an intimate conversation with Ives in November 1899.

36. T. D. Arch Smith, *Love in Earnest* (London: Routledge & Kegan Paul, 1970), p. 137. Summers, together with Allan Wade (Barker's secretary at the Court Theatre and later) and Barker's stage designer Norman Wilkinson, ran the Phoenix Society, the highly successful branch of the Stage Society that specialized in presenting Restoration plays between the first and second world wars. He became well known for his interest in witchcraft and his association with the satanist Aleister Crowley.

37. Shaw also contributed to the Congress of the World League for Sexual Reform in 1929. See "The Need for Expert Opinion in Sexual Reform," in *Platform and Pulpit*, ed. Dan H. Laurence (New York: Hill & Wang, 1961), pp. 432–37.

38. The Clark Collection at the Street branch of Somerset County Library contains Laurence Housman's letters to the Quaker shoe manufacturer, Roger Clark, and his wife, Sarah, which indicates that they were all involved in the B.S.S.P. Laurence's letters to his sister Clemence (both were ardent workers for women's suffrage) are in the same collection and contain many references to Chipping Campden and to Granville Barker, but only a few to Shaw.

39. Note Havelock Ellis's equal caution: "One can appreciate the achievement without having oneself any personal taste for inversion" (quoted in Winsten, *Salt and His Circle*, p. 162).

40. He said much the same in his consolatory letter to Nancy Astor of 15 April 1932 (see *CL* 4, 284).

41. Winsten, *Salt and His Circle*, p. 112.

42. *CPP* 3: 449. His notion of classical form here certainly embraced Greek comedy.

43. He claims, "They joke about the greengrocer, just as they joke about the mother-in-law." Alfred Douglas, who spent a brief while at the play before writing an extraordinary review (in which he claimed that Shaw "does not have a masculine intellect"), took him for a waiter. (On this episode, see Hyde, Appendix I, pp. 207–10.) Could Shaw have been thinking of the vegetable love that crops up in W. S. Gilbert's lines in *Patience*, popular in Wilde's aesthetic days ("a sentimental passion of a vegetable fashion . . . An attachment a la Plato for a bashful young potato")?

44. See Shaw's enthusiastic letter to Herbert Brewer (undated: January 1937) in *CL* 4, 460.

45. I have traced the intertextual relationship between *The Madras House* and Shaw's *Misalliance* in *The Shavian Playground* (London: Methuen, 1972), pp. 188–99.

46. Shaw, "Sir Almroth Wright's Case Against Woman Suffrage," in *Fabian Feminist*, ed. Rodelle Weintraub (University Park: Penn State University Press, 1977), pp. 243–47.

Bernard F. Dukore

SEX AND SALVATION

Sexuality plays a more prominent role in Bernard Shaw's plays than is commonly supposed. In his first play, *Widowers' Houses,* its importance in the last scene between the main male and female characters is manifest, for Shaw's stage directions explicitly describe animal ferocity, eroticism, and lovemaking. Having a character contrast higher and lower centers (brains and genitals) in a later work, *Too True to Be Good,* Shaw also has him call a female character the embodiment of the latter and describe her sexual voracity. In addition, Shaw has her proposition a man for explicitly sexual reasons and has him accept her partly for the same reasons. Whereas the sexual scene in the earlier play steams the proceedings, the sexual talk and action of the later work, in which discussion is far more prominent than in the earlier, is comic. Despite the sexual initiative of the latter female character, neither she nor anyone else in this play does anything as physically erotic as the chief female character of Opus One. Partly for this reason, discursiveness and wit usually register more force-fully than sexuality for readers of this play and of most Shavian comedies. Because these readers include actors and directors, their productions demonstrate the same qualities more powerfully than they do sexuality, and audiences find little sexuality in Shavian comedy. If actors and direc-tors take the erotic aspects more fully into account, the results could en-rich and vivify their productions, grounding the action and the characters' relationships with each other. Such a notion is not as outlandish as may initially appear, for one of the actor's main jobs is to play the character from that character's viewpoint. In other words, treat the lower centers as well as the higher centers.

For good reasons, *Major Barbara* is usually considered a discussion play and an exemplary high comedy. In this article, I will examine it from

I wish to thank Liz Carlin Metz of Knox College for her invitation to deliver a lecture in April 2003 to the college at large, as part of a series for The Caxton Club. The lecture was a different version of this article and helped me to clarify ideas developed here.

another angle—the importance of sexuality. About a quarter of the way through the second act, Shaw gives a prominent clue to the centrality of sex. When Cusins enters, he and Barbara kiss over the drum he carries, *"evidently not for the first time, as people cannot kiss over a big drum without practice. Undershaft coughs."*[1] Anyone who has directed this play, or who has played Barbara or Cusins, can testify that Shaw is right: they need practice to kiss over a large drum. Furthermore, their kiss is not a pro forma peck. It is sexual and lasts long enough to embarrass her father, who coughs in order to stop it. Although the actors should not do anything but kiss, that kiss could convey anything to which it may lead. Let us take this sequence as a point of departure for an examination of the play and as a cue for actors and directors.

The play opens with a duologue between Lady Britomart and her son Stephen. The scene soon reveals that he is twenty-four years old, that he was graduated from Harrow and Cambridge, traditional schools for a young man of his class, and that he traveled to India, then a crown colony, and Japan. We also learn that he has two sisters, whose age Shaw does not cite. We may suppose that Barbara is a year or two younger than Stephen, and that Sarah is probably a year or two younger than Barbara.

A healthy, wealthy aristocrat who attended public (or as Americans would say, private) secondary and tertiary schools that are among the best in the world, Stephen then visited two Asian countries, one of which was ruled by his own. Whether he took advantage of sexual opportunities during his travels, the play does not say. Providing a rich subtext, however, it does say that his mother disapproves of "the present fashion of philandering bachelors and late marriages," which suggests that he is, or that his mother thinks he may be, such a bachelor, and that she is trying to arrange a suitable union for him. His assertion that he had rather arrange it for himself prompts her to exclaim, "Nonsense!" but she tries to mollify him by agreeing to consult him on the matter. Rather than argue the point at this time, he elects to *"close his lips"* and be *"silent,"* which, the actor could suggest, need not mean acquiescence but simply discretion.

Barbara has a fiancé, Cusins, a professor of Greek. She picked him up— yes: she, not he, did it—at a Salvation Army meeting.[2] Lady Britomart describes him as a man who *"pretends* to be a Salvationist" (my emphasis) and plays the drum at rallies "because he has fallen head over ears in love with her." How old is he? Shaw does not say, but Granville Barker was twenty-eight when he played the role, and since Shaw wrote it with Barker in mind, that age is a fair enough estimate. In addition, one may infer such an age since Cusins is young enough to persuade Barbara to pick him up. One recalls that Shaw is careful to distinguish between youth and middle age, and that he considers a union of a young lady and a middle-aged man—Louka and Nicola in *Arms and the Man,* Eliza and Higgins in

Pygmalion—to be a mismatch. At the end of the first act, Lady Britomart tells Cusins she believes he joined the Army "to worship Barbara and nothing else" and warns, "I have found you out. Take care Barbara doesnt." Far from denying her charge, he says, "Dont tell on me."

Independently, Barbara's father reaches the same conclusion about him. In the second act, Undershaft cautions him that Barbara may learn that his drum "is hollow." While Cusins's response is apparently a denial— "you are mistaken: I am a sincere Salvationist"—it is really ironic, for he idiosyncratically defines the Army's religion as one of joy, love, and courage, which unlike hell-obsessed, evangelical sects, battles the forces of evil with music and dance, "as becomes a sally from heaven by its happy garrison."

When, in the third act, Lady Britomart orders Cusins to leave the Army because Barbara has done so, he says he has already obeyed her. "Dolly: were you ever really in earnest about it?" asks Barbara. "Would you have joined if you had never seen me?" A stage direction introduces his reply: "*(disingenuously)* Well—er—well, possibly, as a collector of religions—." Lomax interrupts to conclude, rightly, "Not as a drummer, though, you know."

To return to the play's opening duologue, Lady Britomart explains the Undershaft tradition that prevents Stephen from inheriting his father's business: Stephen's father "pretends to consider himself bound to keep up the tradition and adopt somebody to leave the business to." Pretends? Why would a man whose motto is "Unashamed" pretend? Perhaps her verb reflects the only way she can cope with his decision. Perhaps, though, she is right. She may have recognized that he wanted to keep his options open. As later events reveal, he accepts technicalities and subterfuges to render acceptable someone he wants but who does not strictly conform to the criteria.

Another question arises for us and for the actors. Since Undershaft disinherited Stephen when he was "only a baby," why did she not insist on their separation then instead of two daughters later? The play provides a clue, sex. "You know, my dear," she tells Stephen, "your father was a very attractive man in some ways." This Victorian aristocrat does not count the ways, much less discuss them, and in view of what she just said her statement might astonish Stephen, who could look at her in surprise, awaiting an explanation. Possibly, she thinks the subject concluded and does not continue. He might then stare at her in amazement, which could prompt her to state, "Children did not dislike him," a response that he may consider insufficient and that would motivate her to add, "I did not dislike him myself: far from it," but she gives no specifics, letting "far from it" resonate. They separated, she adds, because she disapproved of him. When she tried to persuade him to change, "he used to laugh and get out of it under cover of some affectionate nonsense." If the last phrase—not to mention "a very attractive man," "I did not dislike him myself," and "far from it"—is code for sex, then she acquires a more earthly dimension. So does Stephen, who recognizes the code. For the actors playing Stephen and Lady Britomart, the scene becomes far richer than it otherwise would.

Another advantage of this interpretation is that it gives the actors who play Undershaft and Lady Britomart an emotional subtext to their curiosity about each other in the dramatic present. He gains a motive for his action when he arrives in Act I—*"Taking her hand with a touch of courtship"*—as well as for his first words when he enters in Act III: "Alone! How fortunate!" and for addressing her as "my love" instead of "my dear," which he uses when others are present and to which he reverts when she pointedly ignores the more affectionate term. If Stephen recognizes that the relationship between his parents continued because of sex, then a director might stage his first appearance in the third act to provide a reason for his behavior. "I beg your pardon," he says upon entering, and immediately prepares to leave. Perhaps his mother has just reverted to the role of a fussy wife who treats her husband as a child when she cannot persuade him to name their son as heir: "And your tie is all on one side. Put it straight." Accepting this role (note the adjective in the stage direction), Undershaft excuses himself, "it wont stay unless it's pinned (*he fumbles with childish grimaces*)." At this point, enter Stephen. If she were to help her husband with his tie, Stephen might, on coming into the room, see them close together, her back toward him, and interpret what he sees as a kiss, or at least as affection. This would provide a subtextual motive (politeness is the surface motivation) for him to excuse himself when he interrupts them. If this moment were tactfully performed, the issue of sex between the parents would help vivify their scenes and humanize both. We would find her more appealing. We would remove him from a pedestal suggestive of omniscience. The issue would also give Stephen a perceptiveness that would add a dimension to his character.

When Bill Walker learns what happened to his girlfriend Mog, sexual jealousy is not the only motivation for his entry. Since she dared to leave him, his ego is damaged. However, sexual pride or a feeling of sexual inadequacy may also be a part of the reason. He comes to the Salvation Army shelter because she left him to go there. It was Jenny Hill, says he, who was responsible for this and who set her against him. He plans to give Mog "a doin" to teach her not to behave that way again and apparently to return to him. To make Jenny hurry in bringing Mog out, Bill strikes her. Soon, Barbara informs him that Mog has a new boyfriend, one of Mog's converts, who "fell in love with her when he saw her with her soul saved"— Barbara might briefly pause as reality enters her memory—"and her face clean, and her hair washed." Bill is *"surprised"* that the "carroty slat" (in

England, the noun does not carry the sexual opprobrium it does in America, where he might call her a carrot-haired bitch) would wash her red hair, evidently believing that washing it would rinse out the color. He then chooses to assert his manhood over his rival's. However, when Bill swears to put the nose of his replacement out of joint, he learns that the man is a former prizefighter who outweighs him. He recognizes that she has got the better of him by gaining a strong protector. Faced with his pugilistic inadequacy, he sulks, feeling his very manhood oozing away. As will happen to Barbara later, he faces a lesson in reality and modifies his behavior accordingly: for having hit Jenny Hill, he aims to start a fight with Mog's new man and get beaten in return. To him, this is fair. Although the result does not go as he plans, he winds up rejecting the Salvation Army, as Barbara will also do.

Before Bill leaves for the fight, Cusins enters and, as described earlier, kisses Barbara over the drum. The punctuation of this kiss by Undershaft's cough is comic and humanizing, as is Barbara and Cusins being unfazed by it. The kiss reminds audiences that the couple is young, and that Barbara's father, until the night before, had not seen her since she was a baby. Thus, it is he, not either of them, who is embarrassed. After all, he must cope with a new fact of life, that his daughter is an adult woman with normal sexual desires. Barbara appears to recognize this to be the case when, after the cough, she says, in a very adult, if not maternal, manner, "It's all right, papa, we've not forgotten you."

Having sized up Barbara, Undershaft examines Cusins, whom he enlists as an ally to win her from the Salvation Army. Mrs. Baines's announcement of Bodger's proposed offer of five thousand pounds if the Army receives a matching five thousand, gives Undershaft the opportunity to achieve his objective. He gives her the matching funds. Barbara tries to prevent the transaction. Noticing that her fiancé is observing her, she might believe that her love as well as her faith is being tested. Her efforts are fruitless. When Cusins *"impishly"* joins Undershaft, she *"almost breaks down as Adolphus, too, fails her."* In other words, she loses the support of her fiancé as well as her religious faith. After Mrs. Baines accepts Undershaft's check, Cusins mischievously declares that Undershaft's unselfishness will inaugurate a new millennium. Cusins's irony devastates her. As he bangs the drum, she pleads, "Dolly: you are breaking my heart."

Still hopeless the next morning, Barbara looks pained when Lomax remarks that she no longer wears her uniform. Comedy returns when he pontificates that the Salvation Army, in contrast to the Church of England, has "a certain amount of tosh." Further signaling the movement from tragedy to comedy—since romantic love, as well as money, is among comedy's usual subjects—Barbara tells him to "go and spoon with Sarah." Obediently, he sits *"affectionately"* beside her. How affectionate is he? Sarah states, "I wish you wouldnt tell Cholly to do things, Barbara. He always comes straight and does them." Does she mean it? Does she not like what he does, or what they do? In productions I have seen, he usually kisses Sarah on the cheek or is stopped from doing so by her remark. Either contrasts with the sexual ardor of Barbara and Cusins in Act II. Another possibility is that the sequence provides a parallel to Barbara and Cusins. Lomax might go straightaway and spoon with Sarah before she delivers the line, after which, or perhaps before which, the two might kiss each other enthusiastically. Either of these actions would give her line and behavior a subtext—she and her fiancé like smooching with each other—and foreshadow Barbara's rejuvenation when she kisses her own fiancé. However, these three are not the only characters on stage. Lady Britomart is also present. Instead of expressing disapproval of her daughter's enjoyment of her fiancé's ardor, which would be a cliché, she herself might take pleasure from watching the couple, which would reverse the audience's expectations and perhaps be funny.

Enter Cusins, who is hung over. "I expected you this morning, Dolly," says Barbara. "Didnt you guess that?" This moment might suggest the depth of their relationship. Sitting beside her, he apologizes. After having greeted each other by kissing over a drum the day before, how do they greet each other here? Possibly, he kisses her before admitting that he has only just breakfasted, which prompts Sarah to reveal how late the hour is: "But weve just finished lunch." If so, what kind of kiss is it? Does she return the kiss? Or do they not kiss? If they do not, how does each cope with this different way of greeting each other and with the attitude the other displays?

In the final scene, Lady Britomart raises the subject of the inheritance. Adopting Undershaft's suggestion, made in Act III, Scene 1, that if she wants to keep the cannon works in the family she should find an eligible foundling and have him marry Barbara, she proposes Cusins as heir. Not contradicting himself, Undershaft indicates that if Cusins were a foundling he would agree. The possibility that Cusins might qualify as a foundling takes everyone, including Lady Britomart, unaware. To audiences, it is a gratifying step that fulfills the expectations of comedy. Because of Undershaft's acceptance of the young man's amusing stratagems—"you have cornered the foundling market"—we know that the lovers will unite in marriage.

After arguing with Cusins, Undershaft cleverly leaves him alone with Barbara to sort matters out. Once they are by themselves, Cusins declares, "I am going to accept his offer." "I thought you would," says she. Since the play is, among other characteristics, a romantic comedy, we are unsurprised that girl gets boy and boy gets girl. Cusins receives the job and will receive, we have little doubt, the legacy as well. Barbara accepts her father's challenge to save the souls of his workers, who are neither poor nor hungry, but who are quarrelsome, proud, and assertive of their rights. Vowing to abjure bribes of bread and salvation, which create hypocrites, not converts, "*She is transfigured,*" according to Shaw. "Glory Hallelujah!" she exclaims, and kisses Cusins. Let this be a long kiss, as sexual as, or more sexual than, the kiss in Act II, because it underscores and seals their betrothal. If it is such a kiss, they will appear more human and more realistic, rather than as a leading lady and leading man who will, according to dramatic convention, live happily ever after. Furthermore, such a kiss would help us to perceive that human ecstasy goes hand in hand with religious ecstasy. Cusins's reaction then becomes fully justified: "My dearest: consider my delicate health. I cannot stand as much happiness as you can." Barbara overwhelms us as well as him. The play is a comedy not only in that its ending emphasizes love, but also in that it is funny. "Yes," she responds: "it is not easy being in love with me, is it? But it's good for you." In addition, it provides an upbeat ending. She has indeed "gone right up into the skies," as Cusins tells Undershaft when he returns, and she brings the audience with her. At the end of the play, she reaffirms her forthcoming marriage, of which sex is a vital part, as well as her commitment to salvation. The play concludes on a note that joins romantic and religious rapture.

Pointedly, Barbara thanks Cusins for finding her a place in which to work at her vocation, which is salvation. But her last line in the play is to her mother: "I want a house in the village to live in with Dolly." She will be a working woman and she will also be a wife. Salvationism is in her future, and so is sex.

Notes

1. Quotations from *Major Barbara* are from *The Bodley Head Bernard Shaw: Collected Plays with Their Prefaces*, vol. 3, editorial supervisor Dan H. Laurence (London: Max Reinhardt, 1971). Because the context makes the source of the quotations clear, I will not bloat the essay with citations.

2. The film version, written by Shaw, dramatizes their encounter at a Salvation Army rally at which Barbara speaks. Although Cusins makes the first move, she elects, almost immediately after he introduces himself to her and declares his love, to take him home to meet her family.

Rodelle Weintraub

WHAT MAKES JOHNNY RUN? SHAW'S *MAN AND SUPERMAN* AS A PRE-FREUDIAN DREAM PLAY

"What makes Johnny run?" What makes Johnny run is what makes *Man and Superman* run. This pre-absurdist play seems deliberately to make no sense. In the first act, what we might now call a Rolls-Royce radical has been named guardian of Ann Whitefield, a young woman who is old enough not to require a guardian and with whom he and his friend, Octavius—also known as "Ricky-Ticky-Tavy"—grew up in a brother-sister relationship, although they are unrelated. Now not only is he emotionally Ann's brother, he has become in effect her father.

On 2 July 1901, Shaw drafted an outline and cast list for "The Superman, or Don Juan's great grandson's grandson." Among the characters who are omitted from the final text of *Man and Superman* are John Tanner's parents: George *Whitefield* Tenorio and Mrs. *Whitefield* Tenorio (Berst 201–2).[1] There is no suggestion in *Man and Superman* that John Tanner is also a Whitefield and in some way actually related to Ann; yet in those intriguing preliminary notes, there is a hint that Shaw was considering, even if not consciously, the suggestion of an incestuous relationship between Ann Whitefield and John Tanner. When in the second act he realizes it is he, not Octavius, whom Ann is determined to marry, Tanner flees in the first automobile ever to be put on the stage.

The next act opens in the Sierra Nevada. A group of brigands is headed by Mendoza, a lovesick Jewish London waiter whose Louisa has rejected him in anti-Semitic England because she is not good enough for him. His brigands, all but one of whom are also British, include an anarchist and socialists who argue about which type of socialism is more correct and who are dressed more for cold London streets than for Spain. Their political argument is interrupted when they carjack John and his chauffeur,

Straker. 'Enry Straker, who has a polytechnic degree and should be an engineer, not a chauffeur, is the brother of Mendoza's Louisa and is more proud of his dropped *Haitches* than the gentlemen are of their Oxbridge accents.

Night falls and John and Mendoza dream. In the "Don Juan in Hell" dream scene, Mendoza is the Devil, John is Don Juan, Ann Whitefield is Doña Ana, and her other guardian, the elderly Roebuck Ramsden, is her father. The four debate ideas about heaven and hell, happiness and fulfillment, life and death, and with the exception of the last line of the dream—Doña Ana's exclaiming, "A father—a father for the superman"[2] (689)—there seems so little connection to the frame play that this long scene can be, and has been, played as a separate, complete drama. In drafting the play, Shaw also gave Ann's line to John (Berst, 201), but in the completed play John says, instead, "Is there a father's heart as well as a mother's?" (729). Shaw wrote the Hell scene interlude before he wrote the social comedy that is the frame play (Berst, 202). The frame play can also be played without the Hell scene. When the five-hour drama is played in its entirety, it is often broken for a supper break, as is opera at Glynnebourne.

The third act ends with the arrival of Ann and party, three men and two women, in the company of an armed escort. It is inconceivable that the group of five, in addition to the unmentioned and unseen but inevitable chauffeur, has managed to get there in Hector's American steam car. The travelers' original plan was to head for Nice, northeast of Granada. Hector says, "When we found you were gone, Miss Whitefield bet me a bunch of roses my car would not overtake yours before you reached Monte Carlo." To Tanner's "But this is not the road to Monte Carlo," Hector replies, "No matter. Miss Whitefield tracked you at every stopping place: she is a regular Sherlock Holmes" (692). The utter impossibility of her having done so, not knowing where he was headed or from which port he had embarked, stretches one's ability to suspend disbelief.

The final act takes place in Granada and Ann's party now includes her mother. Mrs. Whitefield had not been in Ann's party in the third act and would have had no idea that Ann and the others would have wound up in Granada. Hector Malone's father, an Irish peasant who fled the famine—"the starvation" (704)—and has become the wealthiest furniture manufacturer in the United States, turns up in the same hotel at which his son is staying. In an inversion of a Henry James theme, Mr. Malone has sent his son to England to marry a titled lady. But James's millionaires were not Roman Catholic, and such a misalliance between a Catholic peasant's son and an upper-class Anglican British woman could not have been possible. Even though they might be the possessors of an abbey, they would have been cut by the society so dear to Violet. The senior Malone might have softened and not disinherited his son for marrying a woman without a title, but he would never have countenanced his son's marrying outside the faith.[3] Malone, the otherwise shrewd man of business, has bought stock in an enterprise about which he knows nothing except that it is operated by Mendoza, the waiter turned brigand. Ann compromises John by announcing that she has agreed to marry him, even though he has neither proposed to her nor agreed to marry her. And the play ends with the triumphant Ann treating John as a child. All of this, and more, occurs in a frame play that is generally thought to be a somewhat realistic comedy about manners. Just what is going on here?

In a dream play, the latent play—that is, the dream—complements the manifest play and solves the deep-seated emotional problem of the dreamer.[4] Shaw provides us with numerous clues—the nonlinear structure (already described), the language, the splitting of characters, and the symbols—suggesting that he intended Man and Superman to be a dream play, one that includes within it another dream that reflects upon and complements the frame play dream. In both the manifest play and the latent play, John Tanner must overcome the incest taboo in order to become the mate of the woman to whom he is both brother and father, having been named her guardian after the father's death. That he is not actually related to her does not affect his feelings, as the taboo can occur when children who are not related are raised together as they had been. In the Hell scene—the dream play within the frame play—the Commander, Doña Ana's father, has been killed by Don Juan. Having in this way resolved, in the dream, his conflict caused by in effect being Ann's father, John must now deal only with the problem of being her brother.

Many of us take some bedtime reading to our pillows. The text suggests that John Tanner may have read himself, and dreamed himself, into his play. One volume in question seems to have been Rudyard Kipling's The Jungle Book (1895), which includes the story of the heroic mongoose Rikki-tikki-tavi. The mongoose kills a father cobra, whose mate attempts to retaliate on humans. Shaw's ineffectual "Ricky-Ticky-Tavy," the heroine's pet name for her suitor, seems an inversion of the deadly mongoose. Continuing the image, Tanner refers to Ann as a boa constrictor "with ensnaring eyes and hair." The women in Kipling's story outwit and dominate the men (McCauley 23–24), as do the women in Man and Superman.

A second volume is suggested in the Preface to the play, where Shaw writes, "The theft of the brigand-poetaster [Mendoza] from Sir Arthur Conan Doyle is deliberate" (518). Reading Conan Doyle in either The Memoirs of Sherlock Holmes (1894) or in The Strand Magazine, Tanner would have found, in the story "Silver Blazes," a retired jockey named John Straker, who may have metamorphosed into John Tanner's chauffeur, Henry Straker. Hector Malone calls Ann "a regular Sherlock Holmes."

Perhaps the very literary John Tanner, just prior to the opening of Shaw's play, has taken both Kipling and Conan Doyle to bed—and fallen asleep.

In addition, as a gentleman, Tanner would have been familiar with— and perhaps even attended a performance of—Mozart's *Don Giovanni*. There are deliberate references to that opera in the dream sequence, which opens with "*a faint throbbing buzz as a ghostly violincello palpitating on the same note endlessly. A couple of ghostly violins presently take advantage of this bass. . . . It is all very odd. One recognizes the Mozartian strain.*" And Doña Ana's entrance is heralded by a clarinet playing "*Donna Ana's song to Ottavio*" (631–32).

By repeatedly using the word *dream*, even when some other word would have done as well, Shaw reminds us that this might indeed be a dream. From the outset, the play is filled with allusions to dreams. In the first act, when Ann makes her first appearance, the stage directions read, "Ann would still make men *dream*" (549). In describing the unscrupulous artist, Tanner says the artist knows women can "make him see visions and *dream dreams*" (557). In his verbal duel with Ann in the first act, Tanner tells her, "Love played a part in my earliest *dreams*. . . . Yes, Ann: the old childish compact between us was an unconscious love compact. . . . Oh, dont be alarmed." To Ann's "I am not alarmed," aware of the taboo that has not affected her, John responds "Then you ought to be" (571–73).

In Act II, John tells Straker, "I am the slave of that car . . . I *dream* of the accursed thing at night" (586). As a Freudian symbol, an automobile, while more likely to represent a phallus, may also represent a female.[5] John tells Tavy that if he marries Ann she will cease "to be a poet's *dream*. . . . Youll be forced to *dream* about somebody else." Tavy answers, "There is nothing like Love: there is nothing else but Love: without it the world would be a *dream* of sordid horror" (593). In Act III, Mendoza tells Straker and Tanner: "I went to America so that she [Louisa] might sleep without *dreaming*" (627). He then tells Tanner, "these mountains make you *dream* of women—of women with magnificent hair" (629). As symbols, the mountains themselves may represent female genitalia and breasts. Tanner answers, "They will not make me *dream* of women. I am heartwhole." Mendoza cautions him, "This is a strange country for *dreams*" (629).

In the dream play within this dream play, Don Juan tells Doña Ana, "Whilst he fulfills the purpose for which she made him, he is welcome to his *dreams*" (659–60). "The romantic man . . . went to his death believing in his *dream*" (655). "I had been prepared for infatuation, for intoxication, for all the illusions of love's young *dream*" (667). "I had never *dreamt* . . ." (677). "Never in my worst moments of superstitious terror on earth did I *dream* . . ." (682). When morning comes and Tanner and Mendoza awaken, Mendoza asks Tanner, "Did you *dream*?" and Tanner responds, "Damnably. Did you?" At which Mendoza replies, "Yes. I forget what. You were in it." To which Tanner responds, "So were you. Amazing" (690). In Act IV, Ann tells Tavy, "Then you must keep away from them [women], and only *dream* about them" (717). Tanner asks Ann: "When did all this happen to me before? Are we two *dreaming?*" (728).

Tanner and his friend Octavius can be viewed as being different aspects of the young John Tanner. Both were treated as sons by Ann's father, having had unlimited access to his house. Both love Ann. Tanner tries to resist that love, feeling that somehow it would be inappropriate for Ann and him to mate. Tavy, the romantic side of John, desires nothing else but that consummation. While Ricky-Ticky-Tavy thinks he is an artist and poet, it is Tanner, the author of "The Revolutionist's Handbook and Pocket Companion," who is the creative one. He will overcome his fear of incest and marry Ann, while Tavy will be "that sort of man who never marries" (727). Ann tells them that she will have "my dear Granny to help out and advise me. And Jack the Giant Killer. And Jack's inseparable friend Ricky-Ticky-Tavy" (554). Granny is Roebuck Ramsden, Ann's other guardian, who was in his youth a liberal, even a radical. Since he still holds the beliefs and attitudes he had as a young man, Jack considers Ramsden an out-of-date conservative. Ann assures them that "Nobody is more advanced than Granny" (553). We can see in Ramsden another side of Jack, the man Jack will become. Jack tells Ramsden, "You have no more manners than I have myself" (545). Both guardians appear in the dream sequence, Ramsden as Doña Ana's father, Tanner as Don Juan, the libertine who killed Doña Ana's father. In Ramsden we can also see the elderly bachelor that Octavius will become. Ramsden's sister, however, will remain unmarried, unlike Tavy's sister, Violet. Ramsden, the matured John, wants Tavy, the immature John, to reject the friendship of "your schoolfellow" to whom "you feel bound to stand by because there was a boyish friendship between you. Jack could not be turned out of Whitefield's house because "you lived there" (538).

Jack tells Tavy, "you must marry her after all and take her off my hands. And I had set my heart on saving you from her!" (545). Tavy says, "I have no secrets from Jack" (559). In a list of his childhood pranks that Ann describes to Jack, she includes: "You set fire to the common; the police arrested Tavy for it" (572). And when Ann, responding to Jack's description of her as a boa constrictor, throws her arms around him, he exclaims: "My blood interprets for me. Ann. Poor Ricky-Ticky-Tavy!"

Ann: Surely you are not jealous of Tavy?
Tanner: Jealous. Why should I be? But I don't wonder at your grip on
    him. I feel the coils tightening round my very self.
Ann: Do you think I have designs of Tavy!
Tanner: I know you have.

Ann: Take care Jack. You may make Tavy very unhappy if you mislead him
about me.
Tanner: Never fear: he will not escape you.
Ann: If you and Tavy choose to be stupid about me, it is not my fault.
(576–77)

Tavy, having proposed to Ann and been rejected, tells Jack, "You don't
understand. You have never been in love." Tanner: "I! I have never been
out of it. Why I am in love even with Ann." Tavy: "I believe we were
changed in our cradles, and that you are the real descendant of Don Juan.
. . . She has marked you for her own; and nothing will stop her now" (593).
    The act ends when Straker informs Jack that Ann is not interested in
Tavy "Cause she's arter summun else." Pressured by Jack to reveal who it
is, Straker replies, "You." Tanner: "Me!!!" Straker: "Mean to tell me you
didn't know? . . . the marked down victim, that's what you are and no
mistake" (610–11).
    Mrs. Whitefield tells Tavy, "I don't know which is best for a young man:
to know too little, like you, or too much, like Jack" (719). When Ann asks
Octavius to congratulate her on being engaged to John, Ramsden says,
"Jack Tanner. I envy you," to which Mendoza responds, "Sir: there are two
tragedies in life. One is to lose your heart's desire. The other is to gain it.
Mine and yours, sir" (731–32). And one might add: "and John's and
Tavy's." Three characters in the manifest play; three facets of the dreamer
in the latent play.
    In Ann Whitefield and in Violet Robinson, Octavius's sister, we can see
the dream's splitting of the manifest play's Ann. The stage directions describe Violet as "*a personality which is as formidable as it is exquisitely pretty.
She is not a siren, like Ann; admiration comes to her without any compulsion or
even interest on her part; besides there is some fun in Ann, but in this woman none,
perhaps no mercy either: if anything restrains her it is intelligence and pride, not
compassion*" (580). Both women must connive and manipulate in order to
marry the spouse of her choice. Ann must trick John into marrying her,
while Violet is already married but must inveigle her husband's father into
consenting to that marriage. In discussing Violet with her brother, Ann
says: "You are so softhearted! It's queer that you should be so different
from Violet. Violet's as hard as nails."

Octavius: On no. I am sure Violet is thoroughly womanly at heart.
Ann: . . . Is it unwomanly to be thoughtful and businesslike and sensible?
    Do you want Violet to be an idiot—or something worse, like me?
Octavius: Something worse—like you! What do you mean, Ann?
Ann: . . . I have great respect for Violet. She gets her own way always.
Octavius: . . . So do you.

Ann: Yes; but somehow she gets it without coaxing—without having to make people sentimental about her.

Tavy: . . . Nobody could get very sentimental about Violet, I think, pretty as she is.

Ann: Oh yes they could, if she made them. (717)

After it is revealed that Violet is a married woman and everyone is embarrassed by their behavior to her except Ann, Violet says, "Yes: Ann has been very kind; but then Ann knew" (583). In Act IV, Mrs. Whitefield says, "How I wish you were my daughter, Violet." To which Violet answers, "There, there: so I am." Ann, projecting her feelings onto Violet, says: "Fie, mother! Come, now: you mustn't cry any more: You know Violet doesn't like it" (724). As Violet leaves with Mrs. Whitefield, she tells John, "The sooner you get married too, the better." To which he replies: "I quite expect to get married in the course of the afternoon. You all seem to have set your minds on it." Violet: "You might do worse." She and Mrs. Whitefield exit and Ann says: "Violet is quite right. You ought to get married" (724–25).

As in *Arms and the Man*, Shaw's earliest dream play,[6] *Man and Superman* opens to a set permeated by Freudian-type symbols. The study, an enclosed room, and the bookshelves that line the walls can be interpreted as a uterus and, by extension, a woman. To Roebuck Ramsden's right is a window looking out onto a street. Symbolically speaking, the window can be a bodily orifice, and the street, a place for traffic with women. In the center of the wall is a door opening into the house, repeating the symbolism of the window and the room. *"Against the wall are two busts on pillars"* (534). Both heads and pillars are phallic symbols, with the bodyless head—the busts—symbols of fear of castration. Before a word has been spoken, the audience has been prepared for the erotic problem-solving dream that will follow, one in which the dreamer must overcome his fear of incest and the emotional castration it has imposed upon him.

Tavy protests Jack's describing Ann as a boa constrictor (544), and Jack also describes her as a spider, a bee, and an elephant. All four are symbols not of a woman, but of the phallus. And yet when Ann throws her scarf—called a boa—around Jack's neck, he says: "I feel the coils tightening round my very self" (576), inverting the usual symbolism so that Jack becomes the penis within the vagina during intercourse.

Act II opens in a park of a country house, *"a motor car has broken down. It stands in a clump of trees round which the drive sweeps to the house, which is partly visible through them . . . a pair of supine legs . . . protrude"* (585). Both the car and the protruding legs are phallic, but in this case the car is an impotent penis, while the legs protrude from the cavity beneath the car, a symbol for female genitalia. According to Freudian psychoanalyst Leon

Altman, "The number of things reconstituted in the image of man's narcissism with regard to the phallus and endowed with its attributes is truly awesome," and the man who dreams of a broken automobile is "preoccupied with his potency" (Altman 27). The house seen through the clump of trees might represent a woman or her genitalia as seen through a clump of pubic hair.

Act III opens in the Sierra Nevada Mountains of Spain. The description of the mountains in early evening is both realistic and symbolic. *"Rolling slopes of brown, with olive trees . . . in the cultivated patches. . . . Higher up, tall stone peaks and precipices, . . . the high road passes a tunnel . . . in the face of the cliff, a romantic cave . . . towards the left a little hill, commanding a view of the road, . . . and an occasional stone arch"* (613). John Tanner's car drives into this sexually charged atmosphere,[7] and its tires are punctured by the nails the bandits have strewn in the road. The act ends with the arrival of Ann and her party. They are heralded by the sound of a shot fired from a rifle, another phallic symbol. Because of the nails, their automobile has also been rendered inoperable. Ann had bet Hector a bunch of roses if he could overtake John before he arrived at Monte Carlo. Having won the bet, Hector reminds Ann that she now owes him those flowers. "Flowers, like eyes, can stand for . . . female genitalia" (Altman 25). But it is his wife Violet, not Ann, whom he beds.

Act IV opens in a garden. In the background are, of course, more hills, with the Alhambra at the top of one of them. *"If we stand on the lawn at the foot of the garden looking uphill, our horizon is a stone balustrade of a flagged platform. . . . Between us and this platform is a flower garden with a circular basin and fountain in the center"* (696). Since the setting is a garden, there are many flowerbeds, clipped hedges, and the like. Since it is walled and gated and contains furniture, the space can be seen as a room as well as an out-of-doors space. It is in this space that Violet manipulates her father-in-law into accepting her, and that Ann tricks Tanner into becoming her fiancé. While still struggling against his having to marry Ann, Tanner responds to her "you do not love me" with "It is false: I love you. . . . But I am fighting for my . . . honor" (729). In both the manifest play and the dream play, Ann overcomes that delicacy and Jack's resolve. Having conquered the emotional taboo of incest, in both the manifest play and the dream play, Jack Tanner can marry the woman he loves.

Notes

1. Holograph Manuscript, Henry W. and Albert A. Berg Collection, New York Public Library, Astor, Lennox and Tilden Foundations, as quoted in Charles A. Berst, "Superman

Theater: Gusts, Galumphs, and Grumps," in *SHAW, The Annual of Bernard Shaw Studies 16: Unpublished Shaw* (University Park: Penn State University Press, 1996), pp. 202–3 (italics mine).

2. All quotations from *Man and Superman: A Comedy and a Philosophy* and its Preface are from *Bernard Shaw: Collected Plays with Their Prefaces*, vol. 2, ed. Dan H. Laurence (London: Max Reinhardt, The Bodley Head, 1971), pp. 489–733.

3. Later in the century, when rich Catholics sought titles for their daughters, they went to the Continent to purchase Catholic nobles. A notable exception was Joseph Kennedy's daughter Kathleen, who married an English nobleman and whose mother then refused to recognize her as a daughter.

4. For a more detailed discussion of a dream play, see my "Johnny's Dream: *Misalliance*," in *SHAW, The Annual of Bernard Shaw Studies 7: The Neglected Plays*, ed. Alfred Turco, Jr. (University Park: Penn State University Press, 1987), pp. 171–87.

5. Some commonly accepted symbols are listed in Leon L. Altman, *The Dream in Psychoanalysis* (New York: International Universities Press, 1975), pp. 24–30.

6. See my "'Oh, the Dreaming, the Dreaming': *Arms and the Man*," in *Shaw and Other Matters*, ed. Susan Rusinko (Selinsgrove, Pa.: Susquehanna University Press; London: Associated University Presses, 1998), pp. 31–40.

7. Rolling slopes and mountains: female genitalia; tall stone peaks: phalluses; precipices: breasts; caves: bodily cavities; stone arch: female genitalia.

Peter Gahan

JITTA'S ATONEMENT: THE BIRTH OF PSYCHOANALYSIS AND "THE FETTERS OF THE FEMININE PSYCHE"

—The last time we were at the theatre he discussed the play with me. It was a play about love.
—Well, what else would a play be about?
—Bernard Shaw, *Jitta's Atonement* (1922)

Every man who records his illusions is providing data for the genuinely scientific psychology which the world still waits for . . .
—Bernard Shaw, Epistle Dedicatory, *Man and Superman* (1903)

Bernard Shaw's writing of *Jitta's Atonement* raises many questions, not all of which can be addressed in this essay. We know it as an adaptation rather than a literal translation of a German play, *Frau Gittas Sühne* (1920), by Shaw's Viennese translator, Siegfried Trebitsch.[1] Bernard Dukore has compared the two versions and demonstrated how different Shaw's version is in its emphases: "He alters and embroiders every scene, every page, virtually every line" (Dukore 204).[2] Where Shaw claimed in the preface that "the variations" of his translation "affect, not the story itself, but only the key in which it ends" (5:723), Dukore shows that Shaw's changes are spread over the entire play.[3]

The title refers to the atonement that non-Shavian morality, especially that of romantic drama, requires in cases of marital infidelity. In this case the infidelity is the result not of a casual affair but of a love neither partner had ever found in their respective marriages. Unusually for a Shaw play, the question of love occupies center stage, as made clear by Jitta and her lover, Bruno, in Act I:

JITTA. I love you: I love you: we are alive, not dead: you are living with my life as well as your own: your blood surges to be with mine: you cannot die while I hold on to you fast. All the rest is an uneasy dream that means nothing: this is love; and love is life made irresistible.

BRUNO [*carried away*] Life: yes this is life, and this [*he kisses her eyes*], and this [*he kisses her lips*]. What a fool I was with my iron resolutions! one throb of your breast, one touch of your lips; and where are they? (5:743)

And in Act II, when Jitta finally confesses her adultery to her husband, Alfred Lenkheim:

LENKHEIM. You and he were lovers?
JITTA [*proudly*] Yes: you have found the right word at last. Lovers. (5:768)

And a little later:

JITTA [*earnestly*] . . . it was too strong for us.
LENKHEIM. What was too strong for you?
JITTA. Love. You don't understand love. (5:770)

The question in *Jitta's Atonement* becomes: How can the consequences of this phenomenon of the irruption of adulterous love in the context of social and personal relations, and of marriage in particular, be worked out? Or what form should Jitta's atonement and that of her lover, Bruno, take? But it is not as simple as that, and a more immediate question is raised that might set us on the way to answering these others: Why did Shaw set out to "translate" *this* play?

The most obvious and best-known answer lies in the times. In post–World War I Vienna, conditions were desperate, even for such comfortably well-off people as Trebitsch and his wife. To ameliorate their position with some foreign currency, Shaw thought that a translation by him of the latest play by his German translator might, if produced, raise some much-needed cash in Britain and the United States that could be then channeled to the Trebitschs in Vienna. But given the anti-German feelings following the war, even this plan of using the commercial currency of Shaw's name was optimistic. Still, an interrogation of the differences between Anglo-American and German-Austrian sensibilities might have seemed highly appropriate to Shaw in the context of the war and its misunderstandings between cultures, and the situation of translating his translator offered it.

Perhaps there were other reasons as to why Shaw wanted to translate this particular play. It is safe to assume that no text of Shaw's was written entirely disinterestedly, and the correspondence during its composition indicates he was interested in the task quite apart from the challenge of translating the theatrical genre of romantic tragedy into that of serious Shavian comedy. This essay will suggest the following reasons for Shaw's interest in translating a tale of Viennese sexual infidelity, love, and death: first, the context of his own work leading up to and during the rather extended period of two years he spent composing *Jitta's Atonement;* second, the Viennese background of Trebitsch's text, in which is embedded the unspoken name of Freud and his new science of psychoanalysis; third, as a translation of psychoanalysis and its origins into Shavian terms; and finally, as a reformulation of that perennial self-reflexive theme in Shaw's plays, writing, but treated here in terms of translation, where translation as a form of transgression of the "original" writing serves as analogue of the original play's subject of adulterous love viewed as a transgression of the marriage contract.

I

The context for the writing of *Jitta's Atonement* is the play Shaw was finishing as he began the translation: *Back to Methuselah* (1921). There are extraordinary thematic coincidences between Shaw's play-cycle and Freud's contemporaneous text *Jenseits des Lustprinzeps,* published in Vienna in 1920 and translated into English as *Beyond the Pleasure Principle* in 1922, but suffice it to mention here that both were written in the aftermath of the war and that both are centrally concerned with death.[4] Shaw could hardly have known of this text of Freud's in which is posited a death instinct derived from a behavioral pattern called a compulsion-to-repeat, but he had been well aware of Freud and the importance of his work from at least 1910, if not earlier.[5] More to the point, one aspect of life that *Frau Gittas Sühne* highlights is the phenomenon of love, which the metabiology of *Back to Methuselah* largely neglects. Indeed, he deliberately excluded from his play-cycle certain scenes, subsequently published as *The Domesticity of Franklyn Barnabas,* involving the beautiful husband-stealer, Mrs. Etteen. However, there the object of his metaphysical inquiry (in the philosophical sense) was beauty, rather than love. It might well have struck him, as he was finishing *Methuselah,* that he could supply this omission by translating Trebitsch's play about love and marital infidelity. For on the microcosmic level, the couple in love is what his five-part parable play on evolution is about on a macrocosmic level. *Man and Superman* (1903), his earlier attempt at the same thematic, had made sexual attraction between a couple leading to marriage the central action. *Frau Gittas Sühne* very neatly shifts this question to the conflict between a love outside marriage and society's requirements of marriage as its cornerstone, one with which much of Shaw's work is concerned from the early novel *The Irrational Knot* (1880) onward, including such plays as *Candida* (1894), *Man and Superman*, *Getting Married* (1908), and *Village Wooing* (1933).

Shaw's dramatic corpus has something of the shape of a suspension bridge, which starts with the extraordinary achievement of the three collections of early plays and ends with the still under-appreciated group of late plays, with that miscellaneous group stretching from *The Doctor's Dilemma* (1907) through *Pygmalion* (1913) in the middle. But the pillars that support the whole edifice are the two great trilogies: the "Heaven and Hell" trilogy comprising *Man and Superman, John Bull's Other Island* (1904), and *Major Barbara* (1905); and the metaphysical/religious trilogy of *Heartbreak House* (1916), *Methuselah*, and *Saint Joan* (1923). *Jitta's Atonement*, along with *The Domesticity*, should be seen as essential ancillary texts belonging to this second trilogy.

Heartbreak House, in part a play about the disillusionment of love, showed a civilization that had lost its capacity for belief, or rather one in which its educated cultured citizens had lost that capacity, resulting in a vision of a society "on the rocks," to use one of its own metaphors. *Methuselah* makes clear that one of the contributing causes to this state of unbelief was the publication of Darwin's *On the Origin of Species* (1859), and therefore it proposes a counter-myth of belief, a new metaphysical biology that will follow the publication of the texts or gospels of the Brothers Barnabas with consequences for history and evolution analogous to those associated with the gospels of *The New Testament*. I have argued elsewhere that underlying this dramatic myth is a poetic theory of imagination, and John Bertolini has argued that the eponymous heroine of *Saint Joan* personifies poetic imagination.[6] *Saint Joan* returns Shaw from the cosmological perspective of *Methuselah* to a theater of individual character, of an individual in conflict with her society. But Joan, a virgin-martyr warrior-saint, cannot tell us about interpersonal relations. This is precisely what *Jitta's Atonement* does.

Back to Methuselah is not only a dramatic myth and a theory of the poetic imagination, but it proposes a metaphysical science of the phenomenon we call life: a new metaphysics akin, perhaps, to Heidegger's phenomenological existentialism with its investigation of *Dasein* or human existence. This "metabiology" would be a type of phenomenological hermeneutics that would institute critical textual inquiries into any discourse where the phenomenon of life, of human-being, appears, whether it be in the Bible or the modern sciences like psychology and biology. Part of Shaw's critique points to the irony that such a metaphysical science is, in fact, absolutely ruled out in the modern science of biology associated with neo-Darwinism, although in etymological terms it should be just such a science of life. Similarly, *Jitta's Atonement* proposes a new psychological science of the metaphysical phenomenon of love, a concept ruled out in such modern versions of psychology as behaviorism. There is more of an ambivalence in psychoanalysis, which theoretically speaks of the undeniably physical phenomenon of sexual behavior in its therapeutic practice that requires that there be what Freud somewhat disingenuously calls transference between patient and analyst. This sexual transference is what is called in common parlance "falling in love." Further, Freud, the would-be materialist, but endlessly speculative, scientist of the mind, himself recognized in *Beyond the Pleasure Principle* the need for what he calls a "metapsychological" inquiry, and wrote several metapsychological papers, notably "The Unconscious" (1915).

At the time, Albert Einstein was the exemplar of the revolutionary scientist, and Bruno, Jitta's lover, who dies at the end of Act I, is presented in *Jitta's Atonement* as the psychologist who will do for psychology what Einstein has done for physics: "His psychological doctrine was a revelation. It was the beginning of a new epoch in science" (5:777). Einstein was awarded the Nobel Prize for Physics in 1921, after *Frau Gittas Sühne* was written and as Shaw was writing *Jitta's Atonement*. Trebitsch acknowledged that putting Einstein's name in the text was Shaw's idea.[7] Much of the action of the play turns on the hunt by Bruno's wife after his death for the elusive missing manuscript, "The Fetters of the Feminine Psyche," which would make his name as famous as Einstein's. She cannot help but wonder what became of the book on which he worked endlessly, spending "hours and hours and hours in his study, writing, writing, writing, using up paper until it cost as much as the butter and eggs" (5:778–79). The audience knows from Act I, however, that Bruno burned the manuscript of his book, leaving just a typescript behind—not with his name attached, but with that of Alfred Lenkheim, his professional colleague and husband of his lover, Jitta: "I burnt the original manuscript yesterday: there is not a word of it in my handwriting left to prove that I am the author. They will find a book by your husband among my things: that is all" (5:738).

But Bruno's widow, Agnes, after she has herself unwittingly given the typescript that now bears his name to Lenkheim, goes on fruitlessly to search for it through Bruno's manuscript papers:

AGNES. . . . can you pick out . . . one single bit of paper which you could shew to a stranger and expect him to say "The man who wrote this must have been as great as Einstein"?

FESSLER. Well, not exactly Einstein perhaps. But—[*he stops*] (5:778).

Later, Jitta tempts her husband, who "is burning with ambition to have his name connected with a new departure in science" (5:736), to accept authorship of Bruno's book (about which more later) although he does not agree with it, by mentioning Einstein:

JITTA. You will come to believe in it, when it makes [you] as famous as Einstein.
LENKHEIM [*startled by the name*] Einstein! You are tempting me, you devil.
JITTA. You envied Einstein. . . . Well, all that you envied him for is now within your reach. (5:773)

Thus, Bruno's theory is presented as being as revolutionary for psychology as Einstein's was for physics. And Trebitsch and Shaw both knew of the Viennese psychiatrist who had actually proposed just such a revolutionary theory for psychology. But before we consider the place of Sigmund Freud in Shaw's play, we need to follow more closely Shaw's prolonged engagement with Trebitsch's work in order to establish *Jitta's Atonement* as a Shaw text independent of its origins in Trebitsch's work.

Their correspondence reveals that before the war Shaw had twice considered the possibility of translating a Trebitsch play. The first was in 1913, when Trebitsch sent him a literal translation of *Ein Muttersohn* (A Mother's Son). Shaw reported on 12 July that he had "gone very carefully through the first act, reading the German original and using the translation as a dictionary. I will tell you more about it when I have had time to finish it" (Weiss 165).[8] It seems he never did finish it, as on 14 November he confessed to having "neglected the Mother's Son disgracefully; but someday I will finish it" (Weiss 169). But by 8 May 1914, he had turned his attention to another Trebitsch play, *Gefährliche Jahre* (Dangerous Years). His comments are worth bearing in mind in respect of his later approach to the translation of *Frau Gittas Sühne:*

> I have read your play in Jethro's translation, which is far too literal and literary for use on the stage. It is a quite grammatical translation; but it is not English dialogue. . . . The worst of it is that I dont know how to set about getting it right. I must read it in the original, because I cant get the movement of the scenes properly. I have not quite got hold of the characters. . . . I am really afraid to touch it; I should tear the whole thing to pieces. I must read it again and see what I can make of it. (Weiss 173–74)

The war put paid to any Shaw adaptations of Trebitsch's works, but the idea of doing a translation, which they had obviously discussed, had lodged in Shaw's mind. Shaw wrote Trebitsch on 22 August 1919 from Kerry in Ireland, where he was working on *The Tragedy of an Elderly Gentleman*, when *Methuselah* was still conceived as a tetralogy and not yet a "pentateuch." After discussing an edition of his collected works (*Gesamtausgabe*) in German translation, he continues: "The Gesamtausgabe is a colossal achievement for you & me; but what about your own plays? You have not sent me one for five years. You are becoming famous as a playwright, are you not?" (Weiss 207).

Trebitsch's latest play was *Frau Gittas Sühne*, and he must have told Shaw about it in a letter, now lost. Back in London, Shaw wrote on 10 December 1919: "You may tell the Burgtheater that Heartbreak House will not be available until they have produced Frau Gitta. As they will not accept a sentimental reason for this, you had better say that it is important to me that the translation of my play should be by a playwright of the first importance" (Weiss 209).

The Burgtheater, the most prestigious of Viennese theaters, did put on *Frau Gittas Sühne* in February 1920 before, as Shaw had insisted, putting on *Heartbreak House* in November that year. In his autobiography, *Chronicle of a Life* (1951), Trebitsch writes of this production of *Frau Gittas Sühne* as the greatest theatrical success of one of his own plays without revealing the machinations of using Shaw to get the Burgtheater to put it on. That his greatest theatrical success should in some part be due to Shaw is a rather pathetic irony, as a good deal of the autobiography is spent ruefully ruminating on his predicament of being known as "Shaw's translator," rather than as an eminent literary figure in his own right, as were his many literary friends during this golden age of Viennese writing.

On 26 February 1920, possibly following news from Trebitsch of the production of *Gitta*, Shaw writes: "If Frau Gitta's Transgression gets printed, send me a copy" (Weiss 212). As Trebitsch puts it in *Chronicle of a Life:*

> The first night of [*Frau Gittas Sühne*] at the Burgtheater was a great success, as was also the Berlin first night. Since S. Fischer, furthermore, considered the play worthy of being published in book form, it appeared under his imprint, and in fact on the very day of the Burgtheater première. This made it possible to send a copy to my friend Bernard Shaw, who was particularly interested in this work of mine after reading my letters about it, before he read the work itself.
>
> He wrote to tell me that [*Frau Gittas Sühne*] had made a deep impression on him and struck him as very characteristic both of the atmosphere of Vienna and of the author. Of course, he said, he had not been able to read it himself, but a secretary who read German

fluently had given him a vivid picture of it, half reading it in English, half telling him about it. . . . After having a careful draft translation made, which he intended going over very painstakingly with a dictionary, he meant to translate [*Frau Gittas Sühne*] into English and have it performed in England and America.[9]

Trebitsch's account, whether completely trustworthy or not given that it was written in hindsight after Shaw's death, does indicate there might be a letter of Shaw's missing.[10] But by 26 May, Shaw had "read" it and decided he might translate it: "I have read Gitta, though most of your words are not in the dictionary. And I am waiting for a moment when I can write to you. Be patient: I am not wasting my time, and when Methuselah is finished I shall write fully" (Weiss 212).

On 15 September 1920, Shaw informed Trebitsch from Kerry, where he was preparing the preface and five plays of *Back to Methuselah* for the printers from the middle of July: "From time to time, when I had a spare moment in the evening, I devoted it to you by translating scraps of Gitta; and I am sending a complete English version of the first act to my secretary to type out from my shorthand notes" (Weiss 212–13). But Shaw was not only occupied with *Methuselah* and *Gitta* at this time. As Trebitsch had informed him of the impending production of *Heartbreak House* at the Burgtheater, Shaw wrote another long letter about that for Trebitsch to give to the theater's director, Albert Heine. In it, he detailed the perils of producing such "a peculiar play, as dependent on atmosphere and on subtleties of personality in the performers as any of Tchekov's" (Weiss 216). He forecast an inevitable failure.

Back in London, on 28 September he sent Trebitsch a "rough draft" of his translation of Act I of *Frau Gittas Sühne*. After detailing some of his changes ("Charlotte says I have made it brutally realistic"), he advises Trebitsch: "Do not hesitate to tear the thing up if it is impossible. But dont tear it up merely because it is disappointing. Any translation you get will be that. I should even say that you were not likely to get anything much better if it were not that I must admit that it might be an advantage for the translator to know the language the piece is written in" (Weiss 217).

Trebitsch was gracious enough, although he wrote in *Chronicle of a Life*: "Mention must here be made of the fact that Shaw, overwhelmingly self-confident as he was and sure of his skill as a dramatist, in handling this work, which had, after all, been entrusted to his care, took liberties that he would scarcely have forgiven his translator. . . . What could I do but agree? The drama as I had written it existed in print, as evidence of what I set out to do. And as so often happens in life, once again Shaw turned out to be right."[11]

To Shaw himself, he wrote on 1 October 1920 (in his usual idiosyncratic

English): "this morning . . . your version of 'Yittas Atonement' reached me.[12] It is much better than the original and I beg you by all means to continue and finish your version. The end of the act is grand and proves again your stage-genious. But please do put your name on the version, nobody will produce, without that important name, a play from a german author" (Weiss 217).

Shaw's most radical changes, which emphasize the erotic associations of the setting, come at the beginning and end of the act to underline the Freudian emphasis on sex, which might surprise those who think of Shaw solely as a puritanical author.

Whereas Trebitsch has Bruno die just after Gitta has entered—and he is following her to—the bedroom, Shaw makes Jitta go off-stage into the bedroom first, while Bruno, left alone, *"staggers against the door frame; clutches at the wall to save himself; strikes the electric light out by chance; reels back into the middle of the room and drops dead"* (5:744). So by the time Jitta comes back in from the bedroom door *"through which,"* as the stage directions specify at the beginning of the act, *"a bed with rose-colored hangings is partly visible"* (5:725), she is already half undressed—*"her fingers clutch for a moment at her half-naked breast as she thinks of her disordered appearance"* (5:745)—and the room is in darkness, except for the erotic red coloring of the bedroom in the background.

But work was not yet finished on *Methuselah,* which obviously took precedence over *Jitta:* "You are frightfully mistaken about Methuselah. It is true that the manuscript is at the printers; but the proofs are not corrected yet. . . . I have done a little more of Gitta; but the translation will progress slowly until I have cleared off arrears of work" (Weiss 218), Shaw wrote on 13 November 1920. And on 15 January 1921 he confessed: "I have had to lay Yitta aside until Methuselah is off my hands . . . but when Methuselah is finally passed for press I will try to get Yitta under way again" (Weiss 219). By 17 March, "the finally corrected sheets of Methuselah" had been sent on to Trebitsch from the printers, who had finished with them. So while Trebitsch could begin his translation of Shaw's *magnum opus,* there was still no progress on Shaw's translation of *Gitta.* Shaw wanted to know instead about the production of *Heartbreak House* the previous November at the Burgtheater. He also wanted to know about Arthur Schnitzler's *Reigen,* which had just opened in Berlin after a ban of seventeen years.[13] In April, Shaw retired to Harlech in Wales "to recuperate here from the exhaustion of finishing Methuselah" (Weiss 223). Not until August, after *Back to Methuselah* had been published in June, did Shaw report progress on *Gitta.* When Charlotte became ill while visiting Yorkshire, Shaw "set to work hard at Gitta, and nothing but Gitta, and finished her. That is to say, I finished my first draft of the dialogue in shorthand. I have not yet seen the typed transcript; and I have yet to revise that and put in all the stage business; but still the main job is done: the rest is only drudgery and routine" (Weiss 224).

This, along with his labors on "finishing" *Methuselah,* provides a glimpse into the process of Shaw's playwriting technique. Just as a composer writes an opera first in short-score, so does Shaw write his first draft of just the dialogue in shorthand. Then, like the composer who must work out the orchestration in full-score, so must Shaw work out the stage business. For Shaw, the first stage of writing the dialogue was the most essential, the working out and finishing of the second stage being "drudgery and routine." But as *Methuselah* had proved and as *Jitta* in turn would prove, this second stage was a very arduous and exacting process, wherein many of the artistic (as opposed to merely technical) decisions would still have to be taken. The close attention that Shaw gave to this second stage work in *Jitta's Atonement* (including rewriting his first dialogue translation, as we shall see) makes it far more of a Shaw text than has been generally realized.

On 2 October he was finally able to send "Gitta complete as far as the dialogue was concerned." And he excused his changes to Trebitsch's text in genre terms: "I have therefore ventured to shew at the end of your play that the tragedy of the first act, and the melodrama of the second are not the end of the world." More important, he asked: "Will you, when you are sending me back the MS, send me a ground plan of the scenes, showing where the doors are, and how the furniture is placed. I can then work at the stage business and get half a dozen prompt copies typed." Emphasizing how essential this was to him, he repeats the request at the end of his long letter: "Of course I could invent these and arrange the business accordingly; but it will save me trouble if I haven't to think of this" (Weiss 225–28). Trebitsch replied: "Your version is as much better than mine as you are the greater poet of us two. I was puzzeled very much reading your bold alterations." But he did send "the perfect ground plan of the Burgtheater, which probably will satisfy you very much" (Weiss 228–29).

Whether or not it did, devising the stage business turned out to be not nearly as perfunctory as Shaw had supposed. Besides, he was preoccupied with *Heartbreak House* again, rehearsing the first London production, which opened on 18 October 1921. Shaw had probably not been as busy with his plays (writing, publishing, producing, and now translating) since the days of the Court Theater repertory experiment fifteen years earlier. On 17 February 1922, he confessed: "I made a desperate effort the other day to finish Gitta; but I found that much more remains to be done than I thought. I have not only to work out the stage business, but to revise the dialogue a good deal, especially in the first half, which is too German in form to be quite natural and easy for English actors" (Weiss 231). In other words, revising dialogue became a necessary part of working out the stage business.

At this time, the rehearsals for the first production of *Methuselah* were taking place in New York. "A mad enterprize," Shaw called it. On a holiday tour in April, the sixty-five-year-old writer complains: "I have brought Gitta with me; but I cannot get to work on her: I came away because I was utterly worn out; and I am not quite ready to begin again; but at Stratford I hope to get something done. Age and its imbecilities are beginning to tell on me" (Weiss 232).

Back at Ayot, he reported to Trebitsch on 15 May, using some thoughtless language: "I have been working like a nigger at Jitta; and I am only half way through. Mrs Billiter and the flower girl and the planning of their business took me two whole days! I am now postponing everything to it. . . . It is a devil of a job, but not at all uninteresting; and I hope I shall not spoil it" (Weiss 232). Even if he was indulging in some exaggeration for Trebitsch's sake, that the "Mrs Billiter and the flower girl" scene, which occupies hardly more than a single page in the script, took "two whole days" to work out is an indication of the level of close attention that Shaw gave to this aspect of his playwriting.

Finally, on 17 June 1922, over two years after he had decided to translate the play, he reported: "At last I have received from the typist the prompt copies of Gitta, ready for the stage. . . . in this final acting edition of the play I have committed some fresh outrages. . . . Nothing has been lost by this except the characteristic Trebitschian brooding. . . . Still I really think I have kept the story of Jitta there just as it is in the original; so you must forgive me: I have done my best" (Weiss 233).

By December 1922, Shaw was seriously considering writing a new play of his own, *Saint Joan*.[14] It would again be a rewriting and translation of cultures (of historical documents and court records of Joan's trial) and of the successful postwar resurgent anti-British nationalism of his native country, Ireland, into that of fifteenth-century France. But it proved easier to write than "translating" *Jitta*. He began *Saint Joan* on 29 April 1923—by which time *Jitta's Atonement* had opened in New York on 17 January—and finished it less than four months later, on 24 August.

II

Freud is mentioned nowhere in Shaw's extensive correspondence with Trebitsch. In *Chronicle of a Life*, Trebitsch writes of his own ambivalence toward Freud caused by an unsatisfactory consultation with the great doctor that occurred sometime before 1906, part of his fruitless lifelong search for a cure for periodic paralyzing migraine attacks (Shaw was similarly plagued about once a month until he was in his sixties). Trebitsch confessed that this dispiriting encounter "prevented me from making the closer acquaintance of a very great man and his epoch-making work . . . [and] for many years to come from giving my attention to the work of that great psychologist."[15] We may reasonably presume that Trebitsch—friend of Schnitzler, Hofmannsthal, Bahr, Rilke, and Zweig, who all certainly knew of their famous Viennese contemporary—had come to know some of the great doctor's work before writing *Frau Gittas Sühne*. And internal evidence from the play suggests that not only had he arrived by then at his judgment of "epoch-making work," which is close to Shaw's English phrase in *Jitta* of "a new epoch in science," but that he used the phenomenon of Freud's "epoch-making" revolution in the science of the *psyche* as the basis for his play.

Shaw's letter of 11 March 1911 to Gilbert Murray, in which he specifically encourages Murray to write a Freudian version of *Oedipus Rex* (supplying him with a hilarious scenario by way of inducement), shows that by that time he knew about Freud's Oedipus Complex through Ernest Jones's 1910 essay "The Oedipus Complex as an Explanation of Hamlet's Mystery": "I am not very appreciative of the psychiatrists; but there may be something in their theory that repressed instincts, though subconscious, play a considerable part in our lives, and that the first child's jealousy of the second, and even of its father, is the jealousy of Othello in a primitive stage of passion, before the specialization of a part of it takes place for reproductive purposes. The completeness with which that specialization is suppressed does not eradicate the passion."[16]

Shaw knew Jones, Freud's leading English disciple and future biographer, who could have kept him up to date in matters Freudian, and he may easily have come across Freud's name earlier than this in Havelock Ellis's work.[17]

In a review of Julius West's book, *G. K. Chesterton: A Critical Study*, in May 1916, Shaw takes his friend Chesterton to task for not taking into account in his thinking a "Modernist" like Freud. It is perhaps the most succinct, if humorous, expression of Shaw's consistent attitude to Freud and psychoanalysis:

> Freud has neither delicacy nor common-sense. When Mr. Chesterton broke his arm, I deplored it as an accident; but Freud, if he had heard about it, would have concluded that Mr. Chesterton had subconsciously done it on purpose to punish himself for some frightful secret crime. Nobody but a fool would have thought of such a thing; but then wise men are always overlooking things that

are visible to fools; and though I once broke my own arm and therefore vehemently reject the Freudian psychoanalysis of Mr. Chesterton's mishap, I pay a serious if disrespectful attention to Freud.[18]

Shaw probably wrote this with knowing irony, as he had broken his arm as the last in a long chapter of "accidents" just before and after his marriage to Charlotte Payne-Townshend in 1898. "Serious if disrespectful attention" would be exactly the attitude that the text of *Jitta's Atonement* displays toward Freud.

Certainly Shaw knew of Freud through Jones and Ellis, but as to which of Freud's writings Shaw could have read, we can only speculate. The first English translations of the major works, *The Interpretation of Dreams* (1900) and *The Psychopathology of Everyday Life* (1901), came out in 1913 and 1914, respectively, but as a general introduction the most likely possibility is the version of *Five Lectures on Psychoanalysis* (1910), developed from *ex tempore* lectures in German delivered in America in 1909, published in English translation in 1910, prior to the original German version, with the significant title (for us), "The Origin and Development of Psychoanalysis."[19] Among other things, Freud writes in the third lecture of his contention that the interpretation of dreams is the royal road to understanding the unconscious, and mentions the two all-important dream mechanisms of condensation and displacement, of which Shaw seemed to show some knowledge in his later playwriting, particularly in the dream play *Heartbreak House*, but also possibly in *Jitta*, with its constant slippage between what and when the characters know and do not know in relation to their actions. As Bruno puts it in relation to Alfred in the play: "He knows everything: what he lacks is a sense of the significance of what he knows" (5:736).

His various allusions in letters and published writings between 1910 and 1950 show that Shaw was familiar with Freud's ideas on dreams, the Oedipus complex, childhood sexuality, the sexual etiology of neuroses, the technique of word association, the talking-cure involving remembering and speaking, sexual repression, sexual fantasies, and the unconscious.[20] But his attitude remained that of "serious if disrespectful attention," and in 1935 he declined to contribute to a volume on Freud, declaring:

> When I was young I rejected all the standard books on psychology as worthless. I said that a science of psychology was impossible because it could be established only by the personal confession of the workings of the human imagination which nobody would make, and would be unprintable in any case. Dr Freud proved that I was right as to the science, but quite wrong as to the difficulty of obtain-

ing the confessions and the permanence of the Victorian prudery
which inhibited their publication. But that does not qualify me to
contribute to a serious work on psycho-analysis.[21]

Nevertheless, while Einstein, for whom Shaw had immense respect, and
Darwin (another "epoch-making scientist"), for whom he had mixed respect, are both mentioned in the text of *Jitta's Atonement,* the name Freud
is noticeable only by its absence.[22] Yet it cannot be said that either Freud
or psychoanalysis is absent. The "psychological doctrine" that will bring
about "a new epoch in science" is most likely to be taken as an allusion to
Freud's new therapeutic technique of psychoanalysis, and his ideas on the
unconscious are specifically referred to in Act I: "It is a stroke of luck
that he knows nothing—if indeed it is only luck, and not his subconscious
knowledge that he must not let himself know. Yes: he not only does not
know: he *will* not know: he refuses to know. And that refusal . . . is unconscious" (5:737). Psychoanalysis itself, Shaw's addition, is mentioned in Act
II: "You are hiding something from me: I havent experimented with psycho-analysis for nothing" (5:766). [23]

Other echoes of Freudian psychology permeate the text. Is it simply a
coincidence—and again this is Shaw's addition—that Alfred suggests that
Jitta should "lie on the sofa" just when, in Act II, she is putting up her
greatest resistance to wanting to talk about her infidelity? The text's only
mention of psychoanalysis comes immediately afterward. And, although
there is no mention of childhood sexuality, the play does put sexuality
center-stage. As we have seen, Shaw's stage directions (over which he la-
bored so long) stress the erotic associations of the setting in Act I, in particular those of the color red: "*The two photogravure reproductions of pictures
on the walls . . . are of the refinedly aphrodisiac character considered de rigueur in
hotels . . . [Mrs Billiter] goes into the bedroom and switches on the light. The
roseate hangings on the bed appear to great advantage. The flower girl, on her
way to the vase, stops fascinated*" (5:725–26). The "fascination" of the flower
girl who does not enter the room in Trebitsch's version is caused by the
sexual nature of the setting:

THE FLOWER GIRL. Just right for two, aint it?
MRS BILLITER [*incensed*] What do you mean, with your "just right for
two"? (5:727)

And Act I climaxes with Bruno's death immediately following a meta-
phorical analogue of sexual intercourse, as the momentarily rejuvenated
Bruno "*seizes* [Jitta] *round the hips, and lifts her up exultantly*" (5:744).

We are given to believe in the following acts that this place, if not a
brothel, is quite as disreputable as one, and that if Mrs. Billiter is not a

madam, she is not entirely respectable either. Her establishment is used by the professional men of Vienna as a trysting place for their infidelities, and provides a sordid counterpoint to the high romance of love played out beyond the nets of domesticity in the "dreamland" that Jitta and Bruno describe. "Such a house . . . fit neither for him nor for her," as his embittered widow puts it later, is to them a place of dreams, of sleep, from which, like Tristan and Isolde, only death ("the awakening") will awake them. There is also a suggestion of Tristan's "*das Wunderreich der Nacht*" (the wondrous realm of night) when Bruno says, "Our love looks well only by candlelight. It won't stand daylight." To which Jitta replies: "Daylight is for your *work*, for your great book that is to be the crown of your career. But here in the candle light you belong to me, and to me only" (5:734).

This play on sleep, dreams, and waking is carried on throughout the play, and can be read as analogous to the processes of psychoanalysis where one level of knowledge (or rather lack of it) is replaced by a new level of awareness. As the dialogue in Act II between Jitta and Edith, Bruno's father-fixated daughter, puts it three weeks after Bruno's death:

EDITH. I was a child then. I can hardly remember how I felt. It is as if I had been asleep.
JITTA. Your father's death has awakened you: you are looking at life for the first time.
EDITH. I have been looking at death for the first time (5:756).

Or as Agnes puts it in Act III: "that is how things happen. They go on from year to year under your very nose, staring you in the face; and you never notice, never think, because your mind is off the track. And then suddenly your eyes are opened with a bang; and you could kill yourself for having been so blind" (5:782).

Sleep and dreams were of course of the highest importance to Freud, and there seems to be a sly dig at his magnum opus, *Interpretation of Dreams*, when in the search for the manuscript of Bruno's great work, they come upon an unfinished lecture on "Varieties of Sleep":

AGNES. Why, it's only six pages. And what can it mean? There is only one sort of sleep.
LENKHEIM. Not at all. He says that hardly any two people sleep in the same way. Every case is an individual one. (5:780)

And a little later:

LENKHEIM. But the lecture on varieties of sleep—
AGNES. Stuff! I know the variety of sleep he learnt from her. (5:782)

Bruno's widow, Agnes, after talking of her love for Bruno, speaks *à la* Freud of her occasional sexual fantasies: "I have had thoughts myself about our young men at college sports: only fancies of course." Dukore points out that this was a Shaw addition to Trebitsch's text (Dukore 209–10). Bruno also seems to have been given to such day-dreaming (Freud had written a paper in 1908 entitled "Creative Writers and Day-Dreaming").[24] In fact, his astute widow points out—Shaw modified Trebitsch's characters of the adulterers' spouses, Agnes and Alfred, more than any of the others so as to make them less theatrically conventional—that the actual time her husband spent with "the other woman" was only a small part of his infidelity: "One hour is enough for a man. Then he can sit alone at his desk, thinking he is writing some great scientific work, when all the time he is thinking of her, living the hour over again, and looking forward to the next one, right in his wife's face" (5:781).

This off-stage scene, as described by his widow of Bruno day-dreaming while writing, also figures from other points of view in the play and provides an example of Shaw's rare skill in what might be called dramatic counterpoint. Bruno's daughter, Edith, confides to Jitta: "It nearly killed me to see him sitting there, as he often did, staring right through me without seeing me, and sighing as he drew his hand across his eyes and through his hair" (5:758).

Just before this, Edith has described herself as her father saw her on these occasions: "There were moments when I sometimes got beyond my self and became another person; perhaps the woman I am growing into; and he was so responsive to that flash of something different in me, so grateful for it, that I saw quite plainly how he was longing for something else, something more, than we were giving him" (5:758).

As Agnes had brutally put it, and as we learned in Act I that Edith reminds Bruno of Jitta, we know he is thinking of his lover Jitta on these occasions. Indeed, Bruno himself had said to Jitta: "Do you think that my wife and daughter put you quite out of my head when I am at home? They never do: you are everywhere" (5:734). Thus this off-stage scene provides the focus on the combination of writing and sexual fantasy presented through the different perceptions, memories, and individual experiences of the various characters that is crucial to the thematic of the play. Bruno is a writer and lover. Agnes is a bereaved widow, whose love for her husband has been bitterly disabused. Edith is a girl growing into womanhood, and her love for her father in life and now in death is part of that. Jitta, although knowing that Bruno was thinking of her, herself adds to the mix of fantasy, memory, and sex this last mortal element (Shaw would not have needed Freud to underline the old association of sex with death that formed the climax of Act I and, besides, was a feature of the recently completed *Methuselah*): "you must not worry yourself because he sometimes looked straight at you and did not see you. Just think. He was a doctor: he knew his danger better than anyone. When a man finds himself condemned to death, his thoughts and feelings must be overwhelming" (5:758).

Agnes's phrase of Bruno "living the hour over again" is also worth noting as her memory of Bruno remembering. And repetition, like recollection, is a key notion in Freud's theory and plays a prominent theme thematically in this play. Fessler, the young doctor and student of Bruno, gives a concise summary of what Freud calls a compulsion to repeat: "Men's lives consist mostly of their making the same mistake again and again. . . . I knew a man who was married three times; and every one of his wives drank" (5:788).[25]

Fessler says this to his fiancée, Edith, who despises her mother but is sure that her father's lover must be wonderful. So she is "*staggered*" when Fessler, attempting to bring the ideal into focus with the real, *reminds* her that her adored father actually married her hated mother. But she protests that "a man who made a mistake like that once would be the last person in the world to make the same mistake again" (5:788). That people tend to repeat "the same mistake again" expresses the key problem that psychoanalytic psychotherapy tries to deal with: how to escape from a pattern of recurrent behavior. The drama of *Jitta's Atonement* derives from the love of Jitta and Bruno ending in Bruno's death, which, like breaking your arm, can break up the habitual pattern of things and offer an opportunity of coming to understand oneself in symbolic terms. Psychoanalysis, as a story-telling technique of remembering or recollecting, traces such patterns back in time, to a speaking of sexually repressed memories stemming from earliest childhood, to a performance of telling stories of *secrets* that, once spoken, will break the habitual behavior. In Shaw's play, Bruno's death allows the question to be asked: Is Bruno's and Jitta's love illusory or real? And the same question can be asked of Edith's idealized view of her father, as well as to whether or not Bruno's book is the speculative nonsense Alfred thinks it is, or the "new epoch in science" that Bruno believes. Coming to appreciate both sides in such binary oppositions helps cut the Gordian knot of the Freudian compulsion to repeat. And for Shaw, such illusions, whether as a scientific theory or in a romantic affair, are nevertheless necessary, as he explained in a remarkable essay, "The Illusions of Socialism" (1896): "Take from the activity of mankind that part of it which consists in the pursuit of illusions, and you take out the world's mainspring. Do not suppose, either, that the pursuit of illusions is the vain pursuit of nothing: on the contrary, there can no more be an illusion without a reality than a shadow without an object."[26]

The telling of sexual secrets is obviously attributable to Freud. The play makes play with the peculiar logic of the word "secret." A secret can be known only by being repeated, in which case it is no longer a secret: "if secrets dont keep themselves, nobody can keep them" (5:806). "Secret" had figured as a key word in earlier Shaw texts like *Candida* and *The Doctor's Dilemma*, and *Jitta's Atonement* presents a staging of secrets (the affair, the book and its authorship) as a play of knowledge, of revelation, of reading, of translation.[27] A secret that is unspoken / unwritten, nevertheless, demands to be spoken / written. If nothing was secret, everything would be known, and nothing would require writing, rewriting, translating or editing; there would be no need for reading. As a process of knowledge, the play's structure, like psychoanalysis that purports to reveal the hidden truth of one's sexuality, rests on a "mechanism" of secrets, on who knows (and when) and who does not know, on what is known (and when) and what is not known. It is a play of hiding and revelation, of speaking and writing, of understanding and recollecting, analogous to that process of discovery of so-called "truth" in a scientific discourse that would reveal the "secrets" of nature, as proposed, for example, in the writing and reading of such texts as the play's "Fetters of the Feminine Psyche." What instigates this play of secrets and knowledge in *Jitta's Atonement*, as it does also in psychoanalysis as either transference or in a remembered repressed sexual desire, is that necessary illusion: love. Like a secret, love both is and is not, and as transgression, as that which can tear up that piece of writing known as the marriage contract, or not, as the case may be.

But Shaw's drama becomes quite subtle by showing that sometimes the cure can be effected by speaking the secret without consciously understanding its full implications (i.e., the unconscious does understand, in spite of a conscious refusal to acknowledge it, a priority Freud might assent to). We see this in Act III, when with a mighty effort Jitta "cures" her rival and Bruno's wife, Agnes, of her jealousy—another important concern of Freud's, as Shaw knew—as well as herself. That this encounter ends in "hysterical laughter," as we shall see, was Shaw's contribution. According to Dukore, "Nowhere in the original work is there anything resembling [this] scene" (Dukore 209–10). And like Agnes in the scene itself, Trebitsch was blithely unconscious of what Shaw had done in his version, and he lamented: "I only miss the 'ritardando' in the scene between the two women, where Agnes says in my text: 'I am happy to speake at last woman to woman'" (Weiss 229).

Interestingly, Freud had originally used the theatrical metaphor of "catharsis," derived from Aristotle, to describe the treatment of hysterics: the cathartic cure. And psychoanalysis, which involves playing roles, storytelling, dialogue, performance, and catharsis, can itself be viewed as a form of theater. This climactic scene in *Jitta's Atonement* translates Freud's "talking-cure," as psychoanalysis is often called, into a typically Shavian laughing-cure. In 1902, Shaw had written to Trebitsch that "laughter is my sword and shield and spear" (Weiss 27). And Bertolini has very interestingly read some of Shaw's shorter plays as deliberate meditations on how laughter works as part of his dramatic technique.[28] *Jitta's Atonement* seems to belong to this tradition. Laughter can be more effective than simply speaking a secret or a repressed memory because it allows its expression and denial simultaneously, so laughter as his instrument (sword, shield, or spear) is presented as a theatrical alternative to the scene of a psychoanalytic session played out in the doctor's consulting room. However, rather than through Aristotle's pity and terror, Shavian theater, which itself inaugurated a new epoch in modern drama, would effect its catharsis with laughter.

Thus the drama of *Jitta's Atonement* leads toward this cathartic scene of laughter between Agnes and Jitta in Act III. The end is worth quoting almost in full to see how Shaw goes from the equation of "how the mind works" with "funny" in the first line, by way of "smile," "laugh," and "chuckle," to hysteria, convulsions, and agonizing paroxysms at the end, where we may note a difference between the hearty and hysterical laughter of Agnes and Jitta, respectively. This all develops within the context of the knowing/not knowing (conscious/unconscious) thematic so crucial to the play:

AGNES. You know, its very funny how the mind works.

JITTA. How?

AGNES [*slowly and almost roguishly*] I'm so grateful to you, that I am afraid of offending you if I tell you. But I am sure you will only laugh.

JITTA [*with a melancholy smile*] We both need a good laugh, dont we?

AGNES. Have you ever found that you have all along been thinking something that never came into your head for a single moment?

JITTA. That sounds a little difficult. I am afraid I don't quite follow.

AGNES. Of course you dont: it's too silly. But do you know that the moment you took that weight off my mind, and gave me back my peace and happiness—. . . . Well that very moment I knew that I had been believing all along—but I dont think I ought to say it; only it's so funny.

JITTA. What?

AGNES. Why, that YOU were that woman. [*She begins to chuckle*].

JITTA. No!!!

AGNES. Yes I did.

JITTA. But really?

AGNES. Really and truly.

JITTA [*beginning to laugh hysterically*] How funny!

AGNES [*her chuckles now culminating in hearty laughter*] Isnt it? Youre not angry, are you? Oh dear—[*laughing more than ever*].

JITTA. Oh no: of course not.

Jitta has a paroxysm of agonizing laughter; and Agnes accompanies her without a suspicion that she is not enjoying the joke in good faith. (5:794–95)

"Hysteria" has Freudian connotations, specifically in relation to the origins of psychoanalysis, as we shall see. Jitta had displayed a classic hysterical symptom by taking to her bed for three weeks after Bruno died, and the text describes her as "languid" when she appears in her dressing-gown in Act II. But here Shaw metaphorically underlines the use of the word in the stage directions by making Jitta go on to say in the dialogue: "Dont make me laugh any more: I am afraid I shall go into hysterics." When Agnes leaves her alone, Jitta *"begins to laugh again hysterically"* before *"dissolving into convulsive sobs,"* thus effecting for herself a "cathartic cure." The (inter-)textual implication of this hysteria will now be considered in more detail.

III

What *Jitta* proposes, among other things, is a dramatization of the birth of a radically new theory of psychology. To put it at its simplest: Bruno, a professor of psychology, has written a book to which he has given the title: "Fetters of the Feminine Psyche." Knowing that he is going to die soon, he destroys all the manuscript papers of the book, leaving only a typescript behind. But, not wanting his book, his and Jitta's child, to become a textual "orphan," he puts Alfred's name on the title page and asks his lover, Alfred's wife, to ensure that Alfred adopt this ascription of authorship. Now this is not exactly what happened with the birth of psychoanalysis, but it does present uncanny parallels all the same.

The birth of psychoanalysis can be assigned to the publication in 1895 of the co-authored *Studien über Hysterie* by Josef Breuer and Sigmund Freud. One of the peculiarities surrounding this publication is that the younger, ambitious Freud had to persuade the reluctant, established elder physician to co-author the book with him.[29] One would need to be a Freudian analyst to fully understand Freud's motives here, but one of the reasons undoubtedly was to "legitimize" the new science. The origins of psychoanalysis lay in a case of Breuer's of over twelve years previously. By persuading Breuer to co-author *Studies on Hysteria*, Freud was able legitimately to adopt Breuer's case as the first of the new science. So in the first of his *Five Lectures on Psychoanalysis* (1910), Freud expressly assigns to Breuer, not to himself, the invention of psychoanalysis: "If it is a merit to have brought psychoanalysis into being, that merit is not mine. I had no share in its earliest beginnings. I was a student and working for my final examinations at the time when another Viennese physician, Dr. Josef Breuer, first (in 1880–82) made use of this procedure on a girl suffering from hysteria."[30]

Thus Freud could deny what was obvious to everyone else: that Sigmund Freud was the "father" of psychoanalysis. But later, feeling aggrieved that he and not Breuer had taken all the criticism for developing psychoanalysis, he modified his view somewhat to stake an originating claim himself. All in all it contributes to a not-altogether-coherent myth of a birth for psychoanalysis, and this complex aspect of "fathering" both a book and a new science is precisely what *Jitta's Atonement* takes up. Dukore points out that Bruno's rationale—"A book by a dead man is an orphan . . . if Alfred adopts my book it will not perish"—is Shaw's addition to Trebitsch (Dukore 210).

What happened was that in the early 1880s, Freud was still a promising student who was taken up by the highly respected and well-established physician Josef Breuer, as Fessler was taken up by Bruno in the play. (Freud thus might be figured in the three doctors in the play: the young Dr. Fessler, who could mature into a famous psychologist by adopting the ideas of his eminent seniors; the speculative Dr. Haldenstedt, whose ideas will change how we view the workings of the psyche; and the ambitious Dr. Lenkheim, the hardened scientific materialist, who would build his new science on the work of another.) Breuer had treated a patient named Bertha Pappenheim, a friend of Freud's fiancée, Martha. Bertha in later life became a rather remarkable woman. After writing a book of short stories, in 1899 she translated Mary Wollstonecraft's *Vindication of the Rights of Women* and wrote a play, *A Woman's Right,* in which a woman upholds her right to deny her husband sexual relations after discovering an adulterous affair. In addition to her literary career, she came to the forefront of Jewish groups in Germany as a tireless worker for improving social conditions for women, particularly those who had emigrated from the East. She never married. In the early 1880s, however, she was a young woman displaying classic symptoms of female hysteria, which began during her father's serious illness and continued after his subsequent death. Breuer found that by making her talk out the symptoms one by one, they would individually disappear. Daydreaming, which as we have seen figures in *Jitta's Atonement,* played an important part in Breuer's "cathartic cure" of Bertha. At certain times of the day she would have intense daydreams, bordering on hallucinations in which she would be subjectively absent. Breuer would get her to talk about these daydreams or *absences,* which all began with her at her father's sickbed. Breuer described these hallucinatory daydreams as originating in the ordinary daydreams he called "her private theater," in which the bored imaginative rich girl indulged before her father became ill.

This technique, which became the basis of all later psychoanalysis, was initiated more by the patient than the doctor. And as one of her hysterical symptoms was to talk in English, not German, her phrase "talking-cure" was uttered first in English to describe it, ten years before Freud used the term "psychoanalysis" in 1896. However, as Bertha was displaying so many symptoms, it was a practically impossible task to remove them all. Like many hysterics, she had a father-fixation, and when her symptoms went out of control after her father's death, Breuer sent her to be kept under supervision in a sanatorium in the country. In the play, although Edith does not yet display hysterical symptoms (except from her mother's point-of-view, to whom she is extremely antagonistic), her father-fixation is presented in the wake of her father's death. Her father's assistant and her fiancé, Dr. Fessler, warns her: "you mustnt worry too much about your father. It's a sort of hypochondria; and it may make you really ill" (5:786).

Although the end of Bertha's case was somewhat problematic for Breuer, ten years later Freud took up the "talking-cure" as the basis for a whole new direction in psychology. He persuaded Breuer to write up his old case for publication, in which Bertha Pappenheim became famous as "Anna O."—the first patient of psychoanalysis (albeit before psychoanalysis was invented). Freud added four of his own case histories with hysterics, and both wrote separate theoretical chapters as well as a joint preliminary communication to comprise the "epoch-making work," *Studien über Hysterie.*

In spite of hostility toward the new science within Viennese medical and psychiatric circles, the book soon acquired a reputation among the literati. It is worth bearing in mind here that a remarkable work of theater originated in Vienna early in the century that was associated with *Studien über Hysterie:* the drama *Elektra* by Hugo von Hofmannsthal (a friend of Trebitsch's), later transformed into a landmark opera by Richard Strauss.[31] Shaw not only knew the opera well, but there is actually a hint that he was aware of the possible effect of Freud's and Breuer's book on Hofmannsthal's and Strauss's *Elektra.*[32] When *Elektra* opened sensationally in London in February 1910, Shaw engaged in a newspaper controversy with musicologist Ernest Newman on the work's merits, and wrote of diagnosing "the cases of Strauss and Hofmannsthal as psychopathic or neurasthenic, or whatever the appropriate scientific slang might be . . . ," both of which are words that can be associated with Freud.[33] In Act III of *Jitta's Atonement,* the mutual hostility between Edith and her mother, Agnes, comes to a head and becomes that much more understandable if one knows the extraordinary scene in Strauss's opera between the father-fixated Elektra and her hated mother, Klytämnestra. The dialogue between Edith and

Agnes at the end of their scene together could have been lifted from the
opera, and perhaps Shaw intended we might make the connection:[34]

AGNES. You are simply silly, child. Your grief and your crazy love for your
    father have turned your head. I wonder what you would say if you really
    knew.
EDITH [*scornfully*] If I really knew! Do you suppose any girl of my age
    nowadays does not know more than you were ever taught?
AGNES [*shrieking*] What?
EDITH. I know, as well as you do, where my father died, and how he died.
Mrs Haldenstadt covers her eyes in horror. (5:784–85)

Shaw possibly borrowed the theme of displaced sexuality as a result of
father-fixation from the Strauss opera rather than directly from Freud.
Elektra's hysterical desire to avenge her father's death led to the exclusion
of any "normal" expression of sexuality for herself, and she blatantly sets
out to *seduce* her excessively "normal" sister, Chrysothemis, into helping
her murder Klytämnestra and Aegisth. Shaw had approached the subject
of lesbianism, albeit in the muted form of a male-excluding feminism,
with the characters of Sylvia Craven in *The Philanderer* (1892) and Lesbia
Grantham in *Getting Married* (1908). Here Edith, herself trying to come to
terms with her father's death and to rescue his name from what her despised mother would make of it, makes an unconscious declaration of love
to Jitta far more passionate than any feelings she shows to her fiancé. She
will

> find out the secret of his death . . . the woman in whose arms my
> father died. . . . I love her . . . [f]or making my father happy. . . . I
> will take my father's memory and good name out of my mother's
> hands. . . . I will make the world see him as he was, and as I loved
> him, not as she sees him, and as she hates him. . . . I loved him;
> and that makes even his death a glory to me. If [the woman my
> father loved] is lonely why does she not come to me? She *shall* come
> to me. We shall cure one another's loneliness, we two. . . . I will give
> her every right over me that the woman who returned my father's
> love should have over his daughter: the right I deny my mother.
> . . . I can do without any man if I can find the woman to whom I
> am bound for ever and ever." (5:758–62)

This passionate aspiration in Act II lays the ground for the "recognition
scene" between Edith and Jitta in Act III, when Edith "recognizes" Jitta as
her father's lover. Edith and Jitta at that moment become for each other
instruments for "recollection" of Bruno; they become, in a sense, writing.

In Strauss's opera the famous "recognition scene" of Elektra at last recognizing her brother, Orest, who has entered the palace in disguise, is the emotional high point of the opera. Elektra knows that only Orest shares her sense of values, as Jitta does Edith's, and so will be the instrument to vindicate their "father's memory and good name" by murdering their mother and her paramour. Shaw's version is less sanguine.[35] Still as Dukore points out (Dukore 208–9), this demonstration of Edith's passionate love in *Jitta's Atonement* is quite different from Trebitsch's version:

EDITH. There is some woman who was real to my father; and he loved her. I shall love her when she is real to me. Besides, I have a queer sense that I know her quite well as well as a real person; that she is here within reach of my hands if only I could recollect . . .
JITTA. When you are excited like that your voice is his voice. Oh, the agony of hearing it, and the happiness! You bring him to life again for me.
EDITH. Then it was—
JITTA. Only me, dear.
EDITH [*flinging herself into Jitta's arms*] *Only* you! Who better could it be? Of course it was you. I knew it all along, only I couldnt recollect. Oh, darling! Dont you want a daughter? Here I am. *His* daughter. (5:799)

Frau Gittas Sühne's provenance in the Vienna of the early twentieth century is the most likely source for the allusions, direct or indirect, to Freud and the early days of psychoanalysis in Shaw's play. And we may remember that Trebitsch wrote that Shaw found *Frau Gittas Sühne* "very characteristic both of the atmosphere of Vienna and of the author." As it seems that they did not talk about Freud in the context of the translation, we have to assume they both brought to bear on the two separate plays their own individual knowledge of and attitudes to Freud and psychoanalysis.

While we cannot say for certain exactly what Trebitsch knew of Freud, *Frau Gittas Sühne* is itself the best evidence that Trebitsch, at least, knew of *Studien über Hysterie*, co-authored by Breuer and the famous Dr. Freud he had consulted in the early years of the century. The title of Bruno's book within the play, "Fetters of the Feminine Psyche," especially the words "feminine" and "psyche," seems to allude to Breuer's and Freud's *Studies on Hysteria*, which is exclusively concerned with the neuroses of female patients.[36] Trebitsch possibly knew the *Five Lectures* as well, with its summary of the Anna O. case in the first lecture. And as he seems to have known everyone in Vienna and was from a well-off Jewish background like the Pappenheims and their fashionable Dr. Breuer, he might even have learned from Viennese gossip that Anna O. was Bertha Pappenheim.[37] That Bertha's family name and Jitta's married name, Lenkheim, both end with the same significant final syllable, "-heim," common enough among German names, might be simply a coincidence; but (equally) it might not. And as Freud well knew, neither coincidence nor gossip should be under-estimated (what else is psychoanalytic psychotherapy, or literary criticism for that matter?). All we can do here is admit of the possibility of gossip in early twentieth-century Vienna, and *Jitta's Atonement* shows it to be alive and well in a short altercation between Alfred and Jitta.[38]

LENKHEIM. I wonder was she a patient of his?
JITTA. Does it matter? Need we gossip about it?
LENKHEIM [*impatiently*] Dont be so superior. I like gossip. Everybody likes gossip. You like it yourself as well as anybody. (5:752–53)

And who knows what Shaw learned from gossiping about Freud in Lon-don? If Shaw had read Freud's *Five Lectures* ("The Origin and Develop-ment of Psychoanalysis"), dealing with the beginnings of psychoanalysis and with the Anna O. case, or Freud's "On the History of the Psychoana-lytic Movement" (1914), translated by A. A. Brill in 1917, which, as we have said, is possible, he would have known of the Breuer-Freud collabo-ration. So it is not beyond the bounds of speculation, particularly given Shaw's way with names in his plays, that he changed the name of Trebit-sch's Alfons Lenkheim in *Frau Gittas Sühne* to Alfred in *Jitta's Atonement* so that the co-authors of "Fetters of the Feminine Psyche" would become, neglecting orthography for a moment: BR_Uno and alFRE_D.[39]

A final and intriguing parallel between the case of Bertha Pappenheim and Trebitsch's and Shaw's plays would have been unknown to them. In 1932, Freud (in a letter to Trebitsch's friend Stefan Zweig) revealed that the "analysis" of "Anna O." finished when Bertha declared that: "Now Dr. B.'s child is coming."[40] And as Forrester and Appignanesi put it, "there is nothing better suited to become the myth of origin than the story of a birth."[41] Apparently, Breuer was so scared by this intimation of a hysterical pregnancy that he decided to cease treating his patient there and then—and had her incarcerated. The official psychoanalytic accounts main-tained that she was "cured" at that point.[42] According to John Forrester, what seems to have happened is that Breuer realized that "Anna O." was repeating exactly the events of the previous year leading up to the point just before his daughter Dora had been born, three months after his treat-ment of Bertha began. He must have also realized that he himself had become preoccupied with his patient to the detriment of his own mar-riage. A few months later, in October 1883, Freud wrote to his fiancée, Martha Bernays, who knew all the parties, about Breuer's marriage. It sounds very like a description of Bruno's and Agnes's marriage during his affair with Jitta:

> Breuer too has a very high opinion of [Bertha], and gave up her
> care because it was threatening his very happy marriage. His poor
> wife could not stand the fact that he was so exclusively devoting
> himself to a woman about whom he obviously spoke with great in-
> terest. She was certainly only jealous of the demands made on her
> husband by another woman. Her jealousy did not show itself in a
> hateful, tormenting fashion, but in a silently recognized one. She
> fell ill, lost her spirits, until he noticed it and discovered the reason
> why. This naturally was enough for him to completely withdraw his
> attention from B.P.[43]

Breuer's claim that Bertha's sexuality was very undeveloped might account for his failure to notice how she had become so focused on him.
But for ending the treatment at that point, Freud in "On the History of
Psychoanalysis" criticized Breuer for failing to realize what became one
of the key points of psychoanalytical psychotherapy: the phenomenon of
transference, where the patient projects her sexual desires onto the analyst, in a repetition of earlier scenes with other objects of desire. Forrester
points out, however, that in this case what Breuer discovered was, rather,
counter-transference, when the analyst—usually in response to the transference—projects his desires onto the patient. That probably was why he
ran away when, unlike Bruno, he realized the implications for his family
life. He had found himself unwittingly falling in love with Bertha, and her
dependence if not overt sexual interest in him was coming between Breuer
and his wife to threaten their marriage.[44]

In the play, this situation is displaced in several ways. Bruno's consummated love for Jitta comes between him and his wife. The hysteria associated with a father-fixated daughter following the death of the father,
exemplified by Bertha in the history of psychoanalysis, is transferred in
the play to Jitta, although the father-fixated-daughter aspect of Bertha is
figured in Edith, who *is* deeply affected by Bruno's death. Dora Breuer,
who was actually Breuer's and his wife's child born during his treatment
of Bertha, becomes the newborn baby as a phantom or hysterical product
symbolic both of Bertha's relationship with Breuer and of the birth of the
new science. The notion of a phantom child associated with the birth of
"a new epoch in science" is figured in Edith in the play. Edith is Bruno's
and Agnes's child, but as a phantom, hysterical product of Bruno's love
for Jitta she is symbolically his and Jitta's child. And his book, "Fetters of
the Feminine Psyche," where his theory is symbolically worked out, is also
a child of his and Jitta's, born of their love. Like psychoanalysis, its birth
will be the beginning of a new "epoch in science," but "fathered" on another, Alfred, which makes Jitta disavow her responsibility for such a birth,
exclaiming that it will be "no child born of *our* intercourse" (5:741).[45] In

so far as Freud made a paternal claim in connection with the birth of the "science" of psychoanalysis, it was that the merit belonged also to another, to Josef Breuer.

IV

Act I is designed to set up the association between writing and sex, Bruno's book, "The Fetters of the Feminine Psyche," and the love affair. But *Jitta's Atonement* is exceptional in Shaw's plays in that in a play so thematically concerned with writing, no one is actually shown writing. This negation was hardly accidental, as it throws the question of writing into sharper relief, and allows the question as to what extent writing is constituted by other writings, by reading. The setting of Act II, Alfred's study, where "*The walls are crowded with book shelves; and the writing-table [at which the professor is sitting] is heaped with examination papers and manuscripts*" (5:746), underlines the Shavian emphasis on books and writing, in what Bertolini has called "the typical Shavian stage-scape [containing] a writing table, various instruments of writing, and writing itself."[46] Later in the act, this setting becomes a scene of *reading* in a prelude to (and cause of) a big confrontation with Jitta, when Alfred eventually gets a few minutes alone to look at Bruno's typescript, to which he is supposed to attach his name. And this scene of reading may, on another level, be read as a burlesque of Shaw's own reading Trebitsch's play before undertaking to translate and attach his name to it.

> *He carries the dispatch case to his writing-table, and sits down to examine its contents. He is in no hurry. It contains nothing but the manuscript of a biggish book. He leans lazily back with his legs stretched, and turns over the cover without looking at it. He reads a bit, and makes a wry face. He disagrees intensely and contemptuously with every passage he reads, abandoning each with sniffs and pishes, only to be still more disgusted with the next . . .*
>
> *Finally he gives the book up as hopeless; shuts up the pages; and stares at the mass of manuscript as if wondering what to do with such trash. Suddenly his expression changes. His eyes bulge in amazement.* (5:763–64)

Jitta has been silently watching the end of this performance, and when he realizes she is there, he makes her *read* out loud the title page which has caused his amazement: "Fetters of the Feminine Psyche," . . . "By

Alfred Lenkheim." Here, forty years before Roland Barthes, Shaw is predicating his play on "the death of the author." In Act I, the *writer*, Bruno, was represented as dying (along with those in his "tragedies"—of the artist in *The Doctor's Dilemma* and of the Elderly Gentleman in *The Tragedy of an Elderly Gentleman*—one of the few stagings of death in Shaw's theater), and the name of the author was replaced with that of Alfred, the *reader* as represented in this almost silent scene in Act II. Together they encapsulate Barthes's famous dictum that "the birth of the reader must be at the cost of the death of the author."[47] And, sometimes, the reader can be a prospective translator, as both Shaw and Trebitsch (as writers) ruefully acknowledged.

Toward the end of Act III, Jitta, having resolved the respective dramas of Agnes and Edith caused by the circumstances of Bruno's death, now has to resolve her own with Alfred: their marriage and what will happen to Bruno's book. Alfred tells Jitta that, having read Bruno's book (between the acts), he considers it "the most utter tommyrot that was ever put forward as a serious contribution to psychology," and that he will not put his name to it. That Jitta, against Bruno's wishes, has told him of their *secret* affair, Alfred uses as his excuse to renege on his agreement to "father" the book. But Jitta, who knows without having read or been able to understand it, that "that book is the greatest that ever was written," insistently demands: "You will not destroy the book? You will edit it? You will do everything for it that you could for a book of your own?" (5:807). And when Agnes returns, before Alfred can refuse, Jitta tells her: "Alfred has found your husband's book. It is a masterpiece. He will edit it. He will do everything he could for it if it were his own book" (5:807).

And just before this, Shaw cleverly displaced the thematic of writing, as translation and co-authoring as figured in the play of naming involving Bruno and Alfred, onto the figures of the tragically romantic Jitta and the crudely pragmatic Alfred. Many years earlier, with a rare reference to Jane Austen, Shaw had pointed out, in a letter of 27 July 1905, to his translator these same contrasting attitudes as characteristic of Trebitsch and himself: "There is a famous English novel called Sense and Sensibility by Jane Austen, which you ought to keep on your desk to remind you that an empfindlich [sensitive] person is the very opposite of a vernunftig, verständig, gerade [sensible] person who thinks all empfindlich people wahnsinn [mad]. . . . *I* am sensible. *You* are sensitive (empfindlich)" (Weiss 87).

Exemplifying these contrasting theatricalized attitudes, the last scene between husband and wife in *Jitta's Atonement* can be read as a dialogue between Trebitsch and his "translator" describing what Shaw has done in his translation of Trebitsch's play. It also hints as to what Alfred's "editing" of Bruno's book may be like:

JITTA [*tragically*] I am a miserable creature. I betrayed you to please my-self. I deserted him in his extremity to save myself. Please leave me to my disgrace. Nothing that you can say or think can add to the contempt I feel for myself. . . . I did not behave as any decent woman would.

LENKHEIM. That is just where you are mistaken, darling. When you were brought to the point and put to the proof, you didnt behave romanti-cally: you behaved very sensibly. You kept your head, and did just the right thing. You saved your reputation and my reputation. You pre-vented a horrible scandal. You have managed to make his wife and daughter happy. And yet you think you are ashamed of yourself because you were not found stretched on his dead body, with the limelight streaming on your white face, and the band playing slow music.

JITTA. Oh, what a nature you have, Alfred! You are prosaic to the core. (5:802–3)

As we have seen, the Bruno-Alfred authorship problem in *Frau Gittas Sühne* seems to have been inspired by the Breuer-Freud authorship prob-lem. It fitted so well into Shaw's thematic of writing that he could make much more of it than Trebitsch. Dukore states that "Though the questions of whether Lenkheim will allow his name to be put to [Bruno's] work . . . are important in Trebitsch, Shaw makes more of them" (Dukore 205). Moreover, in *Jitta's Atonement* it becomes a self-reflexive questioning of the Shaw/Trebitsch translating/writing co-authorship relation, not only in this particular play but presumably in Trebitsch's life work of translating Shaw into German. To a great degree, Shaw makes translating, writing as rewrit-ing the play's thematic subject, the object of its textual hermeneutics, as figured in the drama around the question of whose name will be inscribed on the title page of "The Fetters of the Feminine Psyche." The resolution is both: the *writer*, Bruno, *edited* by the *reader*, Alfred. Trebitsch, as we saw earlier, had written of his own concern that Shaw might erase his (i.e., Shaw's) name from his translation, but in the end the title page read, "Jitta's Atonement by Siegfried Trebitsch translated by Bernard Shaw."[48] Ironically, if inevitably, this theme did not end there, as, despite Shaw's expressed intentions, his name was used to a greater extent and in larger print than Trebitsch's in early productions of the play.

Jitta's Atonement offered Shaw an opportunity to explore the implications of the illusion of love in relation to marriage, a consistent theme in his work, but here in the context of writing, scientific discovery, and adultery. While the title of Bruno's book, "The Fetters of the Feminine Psyche," might allude to *Studies on Hysteria*, it might also refer to John Stuart Mill's *The Emancipation of Women* (1851), a work Shaw would have known, al-though he probably did not know that Freud had actually *translated* it into German in 1880.[49] Trebitsch, however, could have known this.[50] Mill's essay, which describes what may be justly called the fetters imposed on women in a modern industrial society that must be removed before they can be emancipated, can lead us into a consideration of Shaw's views of marriage in general and in *Jitta's Atonement* in particular. The fetters of the feminine psyche, as Shaw would be quick to point out, are probably much the same as those of the masculine psyche, except that in a patriarchal society where men are generally speaking the money-makers, the fetters of marriage, family, home, and the name of the father/husband, of domesticity in general, are felt more heavily by women. If sex and love enter the picture in the form of a marital "transgression," the presence of those fetters of hearth and home are felt all the more keenly and often thrown right off.[51] However, the irony of Jitta's "atonement" for her "transgression" of the marriage contract, is precisely to accept those fetters of domesticity, to "turn home," which is a literal translation of her *married* name, Lenkheim.[52] Bruno's "atonement," contrary to Jitta's and Edith's wishes, is to suppress his own name and replace it with Alfred's on the typescript of his book: "this sacrifice [is] my atonement to Alfred: It is the price at which I buy his wife from him" (5:740). Thus Alfred and the married state seem to win both ways. However, Jitta as well as Edith, who functions in the play as an analogue both of his writing and of his love for Jitta, both refuse in Shaw's text to be considered as currency in the commerce between men: Jitta: "You have not taken me from him. I belonged to myself: and I gave you myself" (5:737); Edith: "I dont intend to be taken as a legacy, sacred or not" (5:757).

Thus the play both exposes the social structures underlying marriage (akin to Lévi-Strauss's "elementary structures of kinship" based on a system of exchange of gifts between men in which women function as currency) while calling them into question.[53] In the section "Inconsistency of the Sex Instinct" (a subtitle possibly prompted by Freud) in *On the Prospects of Christianity* (1916), Shaw had deconstructed the notion of marriage by showing that it is based on that which would transgress it: sex. But Shaw claimed, in contradistinction to Freud's single overriding instinct of the sexual *libido*, that there were "two tyrannous physical passions: concupiscence and chastity."[54]

> We become mad in pursuit of sex: we become equally mad in the persecution of that pursuit. Unless we gratify our desire the race is lost: unless we restrain it we destroy ourselves. We are thus led to devise marriage institutions which will at the same time secure opportunities for the gratification of sex and raise up innumerable obstacles to it; which will sanctify it and brand it as infamous; which will identify it with virtue and sin simultaneously. Obviously it is useless to look for any consistency in such institutions; and it is

only by continual reform and readjustment, and by a considerable
elasticity in their enforcement, that a tolerable result can be arrived
at. (4:539)

This construction/deconstruction of the "sex instinct" and marriage was
translated by Shaw into a structure of transgression/adherence in relation
to that piece of writing known as the marriage contract, to form the drama
of *Jitta's Atonement.*

Bruno's revolutionary, transgressive theory presents another way of
looking at the phenomena of love and sex that provide such a fragile
foundation for marriage. While Freud might have agreed with Shaw's dictum that "all thinking is wishful," Bruno's theory, unlike Freud's radical
theory of the sexual etiology of neuroses, is based on his "mystical speculation" that unconscious longings have physical consequences. As Bruno
"mystically" puts it in Act I: "Men do not yet realize that no prophetic aspiration of theirs can fall utterly without fruit if its roots lie deep enough in
their innermost conviction" (5:735).[55] This seems to be a restatement of
Franklyn Barnabas's "conviction" about the *unconscious* will underlying
The Gospel of the Brothers Barnabas, to which *Jitta's Atonement* seems to be a
dramatic-thematic supplement: "Do not mistake mere idle fancies for the
tremendous miracle-working force of Will nerved to creation by a conviction of Necessity. I tell you men capable of such willing, and realizing its
necessity, will do it reluctantly, under inner compulsion, as all great efforts
are made. They will hide what they are doing from themselves: they will
take care not to know what they are doing" (5:433).

Both Shaw and Freud were indebted to Schopenhauer's notion of the
Will for their understanding of the workings of the unconscious, but
Bruno's theory seems to be the reverse of Freud's, which would hold that
our past determines our future actions. Here Bruno is saying that it has
been his *unconscious* aspiration toward his future love for Jitta ("before
Edith was born—before I ever set eyes on you") that has brought about
such physical consequences as his speculative theoretical writing as well as
his daughter Edith, who both shares her father's aspiration and incarnates
it. So Freud's idea of forgetting/remembering, of not knowing/knowing,
of not uttering/uttering memories or secrets, gets skewed in Shaw's play.
What has to be remembered or recollected and spoken or written is not a
specific repressed sexual history but a vague unconscious aspiration, made
manifest in love, toward an indefinite future (as Edith says when Jitta reveals herself as her father's lover: "I knew it all along, only I couldn't
recollect"). Bruno's "prophetic aspiration," which later finds its material-
ization in his affair with Jitta, is Shaw's version of Goethe's *"das ewig
Weibliche zieht uns hinan"* (the eternal feminine draws us upward) from
Faust II. And, as he does throughout the text, he is careful to deconstruct

the ideal by contrasting it with the real with Fessler's mention of Goethe's wife, Christiane, who seems to have been about as far from *das ewig Weibliche* as Goethe could get![56] Fessler makes the comparison as a warning to Edith that she may be overestimating the qualities of her father's lover as compared to his wife. The stage directions that introduce Jitta also contrast the illusionary ideal with the real by describing how Bruno sees his lover compared to how she appears to others in her everyday commonplace reality as a Viennese *Hausfrau:*

> *one of those attractively refined women whose wistfully sensitive unsmiling mouths and tragic eyes not only make imaginative men fancy unfathomable depths in their natures, and something undefinably sad and splendid in their destinies, but actually force this conception on the women themselves, however commonplace their characters and circumstances might be. Jitta is nothing more extraordinary than the wife of a college don, and has done nothing more heroic than fall in love with another and more poetic don (also married).* (5:731)

However, real or ideal, *das ewig Weibliche* is what Shaw described as "a necessary illusion," with something like the teleological function of beauty in Plato's *Phaedrus* or Kant's *Critique of Judgement*. And what Jitta represents for Bruno is analogous to the function of the beautiful Mrs. Etteen in relation to Franklyn in *The Domesticity of Franklyn Barnabas*, the discarded first draft of *The Gospel of the Brothers Barnabas:*

MRS ETTEEN. . . . it does not occur to you that Franklyn Barnabas might have had [this "Back to Methuselah" idea] from me. Did he ever speak of it before he met me?
IMMENSO. Now that you mention it, no. But it began with [his biologist brother] Conrad; and you certainly did not work in his laboratory.
MRS ETTEEN. Conrad never saw the scope of his ides. . . . He saw how it affected science. . . . He had the skeleton of the great faith; but it was Franklyn who put the flesh on it. And it was I, the woman, who made that flesh for him out of my own. (5:682)

The similarity of this thematic, in conjunction with the importance of "domesticity" in both texts, suggests that *Jitta's Atonement* may be read as a rewriting of these discarded acts from *Back to Methuselah*, as well as of *Frau Gittas Sühne*. We may further speculate that the romance between Franklyn and Mrs. Etteen, replayed in that between Bruno and Jitta, had deep personal ramifications for Shaw as a fictional replay of his own romance with Mrs. Patrick Campbell of ten years earlier, which nearly wrecked his own domesticity and marriage. Shaw, cutting very close to the bone, even inserts her name, not once but twice into the text of *Domesticity*. The first is by naming the gardener of Franklyn and his wife "Campbell," perhaps playing on the association of the flower girl in *Pygmalion*, Eliza Doolittle, written for Mrs. Campbell (does the flower girl "fascinated" by the lovers' bedroom at the beginning of Act I of *Jitta's Atonement* raise the same association?). The second intrusion of the name Campbell into *The Domesticity of Franklyn Barnabas* is more subtle, if more blatantly indicative, as it breaks in as a piece of music on a dialogue involving Franklyn's wife, Clara (portrayed like Charlotte Shaw as having an interest in Eastern religions):

A hollow chord of G flat and D flat is heard droning from the drawing
 room piano. Then The Campbells are Coming is played on the black
 keys. . . .
CLARA [*indignantly*] Well! (5:671)

And to bring this connection back to *Jitta's Atonement*, Shaw wrote in his letter to Trebitsch of 15 May 1922 that "Mrs Patrick Campbell . . . would have been a wonderful Gitta fifteen years ago" (Weiss 232). As we have seen, Shaw's text slyly suggests that the hours and hours Bruno spent working and writing was a means of escaping from his wife at home in order to fantasize about Jitta. Franklyn's writing in *The Domesticity of Franklyn Barnabas* is similarly derived from Mrs. Etteen. Can we say, by extension, that Shaw's metabiology is derived from Stella Campbell?

This series of loves and the texts that stem from them suggest that writing, whether as *Jitta's Atonement* or "The Fetters of the Feminine Psyche," might be viewed as a supplement to love. As Jitta rather subtly puts it to her lover, Bruno, in Act I in a balanced assessment of that great conundrum of love: Do you love the other for who he or she is or for what he or she is? "You know that I love you as my man, without a thought of your greatness and your work; but all the same your work, your greatness, are a part of you; and I love every bit of you, your body, your soul, your reputation, your work, everything that would not exist if you did not exist" (5:740).

The idea of transgression with which he embarked on the translation of *Frau Gittas Sühne* remained with Shaw, not only in the context of marriage but also of writing as transgressive, as illegitimate, but that could nevertheless inaugurate, as with Einstein and Freud, new epochs in science to question previous lines of paternity.[57] The play of writing as translation raises the question of the transgression of the "original" writing, only for it to be resolved (to be atoned for) "at the end" (i.e., for the moment) of a long series of displacements (from Breuer-Bertha through Freud-Breuer to Trebitsch/Shaw-Breuer/Freud, to Bruno-Alfred, to Jitta-Alfred, to Trebitsch-Shaw). Playing on the word "home," Alfred says: "And now, may I take my good angel home?" after which, Jitta twice says to him: "Come home" (5:807–8). Author and translator, writer and reader, personified in the married couple, Jitta and Alfred *Lenkheim,* live up to their name and decide at the very end of the play *to make for home.* Resuming their marriage, Jitta's atonement for her transgression, for her love of Bruno, will be the fettered domesticity of life with Alfred.

Notes

1. In this essay, the German title will refer to Trebitsch's play and the English one to Shaw's.
2. Bernard F. Dukore, *Bernard Shaw, Playwright: Aspects of Shavian Drama* (Columbia: University of Missouri Press, 1973). All further references to Dukore are incorporated into the text.
3. This essay refers to Shaw's plays and prefaces as published in *The Bodley Head Bernard Shaw: Collected Plays with Their Prefaces,* 7 vols. (London: Max Reinhardt, 1971–74). The first numeral refers to the volume, the second to the page number.
4. In a forthcoming study, I will pursue the comparison between *Back to Methuselah* and *Beyond the Pleasure Principle* in greater detail.
5. See Sidney P. Albert, "Reflections on Shaw and Psychoanalysis," *Modern Drama* 14.2 (September 1971): 169–94.
6. See Peter Gahan, "*Back to Methuselah:* An Exercise of Imagination," in *SHAW: The Annual of Bernard Shaw Studies* 17 (University Park: Penn State University Press, 1997), pp. 215–38, and John A. Bertolini, *The Playwrighting Self of Bernard Shaw* (Carbondale: Southern Illinois University Press, 1991), p. 144: "—the Word made flesh, poetic imagination overcoming the fear of death—Shaw makes her embody as a character and as a symbol, thus helping us to imagine imagination herself, Saint Joan."
7. *Bernard Shaw's Letters to Siegfried Trebitsch,* ed. Samuel A. Weiss (Stanford: Stanford University Press, 1986), p. 229, in a letter dated 11 October 1921. Shaw met Einstein at a dinner in London in June 1921, and had used the phrase "as important as Einstein on Relativity" in an earlier letter to Trebitsch of 15 September 1920, just after he began his translation.
8. All further references to Weiss will be incorporated into the main text. We have most, but not all, of Shaw's side of the correspondence in Weiss, supplemented by "Bernard Shaw's Further Letters to Siegfried Trebitsch," in *SHAW: The Annual of Bernard Shaw Studies* 20 (University Park: Penn State University Press, 2000), pp. 221–45. Trebitsch's few surviving letters are included.
9. Siegfried Trebitsch, *Chronicle of a Life,* trans. Eithne Wilkins and Ernst Kaiser (London: Heinemann, 1953), p. 263.
10. From the correspondence, it does not appear that Shaw worked with a literal translation of *Frau Gittas Sühne.* Trebitsch might have confused this with the literal translation he supplied Shaw for *Ein Muttersohn.* When Trebitsch hinted at the possibility of Shaw translating his next play, *Der Geliebte* (The Beloved), Shaw balked: "A literal translation would be of no use to me: such things are deadly snares" (*SHAW 20,* p. 239).

11. Trebitsch, *Chronicle of a Life*, p. 264.

12. Shaw had altered Gitta to Jitta, because in English he wanted a soft rather than the German hard G sound. Trebitsch then rather comically retranslates the soft G English sound (which does not exist in German) into the silent Y German sound. Shaw somewhat mischievously adopts Trebitsch's spelling, symptomatic of Trebitsch's general misunderstanding in his translations, in subsequent letters.

13. On 21 April 1922, after Schnitzler had sent Shaw a copy of his play (at Trebitsch's request) during the final phase of translating *Frau Gittas Sühne*, Shaw issued his opinion (one must keep in mind that he had read *Reigen* in German presumably with difficulty; *Reigen* became better known as *La Ronde* following Max Ophuls's 1950 French film adaptation): "His plays are just a little *vieux jeu:* life does not consist exclusively of amourettes; and he is a virtuoso in amourettes only. But I enjoy them, and think he ought to persuade Granville-Barker to translate Reigen as a pendant to Anatole" (Weiss 232).

14. He wrote to his friend, the Reverend Joseph Leonard, on 15 December 1922, asking for detailed information on the church's attitude to the recently canonized fifteenth-century Frenchwoman. See *Bernard Shaw: Collected Letters III, 1911–1925*, ed. Dan H. Laurence (London: Max Reinhardt, 1985), pp. 796–800. As with *Jitta*, and almost certainly *Heartbreak House* (which he declared to have started before the war but did not begin to write until 1916), it seems characteristic for there to have been a considerable time gap between Shaw's decision to write a play and his first shorthand draft.

15. Trebitsch, *Chronicle of a Life*, pp. 185–86. Trebitsch specifically states that this experience was the reason he could not draw on Freud's for his story, *Die Frau ohne Dienstag* (The Woman without Tuesday), written just before journeying to Paris to see his friend, the poet Rainer Maria Rilke, and Shaw in 1906.

16. *Collected Letters III*, pp. 13–19.

17. Albert, "Reflections on Shaw and Psychoanalysis," p. 172. Albert suggests that Shaw could have read about Freud as early as 1904 in volume 1 of Ellis's *Studies in the Psychology of Sex*.

18. *Bernard Shaw's Book Reviews, Vol. 2, 1884–1950*, ed. and intro. by Brian Tyson (University Park: Penn State University Press, 1996), pp. 328–29.

19. Translated by Harry W. Chase in the *American Journal of Psychology* 21 (April 1910): 181–218.

20. Albert's "Reflections on Shaw and Psychoanalysis" remains the best resource as to what Shaw definitely knew about Freud and when.

21. *Collected Letters IV, 1926–1950*, ed. Dan H. Laurence (London: Max Reinhardt, 1988), pp. 418–19.

22. Darwin, who had been a major part of the thematic of *Back to Methuselah*, is mentioned here in connection with the metaphor of writing as an orphan (discussed in the last section of this article): "A book by a dead man is an orphan. Orphans sometimes die when they are not adopted. [Gregor] Mendel's masterpiece lay dead for thirty-five years while the fame of the living Darwin spread over the world" (5:739).

23. I would like to thank Sibylle Ferner, a translator by profession, who out of sheer generosity and intellectual curiosity supplied me with a literal translation of *Frau Gittas Sühne* after I wrote the first draft of this essay. This has proved doubly beneficial by enabling me to be more certain than I otherwise could have been about Shaw's additions and embellishments to Trebitsch's German text, while curtailing a few unsupported flights of fancy. Any remaining errors are the sole responsibility of the author, not the translator.

24. In volume IX of the Standard Edition of the complete psychological works of Sigmund Freud, general editor James Strachey, 24 vols. (London: The Hogarth Press and the Institute of Psychoanalysis, 1953–74), henceforth *SE*.

25. See Sigmund Freud, *Beyond the Pleasure Principle* (1920), p. 293. Freud's words are

very close to Fessler's: "There is the case, for instance, of the woman who married three successive husbands each of whom fell ill soon afterwards and had to be nursed by her on their death-beds." The problem is that as Freud's *Jenseits des Lustprinzeps* was published in German in 1920, *after* Trebitsch wrote his play, and the English translation in 1922, *after* Shaw wrote his translation, it is difficult to establish if Shaw/Trebitsch got this notion of a "compulsion-to-repeat" from Freud, except in a general sense that psychoanalysis is based on repeating behavior and remembering forgotten memories of similar behavior all the way back to childhood.

26. "The Illusions of Socialism," *The Home Journal* (New York), 21 and 28 October 1896; reprinted in *Selected Non-Dramatic Writings of Bernard Shaw*, ed. Dan H. Laurence (Boston: Houghton Mifflin, 1966), p. 406. Interestingly Shaw uses "mainspring" to describe Bruno's collapse at the end of Act I: "That lift broke the mainspring" (5:744).

27. See Margery M. Morgan, *The Shavian Playground* (London: Methuen, 1972), p. 68, on *Candida,* and Bertolini, *The Playwrighting Self of Bernard Shaw*, p. 85, on *The Doctor's Dilemma.*

28. Bertolini, *The Playwrighting Self of Bernard Shaw*, pp. 145–65.

29. For the history of the beginnings of psychoanalysis and Breuer's case of Bertha Pappenheim ("Anna O."), this essay is indebted to John Forrester's account in "The True Story of Anna O," in *The Seductions of Psychoanalysis: Freud, Lacan, and Derrida* (Cambridge: Cambridge University Press, 1990), pp. 17–29, as well as to Lisa Appignanesi's and Forrester's *Freud's Women* (London: Virago; New York: Basic Books, 1992), especially chapter 3, "The First Patients," in Part II: Inventing Psychoanalysis, and the section "Anna O.: The First Patient," pp. 72–86.

30. Forrester, "The True Story of Anna O.," pp. 23–24, reprints this extract from *Five lectures on psycho-analysis* (1910) from *SE*, XI. Forrester, p. 321, points out that Freud modified these remarks so as to claim more credit for the invention of psychoanalysis in "On the History of the Psycho-analytic Movement," written in 1914 (*SE*, XIV, pp. 7–66).

31. In "Hofmannsthal's 'Elektra': From Sophocles to Strauss," in *Richard Strauss: Elektra,* ed. Derrick Puffett (Cambridge: Cambridge University Press, 1989), Karen Forsyth suggests that Hofmannsthal "may not have read Breuer's and Freud's *Studien über Hysterie* (1895), often cited as being central to his *Elektra*, until at least 1904." She points out that Hofmannsthal's play, *Elektra*, had opened on 30 October 1903, and then quotes a letter of Hofmannsthal to Hermann Bahr (a literary friend of Trebitsch's) in May 1904: "Could you possibly lend (send) me for a few days the book by Freud and Breuer about curing hysteria by releasing suppressed memories? If not, please write down the exact title for me, so that I can have it sent." *Briefe 1900–1911*, p. 142. However, that might as easily mean that he had already read the book and wanted to consult it again. It certainly reveals that Hofmannsthal knew generally what *Studien über Hysterie* was about.

32. It might have been the experience of this Freudian updating of Sophocles' and Euripides' *Electra* that prompted Shaw's suggestion to Gilbert Murray the following year to write his Freudian version of *Oedipus Rex.* Shaw attended the opera *Elektra* on Saturday, 12 March 1910, with Strauss conducting. Anna von Mildenberg, wife of Trebitsch's friend Hermann Bahr, sang Klytämnestra. Shaw invited Bahr to lunch, but his wife declined. During his "desperate effort" to finish *Jitta's Atonement*, Shaw met Strauss on 24 January 1922. He does not relate whether they spoke of *Elektra* or of Trebitsch, a friend of Strauss's famous librettist. But communication was not easy, as he wrote to his wife: "[Strauss] speaks a little English, but does not understand it very well. . . . My efforts to speak German were pitiable. I kept dropping into French. I told the story of the bear at Mevagissey who danced to the Sinfonia Domestica theme; but as none of the company except S. recognized the theme, and he didn't understand the story, it was a ghastly failure." *Collected Letters III, 1911–1925*, pp. 761–62.

33. See *Shaw's Music: The Complete Musical Criticism of Bernard Shaw*, vol. 3, 2nd rev. ed., ed. Dan H. Laurence (London: Max Reinhardt, The Bodley Head, 1981, 1989), p. 602.

34. Already in *Fanny's First Play* (1911), Shaw had alluded to *Elektra* in the context of the generational conflicts of that play; Fanny's father's taste in music ends with the end of the eighteenth century, and she declares: "I darent let him know that I love Beethoven and Wagner; and as to Strauss, if he heard three bars of Elektra, it'd part us forever" (4:365).

35. Much of *Jitta's Atonement* is concerned with the "father's memory and good name" as Edith puts it (5:760), which obviously has Freudian Oedipal connotations. When Edith speaks of "the honor of father's name," which she feels is being belittled by her mother, Alfred promises to uphold it. In the very next line, Agnes gives Alfred the typescript she herself is looking for, in which Bruno, the father, has already erased his own name in favor of Alfred's! This is yet another example of the slippage between conscious knowledge and action, epitomizing Freud's notion of the unconscious, which pervades the play.

36. Freud had argued, following his teacher in Paris, Jean Martin Charcot, that hysteria was not gender-specific, but in fact all the cases in *Studies on Hysteria* were of female patients treated by male doctors, which thereafter provided the male/female paradigm for the psychoanalytic session invariably involving "transference" between patient and analyst.

37. Appignanesi and Forrester, *Freud's Women*, p. 80, point out that "some people recognized [Bertha Pappenheim] in Anna O. when the case history was published in 1895."

38. See John Forrester's chapter, "Psychoanalysis: Gossip, Telepathy and/or Science?" in Forrester, *The Seductions of Psychoanalysis*, pp. 243–59.

39. Shaw's *Press Cuttings* (1909) provides an example of Shaw's way with names. Two of the characters, Mitchener and Balsquith, caused the short play to be banned because they "were too like Kitchener-and-Milner and Asquith-and-Balfour." See Raymond Mander and Joe Mitchenson, *Theatrical Companion to Shaw* (New York: Pitman, 1955), p. 130.

40. See Forrester, *The Seductions of Psychoanalysis*, p. 17, and Appignanesi and Forrester, *Freud's Women*, pp. 81ff.

41. Appignanesi and Forrester, *Freud's Women*, p. 85.

42. Ibid., p. 76: "Breuer recounted, she was . . . free from all the disturbances she had previously exhibited. But, he added, she took some time to regain her mental balance entirely; since then, however, she had enjoyed complete health."

43. Forrester, *The Seductions of Psychoanalysis*, p. 19.

44. In *Studies on Hysteria*, (1895), *SE* II, pp. 21–22. Breuer wrote: "The element of sexuality was astonishingly undeveloped in her; the patient, whose life became known to me to an extent to which one person's life is seldom known to another, had never been in love, and in all the enormous number of hallucinations which occurred during her illness that element of mental life never emerged." Freud, in "On the History of Psychoanalysis," had no trouble pointing out the obvious symbolic relevance of Bertha's hallucinations about snakes.

45. "if only you will father his book," as Jitta says to Alfred at the end of Act II (5:773).

46. Bertolini, *The Playwrighting Self of Bernard Shaw*, p. 7. Bertolini is possibly the first critic to demonstrate the importance of how often Shaw's writing becomes the subject of his dramatic writing. Such self-reflexive "intentionality" in Shaw's writing is in no way at variance, as Bertolini seems to suppose—"my contra-deconstructionist assumption is that Shaw knew what he was about when he wrote his plays" (5)—with the deconstruction that this writer would propose is at work much of the time in the Shaw text. In fact, deconstruction would not be possible without intentionality.

47. Roland Barthes, "The Death of the Author," in *Image-Music-Text,* trans. Stephen Heath (London: Fontana, 1977), p. 148.

48. The full title page reads: "Jitta's Atonement by Siegfried Trebitsch *Author of* Genesung, Weltuntergang, Das Haus am Abhang, Tagwandler, Ein Muttersohn, Der Tod und die Liebe, Gefährliche Jahre, Spätes Licht, Die Frau ohne Dienstag, Der Geliebte, Die Last des Blutes, etc. etc. Translated by Bernard Shaw."

49. Mill's essay, published in *The Westminster Review*, was co-authored, as was much of his

work, with his lover, Harriet Taylor, whom he had eventually married in 1851, two years after her husband died. After Taylor herself died, Mill continued working on their book, *The Subjection of Women* (1869), with her daughter, Helen Taylor. In connection with the play's theme of books and the name of the author, it may be of interest to note that Mill wrote in his autobiography: "Whoever, either now or hereafter, may think of me and my work I have done, must never forget that it is the product not of one intellect and conscience but of three, the least considerable of whom, and above all the least original, is the one whose name is attached to it."

50. Like Shaw, Freud was strikingly modern in some ways, while maintaining old-fashioned attitudes in others. He detailed a list of his disagreements with Mill's views on women, especially that they should be considered breadwinners equal to men, in a letter to his future wife on 15 November 1883, quoted in Appignanesi and Forrester, *Freud's Women*, pp. 421–22. See *Letters of Sigmund Freud, 1873–1939*, ed. Ernst L. Freud, trans. Tania and James Stern (London: The Hogarth Press, 1970), pp. 90–91. Shaw would have been more in sympathy with Mill's feminism, while *his* old-fashioned Victorianism came out in his consistent criticism of Freud as indelicate.

51. See Weiss, p. 212, who points out that Shaw misread or misunderstood *Sühne* as *Sünde* in the title, and so called it in his letter of 26 February 1920, "Frau Gitta's Transgression."

52. *Lenken* means to guide, drive, direct, steer, and *Heim* means home. Trebitsch was responsible for the name, but Shaw would have known what it meant. *Haldenstedt*, Bruno's and Agnes's married name, has not got such a clear-cut interpretation, as it literally means "place on a sloping hill." This probably had a personal association for Trebitsch, as an earlier novel of his, *Das Haus am Abhang* (1905), translates as "house on the slope."

53. As postulated in Claude Lévi-Strauss in *The Elementary Structures of Kinship*, trans. John R. Von Sturmer and Rodney Needham (Boston: Beacon Press, 1969).

54. As with Wagner's distinction between the chaste Parsifal and the castrated Klingsor, Shaw is careful to distinguish the "passion" of chastity (as found sometimes in artists) from mere sexual repression as found in the psychological type epitomized by Saint Paul, who "suffers from that particular sort of conscience and nervous constitution which brings its victims under the tyranny of two delirious terrors: the terror of sin and the terror of death, which may be called also the terror of sex and the terror of life." From *On the Prospects of Christianity* (1916), published as preface to *Androcles and the Lion* (4:546).

55. See Postscript (1945) to *Back to Methuselah* (5:699).

56. "You know very well that Goethe was a great man; but the fine ladies of Weimar were shocked by his marriage" (5:787). "I have one object in life now, and one only. . . . To find the woman who made my father happy, and to force you to confess that she is high heavens above your Goethe's Christiane" (5:789).

57. See note 51 above on Shaw's mistranslating *Frau Gittas Sühne* as "Frau Gitta's Transgression."

Stanley Weintraub

SHAW'S SCULPTRESS,
KATHLEEN SCOTT

Many years into their long friendship, Bernard Shaw told Kathleen Scott (she had sculpted him, wearing then-unfeminine coveralls or slacks), "No woman ever born had a narrower escape from being a man. My affection for you is the nearest I ever came to homosexuality."[1] Lady Scott, widow of the Antarctic explorer, nevertheless always had trouble deflecting admirers. Nor did she try very hard. Devotees often became subjects for her chisel, and if not then, they became helpless with admiration as they sat for her.

A friend late in her life, who would write Kathleen's obituary in advance (and by request) for *The Times* in 1937, ten years before she died, called her "alleged vamping of distinguished men" empty charges that were "rubbish." Rather, "famous men sought K. out, even those who were not being modelled," and she would claim in pleased vanity that she had "volumes" of letters from them.[2] Shaw's alone would make a small volume.

G.B.S. met Kathleen Bruce in the early 1900s. Born on 27 March 1878, she had studied with Auguste Rodin when just out of her teens, preened at Gertrude Stein's salons, traveled with Isadora Duncan, and volunteered in Macedonia with refugees from Turkish brutality. She introduced Shaw to Isadora, who urged him "to come and sit beside her and hold her hand," Kathleen recalled, because "though I may not be much to look at, I'm very good to feel." Shaw remembered Isadora, who attracted him far less than Kathleen, "clothed in draperies and appearing rather damaged," with a face that "looked as if it had been made of sugar and someone had licked it." Holding out her arms, she appealed, "I have loved you all my life. Come!!" So they sat while "the entire party gathered around us as if they were witnessing a play." If he called on her, Isadora promised, she would dance for him "undraped." He never did.[3]

Kathleen also radiated unconventionality, but she kept her private life prior to her marriage a mystery. Like other men, Shaw was attracted by what he described as her vitality, but he was hardly the first votary. Occultist and magician Aleister Crowley, who met her in Paris at Rodin's studio, penned outrageously bad poetry urging her to "Whip, whip me till I burn! Whip on! Whip on!" Masochistic fantasy? The repellent Crowley claimed that her "brilliant beauty and wholesome Highland flamboyance were complicated with a sinister perversity. . . . She initiated me into the torturing pleasures of algolagny on the spiritual plane. . . . Love had no savour for her unless she was causing ruin or unhappiness to others." Crowley may have merely been frustrated—yet enjoying it.[4] Old Rodin "would flatter me and my work," she wrote, and he would, like so many other admirers, send her fulsome letters. He would call her "*Un petit morceau grec d'un chef-d'oeuvre*," she recalled, "and I would look at my stalwart arms and legs and not feel at all fragmentary."[5]

In Paris, too, was photographer Edward Steichen, whose wife, Clara, identified Kathleen as "the lovestruck young woman" who had allegedly gazed longingly at Steichen across the tables of a cheap café in Paris in 1902.[6] Clara perceived, suspiciously, a sexual overture, and was jealous of the arty women she viewed as rivals for her husband even if the relationships were entirely innocent. At work in England later, Kathleen mingled with politicians and artistic people in circles that intersected with Shaw's own. Her admiration of Shaw was so complete that when she was hospitalized for surgery on an abdominal cyst, and "half-expected to die," she became even more certain of that when a nurse asked her if she would like to have a clergyman visit. No, she said, she would rather see Bernard Shaw.[7]

Her personal world found a focus when she met naval captain and explorer Robert Falcon Scott and determined to make him her husband. He was forty and she was thirty. She had waited almost in eugenic Shavian fashion until she had found the man she wanted to sire her sons (she was sure they would be sons). Scott succumbed.

Peter Scott was born before "Con" left to search for the South Pole in 1910; and with Scott gone, Kathleen resumed much of her former life despite the intrusions of her new celebrity. Later she recalled that among her own searches for excitement she had been the second woman in England to fly, going up in a biplane with dual controls with Thomas Sopwith, and getting her now-familiar face—but to her relief, not her name—in an issue of *The Aeroplane*. Shaw's characters were often real-life composites, and she may have contributed to the personality of Shaw's daring aviatrix in his farce *Misalliance* (1910), who flies tandem with a male companion, and turns men into helpless worshipers. In 1911, while Scott was contending with Antarctic extremes that Kathleen could hardly imagine, she went to the opening night of Shaw's next comedy, the feminist *Fanny's First Play,* after which she chatted happily with G.B.S., who was "awfully hilarious."

Such diary notes were now stockpiled for Robert, to share with him when he was home again, and she planned a voyage to New Zealand to be in the greeting party as he arrived in glory. But Scott, who reached the Pole in January 1912, perished with the team struggling back after the final push. Even making it had been less than a triumph. Arriving at ninety degrees south, they had discovered that Roald Amundsen, the Norwegian explorer, had beaten them by a month and left the evidence. It was almost as if Scott's party would be dying twice.

For Kathleen it was not the way she wanted to become a titled Lady, but she was authorized to use the style that would have been her own, had her husband been knighted on a triumphant return. The wrong kind of fame would continue to come her way. A public subscription for victims' families raised almost £75,000 (a substantial sum in pre-inflationary years), headed by donations from the king and queen. Since such grants were made in order of rank rather than need, Kathleen in 1913 received £8,500. The widow of a petty officer with a naval pension of £48 a year for herself and three children was awarded £1,250.

News of the deaths at the South Pole reached London on 11 January 1913. Kathleen, at sea somewhere between California and Tahiti, only learned of it a month later, as her ship had been too remote from the nearest, still-primitive, radio signals. The three bodies in Scott's tent, Robert included, had been found on 12 November 1912, long after they were presumed dead, and a fourth, located nearby soon after, was that of ailing Captain Laurence Oates, who had left their shelter in a blizzard to die alone, remarking, memorably, "I am just going outside and may be some time."[8]

London intimates vied to comfort her, although, according to Shaw, she "never played the grief stricken lonely widow."[9] Kathleen had long since adjusted to the inevitable, but that was difficult for most friends to accept. Spending an evening with Shaw's Adelphi Terrace neighbor, Scottish playwright James Barrie, also a friend of "Con," on 6 October 1913, she was advised, animatedly, to appear unmournful, although he could not falsify his feelings. "Shaw has just bought a motor-bicycle. He is so happy and excited. My dear, I wish you could tell me something I could buy that would make me happy and excited for one minute." As Kathleen knew, Barrie's comedies masked his own deep melancholy, and she noted in her diary, "Poor wee soul! I wish I could." She was not feeling sorry for herself.

Sculpting commissions—including an inevitable Scott memorial—increased with her widow's visibility, but when war came the next year she sought appropriate work. At an electrical apparatus bench in the Vickers armament works at Erith, east of Woolwich, she felt more fulfilled, but it was a long commute from Peter and their home at 174 Buckingham Palace Road. It also seemed inappropriate for a Lady, especially one who was taken dancing at the Savoy by the Prime Minister, H. H. Asquith, who doted on her.

Midway into the war Lady Scott was persuaded to take a job with the Ministry of Pensions. She became private secretary to the Permanent Secretary, Sir Matthew Nathan, for whom she was working when, at Christmas 1916, she and Peter visited Apsley Cherry-Garrard for the holidays. Then thirty and still a bachelor, and invalided out of the war for Antarctic-related ailments, "Cherry" had survived the "Terra Nova" expedition, not having been among the four that died short of rescue. Shaw's country neighbor at Lamer Park in Hertfordshire, Cherry-Garrard had lived at the idyllic Garrard estate since he was six, when his father inherited it and accordingly hyphenated his name. Sturdy and athletic, and as always without makeup, Kathleen was a striking figure—although perhaps not to the thick-spectacled and brooding "Cherry," who blamed himself rather than circumstances for not having returned with supplies for Scott in time.

Her visits exacerbated his sense of guilt, yet also relieved it. And although Kathleen and Peter took the train in the direction of Lamer at least one weekend in the month to bask in Cherry's devoted hospitality, he was either too overawed to be physically attracted or his sickly conscience got in the way. She coolly found him "a young thing."[10]

Cherry-Garrard invited the Shaws to join them for Christmas Eve, and Kathleen noted in her diary, "Shaw was enchanting; told me I had the blue eye of genius, what he called the Strindberg eye." ("He always flatters me a good deal," she confessed.) On Christmas Day 1916, she and Peter (whom Kathleen dressed for the occasion as a miniature Father Christmas) took several books as gifts to the Shaws at nearby Ayot St. Lawrence, less than a mile down the lane. G.B.S. asked them to stay (with Peter as the excuse) so that he could read to them "what he called a children's story, [although] it was a hyper adult story." It imagined an encounter between the Kaiser and a waiflike girl somehow exposed at night on a Flanders battlefield. Shaw had written it for a gift book in aid of a Belgian children's charity, the *Vestiaire Marie-José*. When he had delivered it some months earlier, the charity had bypassed its own book for ready money, selling it instead, for £400, to the *New York Herald Tribune*. The fantasy had already appeared on the front page of the *Tribune*'s Sunday magazine on 22 October 1916, illustrated (above a sentimental caption) by Boardman Robinson.

Kathleen was still fixated on death and sacrifice, as were the many who mourned loved ones lost in the continuing carnage of the war. It may have seemed to her as if Shaw, anticipating Joan of Arc's death, had suggested what the Maid of Orleans was like when she was a girl. Simple yet shrewd, and irreverent toward authority figures, the child is the Kaiser's intellectual match in their brief exchange, and the blustering Wilhelm II is seen as the helpless pawn of his position. As they debate amid the shellfire, a round explodes nearby, obliterating the child but leaving her disembodied voice, in which fashion she reappears to him as if in a waking dream. Although the bewildered and bespattered monarch remains alive, he is now alone. The child has been "set free by the shell" from the pain and privation of existence much in the manner the lively Joan of the epilogue of Shaw's play to come (in 1923) is freed from the body by her burning.[11]

Sixty, but younger in heart when it came to attractive women, even when he thought of them only as the daughters he never had, G.B.S. was exhilarated by reading the story to Kathleen and her fatherless little son. He would see much more of her through the war years and later. When she learned that he was going to Flanders by army invitation in January and February 1917, which he would write up as "Joy-Riding at the Front," she used her connections to get him a follow-up invitation to visit the Austro-Italian lines. He knew it would disappoint her, but he responded to General Charles Delme-Radcliffe of the British Military Mission that although the Trentino in the spring was a pleasant thought, he would be of no propaganda use there. Few Englishmen were involved in the fighting, and the public considered the war in Italy a sideshow to the main stage.[12]

Kathleen would be among the select few in his Adelphi Terrace flat late in the afternoon of 8 June 1917, when he read the opening scenes of his newest play, *Heartbreak House*, taking all the roles himself. "Very, very funny," she noted in her diary about the first act. Halfway through came tea, and the remainder of the play followed, but while others stayed to the end, Lady Scott had to return to her office at the Ministry of Pensions to work late.

The next day Shaw traveled to Lamer with her, and after Peter had gone to bed that evening, G.B.S. read to her and to Cherry parts of what she had missed. She was baffled by it, its dreamlike elements escaping her: "All the people develop as you least expect." On Sunday she and Peter lunched at the Shaws', and afterward, as she dozed intermittently in the sunlit garden, G.B.S. completed his reading, more for himself, it seemed, than for her. According to one of her diary entries in May 1917, after lunch at Ayot, G.B.S. walked back with her to Lamer, "and we discussed the propagation of the race." The new play he was planning, the *Back to Methuselah* cycle, would deal in part with longevity and futuristic evolution, and he was apparently trying out ideas with her.

He would see a lot of Kathleen. Both in London and in Ayot St. Lawrence he had his work, and nearby in both places (as she often frequented Lamer Park) there was almost always Lady Scott on weekends. She had emerged as a trusted figure in whom he could confide those things he was reluctant to tell Charlotte. Once, encountering Kathleen and Peter on the train, he "descended from first class to third class to play with us." At Lamer he would turn up for tea, and remain for the evening, telling bedtime stories for Kathleen's son, which he would invent on the spot. Ever since he was very little, Shaw explained to Peter, he always told himself a story each night before he went to sleep, some of them continuing as serials over several nights. He repeated his favorite stories, Shaw confessed, over and over again.

One evening that November, after Peter went off contentedly to bed, the Shaws and Kathleen had dinner with Cherry, at which G.B.S. confessed for reasons unknown that he had never learned to dance. Kathleen offered to give him a lesson, and he glided across the floor with her to music from Cherry's phonograph, pleased with himself. Following another dinner at Lamer, with the artist pair Charles Ricketts and Charles Shannon, she urged Shaw to demonstrate his new dancing skills. Again in December at Lamer they danced, and she "gave Shaw a lesson, both practical and demonstrative." While Charlotte watched placidly (she bridled at his attentions to other women, yet never to Lady Scott), Shaw happily went through his paces with Kathleen. "To begin to learn to dance at sixty-one is rather delicious," she had written in her diary two weeks earlier. "I love old Shaw." He wrote to a friend, Henry Salt, "I was found to possess a senile and lumbering diable au corps which made my King David-like gambols amusing to myself and not so utterly unbearable for my unfortunate partner as might have been expected." Given the biblical David's lusty reputation, Shaw may have intimated more than daughterly feelings when in Kathleen's arms.

Late in December 1917, Kathleen became a war casualty, falling ill from overwork. She had often worked at the Ministry far into the evenings, and loathed the dull job, considering it "very little different from a grave." On 8 January 1918, Shaw visited and sat for hours at her bedside, returning two days later, after which she was able to pen a diary note, "Still in bed, fainting a good deal. Bernard Shaw came, and we discussed dreams, deliriums, and happiness." He often told her his dreams, never revealing them to Charlotte.

Shaw often visited, alone, at Buckingham Palace Road, dining with Kathleen and reading scenes from his overly talky new play about characters based on her friend Asquith and his Downing Street successor, David Lloyd George. "Ll.G. the bouncing rhetorical fraud, and Asquith, the bland, benign old gentleman—very funny, but not quite right," she observed loyally about the ousted Asquith. When she next went to Lamer, this time without Peter, Shaw was again there because he expected her. If the weather proved mild, some of Cherry's overnight guests slept outdoors, and Kathleen uninhibitedly danced barefoot in her nightgown.

Shaw "amazed me," she wrote (29 June 1918). "I have known him for fifteen years, and this was the first time I knew he sang. He went almost through the score of Rheingold on the piano, singing in a charming baritone voice. He plays amazingly well. He is a marvellous man." Alone with her, he often reminisced about his past indiscretions—his affair with actress Florence Farr, whom Kathleen met only after her looks had faded; children's writer Edith Nesbit's failed passes at him; his own frustrations in trying to seduce "Mrs. Pat" Campbell, his Eliza in *Pygmalion.*

What Shaw did not tell Kathleen—if he knew himself—is that he may have put aspects of her into a character in the next futuristic playlet, after the Asquith–Lloyd George segment, in his *Methuselah* cycle, "The Thing Happens." It includes a female Domestic Minister, perhaps a promotion from Kathleen's job at the Ministry of Pensions, who wears a tunic and dresses *"not markedly different from . . . the men."* Mrs. Lutestring, who, from experience, discusses, among other matters, "Old Age Pensions," is *"a handsome woman, apparently in the prime of life, with [an] elegant, tense, well held-up figure, and the walk of a goddess."* Among men she inspires *"instinctive awe."* Although never an artist, her late husband was "a great painter." Only the smallest of hints, perhaps, but the stately Cabinet Minister may be a Shavian bow to Lady Scott.

For July and August 1918, Kathleen rented Streatley Vicarage in Berkshire, up the Thames from London, using it also as a studio. Shaw agreed to visit and pose for her while she did a statuette—if he did not have to dress "respectably." And while Charlotte went off to visit her sister in Ireland, Shaw paid visits to Kathleen and Peter. His first full day at the Vicarage was 26 July, his sixty-second birthday. As he had been about to leave Ayot, a telegram had arrived for him as "next of kin." In the war years one dreaded a messenger at the door. Robert Loraine, who had played John Tanner in the American run of *Man and Superman,* and now was a major in the Royal Flying Corps, had been shot down.[13] To Shaw, who had visited Loraine on the Flanders front, he was a surrogate son, and Loraine had duly listed the Shaws as next of kin. It was not the first such telegram. Loraine had been wounded before, and Shaw returned a hasty note hoping that "it is a cushy one this time."

Brooding over the news, and cold and wet from a soaking rain, he arrived unhappily at Lady Scott's. Shaw was cross, and she was shy and dull, Kathleen told her diary. "I am not good at sustained efforts of niceness." Besides, the food was "bad," and the prospects for improvement, given wartime rationing, were "hopeless." Still, G.B.S. remained for ten days, swimming in the Thames when the sun shone, sitting for a statuette when it did not. And he wondered to her whether an artist's own gender and character revealed itself in the work, guessing that in her androgynous case it did not. Although husbandless since 1912, Kathleen was uncon-

Fig. 1. Statuette of Shaw (1918), one of eight casts, 20 1/2 inches high, for the Fine Arts Society. Only two bronzes were cast in Kathleen's lifetime.

Fig. 2. Kathleen in her studio-gallery, 1933. From left to right, the sculptures are of Adam Lindsay Gordon (for Westminster Abbey), William of Wykeham (Winchester Chapel), David Lloyd George (National War Museum), and Bernard Shaw (Bournemouth Municipal Gallery).

cerned about having Shaw on the premises, however her rather remote neighbors might talk. Their relationship was as much father-daughter as that with Loraine was father-son. She could be just as irreverent as an emancipated daughter, too, as she noted in her diary on Sunday, 4 August, when the grave and sober Frederick Watson, a leader in crippled children's causes, whom she knew from the Ministry of Pensions, came to visit for the afternoon.

Watson found himself greeted by the overpowering Shaw, who "at once took up the duties of a host, and behaved through the day in a manner reminiscent of Queen Victoria and the annual Wesleyan Conference." While Watson seemed "extremely promising in occasional asides," he was "instantly submerged and rejected by the reminiscences instantly inflamed in the mind of Shaw." Even at dinner, when Watson hovered "on the point of a joke," the vegetarian Shaw "set up a strident noise for cheese," and poor Watson's moment passed, "never to return."

At Streatley, Shaw received word that Loraine's wound had shattered his knee and that he would be evacuated to an English hospital, possibly for amputation. Preparing a telegram for Shaw to Loraine, Lady Scott quoted Shaw as advising, "Oh, tell him to be sure not to take any leg they recommend at Roehampton." He was attempting, with whatever humor was possible under the circumstances, to prepare Loraine for the most extreme solution. (Loraine preferred keeping his stiffened and unusable leg.)

From Streatley, Shaw was to travel further, by bus and rail, to visit Beatrice and Sidney Webb in Wales. Since that meant lunching en route, Kathleen asked her cook to pack cucumber sandwiches for Shaw. When he unwrapped the first one he discovered that the thoughtful cook had enhanced the dreary vegetarian repast with potted meat. G.B.S. threw them away and hungered all the way to Wales. He was in Ireland with Charlotte when Kathleen went to the pre-opening private view of the International Art Show in London, where her already completed bronze statuette of Shaw, standing, with arms folded across his chest, appeared to her "alone on the central table of the principal room, looking very small." After seeing it, Shaw would call it "a masterpiece."

To G.B.S., Kathleen could do no wrong—unless it was her marrying Scott. (Shaw forgave her even that because the union produced Peter.) To her second husband, who was not amused, Shaw confided indiscreetly that Kathleen should have only been "secondarily famous as the wife of the world renowned wonderful Scott." Her authentic achievement was in art. "Now Scott was not wonderful: there was nothing wonderful nor uncommon about him; and he was so unsuited to the job he insisted on undertaking that he ended as the most incompetent failure in the history of exploration. Kathleen, on the other hand, was a wonderful woman, first rate at her job, adventurously ready to go to the ends of the earth at half an hour's notice with no luggage but a comb with three teeth left in it, and always successful. Scott's best right to his celebrity is that he induced her to marry him."

Although in part Shaw was indulging in his love of paradox, Kathleen would have remained far less friendly had she known of Shaw's private disloyalty to Scott, and how Cherry, with Shavian assistance, was treating her hero in the memoir he had begun early in 1917 as *Never Again: Scott, Some Penguins, and the Pole.* Cherry had been invited by the Captain Scott Antarctic Fund to write the official history of the doomed second Scott expedition. The Shaws lunched with Cherry-Garrard nearly every Sunday they were in the country, and on one crucial Sabbath he revealed the offer. But he was no explorer, he said dismissively: he had only been the young naturalist of the expedition, who as a boy had "a taste for snails and solitude." G.B.S. and Charlotte urged him to undertake it, although he had never written for publication. He felt daunted by the prospect, but Shaw offered editing help, and Charlotte even promised to correct his proofs.

Kathleen was delighted. In the circumstances, she felt, loyally, how could the result be anything but a hagiographic masterwork? But Shaw saw the project as more than a saint's life. First he set down for Cherry a half-page rules of punctuation, Shavian style, that emphasized the colon and semicolon. Then Shaw criticized the text, Cherry noted, "as it was written, word by word and chapter by chapter." As self-appointed editor, he asked questions to establish clarity, as in "What is pack?" Some of the questions, as this one, became rhetorical devices, as it introduced an explanation of pack ice. Beyond the pathetic end for Scott, Shaw also saw a drama in the race to the Pole—two protagonists on the Antarctic stage.

Cherry, Shaw recalled at the start, "still retained his boyish notions of Scott and his expedition. . . . One day, in his library, I asked him if there was any extant account of Amundsen's venture." Roald Amundsen, the Norwegian adventurer who had reached the Pole a month before Scott (as Scott discovered to his consternation), on 14 December 1911, had published a book about the enterprise, *The South Pole,* in 1912. Cherry took down the book, which Shaw guessed had not been opened. "I read it and found he was an explorer of genius, who had got to the Pole and back without losing a single man, having found a new route . . . by two inspired guesses and taking two big chances, and knowing exactly how to treat his men. Everything he did was original and right: Scott did what was done last time; and everything he did was wrong." Thus Cherry writes, undoubtedly with Shaw's hand guiding him, of Amundsen's "sort of sagacity that constitutes the specific genius of the explorer," and that his expedition "was more highly endowed in personal qualities than ours."

During the three years when Cherry was writing, and the Shaws assisting—he was a wealthy country gentleman and had no working dead-lines—he began to realize that harrowing deaths during "Scott's folly," however heroic, had their ambiguous dimension. Overextending his re-sources, "Scott had nothing to gain and a good deal to lose by taking an extra man to the Pole." Cherry had access to several of the journals of the men, and, unnervingly, had discovered the mottled, frozen corpses of his dead companions in their tent in 1912 as rescue arrived too late. Whatever their physical and moral resilience, they had failed in their quest for the Pole and return. The elements had won. The buck stops with the expedi-tion's leader, and his handling of the logistic details, and Cherry was tor-mented by having to bear witness to that, and to his pervasive gloom about not having returned in time, with supplies, to Scott's frozen and snow-swept tent. Cherry quoted Scott from the journal he left behind, "We took risks, we knew we took them; things have come out against us, and there-fore we have no cause for complaint." Although Cherry added, "No better epitaph has been written," with an uneasy conscience he withdrew from his commitment to the Fund, and opted to publish independently.

G.B.S. had been drafting and rewriting passages for Cherry, and both Shaws, as Cherry wrote, made marginal comments and textual emenda-tions. (The plethora of full colons is also likely to have been Shaw's hand, as well as the discussion, recalling *Man and Superman,* of exploration as "the physical expression of the Intellectual Passion.") Shaw even arranged with his own printer, R. & R. Clark in Edinburgh, and his longtime pub-lisher, Constable, for publication, and the proofs of the book, under its original title, were delivered on 9 April 1920. But Cherry was morbidly displeased with the seeming facetiousness of his "Penguins" allusion, al-though a central portion of the narrative dealt with his trekking to Cape Crozier in the minus-75-degree temperatures over five terrible winter weeks in 1911 with two companions to collect the substantial eggs of em-peror penguins from their rookery for desperately needed food. It was, he concluded, "the worst journey in the world." It would have taken a saw to open his frozen outer clothes. "There's your title," said Shaw.

As the book moved closer to publication, G.B.S. deflected Cherry's re-quest that his considerable assistance be acknowledged. "It would be fatal," he advised on 26 April 1922, "to make any suggestion of collabora-tion on my part. The book would be reviewed on the assumption that I had written all the striking parts of it, and that they were 'not serious.' As my experience on the ice dates from the great frost of 1878 (or there-abouts) when I skated [in London] on the Serpentine, my intrusion into the Arctic Circle would be extraordinarily ridiculous. Besides, the sugges-tion would be misleading. Beyond proofreading work, and paraphrasing your conversation here and there," he downplayed, "I have done nothing that is not covered by your device of quoting the practical man. You should not be at all uneasy as to the integrity of your authorship." Cherry would confess about the Shaws, "They taught me to write," and among the well-chosen epigraphs to chapters of the book he included one from *Man and Superman,* in which Don Juan in the interlude in Hell declares that men can be driven by ideas—"I tell you, . . . if you can show a man a piece of what he now calls God's work to do, and what he will later call by many new names, you can make him entirely reckless of the consequences to himself personally."

That concept as it applied to Scott should have appealed to Kathleen, but since Shaw realized, too, how she would react to other implications in the book, he had, accordingly, another and unconfessed reason to keep his distance. For when he (and Charlotte) began helping T. E. Lawrence, later that year, to turn his heat-drenched masterpiece about Arabia in 1917–18, *Seven Pillars of Wisdom,* into a publishable book, he permitted a wry but open acknowledgment. It was remarkable that in the same decade G.B.S. should have an editorial hand in perhaps the two greatest memoirs of adventure in English in the twentieth century, both at the climatic extremes—one set in ice, the other in sand.

Adventurers always intrigued Kathleen, and she would become friendly, too, with T. E. Lawrence, and sculpt him as well. When back in England, having reduced himself from lieutenant colonel to private, and concealed himself luridly in his own limelight by changing his name to *Shaw,* he would pop in and out of friends' homes (like the Shaws) within motorcycling range. Once, on a Sunday in July 1926, Kathleen was in her bath when her maid tapped and announced that Mr. Shaw was there. "Mr. Bernard Shaw, all right," she said. When her maid said no, Kathleen shouted through the door to ask the visitor what his business was. The maid went off, then returned with word that the stranger would not tell his business. "Probably a beggar," Kathleen dismissed.

"I don't think so," said the maid. "He was in Air Force uniform."

"Colonel Lawrence! Dash after him!"

Off flew the maid to retrieve "Shaw." Brought back, he explained that he could not imagine what to say his business was, for "obviously" he had none. He was only an unskilled mechanic in the ranks, and was only dropping by.[14]

A few days later she had lunch with the other Shaw, and mentioned the unexpected visit and surprise name. She had not known that Lawrence had become *Shaw.* The talk turned to *Seven Pillars of Wisdom* and G.B.S.'s role in it. Other than confessing that he recommended that a chapter be cut, Shaw said evasively, he had little share in it. But Kathleen confided to her diary that Lawrence had told her that "there was scarce a paragraph that G.B.S. had not amended." She had no idea what Shaw's part had been in Cherry's book either, which among other things had included writing at least some of the lines that praised Amundsen at Scott's expense. (G.B.S.'s later role was a jacket blurb for the Chatto & Windus reprint that hinted only slightly at that. Compared with Scott's "extraordinary and appalling" expedition," Shaw wrote, "Amundsen's victorious rush to the South Pole seems as cheerful as a trip to Margate. Even Dante's exploration of the icebound seventh circle of hell shews that men cannot imagine the worst that they can suffer." In a way, that toned down for Kathleen the criticism in the book itself.)

Kathleen's first postwar years included hectic travel that the war had precluded, in part to escape her past, in part to escape a new and intent admirer. In 1919 she recorded a March weekend at Lamer Park with the Shaws, their Irish playwright friend Lady Gregory, and Norwegian Arctic explorer and war relief activist Fridtjof Nansen. A hero at the new League of Nations, Nansen, in his late fifties, was, to Kathleen, "simple, frank, humble, childish, and altogether adorable"—and almost instantly in love with her. He would follow her around the world had she let him. But she wanted to remarry, and noted in her diary from Cherbourg, after travels across both Americas, "Lord will I ever find a man I altogether like—who do I want? No one will do. Maybe I am utterly and completely spoilt."

Another aspirant, however, had emerged from her surfeit of adventurers and heroes. In November 1922 she had Shaw and H. G. Wells to lunch, when they learned about her betrothal by accident. Kathleen had Shaw promise to read his new and yet-unproduced *Saint Joan* to her, and she asked him "if he was never coming to an end." He confessed, "I thought I must have dried up after producing *Methuselah,* but to my astonishment I found the sap rising again." The discussion turned to her show of recent work at the Grosvenor Gallery, to which Wells had taken Shaw, and he was "awfully impressed," Kathleen noted, by her nudes, especially one she had titled, obscurely, *I Want.* Since she sculpted from life, he wondered about its origin. "Bill did it," she said.

Shaw looked puzzled. "Bill" was Edward Hilton Young, the Liberal M.P. and lawyer she married the following March. But the statuette had two arms. In 1918 Hilton Young, then a naval officer, had lost his right arm in Belgium during the siege of Zeebrugge, and Kathleen had restored it in her bronze. She had felt immensely sorry for Hilton, and as her feelings for him intensified Shaw tried to console her as he had done, wryly and unsuccessfully, with Robert Loraine. "I said," he recalled, his propensity for paradox again unsuccessful, "that as a man with two arms is not unhappy because he has not three, neither is he unhappy if, having one, he hasn't two, and she flew out at me so furiously that I discreetly shut up."

Kathleen was well past forty-four when she and Hilton were married in the crypt of the House of Commons by an Anglican bishop; he was younger by nearly a year. It was an opportune time for Shaw (23 March

1923) to caution her as gently as he could about Cherry's just-published deflation of Scott, which Shaw had abetted but described to her as "a classic story of travel." Kathleen had the two-volume boxed set sent by Cherry, inscribed "with very grateful thanks," and had already begun to pen "Rots!" in the margins. If she were able to bear "to treat the expedition judicially . . . by a man who was only 23 when it occurred," Shaw wrote, too late, she would put aside "every impression that has been made on you by selected scraps" in the press. He was "more or less a witness" to Cherry's writing the book, was all he admitted to. But he also suggested that she not visit Ayot as Cherry might be there; and he confessed that he had recommended to Cherry "that international courtesy and sportsmanship made it advisable to be scrupulously just and polite to Amundsen. I suspect this was the hardest pill he had to swallow; for the moment he went into the question he had to admit Amundsen was no scallywag, but a very good explorer." Then Cherry "was forced to contrast Amundsen's triumph with Con's tragedy."

Shaw wrote two long, delicate letters to Kathleen about Scott and *The Worst Journey in the World,* attempting to make the distinction between hagiography, a word he left unsaid, and history. "Keep this," he began one letter defensively, "for a quiet hour: it is about Cherry and old times and sorrows." The facts would come out by some means or other, and as in "Cherry's narrative" Scott would be proved "reckless in travelling without sufficient margins in provisions and fuel; and he had accepted the official scientific formula for rationing, which was of course all wrong, and produced a starvation which was disguised until it was too late." The book, he explained, gently but unpersuasively, in his second letter, was not "an act of personal disloyalty to Con."

Loyally, Hilton was even more outraged than Kathleen, seeing on Cherry's part "a grievance against his leader, whom he believed to have neglected his, C.G.'s, merits, on the expedition." Although he saw Shaw's (and Cherry-Garrard's) undiplomatic assessment of Scott as irresponsible, it has stood up.

Shaw "seems unconsciously determined to make me angry and resentful against Cherry," Kathleen wrote in her diary, "a thing I do not want to be at all. I have never admired Cherry but I am fond of him and don't want to have to cease to be . . . [but] his rendering of Con's character is so ludicrous it should not even make one cross, only Shaw seems determined I should be cross!"

Scott had become a national icon for stoic endurance in terrible adversity, a quality glorified by a world war. Cherry (and Shaw) had tarnished the shining moment. Yet she waited until early 1927 before she went to the publishers of *Worst Journey* to urge "that some effort be made to prevent a passage in Cherry-Garrard's book"—the use of his full, hyphenated surname suggested her hostility—"from gaining credence." The words about Scott she wanted expunged ("this silly opposite of the truth") were "weak and peevish." They might have been Shaw's.

Kathleen's friendship with Shaw survived *The Worst Journey in the World* because she never knew the extent of Shaw's hand in it. Cherry-Garrard would see little of her afterward, but he was gradually withdrawing into chronic, debilitating depression. "My own bolt is shot," he wrote near the close of his book; "I do not suppose I shall ever go south again before I go west." He had not been able to save Scott's marooned team. The memoir had attempted to explain why, but it could not purge him of his demons. One of the few people he was willing to see over the full course of his forty-six post-polar years was Shaw.

In August 1923, at forty-five, after four days of difficult labor, Kathleen gave birth to her second son, Wayland. The late, risky pregnancy had not kept her from working. On Armistice Day, a cold, sunny morning, her war memorial, a larger-than-life brooding soldier, was unveiled at Huntingdon. Shaw remained in her life, now given over substantially to her husband's career in the Commons. "I was awfully pleased to see him," she wrote of Shaw on 11 March 1924. "He sat holding forth on life, politics, and the drama, with our babe comfortably tucked up on his arm. There's summut [Scots for *something*] in a white-haired old man with a little baby that stirs all my heart."

In 1926, Hilton Young switched allegiance to the Conservatives, and politics became more intrusive in Kathleen's life. It was hard to be a sculptor, she wrote, when "there are . . . political parties in the world." People were beginning to forget exactly who her first husband was, other than that he was somehow connected with polar exploration. At a political dinner party in the Commons, a guest greeted her with, "I knew your dear husband [Ernest] Shackleton." (At Charles Shannon's house, a servant once asked him, as he ushered G.B.S. out, "Excuse me, sir, is that the gentleman who wrote Shakespeare?")[15] Despite her remarriage, she could not escape Scott's shade, even when it was misidentified.

With Hilton's change of party, he was now seeking a seat from the Sevenoaks division, and early in 1928 Kathleen made speeches for him while he was on political business in East Africa. She served her "lord god" by hosting dinner parties, made time for overseeing her sons, now nineteen and six, and worked on a statue commission of a former secretary of state for India, Edwin Montagu, for Calcutta. At one party, she recalled, Mrs. Stanley Baldwin, wife of the Tory prime minister, "looked down her nose at Bernard Shaw, and didn't get hold of him at all." Shaw often came to lunch, "which is fun," and on one occasion when she had the stellar Portuguese cellist Guilhermina Suggia also as guest, the one-time music critic (as "G.B.S.") "chid Suggia teasingly for having such a cumbrous instru-

ment as a cello. Why not a nice little fiddle?" It reminded Shaw of the
elderly removals laborer who, while weighed down by a grandfather's
clock he was carrying, was stopped and asked, "Excuse me, but at your
age, wouldn't you find a wristwatch more convenient?"

Shaw was again at Buckingham Palace Road in April 1929 to lunch with
American banker Otto Kahn and several English politicians. Kathleen and
Hilton "had a bet" as to whether Shaw or Austen Chamberlain would "talk
the other down." To their surprise, Kahn "beat them both, and Shaw came
in a poor third." On one occasion the millionaire playwright boasted to a
party of economists and financiers that he was a communist, a paradox
that Kathleen found "unconvincing." At another, in 1932—he was often a
raisin in her social cake—he brought her his newest book, the *Candide*-like
The Adventures of the Black Girl in Search of God, and "got on like a house on
fire" with fashionable conductor Malcolm Sargent. Afterward she walked
across Green Park with Shaw "at an immense rate." She was amazed at his
stamina. "He is a grand old man. . . . May I be like him when I am seventy-
five." Kathleen would have been peeved had she known that in Cherry-
Garrard's gift copy of *The Black Girl* G.B.S. would write,

> For Cherry and Angela
> Greatest of my friends.[16]

Only once in her own later years did Kathleen run into Cherry. Although she had put him out of her life, she had been telling people—
ignoring the neighborly connection—that it was she who had introduced
him to G.B.S. Cherry and Angela (he had married belatedly in 1938) were
having tea at a London hotel, a rare occasion for a chronic depressive,
when Kathleen entered with her husband and a son. "Now, Cherry," she
admonished on spotting him, "don't pretend you don't know me!" Cherry
stood up politely, looked at the boy and said, "This must be Wayland."
"It's Peter," she crowed.

Also in 1938, when Shaw was eighty-two, she had Shaw sit for a head-
and-shoulders sculpture. She was sixty, and in dark slacks and Nehru-like
blouse she looked youthful. Watching her results, Shaw, who materialized
under her fingers with his head in his hands, framing his face, deplored
it facetiously as "a Shakespearean tomb." It did look remarkably like the
iconic portrait of the Bard. For it (and her) Shaw wrote a rhyming commentary, on green paper, beginning, "Weep not for old George Bernard:
he is dead"—a copy of which he sent to Lord Alfred Douglas, once Wilde's
young friend and a minor poet. Kathleen, he wrote, rejected his "epitaph"
(jokingly intended as inscription for a pedestal) as "nonsense verse"—
which might have been too kind. He had once written of his likeness in
marble by Auguste Rodin that he—G.B.S.—would be remembered mainly

as "subject of a bust by Rodin: otherwise unknown." Now he closed by versifying that "Kathleen plied" at his head

> Until one day the Lord said "No, my lass:
> Copy no more. Your spirit shall be your guide."
> Carve him *sub specie aeternitas*
> 'So, when his works shall all forgotten be
> He yet shall share your immortality.'[17]

At the Royal Academy exhibition in the spring of 1940, while the *Luftwaffe* rained incendiary bombs on London, she exhibited in bronze what she called "a half-figure, almost," pleased with the outcome. Under wartime restrictions, people got around far less, and Shaw saw little of Kathleen then and nothing of Peter, who commanded a destroyer. Shaw lived largely in the country, as Charlotte was very ill, and the bombings made matters worse for her. Kathleen, too, lived more at Leinster Corner, the country place she and Hilton had acquired.

Returning painfully to London to be close to her doctors, Charlotte died on 13 September 1943 at eighty-six. At the end of October, after her private funeral and cremation, Shaw remained to help sort out her effects at Whitehall Court, and on 30 October Kathleen wrote, still maintaining her diary, that Shaw, eighty-seven, came to tea, traveling alone by tube. "He was more amazing than ever, and better company. He told us all about Charlotte's illness and death." Charlotte, G.B.S. told Kathleen and Hilton—he was now Lord Kennet of the Dene, and she was Lady Kennet—had illusions that the service flat in which the elderly Shaws had lived since the mid-1920s was full of people who did not belong there. "You must get up the housekeeper and the manager," Charlotte appealed. "We pay for the flat and it is very expensive: we have a right to have it to ourselves." Shaw explained the phenomenon to her imaginatively as her clairvoyance—"all these people existed but they were in Australia or Oxford or anywhere," and the manager would not be able to see them.

Three years later, after Shaw had a fall, Kathleen went to see him, finding him sitting up in a dressing gown and "looking really very frail. . . . Oh dear he is the oddest maddest mixture. He told me yet again how [since Charlotte's death] many women wanted to marry him, knowing that they would only have to look after him for a year or two and then have his fortune." It was 14 October 1946. "He is ninety, but his mind and gestures are as active as ever and his memory for what we had said and done thirty years ago quite prodigious, and putting me to shame." Feeling his mortality, at his suggestion they talked of possible Shavian memorials, including her bust. "I tried to go lots of times, lest he should get tired, but he wouldn't let me. He was a little sentimental, finally. Waning is a sad, sad thing."

Kathleen said nothing about herself, but she was waning more seriously, stricken by painful angina. Soon after Christmas she was bedridden. A few months into 1947, she went into St. Mary's Hospital, Paddington, realizing that it was the end. When she died on 24 July 1947, a year short of seventy, it was two days before Shaw would reach ninety-one. He wrote to Peter, now an eminent ornithologist, "The news from Leinster Corner reached me on my birthday, and for a moment struck it all of a heap. But I cannot feel otherwise than gladly about her, nor imagine her old. She was a very special friend."

At the time, Shaw was contemplating publication of his admittedly lightweight *Rhyming Picture Guide to Ayot Saint Lawrence*. He could not imagine a year without producing something between hard covers. Its origin, years before, had been picture-postcard doggerel verses for Ellen Terry. The last contribution to it was a photograph he had taken of Kathleen at Ayot. Accompanying it were his unmemorable yet deeply felt lines,

> Widow of Scott, whose statue [I] cherished
> She wrought when at the Pole he perished;
> A later union of two hearts
> Was with a man of many parts.
> She wedded him, and then was seen
> As Lady Kennet of the Dene.
> Lest she should have her looks undrawn
> I photographed her on my lawn;
> And me she modelled at her Dene house
> As I was sitting in its greenhouse.[18]

It was the last book on which Shaw worked, published in December 1950, six weeks after his own death.

Notes

1. Kathleen recalled the remark in her diary entry for 19 September 1929. All her diary entries following, unless otherwise cited, are from her *Self-Portrait of an Artist*, ed. Lord Kennet (London: John Murray, 1949).

2. James Lees-Milne, *Fourteen Friends* (London: John Murray, 1996), pp. 8–16.

3. Shaw would deny the oft-repeated canard that Isadora had offered to have a child by him in order to produce the perfect child—her body matched to his brain—and that he had retorted, unkindly, "What if it turned out to have my body and your brain?"

4. Aleister Crowley, *The Confessions of Aleister Crowley*, ed. John Symonds and Kenneth Grant (London: Jonathan Cape, 1969), p. 600. The *OED* defines *algolagnia* (the spelling by Crowley in his *Confessions* is his own) as the practice of obtaining sexual pleasure from pain inflicted on oneself or another.

5. Frederic V. Grunfeld, *Rodin: A Biography* (New York: Holt, 1987), p. 425.

6. Penelope Niven, *Steichen* (New York: Clarkson N. Potter, 1997), p. 313; Louisa Young, *A Great Task of Happiness: The Life of Kathleen Scott* (London: Macmillan, 1995), pp. 29–30.

7. Young, *A Great Task of Happiness*, p. 77.

8. Shaw to Lord Kennet of the Dene, 16 August 1947, in *Collected Letters IV*, ed. Dan H. Laurence (London: Constable, 1988), p. 798. All G.B.S. letters, unless otherwise described, are from vols. II and IV of this edition.

9. Quoted in Cherry-Garrard, *The Worst Journey in the World* (London: Chatto & Windus, 1965), p. 537. Further quotations are from this edition.

10. The three-way relationship with Kathleen, Cherry, and Shaw, and how it was affected by *The Worst Journey in the World*, is drawn from Kathleen's diaries, Shaw's letters, and Sara Wheeler's *Cherry: A Life of Apsley Cherry-Garrard* (London: Jonathan Cape, 2001), pp. 203–76.

11. For additional details on Shaw's Great War story, see Stanley Weintraub, *Journey to Heartbreak* (New York: Weybright and Talley, 1971), pp. 204–5.

12. Shaw's story of the Flanders episode as a war correspondent appeared in the *Daily Chronicle* on 5, 7, and 8 March 1917, later collected, with additions, in "Joy Riding at the Front," in *What I Really Wrote About the War* (London: Constable, 1931), pp. 248–79. That Lady Scott had procured the invitation is clear from Shaw's letter to Delme-Radcliffe, 23 April 1917.

13. The Robert Loraine details also appear in *Journey to Heartbreak*. Kathleen's diary describes the Streatley visit.

14. See Stanley Weintraub, *Private Shaw and Public Shaw* (New York: G. Braziller, 1963), pp. 98–99, and Lady Scott's diary.

15. Young, *A Great Task of Happiness*, p. 225.

16. George Seaver, in the foreword to the Chatto & Windus reprint of *The Worst Journey in the World* (London, 1965), p. xxiv.

17. Shaw to Kathleen, 12 November 1938, in *Bernard Shaw and Alfred Douglas: A Correspondence*, ed. Mary Hyde (New Haven and New York: Ticknor & Fields, 1982), pp. 98–99. The bust is illustrated on page 100.

18. *Bernard Shaw's Rhyming Picture Guide to Ayot Saint Lawrence* (Luton: Leagrave, 1951), p. 31. Although dated 1951, it was released on 14 December 1950.

Karma Waltonen

SAINT JOAN: FROM RENAISSANCE WITCH TO NEW WOMAN

Many have accused Bernard Shaw of sharing the sentiments of Henry Higgins (as expressed in lines written by Alan Jay Lerner): "Why can't a woman be more like a man?" This repeated refrain in the musical version of *Pygmalion* does indeed seem to fit Shaw's mind; several critics have noted that Shaw, a crusader for women's rights, wanted to enable women to become more like men. This article will explore the problematic picture of the masculine "New Woman" by tracing Shaw's recuperation of a woman who was burned for trying to "be more like a man." Saint Joan, vilified by her contemporaries and in Shakespeare's representation of her, is presented to Shaw's audience as a paragon of rational thought. Yet it would be simplistic to argue that Shaw was praising the maid merely for her masculine qualities. Rather, we shall see that Shaw's high estimation of Joan is due to his view that she shares many qualities with him. Perhaps Lerner hit upon the right line when he had Higgins end his song with the question: "Why can't a woman be like me?"

Bernard Shaw apparently had William Shakespeare quite often on his mind. Not only does he praise Shakespeare—"He has outlasted thousands of abler thinkers, and will outlast a thousand more . . . people he has created become more real to us than our actual life" (quoted in Smith 127)—but he also expresses jealousy, or what Harold Bloom would call the anxiety of influence: "With the single exception of Homer, there is no eminent writer . . . whom I can despise so entirely as I despise Shakespear when I measure my mind against his" (quoted in Mason 47). Shaw has written several plays based on the events previously dramatized by Shakespeare. Are we to understand Shaw's "rewrites" of Shakespeare's plays as a modern man's attempts at improving the Bard's work, or as the highest compliment? After all, Shaw maintained: "the stage is still dominated by Garrick's conviction that the manager and actor must adapt Shakespear's plays to the modern stage by a process which no doubt presents itself to the adapter's mind as one of masterly amelioration, but which must necessarily be mainly one of debasement and mutilation whenever, as occasionally happens, the adapter is inferior to the author" ("Mainly About Myself" 20).

Shaw obviously felt that his adaptations were not debasements or mutilations. His treatment of Joan of Arc was perhaps even more justified in his mind, as he did not consider Shakespeare's Joan to be entirely authentic. Shaw believed that Shakespeare, "having begun by an attempt to make Joan a beautiful and romantic figure, was told by his scandalized company that English patriotism would never stand a sympathetic representation of a French conqueror of English troops, and that unless he at once introduced all the old charges against Joan of being a sorceress and a harlot, and assumed her to be guilty of all of them, his play could not be produced" (quoted in Hardin 25). While Shaw made excuses for Shakespeare's negative treatment of Joan, it is doubtful, however, that he fully considered his own reasons for rewriting her myth. That is not to say that Shaw was not prolific in his explanations or justifications—his Preface to Saint Joan is almost half as long as the text of the play. Among his other proclaimed goals, Shaw is eager to show us Joan as the embodiment of modern ideals: "she was in fact one of the first Protestant martyrs . . . one of the first apostles of Nationalism, and the first French practitioner of Napoleonic realism in warfare" ("Preface" 7).[1] As she is a woman, she also becomes one of Shaw's "unwomanly women." Shaw's modernization of Joan is indicative of his desire to change the Victorian sex-gender system, which denigrated women to a lesser status because of their sex.[2] Joan's historical contemporaries labeled her a witch, in part because she chose to break free of the sex-gender system of her time.[3] Shaw did not adhere to notions of sexual difference as dictated by the body—he was more interested in the individual, the spirit and genius that were capable of transcending the body. In Shaw's vision, Joan has at least partially fulfilled that transcendence and, like himself, has been made abject because of her superiority.

Shaw's Joan comes to us three years after her canonization in 1920. He even makes a point to include what he believes would have been her reaction to sainthood in the epilogue scene: "Woe unto me when all men praise me!" (158). Shaw's Joan is the polar opposite of Shakespeare's, whose portrait of Joan la Pucelle in I Henry VI is very different from the picture we have of the canonized saint now. She is not the brave young girl who, led by the voice of God, defeated the English in battle, only to be doubted and burned at the stake when the tide turned against her. Instead, she is little more than a side note in the battles England waged against France when Henry VI was coming to power. According to one critic, Shakespeare's play is "an exemplar of authorial chauvinism both national and sexual" (Jackson 40). France does not win battles because of its military power or strategy, but because a woman uses the powers of evil to defeat the God-fearing English. The nation of France ends up deceiving itself by placing its trust in the maid. When, however, the English forces gain ground, the audience sees Joan summoning her demons, who, in the ultimate revenge against the French, abandon her. Her deceitful nature is revealed in her final scene, when she first claims virginity and then claims to have been impregnated, although she cannot decide which father would be the most politically advantageous. Although Joan is admired for her skill as a warrior, she will never be, for Shakespeare, anything other than a woman in a soldier's dress. Through her transvestism, Joan becomes not just a French idolater, but also a sexual deviant: "Holinshed has the captive Joan charged with witchcraft at her trial, but never questions her virginity. . . . Shakespeare, then, goes out of his way to invent the most unpleasant part of his portrayal of Joan, the scene where she debases herself into a camp whore" (Hardin 30). Shaw immediately dismisses the base attributes Shakespeare endowed her with: "Nevertheless the rehabilitation of the 1456, corrupt job as it was, really did produce evidence enough to satisfy all reasonable critics that Joan was not a common termagant, not a harlot, not a witch, not a blasphemer, no more an idolater than the Pope himself, and not ill conducted in any sense apart from her soldiering, her wearing of men's clothes" ("Preface" 9–10).

Shaw is, in fact, able to produce a more historically precise portrait of Joan than Shakespeare, if modern knowledge is taken as accurate. He not only had access to Shakespeare's sources, Shakespeare's works, and numerous later renditions of Joan's stories but also the trial transcripts, which he liberally used in his text. These were not, however, the only influences on Shaw's Joan. Whatever Joan we have will always be a product of her time and her author's reaction to it.

Although the Rehabilitation cleared Joan of the charges of witchcraft, the belief in witches persisted well into Shaw's time in varying degrees. Through the benefit of anthropology, the idea of Joan as witch was revived in the 1920s. Margaret Murray had written of Joan in her 1921 *The Witch Cult in Western Europe*. She believed Joan was part of an "underlying organization" of witches (271). Her evidence shows a predisposition for belief in supernatural forces, as when she notes Joan "first heard the 'Voices' at the age of thirteen, the usual time for the Devil and the witch to make paction [a pact]" (275). Although Shaw did not choose to emphasize this lingering belief in actual witchcraft, he alludes to Murray's findings when his characters declare how prevalent Joan's supposed activities were in Domremy, her childhood home: "There is not a village girl in France against whom you could not prove such things: they all dance round haunted trees, and pray at magic wells" (120). It was precisely these village activities that led Murray to her conclusions.

The lingering belief in the witch, coupled with the legacy of Shakespeare's Joan and her infamous trial, necessitated Shaw's confrontation of Joan as witch. After all, despite Shaw's disbelief in witchcraft and his sympathy for the abject, witchcraft is what she was burned for. He uses Charles to introduce the subject when he first meets her: "Can you do any cures? Can you turn lead into gold, or anything of that sort?" (53). Although Charles seems to be asking about her potential for miracles, wise women who produced cures were often suspected of being witches. Joan's critics are quick to suspect her of being a witch. In the English camp, the Chaplain and Bishop Cauchon debate the source of the powers that result in her stunning victories. The Chaplain believes that she has the forces of darkness on her side: "that was a clear case of witchcraft and sorcery" (58). Her enemies are not united in believing her a witch, however. Cauchon prefers to believe that she is not a witch, but a heretic, which he finds to be the more dangerous crime. Warwick, the soldier, defends her from being convicted of a Catholic crime when he does not believe she stands for Catholicism: "It is the protest of the individual soul against the interference of priest or peer between the private man and his God. I should call it Protestantism if I had to find a name for it" (66). Of course, Shaw has Warwick making this argument in a time before Protestantism existed in England. These problems of definition do not alleviate the Bishop's aggressive condemnation of Joan: "Call this side of her heresy Nationalism if you will: I can find you no better name for it. I can only tell you that it is essentially anti-Catholic and anti-Christian; for the Catholic Church knows only one realm, and that is the realm of Christ's kingdom" (67).

While Joan's association with modern feminism and nationalism sparked the imagination of Shaw, he was most taken by his interpretation of her religious inclinations. He holds her up as the martyr for Protestantism even though she was ordained a Catholic saint. Joan was not only an individualist: she was passionately committed to her religious conviction. In Shaw's time, religious conviction was waning because of new discoveries in science. Darwinism, in particular, had an effect on the mind-set of Shaw's contemporaries. Darwin held that the belief in "unseen spiritual agencies" led to

> various strange superstitions and customs. Many of these are terrible to think of—such as the sacrifice of human beings to a blood-loving god; the trial of innocent persons by the ordeal of poison or fire; witchcraft, &c—yet it is well occasionally to reflect on these superstitions, for they shew us what an infinite debt of gratitude we owe to the improvement of our reason, to science, and to our

accumulated knowledge. . . . These miserable and indirect consequences of our highest faculties may be compared with the inciden-
tal and occasional mistakes of the instincts of the lower animals.
(Darwin 68–69)

Although Shaw was not a conventionally religious man, he still believed in
what he called the Life Force. His skepticism of Darwinism is notable given
his belief in "evolutionary socialism brought about by legal and democratic means" (Kermode and Hollander 31). He did believe in religious
conviction, however, as he "apparently developed this view of the dependence of heroic commitment upon religious conviction in reaction against
the biological determinism of the followers of Darwin" (Searle 100). That
is, Shaw did not believe in the social Darwinism that capitalism fed upon,
but did believe that socialism would evolve to be the dominant economic
and social form. Shaw was also equitable in his judgments concerning
those who had faith in religion and those whose faith relied on science:
"But why the men who believe in electrons should regard themselves as
less credulous than the men who believed in angels is not apparent to me"
("Preface" 41).

While Shaw celebrated devotion to the Life Force in his play, it is clear
that the Joan he constructed held a belief in God that was quite different
from his own. Shaw holds up Joan as a champion of faith, but he questions
one of the most basic assumptions of her sainthood: miracles. Joan never
performs a miracle in his play, "a fact which points up a fundamental
difference between her conception of the God she is serving and that of
her creator. God, as Shaw conceived him, is not a transcendent Being,
capable of interfering in the orderly processes of nature. . . . 'It is not an
omnipotent power that can do things without us,' Shaw remarked of the
Life Force in 1912; 'it has created us in order that we might do its work.
In fact, that is the way it does it work—through us'" (Searle 101).

Despite Shaw's less-than-miraculous explanation of many of Joan's miracles, he still must contend with the voices that lead her into battle. If the
Life Force does not interfere with "the orderly processes of nature," how
did Joan hear the voice of God? Shaw treats the subject early in the play,
when Robert confronts Joan in her first meeting with Charles:

JOAN: I hear the voices telling me what to do. They come from God.
ROBERT: They come from your imagination.
JOAN: Of course. That is how the messages of God come to us. (41)

This exchange is representative of Shaw's beliefs about how God operates
in our world. As he wrote to Lady Gregory in 1909, "To me the sole hope
of human salvation lies in teaching Man to regard himself as an experi-

ment in the realization of God, to regard his hands as God's hand, his brain as God's brain, his purpose as God's purpose" (Laurence 2, 858). If Shaw's belief is correct, then any voice in our imagination is indeed the voice of God, making it possible for his Joan to hear the voice of God without necessarily being singled out by Him for sainthood. Joan's voices, therefore, only betray her when her intellect does: "That the voices and visions were illusory, and their wisdom all Joan's own, is shewn by the occasions on which they failed her, notably during her trial, when they assured her that she would be rescued" ("Preface" 18). The voices that deceived her, however, fostered the Protestant ideas that got her into trouble: "The girls in the field praise thee; for thou hast raised their eyes; and they see that there is nothing between them and heaven" (157). Although Joan died a Catholic martyr, Shaw holds that she was condemned in part because she did not show the proper respect for the Church.

Shaw also recognizes that Joan's nationalistic tendencies were at odds with the feudal system under which she lived. Shaw admires her loyalty to her country, although he feels no such pride: "As an Irishman I could pretend to patriotism neither for the country I had abandoned nor the country that had ruined it" ("Mainly About Myself" 7). In contrast to Shakespeare, Shaw is much more sympathetic to the French than the English, and he affords himself a few opportunities to satirize English pride (which is possible only when there is the assumption that witches do not exist). For example, the English troops immediately assume Joan is a witch simply because she defeats them: "We are not fairly beaten, my lord. No Englishman is ever fairly beaten" (89). The trial scene, so judiciously written in light of the horror that resulted from it, includes a short exchange in which the English offer as evidence of diabolism Joan's voices speaking to her in French (119). Apparently, that is heresy enough to the English.

Although Shaw favored certain religious and nationalistic tendencies, his didactic purpose necessitated that he render all the players fairly. If he allowed his audience to decide that it was English pride or Papist zealots who were wrongly responsible for Joan's death, that audience would be able to distance itself from its own intolerance of difference. (In a speech on Saint Joan given in 1931, Shaw compared Joan's treatment with the reactions to Leon Trotsky and Sylvia Pankhurst, indicating to his audience that they are not above supporting the persecution of "dangerous" ideas.) Instead, he posits, "it is hardly surprising that she was judicially burnt, ostensibly for a number of capital crimes which we no longer punish as such, but essentially for what we call unwomanly and insufferable presumption" ("Preface" 7). Although Marina Warner, in her *Saint Joan: The Image of Female Heroism* (1981), shows the same judicious sympathy for Joan's accusers ("Joan was not contending with a gang of depraved and ignorant individuals, as her hagiographers have sometimes suggested.

She was trapped in a situation of extreme delicacy and complexity, which gave major reasons for struggle to all sides" [48]), Shaw's critics have up-braided him for his reluctance to clearly label the villains and heroes. He maintains, however, that "Joan's judges were as straightforward as Joan herself," and "it cannot be too clearly understood that there were no vil-lains in the tragedy of Joan's death. She was entirely innocent; but her excommunication was a genuine act of faith and piety; and her execution followed inevitably" (Shaw, quoted in Kaul 324). This straightforwardness of all the characters, along with the lack of villains, is characteristic not only of Shaw but also of his age. Following the Great War, it was increas-ingly difficult to tell the heroes from the villains. If one cannot distinguish between them, how can any argument be completely discounted? "It is also the way in which Shaw starts to pit his own ideas against each other, to surprise himself not with the soundness, but even with the imagination and generosity behind a position which he is in the process of showing to be wrong" (Kermode and Hollander 32).

It is possible to detect Shaw's egotism here as well. Joan is reminded that the God she prays to must be evenhanded: "For He has to be fair to your enemy too: don't forget that" (107). Shaw, then, is godlike in his fairness. And just as there are those who question God's fairness in battle, Shaw's gentle treatment of the inquisitors has been critiqued. I do not wish to add to the argument so generously described by Lorichs.[4] I will, however, point out the comparison between these inquisitors' methods and Shaw's. We are assured by the Inquisitor that "The Maid needs no lawyers to take her part: she will be tried by her most faithful friends, all ardently desirous to save her soul from perdition" (116). Quite clearly the Maid has already been condemned by this moment in the drama, yet the Churchmen believe themselves just in trying to save her from herself. Shaw, in his alterations of Joan's character to suit the modern age, has also already judged Joan as a modern soul and seeks to save her from those who are not as enlightened as himself.

Although Joan's nationalism, nationality, and religiosity troubled those men who sought to save and/or burn her, Shaw reminds us often of that which condemned her utterly, her "unwomanly and insufferable pre-sumption." Throughout *Saint Joan*, Joan actively denies her femininity in every way possible: "[*matter-of-fact*] I will never take a husband. A man in Toul took an action against me for breach of promise; but I never prom-ised him. I am a soldier: I do not want to be thought of as a woman. I will not dress as a woman. I do not care for the things women care for. They dream of lovers, and of money. I dream of leading a charge, and of plac-ing the big guns. You soldiers do not know how to use the big guns: you think you can win battles with a great noise and smoke" (83). Inherent in this speech are the many ways in which Joan goes against the sex-gender system of her time: as Shaw reminds us, "she refused to accept the specific woman's lot, and dressed and fought and lived as men did" ("Preface" 7). Joan not only declines to submit herself to a husband, but the very fact that she speaks this way to men indicates her repudiation of her role as wife. Shaw's picture of Joan resembles in many ways Marina Warner's positive depiction. They both believe "[s]he is anomalous in our culture, a woman renowned for doing something on her own, not by birthright" (Warner 9). Warner does point out, however, that Shaw makes Joan a much more clever woman than she was. It is with a sense of regret that Warner points out the discrepancies between the historical Joan and Shaw's character: "Shaw made Joan's defiance of the ordinary procedure of a trial the mark of her individualism and disdain for institutions' coercion. His image of the young, plainspoken peasant taking on the mighty pillars of the Church and sundering them like Samson has an eloquence that has made it stick in the minds of many as the true Saint Joan. But it is an anachronism; Joan was not against compromise for purposes of modern self-determinism" (Warner 173). Unlike Shaw's, Warner's Joan is no great talker, but rather a young girl who was often confused by the language of her prosecutors and clearly no match for them (92). And that which Shaw holds up as so important (perhaps because those at the trial did as well)—Joan's transvestism—is quite different in his version. Warner reminds us—and this is in the transcripts Shaw perused—"neither at this point in the trial nor at any other time, until the very end, did she specifically give a practical reason [for cross-dressing]. She never said she had done it to live with greater safety among soldiers, to preserve her chastity, or to ride a horse" (Warner 144). Yet this is precisely what Shaw has her say: "what can be plainer commonsense? I was a soldier living among soldiers. I am a prisoner guarded by soldiers. If I were to dress as a woman they would think of me as a woman; and then what would become of me? If I dress as a soldier they think of me as a soldier, and I can live with them as I do at home with my brothers. That is why St Catherine tells me I must not dress as a woman until she gives me leave" (132). In both speech and dress, Shaw's Joan is a creature of our era, an inspiration for women who wish to transcend society's limiting sex-gender system.

While Shaw holds that "She was the pioneer of rational dressing for women" ("Preface" 7), Joan's enemies conflate every imaginable crime with her cross-dressing. The Archbishop is seen as prejudiced against her because of her dress as he warns Charles about her: "This creature is not a saint. She is not even a respectable woman. She does not wear women's clothes. She is dressed like a soldier, and rides round the country with soldiers" (67). The dangers Joan's transvestism posed are explained by the Inquisitor: "Mark what I say: the woman who quarrels with her clothes, and puts on the dress of a man, is like the man who throws off his fur gown and dresses like John the Baptist: they are followed, as surely as the night follows the day, by bands of wild women and men who refuse to wear any clothes at all" (121–22). D'Estivet sounds remarkably like Holinshed, whose description of Joan of Arc's death is clearly without sympathy: "Wherein found, though a virgin, yet first, shamefully rejecting her sex abominably in acts and apparel, to have counterfeit mankind, and then, all damnably faithless, to be a pernicious instrument to hostility and bloodshed in devilish witchcraft and sorcery, sentence accordingly was pronounced against her" (Hosley 157), when he summarizes the case against her, illustrating that Shaw understood perfectly what Joan's repudiation of the masculine role meant to her contemporaries: "I must emphasize the gravity of two very horrible and blasphemous crimes which she does not deny. First, she has intercourse with evil spirits, and is therefore a sorceress. Second, she wears men's clothes, which is indecent, unnatural, and abominable; and in spite of our most earnest remonstrances and entreaties, she will not change them even to receive the sacrament" (86). There is also the possibility that D'Estivet and the Inquisitor sound much like members of Shaw's audience. Shaw had campaigned for women's newly won suffrage (1918), and apparently believed that his contemporaries were as irrational about women's garments as Joan's prosecutors were. He notes that only those women who are "in a position to defy public opinion" may escape being labeled abject for their "rational dressing" ("Preface" 20). The results of Joan's rationality are stressed in every story that includes scenes from her imprisonment, as she agonizes over not being allowed to take the sacrament. Her decision to remain in men's garments cost her dearly.

Of course, in contrast with Shakespeare's play, where Joan's transvestism was tied to her supposed diabolic sexuality, Shaw never questions Joan's virginity or sexuality. There is one moment where Joan seems to be flirting with her fellow soldier, Dunois, but Shaw uses the moment to show her devotion to her cause:

JOAN: . . . I wish you were one of the village babies.
DUNOIS: Why?
JOAN: I could nurse you for awhile.
DUNOIS: You are a bit of a woman after all.
JOAN: No: not a bit: I am a soldier and nothing else. Soldiers always nurse children when they get a chance. (103)

This exchange is significant in that it reverses the expectation for both male and female behavior. Joan wishes to nurse not because she is female—but because she is a soldier. Likewise, soldiers, who are often thought to be the epitome of masculinity, are shown to have the desire to nurture.

Some critics have pointed out that the feminine way of life is not entirely foreign to Joan. When she says, "Nay: I am no shepherd lass, though I have helped with the sheep like anyone else. I will do a lady's work in the house—spin or weave—against any woman in Rouen" (128), she seems to be admitting that soldiering is not her only skill. Gainor recognizes that in this short exchange "she makes her distinctive calling explicit" (143). That is, once again, Shaw shows us the feminine world to show us how far Joan is outside of it: "There are plenty of other women to do it [women's work]; but there is nobody to do my work" (128), she says.

There are feminine ties to Joan that other critics have not apparently noticed, however. Shaw opens his play with a problem: there's no milk and the chickens won't lay. When Joan is given her way, the eggs come. Although she is apparently unconscious of this (all discussion of the eggs happens in her absence), this first scene serves to tie her to the domestic sphere. She is also constructed to resemble more a polite young girl than a soldier in the making. In the first scene, she "curtsies" (58) and plumps "down on the stool again, like an obedient schoolgirl" (61). Her request for men's clothing, so instrumental to her fate, is also almost begged for, as a child would request a Christmas doll: "And the dress? I may have a soldier's dress, maynt I, squire?" (62). Although she matures throughout the course of the play, we also see glimpses of her childishness: "*She squats down on the flags with crossed ankles, pouting*" (107).

In these actions, Shaw's Joan resembles his Cleopatra, "the kitten turned tiger, who against Caesar's advice stains her hands with her enemy's blood" (Adams 157). Shaw's Cleopatra, in his *Caesar and Cleopatra*, does not initially behave as one might expect of a queen. She runs after Caesar, "*clinging to him*" (31). This woman, who "*quails like a naughty child*" (32), is "*rent by a struggle between her newly acquired dignity as queen, and a strong impulse to put out her tongue*" (48). Although this behavior certainly does not seem to be in line with Shaw's theories of the emancipated woman, she is accused of being exactly what Shaw wanted: "You are like the rest of them. You want to be what these Romans call a New Woman" (92). This seeming contradiction is possible because Shaw did not see Cleopatra's behavior as necessarily tied to her sexuality. "The childishness I have ascribed to her, as far as it is childishness of character and not lack of experience, is not a matter of years," writes Shaw in his notes to the play (131). It is not her youth or her sex that allows Shaw to treat her this way. Rather, it is her lack of education. Despite all evidence to the contrary, Shaw does "not feel bound to believe that Cleopatra was well educated" (131). If Joan's childishness is explained in the same way—she was indeed uneducated—her behavior then becomes another reason for mod-

ern education reform, not an example of her femininity. Both of Shaw's
historical witches are held back from transcendence when their lack of
education gets in the way:[5] "[Joan's] want of academic education disabled
her when she had to deal with such elaborately artificial structures as the
great ecclesiastical and social institutions of the Middle Ages" ("Preface"
22). Shaw's Joan indeed displays an innocence in the face of her accusa-
tions: "What I have done is according to God. They could not burn a
woman for speaking the truth" (110).

Many critics have noted Shaw's self-serving alterations to the historical
Joan: "Of course, he made Joan a nationalist, a Protestant, a champion of
individual conscience and the inner light, before either Protestantism or
nationalism was formally inaugurated, and he knew exactly what he was
doing" (Kaul 322). What Shaw was doing was giving his audience a picture
of the modern woman caught in a patriarchal society—a woman labeled a
witch because she violated the rules of an oppressive sex-gender system.
"For Shaw she stands for an early and divinely inspired heroine of the
long crisis out of which was born a new culture—his own" (Kaul 322–23).
This new culture was comprised of new ideas, including the idea of wom-
en's equality, of which Shaw wholeheartedly approved. Joan has been singled out as the paragon of the New Woman, "contrasted to the 'womanly
woman' who had been the ideal, he labeled the *Unwomanly Woman*": "Joan
is, beyond comparison, the most Unwomanly Woman in the Shavian
canon" (Lorichs, "The 'Unwomanly Woman'" 99 and 110). The casual
observer can easily see how Joan might fit the bill: "The literary treatment
of this type has been a portrait of a woman who is unmarried, plain and
'masculine' in dress and manner" (Adams 160). Above all things, Shaw
believed it was Joan's status as unwomanly which led to her burning and
accounted for the four hundred years between her death and her full rehabilitation by the Church: "Had Joan not been one of those 'unwomanly
women,' she might have been canonized much sooner" ("Preface" 20). In
other words, the behavior that was expected of a woman in Joan's time
and in Shaw's time was similar—and violations of that behavior were dealt
with similarly. Shaw does not believe his contemporaries are any more
enlightened than Joan's—in fact, her canonization shows not that civilization is improving, but rather emphasizes how long it takes for any slight
change in the sex-gender system to take place: "If Joan had to be dealt
with by us in London she would be treated with no more toleration than
Miss Sylvia Pankhurst, or the Peculiar People, or the parents who keep
their children away from the elementary school, or any of the others who
cross the line we have to draw, rightly or wrongly, between the tolerable
and the intolerable" ("Preface" 27).

In order to understand Shaw's Joan, one must examine the idea of the
New Woman in some detail. Numerous critics have investigated Shaw's

sources. He was a devotee of John Stuart Mill and Mary Wollstonecraft, among others, and he professed to have inherited the notion of the New Woman from Henrik Ibsen. Nora, the protagonist of *A Doll's House* (1879), is the acknowledged precursor of all Shaw's independent women (Lorichs, *The Unwomanly Woman* 17). Shaw took this woman and developed "a major thesis he would propagate—that 'woman's nature,' a principle on which capitalist society based its prevailing morality and corresponding modes of behavior, was merely an artificial construction" (Greiner 90). This idea—that gender was socially constructed—went against everything science believed about biological determinism.

The four hundred years between Shakespeare and Shaw saw enormous changes. The one-sex sex-gender system, explained by Thomas Laqueur in his *Making Sex: Body and Gender from the Greeks to Freud* (1990), changed into the two-sex sex-gender system we understand today. This two-sex system was used to justify a strict two-gender system through biological beliefs. Further, "the body was no longer regarded as a microcosm of some larger order in which each bit of nature is positioned within layer upon layer of signification" (Laqueur 10). That is, the body was not necessarily a reflection of the social order, though it was used biologically to justify social consequences. Nevertheless, the body was entirely dispensable for Shaw: "Independent of the scientific writings, Shaw had constructed a theory of human similarity, developed from his culture's sense of gender codes. Rather than identify the feminine and masculine elements dominant in any individual, Shaw propounds an essential likeness among all people" (Gainor 82).

Watson examines Shaw's beliefs as revealed in his treatment of Joan:

> Her accusers dwell on witchcraft and unfeminine behavior. Her defense against these charges shows how necessary it is for women to unsex themselves to succeed in great enterprises, how the woman's role is a trap to be wary of and is, furthermore, the best example of the way all such traps as stereotypes work. . . . Soldier is a role, bishop is a role, shepherd is a role (although shepherdess turns it into a mythological fancy), even saint is a role, but woman is an antirole and therefore a woman must be a rebel or nothing. (124)

Unsexing oneself was not always the way to gain favor. Indeed, to be a woman in a patriarchal world has been historically to fit a role of harlot, lunatic, or witch. It is also curious that Watson would choose the word "unsex" in describing Shaw's strategy. Shaw might perhaps accept this word as an accurate description. He has practically said as much himself: "The sum of the matter is that unless Woman repudiates her womanliness, her duty to her husband, to her children, to society, to the law, and to everyone but herself, she cannot emancipate herself. . . . Therefore woman has to repudiate duty altogether" (quoted in Lorichs, *The Unwomanly Woman* 31). Luckily for Joan, duty to the Lord is duty to herself, but it is clear that Shaw does not believe in mandatory femininity.

It must be noted, however, that the reverse does not seem to be true: "Shaw's was a biased androgyny, in that he virtually ignored this phenomenon in men—who were at the time of equal interest to the scientific community—focusing almost exclusively on instances in women" (Gainor 68). Gainor goes beyond feminist critics who seek to claim Shaw as one of their own. While Shaw was part of the suffrage movement, tried to repeal laws criminalizing sodomy, and wrote many letters calling for the more practical dress of women (Gainor 85), his feminism left something to be desired. Most telling is his famous "petticoat speech" of 1927:

> People are still full of the old idea that woman is a special creation. I am bound to say that of late years she has been working extremely hard to eradicate that impression, and make one understand that a woman is really only a man in petticoats, or if you like, that a man is a woman without petticoats. People sometimes wonder what is the secret of the extraordinary knowledge of women which I shew in my plays. They very often accuse me of having acquired it by living a most abandoned life. But I never acquired it. I have always assumed that a woman is a person exactly like myself, and that is how the trick is done. ("Woman—Man in Petticoats" 174)

Gainor's analysis of Shaw's point is well made: "Essentially, if one puts petticoats on a man one gets a woman; or, conversely, if one takes the petticoats off a woman, one has a man. In either case, the fundamental identity is male, which corresponds to Shaw's sense that a woman is a person like himself, albeit with the additional petticoats, that is, with certain external, unimportant distinctions" (Gainor 84). That is, biological distinctions mean nothing—so long as one is prepared act in a masculine fashion.

It does not necessarily follow, however, that Shaw's attitude arises from any ideas he held about the superiority of man over woman. He has often held the opposite view. As a follower of Mills and Wollstonecraft, he most likely assumed, as they did, that "Whether through inherent nature . . . or through centuries of suffering, women are construed, in and through their bodies, as being less in the thralls of passion and unreason and hence morally more adept than men" (Laqueur 203), which would have appealed to his love of reason. In body, he believed "women are hardier than men" (Shaw, "Torture" 229). His answer to critics who thought of women as lesser in nature is most telling: "Of course, it's usually pointed out that women are not fit for political power, and ought not to be trusted with a vote because they are politically ignorant, socially prejudiced, narrow-minded, and selfish. True enough, but precisely the same is true of man" (quoted in Braby 240). Shaw believed women should be like him not in the masculine sense; it was only that he happened to be male. Shaw believed that *everyone* should strive to be like him. Joan is the incarnation of everything he admired about himself: strong-willed, inspired, clever, determined, and innovative.

Shaw did not agree with most of the men of his time, who tried to divide the world into separate spheres: "The creation of a bourgeois public sphere, in other words, raised with a vengeance the question of which sex(es) ought legitimately to occupy it" (Laqueur 194). Shaw was not concerned about the issue of sex in terms of public influence—he believed intellect was the only true measure of a person—and that most people were significantly lacking it. His opinions on his fellow humans were not held back any more than his social beliefs: "Shaw has said that no great writer uses his skill to conceal his meaning. . . . He was a practical man of the theater; he was also an artist of integrity who never tailored his ideas to fit an audience, but deliberately and invariably presented what he thought and exposed the folly of what everybody else accepted" (Gilmartin 144). It was Shaw's belief that modern people must be confronted with their own prejudices and a multitude of ideas. Thus, he justifies his rewrite of Shakespeare's subject because he had the "conviction that Shakespeare, even in his restored integrity, could not satisfy the spiritual and intellectual needs of a genuinely modern person: great as he is, he is not good enough" (Smith 133). The critique that "I feel sure that there is no more relation between the historical Joan of Arc and his theatrical heroine than there is between the historical Macbeth and Shakespeare's" (Charles Sarolea, quoted in Lorichs, *The Unwomanly Woman* 176) would not have bothered Shaw at all. He believes the Joan he portrays is accurate: "'I have done nothing but arrange her for the stage. There really was such a woman. She did and said all these things,' Shaw declares. He found his heroine 'ready-made' and 'the play wrote itself'" (Lorichs, *The Unwomanly Woman* 172).

Joan is quite self aware in the epilogue Shaw creates for her. She first recognizes that her chief sin was her sex: "I might almost as well have been a man. Pity I wasn't: I should not have bothered you all so much then" (148). Her hindsight also allows her to forgive, as Shaw has, her persecutors: "I hope men will be the better for remembering me; and they would not remember me so well if you had not burned me" (149). Indeed, at no point in the play does Joan sound more like Shaw as when she laments the lot of those who die unappreciated and despised because of their superiority to the common man: "Must then a Christ perish in tor-

ment in every age to save those that have no imagination?" (154). Shaw's
Joan is not so upset that she was killed—indeed she seems amused at her
canonization—but what seems to distress her most is the reaction of those
who praise her when she asks if it is time to return: "shall I rise from the
dead, and come back to you a living woman? . . . What! Must I burn again?
Are none of you ready to receive me?" (158). The critique is clear.
Throughout the play, Shaw has shown his audience that they are no more
enlightened than Joan's judges—if anything, they are less so. In the modern era, Shaw's Joan would not be criminalized as a witch. Not in Shaw's
eyes, at least. Instead, Joan is Shaw—and is punished for her genius: "A
genius is a person who, seeing farther and probing deeper than other
people, has a different set of ethical valuations from theirs, and has energy
enough to give effect to this extra vision and its valuations in whatever
manner best suits his or her specific talents" ("Preface" 10). Those who
would ban Shaw's plays would burn Joan as a witch.[6]

Despite Shaw's feminist leanings, scholars have criticized his use of the
'unwomanly woman' in that he so often "compromises" her (Gainor 20).
That is, too often after his female characters declare their independence,
they must lower themselves somehow to achieve what they want. These
compromises lead to another criticism: "Shaw's frequent reference to his
didactic purpose in playwriting leads one to expect a dramatic environment that would illustrate both the social evils he observed and some
movement toward their rectification" (Gainor 21). If the problems Shaw
dealt with—prostitution, slums, war mongering, etc.—were surface issues,
he might have been able to provide answers. All problems, however, can
be traced back to the lack of genius or to humanity's fear of genius once
it is discovered. His heroines (and his heroes) often have to compromise
because the world is not suited to them. Joan is killed because she refuses
to compromise—hers is the picture of what happens when the New
Woman is not aware enough (through a lack of education) of the social
forces at work. Her principal crime is not that she tries to appropriate
male power, although Shaw is arguing for a change in the sex-gender
system when he notes that "her ideal biographer . . . must be capable of
throwing off sex partialities and their romance, and regarding women as
the female of the human species, and not as a different kind of animal
with specific charms and specific imbecilities" ("Preface" 10–11); and certainly it is not the crime of witchcraft. Rather, Shaw's witch is put before
the audience to show the potential consequences that any modern hero
may face in the pursuit of genius. The witch label that Shakespeare used
in his plays is, for Shaw, a way of singling out those who do not subject
themselves to the dominant mode of behavior. Shaw is, of course, aware
that this label was most often used to abject women within an unjust sex-
gender system that had persisted into his own time. Shaw is able to exploit

the memory of Joan as a Renaissance witch by constructing her as a symbol of Modern genius. As Shaw notes, "Now it is always hard for superior wits to understand the fury roused by their exposures of the stupidities of comparative dullards. . . . Fear will drive men to any extreme; and the fear inspired by a superior being is a mystery which cannot be reasoned away" ("Preface" 8). Joan is created in Shaw's own image, and only era and gender prevent him from being labeled for his own transgressions, as she was.

Notes

1. All quotations from *Saint Joan* and its Preface are from the 1966 Penguin edition.
2. The phrase "sex-gender system" was theorized by Teresa De Lauretis in her *Technologies of Gender* (1987). Each society has its own historically situated system of interlocking ideologies that define the parameters of genders and how gender relates to biological sex. De Lauretis notes that "[a]lthough the meanings vary with each culture, a sex-gender system is always intimately interconnected with political and economic factors in each society" (5).
3. Anne Llewellyn Barstow's *Witchcraze: A New History of the European Witch Hunts* (1994) is an excellent source for understanding the unique role gender played in witchhunts.
4. The debate surrounding Shaw's portrayal of Joan's inquisitors is detailed in Sonja Lorich's *The Unwomanly Woman* (1975). Lorichs ultimately defends Shaw's revision of history as accurate.
5. Shaw playfully refers to Cleopatra as a witch, while the Romans used the term with more venom. *Caesar and Cleopatra* does contain a witch, however. Cleopatra's aged, mysterious servant, Ftatateeta, takes on all the negative characteristics the Romans assigned to Cleopatra. She is called many names, among them "witch," and made abject from the Roman world—while Cleopatra embraces the Roman reason Caesar stands for. In her devotion to her mistress, Ftatateeta kills a Roman soldier who means to harm Cleopatra. Not surprisingly, Ftatateeta is killed for her unwomanly behavior.
6. Shaw considered his misunderstood genius to be the reason his plays were so often censored. His railings against censorship of genius can be found in "Mainly About Myself," the Preface to his *Plays Unpleasant.* He quite clearly sees himself as having a "different set of ethical valuations" from the Lord Chamberlain, whom he cannot read "without boiling of the blood" (15).

Works Cited

Adams, Elsie. "Feminism and Female Stereotypes in Shaw." In *Fabian Feminist: Bernard Shaw and Woman.* Ed. Rodelle Weintraub. University Park: Penn State University Press, 1977: 156–62.

Barstow, Anne Llewellyn. *Witchcraze: A New History of the European Witch Hunts*. San Francisco: Pandora, 1994.

Braby, Maud Churton. "G.B.S. and a Suffragist." In *Fabian Feminist: Bernard Shaw and Woman*. Ed. Rodelle Weintraub. University Park: Penn State University Press, 1977: 236–42.

Darwin, Charles. *The Descent of Man, and Selection in Relation to Sex*. Princeton: Princeton University Press, 1981.

De Lauretis, Teresa. *Technologies of Gender*. Bloomington: Indiana University Press, 1987.

Gainor, J. Ellen. *Shaw's Daughters: Dramatic and Narrative Constructions of Gender*. Ann Arbor: University of Michigan Press, 1991.

Greiner, Norbert. "Mill, Marx, and Bebel: Early Influences on Shaw's Characterizations of Women." In *Fabian Feminist: Bernard Shaw and Woman*. Ed. Rodelle Weintraub. University Park: Penn State University Press, 1977: 90–98.

Hardin, Richard F. "Chronicle and Mythmaking in Shakespeare's Joan of Arc." In *Shakespeare Survey: An Annual Survey of Shakespeare Studies and Production*, vol. 42. Ed. Stanley Wells. Cambridge: Cambridge University Press, 1990: 25–35.

Hosley, Richard, ed. *Shakespeare's Holinshed*. New York: G. P. Putnam's Sons, 1968.

Jackson, Gabriele Bernhard. "Topical Ideology: Witches, Amazons, and Shakespeare's Joan of Arc." *English Literary Renaissance* 18.1 (1998): 40.65.

Kaul, A. N. *The Action of English Comedy: Studies in the Encounter of Abstraction and Experience from Shakespeare to Shaw*. New Haven: Yale University Press, 1970.

Kermode, Frank, and John Hollander. "Foreword to *Saint Joan*." *Modern British Literature*. New York: Oxford University Press, 1973: 31–34.

Laqueur, Thomas. *Making Sex: Body and Gender from the Greeks to Freud*. Cambridge, Mass.: Harvard University Press, 1990.

Laurence, Dan, ed. *Bernard Shaw: Collected Letters, 1898–1910*, vol. 2. London: Reinhardt, 1972.

Lorichs, Sonja. "The 'Unwomanly Woman' in Shaw's Drama." In *Fabian Feminist: Bernard Shaw and Woman*. Ed. Rodelle Weintraub. University Park: Penn State University Press, 1977: 99–111.

———. *The Unwomanly Woman in Bernard Shaw's Drama and Her Social and Political Background*. Uppsala: University of Uppsala Studies in English, 1973.

Mason, Ronald. "Shaw on Shakespeare." *The Shavian* 4 (1970): 46–51.

Murray, Margaret. *The Witch-Cult in Western Europe*. Oxford: Clarendon Press, 1921.

Searle, William. *The Saint and the Skeptics: Joan of Arc in the Work of Mark*

Twain, Anatole France, and Bernard Shaw. Detroit: Wayne State University Press, 1976.

Shaw, George Bernard. *Caesar and Cleopatra.* Baltimore: Penguin, 1966.

———. "Notes to *Caesar and Cleopatra.*" *Caesar and Cleopatra.* Baltimore: Penguin, 1966: 126–36.

———. "Woman—Man in Petticoats" (1927). *Platform and Pulpit.* Ed. Dan H. Laurence. New York: Hill & Wang, 1961: 172–78.

———. "Preface: Mainly About Myself." *Plays Unpleasant.* Baltimore: Penguin, 1958.

———. "Preface to *Saint Joan.*" *Saint Joan.* Baltimore: Penguin, 1966: 7–47.

———. *Saint Joan.* Baltimore: Penguin, 1966.

———. "Saint Joan" (1931). *Platform and Pulpit.* Ed. Dan H. Laurence. New York: Hill & Wang, 1961: 208–16.

———. "Torture by Forcible Feeding is Illegal." In *Fabian Feminist: Bernard Shaw and Woman.* Ed. Rodelle Weintraub. University Park: Penn State University Press, 1977: 228–35.

Smith, J. Percy. "Superman Versus Man: Bernard Shaw on Shakespeare." In *Stratford Papers on Shakespeare.* Ed. B. W. Jackson. Toronto: W. J. Gage, 1962: 118–49.

Warner, Marina. *Joan of Arc: The Image of Female Heroism.* Berkeley and Los Angeles: University of California Press, 1981.

Watson, Barbara Bellow. "The New Woman and the New Comedy." In *Fabian Feminist: Bernard Shaw and Woman.* Ed. Rodelle Weintraub. University Park: Penn State University Press, 1977: 114–29.

Harold Pagliaro

TRUNCATED LOVE IN *CANDIDA* AND *HEARTBREAK HOUSE*

Shaw's imagination as it is revealed in the plays is intensely and complexly heterosexual. My claim is obviously supported by such works as *Man and Superman, Major Barbara,* and *Misalliance,* where the Life Force works remorselessly until it triumphs. But Shaw's heterosexual couples are not confined to those the Life Force has thrown together imperiously, "intending," as it were, to promote its evolutionary mission through them. Among these other couples, some marry (reproduce) only generally prompted by Evolution to do so, like Violet and Malone or the Collinses, the Tarletons, and the Utterwords. Others develop a relationship because they are drawn to each other or because they are brought together by circumstance, only to conclude that it should not lead to marriage, like Vivie and Frank or Lavinia and the Captain or Lesbia and the General.

One may regard these relationships as failures of the Life Force, as in some sense they are. But one may also think of them as experiments whose biological truncation enables Shaw to display in dramatic terms a range of heterosexual configurations. For example, Marchbanks, Higgins, Lavinia, Lina, and Cicely (with help from Brassbound) end a heterosexual relationship or resist allowing it to come to sexual fulfillment for essentially artistic, religious, or intensely held private reasons. Ellie, Vivie, and Lesbia do so too, but for them at least part of the reason is that society has failed to give the Life Force a setting they find acceptable. All these and other Shaw characters share an obvious common ground—they think and feel about a possible sexual partner, even if they do so only negatively, as Vivie does of Crofts.

Shaw's invention is varied enough that the psychosexual dynamic at work between potential partners is individually engaging, inviting separate critical attention. Here I shall confine myself to looking at the heterosexual dynamic of two plays, *Candida* and *Heartbreak House.* In both, Shaw proposes couplings that are unlikely to come to happy endings—young Marchbanks and mature and married Candida, young Ellie and mature and married Hector, young Ellie and mature and unattractive Mangan, young Ellie and very old Shotover. The Life Force is sometimes at a disadvantage in the mating game.

Candida is a difficult play because all three principals, especially Candida, seem to invite fixed appraisals, when in fact they are complex characters.[1] The hardest by far to read is Candida, who is not simply an intelligent, liberated, frank, and beautiful maternal comforter (the Virgin Mother); she is also self-indulgent, cruel, narrow in her interests, and less sound in "instinctual intelligence" than she thinks she is. Marchbanks is not only a Shelleyan-sensitive poet who sees into the human heart with unerring accuracy, but he is also sexually immature and so maladroit socially as to be dangerous. Finally we may see Morell as Candida and Marchbanks do—as an overly indulged windbag, utterly dependent on his wife—when in fact he has won the remarkable Candida's love to begin with, and despite his fear of losing her, deliberately leaves her and Marchbanks alone to bring their amatory gymnastics to a head.

It is possible, of course, that Shaw himself was ambivalent about his characters, especially Candida and Marchbanks, giving the title and the first two acts, more or less, to her, and the remainder, especially his mission-heavy departure into the night with an important secret, to him, not having known at first that Marchbanks was to become radically independent of Candida. But I think Shaw had a thorough artistic grasp of their characters from the start, however unconsciously. Candida had to be attractive enough to take possession of Marchbanks's perceptive young mind. And Marchbanks had to be vital and intelligent enough to choose, finally, an independent life; but early on, he had to be immature enough to be engulfed by Candida.

A look at Shaw's stage directions describing Candida on her first appearance may help to clarify this claim about Shaw's control. He says of Candida, "she is like any other pretty woman who is just clever enough to make the most of her sexual attractions for trivially selfish ends; but Candida's serene brow, courageous eyes, and well set mouth and chin signify largeness of mind and dignity of character to ennoble her cunning in the affections" (*Bodley Head Shaw*, 7 vols., ed. Dan H. Laurence [London: Max Reinhardt, 1970–74], I, 532. Hereafter I locate quotations by volume and page number in the *Bodley Head* edition). Candida's sphere is the affections, where she works with "ennobled cunning," Shaw tells us—a strange formulation, suggesting that in human affairs Candida is capable of wide-ranging, independent behavior. Shaw himself says of his heroine, "Candida is as unscrupulous as Siegfried: Morell himself sees that 'no law will bind her.' "[2] Shaw also makes it clear that Marchbanks is responsible for the contrasting view of Candida as the Virgin of the Assumption.[3]

We are also given an alternative to the almost universal male approval of Candida; it is a woman's view, Prossy's. Fed up with Lexy the Curate's praises of Candida, she yells, "Her eyes are not a bit better than mine: now! And you know very well you think me dowdy and second rate" (I, 523). Half accusing, half apologizing, Lexy says, "I had no idea you had any feeling against Mrs Morell." To this Prossy answers with Shavian assurance, "I have no feeling against her. She's very nice, very good hearted: I'm very fond of her, and can appreciate her real qualities far better than any man can. . . . You think I'm jealous? . . . It must be so nice to be a man and have a fine penetrating intellect instead of mere emotions like us, and to know that the reason we don't share your amorous delusions is that we're all jealous of one another!" (I, 523–24). Shaw's varied representations of Candida suggest not his gradual recognition and control of the character he wants her to be, but the display of her complexity.

Candida's initiatives are important. She decides not only what she will do but in large measure what the men will do. There is plenty of evidence that Morell is an effective clergyman socialist by profession, but it is largely as Candida's husband that the dramatic action gives him to us. Similarly, Marchbanks is unmistakably represented as an aristocrat and a poet, but it is largely as Candida's lover that we get to know him. Shaw generates and controls Candida's emotional centrality as a means (among other things) of developing the characters of the men as lovers.

The second act opens with a curious scene between Marchbanks and Prossy, during which she tries to maintain a conventional reticence about her fantasy lovelife, and Marchbanks insists upon demonstrating that the primal activity of all human minds is amatory longing. He is remorseless, hitting Prossy with the claim until she finally breaks down, protecting herself only with the promise of denial should Marchbanks divulge her secret.

PROSERPINE. [*suddenly rising with her hand pressed on her heart*] Oh, it's no use trying to work while you talk like that. [*She leaves her little table and sits on the sofa. Her feelings are keenly stirred*]. It's no business of yours whether my heart cried or not; but I have a mind to tell you for all of that.
MARCHBANKS. You neednt. I know already that it must.
PROSERPINE. But mind if you ever say so, I'll deny it. (I, 550)

The longish scene serves several dramatic purposes, telling us more about Prossy than we knew and especially more about Marchbanks. We learn that he is both aware of his compulsive dwelling on love and that he is convinced that such mental behavior is normal in that all except wicked people enjoy and endure an interior life very like his own, the wicked being those who have no love to give and no power to receive it (I, 549). In the world of the play, heterosexual love is humanity's chief interior activity. Love is also its chief social activity.

But the scene does an even more important thing. It provides Marchbanks and us with vital information about Morell. We already know that Morell, Marchbanks, and Lexy—"all" the men—love Candida. But we have not yet been made to see that Morell is sexually a very attractive man. Indeed the exchange between him and Marchbanks that ends the first act seems to go dead against him in that regard, with the young intruder and Candida, arm in arm, leaving the desolate husband on the ropes. "I am the happiest of mortals," Marchbanks says. To this Morell adds, "So was I—an hour ago" (I, 546).

But we soon learn that Marchbanks still thinks of Morell as a dangerous rival. For it turns out that his seduction of Prossy into sexual self-revelation leads him to an overwhelming question that he may not have consciously intended to ask at the outset.

MARCHBANKS. No: answer me. I want to know: I must know. *I* cant understand it. I can see nothing in him but words, pious resolutions, what people call goodness. You cant love that. (I, 552)

But Prossy resists Marchbanks. She has admitted her interior preoccupation with matters of the heart, but she has not of course identified her lover. Marchbanks will not let go.

MARCHBANKS. . . . [*Determined to have an answer*] Is it possible for a woman to love him?
PROSERPINE. [*looking him straight in the face*] Yes. [*He covers his face with his hands*]. (I, 552)

Despite his self-confidence in most matters, Marchbanks regards the husband as a rival almost to the end. As I have said, Morell arranges for Marchbanks and Candida to be alone while he and the others attend a meeting of the Guild of St. Matthew. Inevitably, the two men confront each other later. But before Marchbanks makes it clear that he and Candida were lovers in spirit only, he is compelled to inquire about Morell's credentials as lover: "The man I want to meet is the man Candida married" (I, 577). Morell assures him that the man she married stands before him—"the same moralist and windbag [he was then]," he adds ironically (I, 578).

Shaken as he is, Morell shows courage in bringing matters between Marchbanks and Candida to resolution. He is a good man, even by Shavian standards. We meet him well before we meet Candida, and we learn that he sees through and easily manages the greedy reprobate Burgess, his father-in-law. If not quite the Unofficial Bishop of Everywhere, Morell is an effective Anglican priest, and an ardent socialist who may speak as well as Shaw himself. And like Marchbanks, he too is attractive, to Candida, Prossy, and all the women who have ever watched and heard him in the pulpit or on the platform. If Marchbanks is ultimately the stronger man, it is in the sense that he will not play Tanner to Candida's Ann.[4]

What does Candida mean by saying she will choose the weaker of the two? Her last long speech of the play is an extravagant explanation of Morell's lifelong dependence on women—first his mother and sisters and, later, Candida and the Prossys, who have worked for him. If one accepts what Candida says, Morell is reduced to a nullity, except as the sire of her children. But dramatic actions are synergies. We do better to locate her last long speech in the context of her behavior toward Morell throughout the play. Her first serious exchange with him takes place soon after Marchbanks has told Morell that he loves Candida, and pointed out to him in brutal language his disqualifications as her husband. Candida thereafter finds him looking "very pale, and grey, and wrinkled, and old," and acts as if she wants to comfort him (I, 561). But she soon tells him that he gets too much love and Marchbanks too little; she derides Morell's work as nothing but an aphrodisiac, inducing "Prossy's complaint" among London's women. Then she confides that Marchbanks is falling in love with her, without realizing it. Her unintended irony reminds us of Marchbanks's brutal treatment of her husband just a short time before: it has left him looking "very pale, and grey, and wrinkled, and old," just the state that has moved Candida to comfort him. Comfort indeed. But she is yet to deliver the hammer blow. This she does by candidly telling her husband that if she slept with Marchbanks, she would save him from the terrible fate of finding out about love from "bad women" (I, 565).

Candida is genuinely "amazed" that Morell does not "understand" her suggestion and is confounded that when she kisses him he is outraged. She asks, "My dear: whats the matter?" To this he replies, "[*frantically waving her off*] Don't touch me" (I, 566). If Candida is Morell's chief mainstay, she is also his emasculator, perhaps unconsciously.[5] Can she really believe Marchbanks does not realize he is in love with her? Or does she know, and does she decide to be coy about it, intending to save Morell's feelings? If her aim is to spare his feelings, how can she possibly say it might be a good idea to sleep with Marchbanks to save him from bad women? If Candida wants to sleep with him, can she really believe it is to save him from bad women? Whatever the answers, she is being either wantonly cruel to her husband or improbably inept, not to say stupid. Candida has unintentionally warned us not to take her appraisals of Morell at face value.

But the best demonstration that Candida's willingness to spill this interior baggage is destructive is not my argument. It is Marchbanks's appraisal of what she has done and his reaction to it. He and Burgess enter just as Morell says, "Don't touch me," and waves Candida off. And she, insensitive to her husband's pain, says, "greatly amused," pointing to Morell, "look at him! Just look!" (I, 566). Moved by Morell's pain, Marchbanks urges, "Oh, stop, stop. . . . You have made him suffer frightfully. I feel his pain in my own heart" (I, 567). Marchbanks is both the most mature and the most immature of the three principals. He sees people and things with great clarity. Nevertheless, his actions are sometimes disastrous because of his lack of experience. But he is a quick study; indeed he matures before our eyes.

Let me now return to Candida's last long speech of the play and its complex ending. Candida is surely an attractive person—energetic, loving, and generally constructive. But she also overestimates her insight into the interior lives of others, and she underestimates her husband's ability to stand alone if he must. Could he, in a pinch, do the work of the Reverend Anthony Anderson? Morell needs the mother-sister-wifely presence of his Candida, on whom he has fixed an abiding love. He also needs her in the deep sense that he is a strong heterosexual male who would be a very uncomfortable celibate. Recall that very early in the action Candida tells Marchbanks not to accept an invitation to lunch upon their return from her three weeks away, obviously anticipating that Morell will want to make love immediately. Recall, too, that Marchbanks quite misses the point even after Morell explains the matter. When finally he gets the message, he is "horrorstricken" (I, 538–39).

In the final scene, Candida plays the role of mother-wife to the hilt, scorning Morell's notion that she must choose between the men, detailing with extravagant self-justification his dependency on her (and yet "leaning forward to stroke his hair caressingly at each phrase" [I, 593]), expressing solicitude for the young and lonely Marchbanks, and finally choosing the "weaker" of the two men as soon as she requires Marchbanks to admit what she may already know. Morell gives her the chance.

MORELL. You are my wife, my mother, my sisters: you are the sum of all loving care to me.
CANDIDA. [*in his arms, smiling, to Eugene*] Am I your mother and sisters to you, Eugene?
MARCHBANKS. [*rising with a fierce gesture of disgust*] Ah, never. Out, then, into the night with me! (I, 593)

The young poet's secret is that he has come to understand the reality of domestic life, and he instinctively knows it is not for him. An aspect of this recognition is his sense that Candida's strength is a direct function of her husband's dependency. She needs him (or someone like him) as much as he needs her (or someone like her). They are mutually dependent heterosexuals, whatever Candida (or Morell) may suppose. Moreover, Marchbanks knows that Candida is capable of cruelty, consciously or not. And, of course, so is he, working over the same victim (I, 539–46). But however human she may show herself to be, Marchbanks cannot conceive of her in sexual terms—she remains the Virgin Mother until the moment before he leaves, accepting a farewell kiss on the brow while he kneels. Spiritually far better endowed than that other poet, Ricky Ticky Tavy, who has what Ann calls "an old maid's temperament" (II, 727), Marchbanks has yet to come to terms with his sexuality. Candida has tried (not quite in earnest) and failed to seduce him. While she waits placidly, and then impatiently, he reads poetry, missing the main chance, feeling noble in matching the nobility of the husband, who has given them their opportunity to be alone. Maybe Marchbanks's noble feeling is a mask for his fear of sex. By play's end, he may have chosen celibacy and work; he has certainly rejected the mutual dependency of a protracted heterosexual love. Up to this point at least, the Life Force has failed to work through him.

Heartbreak House is a play with a strong social message that works out its warning about humanity's socioeconomic disarray largely in the terms of failed human relations, with a strong emphasis on heterosexual relations. I do not mean to say that Shaw uses a human relational code with explicit social equivalents, but rather that he uses unsatisfactory relations between people, and especially between the sexes, to represent the uncertain foundations on which society is structured.[6] "Heartbreak House" is obviously a complex metaphor standing not only for Western Europe, with emphasis on England, but for the whole world, as Shaw in several instances has his characters suggest and, in at least one instance, make explicit. It is in the response to Mangan's question to the Captain, "Am I in [Hesione's] house or yours?" (V, 88).

CAPTAIN SHOTOVER. You are beneath the dome of heaven, in the house of God. What is true within these walls is true outside them. Go out on the seas; climb the mountains; wander through the valleys. (V, 88)

I shall argue that "what is true within these walls [of Heartbreak House]" is expressed preponderantly in the terms of heterosexual relations.

The play gives us a few good relations between the sexes, but they are in the past. All the many others in the play are unfulfilling or destructive or both. The exceptions are Captain Shotover's two-year marriage in Jamaica to a black woman, who redeemed him (V, 89); Mazzini Dunn's love-match with his wife, which he says accounts for Ellie's being lovely (V, 120); and the Hushabyes' marriage during the early years, when they were in love (V, 98). But even these exceptions are marred. The Captain's West Indian wife may still be alive (V, 148), and we are left to wonder why he left her; and we know nothing of his second, presumably bigamous marriage nor of Hesione's and Addy's mother. Does each have a different mother? Mazzini admires his wife, but she accepts his inability to earn money with resignation, so that he feels inadequate (a "footling" person) (V, 118). No longer in love, the Hushabyes make liberal use of their sexual powers of attraction in a continuing round of barren flirtations.

The play has no character like Caesar or Undershaft or Don Juan, who are all (allowing for obvious differences) quintessential Shavians, in possession of insights that guide them and may serve as lessons to others. It is a clear possibility that Ellie may become such a person, for she matures as we watch her; but we are left uncertain because the play seems to imply that all its characters have unresolved problems of identity.[7] Captain Shotover comes closest to being a Shavian hero, but he is seriously limited. He is very old, and yet no Ancient, having failed to reach the seventh degree of concentration (V, 100). He refers to former times when he did inspired work, but he himself tells us his ideas are only echoes of the past (V, 176). He identifies his sense for his own status by saying of Heartbreak House, "It is not my house: it is only my kennel" (V, 171). He drinks rum, not to get drunk but to keep from dreaming, a dangerous escape from reality in his view (V, 147). And forgetting that we are members of one another, he vents his frustration with life as he knows it by saying he wants his "seed" to destroy "hogs" like Mangan, "for whom the universe is nothing but a machine for greasing their bristles and filling their snouts" (V, 100).

What is wrong with Heartbreak House? Near the very end of Act I, Shotover begins a weird chant that Hector and Hesione conclude. "I builded a house for my daughters, and opened the doors thereof / That men might come for their choosing, and their betters spring from their love; / But one of them married a numskull; / The other a liar wed; / And now must she lie beside him, even as she made her bed" (V, 105).

The daughters chose husbands badly, and betters seem not to have sprung from their love. The Hushabye children are not youthful, Shotover tells us (V, 68). And there is nothing to suggest that the Utterword children are at all remarkable. Shotover says "gloomily," "Youth! Beauty! Novelty! They are badly wanted in this house" (V, 68). But there, only restless, flirtatious adults display themselves as flawed lovers, as if they had failed to generate a sound biological future and were vainly trying to do so, unconsciously it seems. Their restless dissatisfaction reminds one of the basis of Lilith's hope at the end of *Back to Methuselah*—dissatisfaction is promising for the future of the race (V, 630). But what those in Heartbreak House feel is better represented by Hesione: "When I am neither coaxing and kissing nor laughing, I am just wondering how much longer I can stand living in this cruel, damnable world" (V, 123).

The chief flirtations revolve around Hesione and Hector, and they make up much of the fabric of the play. They are obvious enough to need no special attention. Hector, playing a latter-day white Othello with bronze mustaches, has moved Ellie to fall in love with him before the action begins. He starts his other flirtation, with his wife's sister, Addy, strenuously kissing her; but he regrets the move, calling himself fool and goat (V, 97–98). Having discovered that Hector is married, Ellie is broken-hearted, and she says that Hesione has stolen her babies (V, 126). At one level, her maternal sense of loss may seem childish, but at another it suggests the primal nature of her wound. Men and women in Shaw's world fall in love once only. Ellie's one turn with Hector has proved barren. Hesione feels sorry for Ellie and does not want her to marry middle-aged Boss Mangan; mistakenly assuming that her father, Mazzini, is behind the marriage plan, Hesione flirts with him to move him to her view of things. He resists her, having known the real thing with Ellie's mother. Hesione also flirts with Mangan, to pry him away from Ellie, and succeeds in making him fall in love with her. Mangan, like Ellie, suffers a broken heart. Despite Hector's conquest of Ellie and Mazzini's resistance to Hesione, the women seem to control the flirtations in the world of the play, including Addy's long-standing, apparently unconsummated affair with Randall and Ellie's and Captain Shotover's mutual (limited) seduction.

This complicated sexual relation is begun by Captain Shotover.[8] It takes place in a context of the Captain's repudiation of conventional marriage, of which the following statement by him to Randall, whom he believes to be Addy's husband, is but an example: "You have been boiled in bread and milk for years and years, like other married men. Poor devil!" (V, 90–91). He makes a similar statement to Hector: "[Hesione] has used you up, and left you nothing but dreams, as some women do" (V, 102).

The Captain has reservations not only about marriage, but about the company of women generally. To Mangan, who wants to leave Heartbreak House, he says, "Go, Boss Mangan; and when you have found the land where there is happiness and where there are no women, send me its latitude and longitude; and I will join you there" (V, 131). Nevertheless, the old man is drawn to Ellie at first sight, we learn in the opening scene, where he refers to her as "A young and attractive lady" (V, 62); and he acts on this attraction throughout the play. He makes China tea for her, leaving Nurse Guinness and Hesione amazed at his attention (V, 68); he chooses Ellie's room (V, 69); and he discards her bed's damp sheets and replaces them with clean ones, pointedly leaving Addy to shift for herself[9] (V, 72). Beyond that, he tells Mangan, probably quite sincerely, not to marry Ellie because he is too old (V, 87). And when Ellie asks him whether she should marry Mangan, he argues strenuously against her doing so, again, probably sincerely (V, 142–47). Ellie responds to the old man with trust and affection, not only asking his advice about her planned marriage, but confidently holding on to him when he wants to take one of his many trips to the pantry for a glass of rum. She tells him, "You shall not run away from me. . . . You are the only person in the house I can say what I like to. I know you are fond of me" (V, 145). As Hector says of her influence over the Captain, "That's an extraordinary girl. She has the Ancient Mariner on a string like a Pekinese dog" (V, 149).

The Captain thinks well of Ellie because she is a young and attractive woman in a house that needs someone like her. But we see that he has reservations about his perception of her, afraid that he is romanticizing what she is. Nevertheless, he is too old to resist the happiness she promises.

CAPTAIN SHOTOVER. I am too weary to resist or too weak. I am in my second childhood. I do not see you as you really are. I cant remember what I really am. I feel nothing but the accursed happiness I have dreaded all my life. (V, 148)

For her part, Ellie is up against it in the love game. She would have had wonderful babies with Hector, and she would not have turned him into a house pet, as she says Hesione has done (V, 125). She can marry Mangan, though she has some trouble keeping him to the bargain after he falls in love with Hesione. But he is not at all attractive, in body or spirit—just the kind of bad seed Shotover would like to destroy. She has no good choices. In giving her "broken heart and strong sound soul to its natural captain, my spiritual husband and second father" (V, 168), she is settling for an affectionate celibacy—the end of the road for begetting and the end of the road for Heartbreak House. Their marriage, such as it is, may be amiable, but it is the grotesque symbol of sexual failure for both of them. The Life Force seems to have abandoned Heartbreak House.[10]

Notes

1. For example, Eric Bentley, *Bernard Shaw* (Norfolk, Conn.: New Directions, 1947), thinks of Candida as a capable unromantic woman (167), and of Morell and Marchbanks as

"the two halves of Shaw's nature: his outer, glib, and confident half, at once socialist and social, and his spiritual, lonely, artistic half, the half that puts him beyond the pale of society" (204–5). He also believes that at play's end Morell is "crushed and speechless" (137); that Marchbanks is "strong enough to leave the homestead and live with himself and his vision" (205); and that Candida is immensely stable: "[She] really assumes that she has inherited the earth" (206–7). But in regarding Candida as unchangeable, Bentley means to praise her, not to suggest that she has overestimated her "mastery" of the two men. For an interesting early (and still representative) fixed opinion about the play's principals, see Arthur H. Nethercot, *Men and Supermen* (Cambridge, Mass.: Harvard University Press, 1954), pp. 7–17.

2. Shaw's comparison of Candida to Siegfried occurs in a letter to James Huneker, 6 April 1904. See *Bernard Shaw: Collected Letters*, 4 vols., ed. Dan H. Laurence; vols. I and II (New York: Dodd, Mead, 1965, 1972); vols. III and IV (New York: Viking, 1985, 1988). The letter to Huneker is in II, 414–16. Margery M. Morgan, in *The Shavian Playground* (London: Methuen, 1972), reviews various appraisals of Candida, including some of Shaw's own. We learn that she has been regarded as everything from Virgin Mother to unscrupulous manipulator to seductress to sentimental prostitute (72–73).

3. Though in a letter to Ellen Terry, 6 April 1896, Shaw refers to Candida as the Virgin Mother, his bantering tone suggests less that he shares the early-Marchbanks view of her than that he was immensely proud of his creation, and was trying to interest Ellen in the play, which he offered to read to her (see *Collected Letters I*, 623).

4. The very idea that Candida's choosing is significant is open to question. Nethercot (10) identifies Candida as a spiritually "static Philistine." In an essay in progress, I argue that Candida is spiritually her father's daughter, like many of Shaw's heroines; there I return to the value of her choosing.

5. In a letter to William Archer, 24 January 1900, Shaw refers to Candida as "mother first, a wife twentyseventh, and nothing else" (*Collected Letters II*, 137).

6. A. M. Gibbs, in *Heartbreak House: Preludes of Apocalypse* (New York: Twayne, 1994), offers an excellent and thorough treatment of the play. He makes the point (e.g., pp. 61–69) that marred human relations comprise a metaphor representing the dissolute state of society.

7. Gibbs observes, "It can be argued that Ellie Dunn's progress through the play is a process of emancipation; but her portrayal is also deeply ambiguous" (34).

8. See Gibbs, *Heartbreak House*, pp. 38–40, for an interesting connection between the Ellie Dunn–Shotover and the Erica Coterill–Shaw relations.

9. Shotover responds to Addy with varied emotions during the course of the play. Almost certainly recognizing her at once, he pretends not to know her. He sends her to her former bedroom, which turns out to be a "little hole" (V, 72). But he feels compassion enough for her that when she says, "Papa: don't say you think I have no heart," he comforts her: "If you had no heart to break how could you want to have it broken, child?" (V, 141).

10. What the bombing that ends the play may portend is ambiguous. It may signify the end of things altogether. Or it may be the necessary obliteration of what is—the failed Heartbreak House—for the sake of what is to come. See Gibbs, *Heartbreak House*, pp. 86–110, for an interesting discussion of the play's ending.

Bernard Shaw

SHAW'S SEX CREDO

[Shaw's letter to Frank Harris, 24 June 1930, is published in Dan H. Laurence, ed., *Bernard Shaw: Collected Letters IV, 1926–1950* (New York: Viking, 1988), pp. 190–93. A slightly bowdlerized version appears at the end of the chapter entitled "Shaw's Sex Credo" in Harris's *Bernard Shaw: An Unauthorized Biography* (New York: Simon & Schuster, 1931; London, Victor Gollancz, 1931). Substantial changes, deletions, and additions were made for republication as "To Frank Harris on Sex in Biography," chapter XVI of Shaw's *Sixteen Self Sketches* (London: Constable, 1949). The letter is also found in Stanley Weintraub, ed., *The Playwright and the Pirate: Bernard Shaw and Frank Harris: A Correspondence* (Gerrards Cross: Colin Smythe, 1982), whose Introduction summarizes the Shaw/Harris relationship.

For their published versions (upon which the one below is based), Laurence and Weintraub consulted the text of the original manuscript letter in the Harry Ransom Humanities Research Center, University of Texas at Austin. However, the letter as it appears below is a conflation of three documents: Shaw's 1930 letter, the changes made for the 1931 Harris biography, and those made for the 1949 sketches. In one instance, for example, Shaw goes from "copulations" (1930) to "gallantries" (1931) to "sex histories" (1949).

Given the context of certain publication by Harris, either verbatim or as (possibly distorted) narrative, Shaw's 1930 letter is surprisingly frank. Even his friends H. G. Wells and Arnold Bennett, both incorrigible womanizers, never publicized their sexual experiences in as much detail or with such *désinvolture* as Shaw does here. A few years earlier, on the other hand, the priapic Harris had unabashedly described his own sexual adventures in his notorious memoirs, *My Life and Loves* (4 vols., 1922–27; vol. 5, 1954)—"more fantasy than fact," cautions Weintraub (xiii)—the first volume of which was burned by Charlotte Shaw in the fireplace!

The reasons for Shaw's frankness on 24 June—and for his closing ca-

veat: "above all no pornography"—are found in the post scriptum to his
previous letter of 20 June. There he cautions Harris that his letter "does
not answer the modern biographer's first question nor satisfy the modern
reader's Freudian curiosity, which is 'How did you respond to your sexual
urges?'" Shaw promises to write further about what he calls "a very wide
and complex subject" (quoted in Weintraub, 233). Four days later, he did.

For publication the following year, however, Shaw cleaned up his language: "copulations" was softened to "gallantries and "whore" became
"mistress." And an allusion to Jenny Patterson as "sexually insatiable" was
deleted, perhaps out of consideration for Charlotte. By 1949 (Charlotte
having died in 1943), Shaw was free to thoroughly revise (in some cases
rewrite) his 1930 letter, referring to prostitutes and "Sunday husbands,"
to sexual experience as a "natural appetite," and to his marriage as a "relation in which sex had no part." At ninety-three, Shaw was still concerned
about the wide and complex subject of his sexual urges.[1]

A note on the text: Brace brackets { } indicate the few 1931 changes, while
square brackets [ ] mark the numerous 1949 emendations. Passages in
bold are additions; all other bracketed passages indicate deletions. Minor
changes—in syntax, punctuation, phrasing, verb tense, pronoun use—
have not been included.—M.W.P.]

Dear Frank Harris,
First, O **[sex-obsessed]** Biographer, get it clear in your mind that you
can learn nothing about your [sitter (or Biographee—) from a mere record
of his {copulations.}] **{gallantries.}** **[biographees from their sex histories.]** [You have no such record in the case of Shakespeare, and a pretty
full one for a few years in the case of Pepys: but you know much more
about Shakespeare than about Pepys. The explanation is that the relation
between the parties in copulation is not a personal relation.] **[The sex
relation is not a personal relation.]** It can be irresistibly desired and rapturously [executed] **[consummated]** between persons who could not endure one another for a day in any other relation. If I were to tell you every
such adventure that I have enjoyed you would be none the wiser as to [my
personal, nor even as to my sexual history.] **[the sort of man I am.]** You
would know only what you already know: that I am a human being. If you
have any doubts as to my normal virility, dismiss them from your mind. I
was not impotent; I was not sterile; I was not homosexual; and I was extremely, though not promiscuously, susceptible.

Also I was entirely free from the neurosis [(as it seems to me)] **[(as I
class it)]** of Original Sin. I never associated sexual intercourse with delin-
quency[.] [,] [I associated it always with delight, and had no] **[nor had any]**
scruples nor **[or]** remorses nor **[or]** misgivings of conscience. **[about it.]**

Of course I had scruples, and effectively inhibitive ones too, about getting women "into trouble" [(or letting them get themselves into it with me)] or cuckolding my friends; and I [understood that chastity can be a passion] **[held chastity to be a passion]** just as intellect is a passion; but St Paul was to me always a pathological case. Sexual experience seemed a [necessary completion of human growth; and] **[a natural appetite, and its satisfaction a completion of human experience necessarily for fully qualified authorship.]** I was not attracted [to] **[by]** virgins as such. I preferred **[fully matured]** women who knew what they were doing.

[As I have told you,] **[You were amazed and incredulous when I told you that]** my adventures began when I was 29. But it would be a prodigious mistake to take that as the date of the beginning of my sexual life. Do not misunderstand this: I was perfectly continent except for the involuntary incontinencies of dreamland, which were very infrequent. But as between Oscar Wilde, who gave 16 as the age at which sex begins, and Rousseau, who declared that his blood boiled with [sensuality] **[it]** from his birth [(but wept when Madame de Warens initiated him)] my experience confirms Rousseau and [is amazed at] **[confutes]** Wilde. Just as I cannot remember any time when I could not read and write, so I cannot remember any time when I did not exercise my [overwhelming] imagination in telling stories about women.

[I was, as all young people should be, a votary of the Uranian Venus.] **[All young people should be votaries of the Uranian Venus to keep them chaste: that is why Art is vitally important.]** I was steeped in romantic [music] **[opera]** from my childhood. I knew all the pictures and [the] **[antique Greek]** statues in the National Gallery of Ireland [(a very good one)] by heart. I read **[Byron and]** everything **[or romantic fiction]** I could lay my hands on. Dumas père made French history like an opera by Meyerbeer for me. From our cottage on Dalkey Hill I [contemplated an eternal Shelleyan vision] **[surveyed an enchanting panorama]** of sea, sky, and mountain. [Real life was only a squalid interruption to an imaginary paradise.] I was overfed on honey dew. The Uranian Venus was bountiful.

The difficulty about the Uranian Venus is that though she [saves you from squalid] **[can save us from premature]** debaucheries and enables you to prolong your physical virginity long after your adolescence, she may sterilize you by giving you imaginary amours on the plains of heaven [with goddesses and angels and even devils so enchanting] **[so magical]** that they spoil you for real women [or—if you are a woman—] **[and]** for real men. You become inhuman through a surfeit of beauty and an excess of voluptuousness. You **[may]** end as an ascetic, a saint, an old bachelor, an old maid [(in short, a celibate)] because, like Heine, you cannot ravish the Venus de Milo or be ravished by the Hermes of Praxiteles. Your love poems are like Shelley's Epipsychidion, irritating to *terre à terre* sensual [men and] women, who know at once that [you are making them palatable by] [we are in love with our own vision and only] pretending they are something that they are not, [and cannot stand comparison with.] [neither desire nor hope to be.]

Now you know how I lived, a continent virgin, [but an incorrigible philanderer] until I was 29, and ran away even when the handkerchief was thrown at [to] me. [; for I wanted love, but not to be appropriated and lose my boundless Uranian liberty.]

From that time until my marriage there was always some lady at my disposal; {some kindly lady available} [During the 14 years before my marriage at 43 there was always some lady in the case;] and I tried all the experiments and learned what there was to be learnt from them. [They were "all for love";] [The ladies were unpaid;] for I had no spare money; I earned [only] enough to keep me on a second floor, and took the rest out, not in money, but in freedom to preach Socialism. [Prostitutes, who often accosted me, never attracted me.]

When at last I could afford to dress presentably, I [soon] became accustomed to women falling in love with me. I did not pursue women: I was pursued by them.

Here again do not jump at conclusions. All the [my] pursuers did not want sexual intercourse. [They wanted company and friendship.] Some were happily married, and [were affectionately appreciative of my understanding] [appreciated our understanding] that sex was barred. [They wanted Sunday husbands, and plenty of them.][2] Some were prepared to buy friendship with pleasure, having [made up their minds] [learnt from a varied experience] that men were made that way. Some were [sexual geniuses, quite unbearable in any other capacity.] [enchantresses, quite unbearable as housemates.] No two cases were alike: William Morris's dictum "that all taste alike" ["they all taste alike"] was not, as Longfellow puts it, ["spoken of the soul."] ["spoken to the soul."]

[I found sex hopeless] [I was never duped by sex] as a basis for permanent relations, [and never] [nor] dreamt of marriage in connection with it. I put everything else before it, and never refused or broke an engagement to speak on Socialism to pass a gallant evening. [I liked sexual intercourse] [I valued sexual experience] because of its [amazing] power of producing a celestial flood of emotion and exaltation [of existence] which, however momentary, gave me a sample of [what may one day be the normal state of being for mankind in intellectual ecstasy.] [the ecstasy that may one day be the normal condition of conscious intellectual activity.] [I always gave the wildest expression to this in a torrent of words, partly because I felt it due to the woman to know what I felt in her arms, and partly because I wanted her to share it. But except perhaps on one occasion I never felt quite convinced that I had carried the lady more than half as far as she carried me: the capacity for it varies like any other capacity. I remember one woman who had a {quite innocent} sort of affectionate worship for me {saying} {explaining} that she had to leave her husband because sexual intercourse {felt, as she put it,} {hurt her physically,} "like someone sticking a finger into my eye." Between {her} {this extreme case} and the heroine of my first adventure, {who was sexually insatiable,} there was an enormous range of sensation; and the range of celestial exaltation must be still greater.

When I married I was too experienced to make the frightful mistake of simply setting up a permanent {whore} {mistress}; nor was my wife making the complementary mistake. There was nothing whatever to prevent us from satisfying our sexual needs without paying that price for it; and it was for other considerations that we became man and wife. In permanence and seriousness my consummated love affairs count for nothing besides the ones that were either unconsummated or ended by discarding that relation.]

[Not until I was past 40 did I earn enough to marry without seeming to marry for money, nor my wife at the same age without suspicion of being driven by sex starvation. As man and wife, we found a new relation in which sex had no part. It ended the old gallantries, flirtations, and philanderings for both of us. Even of these it was the ones that were never consummated that left the longest and kindliest memories.]

Do not forget that all marriages are different, and that a marriage between [two] young people followed by parentage cannot [must not] be lumped in with a childless partnership between [two] middle aged people who have passed the age at which [it is safe to] [the bride can safely] bear a first child.

And now, no romance and above all no pornography.

[1930]   G.B.S.

Notes

1. For details about the quarrel over quoting verbatim from Shaw's letters, see Sheila Hodges, *Gollancz, The Story of a Publishing House, 1928–1978* (London: Victor Gollancz, 1978), pp. 79–88.

2. Shaw used "Sunday husband" for the first time in *Getting Married* (written 1907–8): "THE BISHOP. Oh. I should say most imaginative and cultivated young women feel like that. I wouldnt give a rap for one who didnt. Shakespear pointed out long ago that a woman wanted a Sunday husband as well as a weekday one. But, as usual, he didnt follow up the idea" (Dan H. Laurence, editorial supervisor, *Bernard Shaw: Collected Plays with Their Prefaces,*

vol. 3 [New York: Dodd, Mead, 1975], p. 573). See *Much Ado About Nothing* 2.1, where Beatrice refuses to take Don Pedro as a husband "unless I might have another for working days." (My thanks to Rodelle Weintraub for tracing the allusion.) In *The Millionairess* (1934), Epifania defines "Sunday husband" as "a gentleman with whom I discuss subjects that are beyond my husband's mental grasp, which is extremely limited" (6:897–98); and in *Buoyant Billions* (1947), Tom Buoyant explains: "My wife needed some romance in her life when I ceased to be romantic to her and became only her matter-of-fact husband. To keep her in good humor and health I had to invite and entertain a succession of interesting young men to keep her supplied with what I call Sunday husbands" (7:346–47).

Michel W. Pharand

A SELECTED BIBLIOGRAPHY OF WRITINGS BY AND ABOUT BERNARD SHAW CONCERNING LOVE, SEX, MARRIAGE, WOMEN, AND RELATED TOPICS

This selected bibliography attempts to gather Bernard Shaw's pronouncements on sexuality and related topics (Section A), as well as some pertinent critical commentaries, including the essays in this volume (Section B). As the keywords here are "selected" and "attempts," the editor apologizes in advance for the inevitable omissions and welcomes any additions and corrections to what must be considered merely a preliminary compilation. It is hoped that the items listed below will open new avenues of research into an important Shavian arena.

References in brackets are to Dan H. Laurence's *Bernard Shaw: A Bibliography,* 2 vols. (Oxford: Clarendon, 1983), and to his *Supplement* (entries marked ['-S']) published in *SHAW: The Annual of Bernard Shaw Studies 20* (University Park: Penn State University Press, 2000), pp. 3–128. In Section B, I have used two important sources: *G. B. Shaw: An Annotated Bibliography of Writings about Him* (DeKalb: Northern Illinois University Press), vol. 1: 1871–1930, ed. J. P. Wearing (1986); vol. 2: 1931–56, ed. Elsie B. Adams, with Donald C. Haberman (1987); and vol. 3: 1957–78, ed. Donald C. Haberman (1986) [K310-S, K311-S, K312-S]; and Lucile Kelling Henderson, "Shaw and Woman: A Bibliographical Checklist," *Shaw Review* 17.1 (January 1974): 60–66; reprinted (and expanded) as "A Bibliographical Checklist" in *Fabian Feminist: Bernard Shaw and Woman,* ed. Rodelle Weintraub (University Park: Penn State University Press, 1977), pp. 262–71 [B437].

Section A: Works by Bernard Shaw

"About Sex and Marriage." Ruth Adam. *What Shaw Really Said.* New York: Schocken Books, 1966, pp. 37–46. [K204]

"As Bernard Shaw Sees Woman." *New York Times,* 19 June 1927, 4, 1–4, 2:1–5. [C2651; see B167]

Bernard Shaw: Agitations, Letters to the Press, 1875–1950. Ed. Dan H. Laurence and James Rambeau. New York: Frederick Ungar, 1985. [A316-S; on censorship: 93–105, 252–55; morality: 153–59; obscenity: 239–41; prostitution: 25–35; sex and marriage: 89–92, 106–13, 137–38, 279–81]

"Bernard Shaw on American Women." *Cosmopolitan* 40 (December 1905): 247–48. Reprinted in *The Independent Shavian* 10 (Winter 1971–72): 1–5.

"Bernard Shaw Extols Divorce" (symposium). *Globe and Commercial Advertiser* (New York) (28 March 1905): 4:2–4. [C1476]

Bernard Shaw and Mrs. Patrick Campbell: Their Correspondence. Ed. Alan Dent. London: Gollancz, 1952; New York: Knopf, 1952. [A266]

Bernard Shaw: Selections of His Wit and Wisdom. Compiled by Caroline Thomas Harnsberger. Chicago and New York: Follett, 1965. [see under Divorce, Man and Woman, Marriage, Women, and Sex]

"The Bishop Would be a Nudist" (statement). *Daily Mirror,* 2 November 1935, 1:4, 28:2. [C3127; see "Nudism" and "Mr. G. Bernard Shaw" in this section]

"Book Ban Denounced: Eminent People Defend 'Well of Loneliness'" (letter). *Daily Herald,* 22 November 1928, 5:4. [C2755a; drafted by Shaw; 45 signatories supporting Radclyffe Hall's 1928 Lesbian novel. See "Shaw and Wells" in this section]

"Brieux: A Preface." *Three Plays by Brieux.* London: A. C. Fifield; New York: Brentano's, 1911, pp. 9–53. [A104] Reprinted in Bernard F. Dukore, ed., *Bernard Shaw: The Drama Observed. Volume III: 1897–1911* (University Park: Penn State University Press, 1993), pp. 1188–222. [A326-S; on venereal diseases, 1216–20]

"The Cleveland Street Scandals" (letter of 26 November 1889). *Encounter* 3 (September 1954): 20–21. [C3942; on homosexuality]

"Divorce Law Reform" (letter). *The Times,* 14 July 1950, 7:5. [C3921]

Ellen Terry and Bernard Shaw: A Correspondence. Preface by Shaw. Ed. Christopher St. John. London: Constable, 1931; New York: G. P. Putnam's Sons, 1931. [A205]

"The Empire Promenade" (letter). *Pall Mall Gazette* 59, 16 October 1894, 3:2. [C1038; on prostitution]

"Fifth Fable." *Farfetched Fables* (1948). *Bernard Shaw: Collected Plays with Their Prefaces*, vol. 7. Editorial Supervisor Dan H. Laurence. New York: Dodd, Mead, 1975, pp. 449–54. [A296b; on nineteenth-century sex practices and beliefs]

"'Flog Every Brothel Keeper,' Says Shaw." *Daily Worker*, 30 March 1944, 3:4. [C3519; statement on the findings of an inquiry committee into prostitution]

"Forcible Feeding . . . Mr. Shaw on Suicide as a Solution" (letter). *Daily Mail*, 17 September 1912, 5:2. Extracts reprinted as "Let Suffragists Die, Says G. B. Shaw" in *New York Times*, 17 September, 4:1. [C1836]

"Forcible Feeding" (unsigned). *New Statesman* 1 (12 April 1913): 8–9. [C1870; see C1873 and "Torture by Forcible Feeding" in this section]

"G.B.S. and a Suffragist" (interview, extensively revised by Shaw). *Tribune* (London), 12 March 1906, 3:3–4. [C1534] Reprinted in Rodelle Weintraub, ed., *Fabian Feminist*, pp. 236–42.

"G.B.S. and Birth Control." *Manchester Guardian*, 23 November 1922. [C2468a-S]

"G.B.S. Wants Women Rulers" (interview). *Sunday Express*, 28 December 1924, 3: 1–3.

"George Bernard Shaw's Advice to the New York Vice Society" (letter). In Alfred Kreymborg's pamphlet, *Edna: The Girl of the Street*. New York: Guido Bruno, 1919, p. 3. [B107]

"The Husband, the Supertax, and the Suffragists" (letter). *The Times*, 10 June 1910, 7:1–2. [C1733]

The Intelligent Woman's Guide to Socialism and Capitalism. London: Constable, 1928; New York: Brentano's, 1928. [A187]

"Is the Servile State Coming? Bernard Shaw's Strange Suggestion." *Woman's Dreadnought* 3 (16 September 1916): 547. [C2090; reply to query on woman suffrage by Sylvia Pankhurst]

Letters from Margaret: Correspondence between Bernard Shaw and Margaret Wheeler, 1944–1950. Ed. Rebecca Swift. London: Chatto & Windus, 1992. [A323-S]

"Letters to Alice Lockett." *The Armchair Esquire*. Ed. Arnold Gingrich and L. Rust Hills. New York: Putnam, 1958, pp. 331–39.

"Literature and the Sex Instinct." From Preface to *Three Plays for Puritans* (1900). Reprinted in Stanley Weintraub, ed., *Bernard Shaw's Nondramatic Literary Criticism*. Lincoln: University of Nebraska Press, 1972, pp. 203–8. [A302]

"The Logic of the Hunger Strike." *Manchester Guardian Weekly Edition*, 10 September 1920, 213–14. Reprinted in *Living Age* 307 (2 October 1920), 30–31. [C2297]

"Love Affairs." Reprinted in *Shaw: An Autobiography, 1856–1898*. Ed. Stanley Weintraub. New York: Weybright and Talley, 1969, pp. 163–71. [Excerpts from Shaw's writings]

"Marriage and Its Critics" (letter). *Pall Mall Gazette* 85, 2 December 1907, 1:3, 2:1–2. [C1620]

"Marriage and Its Critics" (letter). *Pall Mall Gazette* 85, 10 December 1907, 3:2. [C1621]

"Martyrdom and Woman Suffrage" (letter). *The Times*, 25 June 1913, 10:4. [C1902; see C1900]

"The Menace of the Leisured Woman." *Time and Tide* 8 (4 February 1927): 106–7. [C2634; verbatim report of Shaw's summation from the Chair after 27 January debate between G. K. Chesterton and Lady Rhondda]. Reprinted in Dan H. Laurence, ed., *Platform and Pulpit* (New York: Hill & Wang, 1961), pp. 168–71. [A281]

"Modern Novels and Sex." *Evening Standard* (London), 26 May 1922, 5:1–2. [C2397] Reprinted in Stanley Weintraub, ed., *Bernard Shaw's Nondramatic Literary Criticism*, pp. 209–10.

"Morality and Birth Control." *Physical Culture* (New York) 42 (July 1919): 17–19. [C2227] Reprinted in *The Independent Shavian* 10 (Spring 1972): 33–36.

"Mr. G. B. Shaw on Women's Rights" (letter and statement). *Manchester Guardian*, 4 November 1933, 16:6–7. [C3017]

"Mr. G. Bernard Shaw on Excessive Clothing" (letter extract). *Sun Bathing Review* 1 (Summer 1933): 6. [C3002; see "Nudism" and "The Bishop" in this section]

"Mr. Shaw and Girl Strikers" (cable). *Daily Mail*, 7 January 1910, 7:6. [C1719]

"Mr. Shaw and the Unprotected Child" (letter). *Time and Tide* 4 (16 March 1923): 305. [C2448; on venereal disease. See "The Unprotected Child and the Law" in this section]

"Mr Shaw on Morals" and "Public Morals" (letters of 8 and 15 November 1913). Reprinted in Bernard F. Dukore, ed., *Bernard Shaw: The Drama Observed. Volume III: 1897–1911*, pp. 1303–9.

My Dear Dorothea: A Practical System of Moral Education for Females, Embodied in a Letter to a Young Person of that Sex. London: Phoenix House, 1956; New York: Vanguard, 1956. [A271]

Not Bloody Likely! and Other Quotations from Bernard Shaw. Ed. Bernard F. Dukore. New York: Columbia University Press, 1996: [A333-S; see under feminism, homosexuality, love, marriage, men and women, nudity, pornography, sex, wives, women]

"Nudism" (interview). *Dress and Beauty* 1 (April 1935): 14–15. [C3098; see B315, "George Bernard Shaw Gives His Views on Nudism," abridgment of C3098; see "The Bishop" and "Mr. G. Bernard Shaw" in this section]

"On the Economic Disabilities of Women" (verbatim report of 1 July 1907 speech at annual meeting of Association of Post Office Women Clerks). *Association Notes* (July 1907). Reprinted in *The Independent Shavian* 19.2 (1981): 27–31. [C3974]

"On Stage Morals and Censorship, Religion, Art, and Spiritual and Physical Love," "On Love, Marriage, the Nature of Sex, and Sex Ethics," and "On Sexual Reform." In Allan Chappelow, *Shaw—"The Chucker-Out": A Biographical Exposition and Critique*. London: George Allen & Unwin, 1969, pp. 61–102. [Excerpts from Shaw's writings]

"Our Morals and Our Police" (unsigned). *New Statesman* 1 (10 May 1913): 133–34. [C1887]

"Pensions for Mothers." *The Western Daily Mercury* (Plymouth), 26 September 1918.

"The Play and Its Author." Souvenir Program of a production of Eugène Brieux's *Woman on Her Own* (8 December 1913). [B77] Reprinted in Bernard F. Dukore, ed., *Bernard Shaw: The Drama Observed. Volume III: 1897–1911*, pp. 1309–12. [on prostitution]

"The Prosecution of Mr. [George] Bedborough" (letter). *The Adult* 2 (September 1898): 230–31. [C1287; on homosexuality]

"Preface." *Getting Married. Bernard Shaw: Collected Plays with Their Prefaces*, vol. 3. Editorial Supervisor Dan H. Laurence. New York: Dodd, Mead, 1975: 451–545. [A296b]

"Preface." *Mrs Warren's Profession. Bernard Shaw: Plays Unpleasant*. Ed. Dan H. Laurence. Harmondsworth: Penguin, 2000, pp. 181–212.

"The Rights of Women Now" (interview). *News Chronicle* (London) (17 November 1943): 2:5–8. Reprinted as "Shaw Asserts British Law Handicaps Men; Finds Women Really Running Country Now" in *New York Times*, 18 November, 27:5. [C3499]

"Romance and Real Sex." From *Table Talk of G.B.S.* (London and New York: Harper & Brothers, 1925). [A173] Reprinted in Stanley Weintraub, ed., *Bernard Shaw's Nondramatic Literary Criticism*, pp. 211–15.

"The Root of the White Slave Traffic." *The Awakener* 1.1 (16 November 1912): 7–8. [C1848] Reprinted in Rodelle Weintraub, ed., *Fabian Feminist*, pp. 255–59.

"Scientists Plead for Birth Control Idea" (statement). *New York Times*, 29 March 1925, 9, 6:1. [C2544; sent to Sixth International Neo-Malthusian and Birth Control Conference, New York]

"Sex Education." Louis Simon. *Shaw on Education*. New York: Columbia University Press, 1958, pp. 198–203. [Excerpts from Shaw's writings]

"Sex, Love and Marriage: I, II, and III." *Shaw: Interviews and Recollections*. Ed. A. M. Gibbs. Iowa City: University of Iowa Press, 1990, pp. 419–23. [I: 1914 conversation; II: 1927 interview; III: 1929 recollection]

"Shaw Gets Laughs as Expert on Sex" (expurgated verbatim report of speech, "The Need for Expert Opinion in Sex Reform"). *New York Times*, 14 September 1929, 2:6–7. Extracts from speech published as "Bernard Shaw on Sexual Reform" in *Time and Tide* 10 (20 September 1929): 1113–14. [C2805; see B195] Reprinted in Dan H. Laurence, ed., *Platform and Pulpit*, pp. 200–207.

"Shaw and Wells in Banned Book Battle." *Daily Herald*, 6 October 1928, 1:1–2. [C2745; on Radclyffe Hall's *The Well of Loneliness*. See "Book Ban" in this section]

Shaw on Women. Edited by Mary Chenoweth Stratton. Illustrated by Linda Holmes. Bucknell University: The Press of Appletree Alley Limited Editions, 1992.

"Shaw on Women: 'Monsters of Ingratitude'" (letter). *Daily News*, 26 June 1928, 6:7. [C2731]

"Shaw's Garden of Love." *A Curmudgeon's Garden of Love*. Ed. Jon Winokur. New York: New American Library, 1989, pp. 113–15. [see also at 30, 133, 164, 174, 179, 196]

"Shaw *versus* Roosevelt on Birth Control" (letters). *The World To-Day* 46 (September 1925): 845–50.

"Should Wives Be Paid?" (symposium). *Sunday Express*, 30 March 1919, 4:3. [C2210]

"Should Women Stop War?" (letter). *Free Lance* 3 (25 January 1902): 429. [C1382]

"Sir Almroth Wright's Polemic." *New Statesman* 2 (18 October 1913): 45–47. [C1910] Reprinted as "Sir Almroth Wright's Case Against Woman Suffrage." In Rodelle Weintraub, ed., *Fabian Feminist*, pp. 243–47.

"Some Opinions on Sex Training" (symposium). *New Era in Home and School* 5 (January 1924): 34. [C2476]

"The 'Suffragette' Case: Messages from Public Men." *Labour Leader* 10 (22 May 1913): 5:4. [C1889]

To a Young Actress: The Letters of Bernard Shaw to Molly Tompkins. Ed. Peter Tompkins. New York: Clarkson N. Potter, 1960; London: Constable, 1961. [A277]

"To Frank Harris on Sex in Biography." *Sixteen Self Sketches*. London: Constable, 1949; New York: Dodd, Mead, 1949, pp. 113–15. [A259; substantially revised version of letter dated 24 June 1930; first published (slightly bowdlerized) in Frank Harris's *Bernard Shaw* (1931); reprinted in this issue]

"Torture by Forcible Feeding is Illegal" (verbatim report). *London Budget* (23 March 1913): 4:1–7. [C1867] Reprinted in Rodelle Weintraub, ed., *Fabian Feminist*, pp. 229–35.

"Two Notable Occurrences" (letter to Margaret Sanger). *Birth Control Review* 9 (January 1925): 5. [C2535; see C2763] Reprinted in G. *Bernard*

Shaw on Birth-Control (The Madras Neo-Malthusian League, 1930). [A196]

"The Unmentionable Case for Women's Suffrage." *The Englishwoman* 1 (March 1909): 112–21. [C1674] Reprinted in Lloyd J. Hubenka, ed., *Bernard Shaw, Practical Politics*. Lincoln: University of Nebraska Press, 1976. [A303]

"The Unprotected Child and the Law." *Time and Tide* 4 (23 February 1923): 210–12. [C2442; on venereal disease]. Reprinted in *Doctors' Delusions, Crude Criminology, and Sham Education*, London: Constable, 1931, pp. 234–40. [see "Mr. Shaw and the Unprotected Child" in this section]

Unsigned note on White Slave Act sentence. *New Statesman* 1 (19 April 1913): 36. [C1874]

"What I owe to German Culture." *Adam International Review* 337–39 (Spring 1970): 5–16. [C1765; written 21 December 1910, published in German as the preface to the first volume of *Dramatische Werke* in 1911] Reprinted in Dan H. Laurence and Daniel J. Leary, eds., *The Complete Prefaces. Volume 1: 1889–1913* (London: Allen Lane, The Penguin Press, 1993), pp. 331–44. [see comments on "moral and immoral romance," 333–38]

"What is Mr. Asquith Up to Now?" *Independent Suffragette* 1 (October 1916): 10–11. [C2091]

"Why All Women Are Peculiarly Fitted to Be Good Voters." *New York American* (21 April 1907) 3.2:1–5. [C1584] Reprinted in Rodelle Weintraub, ed., *Fabian Feminist*, pp. 248–54.

"Why Not Personify God as a Woman?" (transcription of London lecture, "Some Necessary Repairs to Religion," 29 November 1906). *New York Times*, 30 November 1906. Reprinted in *The Independent Shavian* 10 (Fall 1971): 1–2, and in *SHAW: The Annual of Bernard Shaw Studies 1*. University Park: Penn State University Press, 1981, pp. 81–84. [B442]

"Why Women SHOULD Have the Vote: From Man's Point of View" (symposium). *Pall Mall Magazine* 51 (March 1913): 305. [C1860]

"Wives' Ideas on Rights are 85 Years Old." *Daily Sketch* (19 October 1945): 1:1–3. [C3614; debate with Married Women's Association. See C3606 and C3611]

"Woman—Man in Petticoats" (speech). As "As Bernard Shaw Sees Woman," in *New York Times Magazine*, 19 June 1927. [B167; see C2651] Reprinted in Dan H. Laurence, ed., *Platform and Pulpit*, pp. 173–78.

"A Woman Must Have a Home" (interview). *Cheltenham Chronicle*, 27 May 1950, 7:3–5. [C3916]

"Woman Since 1860 as a Wise Man Sees Her." *McCall's* (New York) 48 (October 1920): 10–11, 27. As "Woman Since 1860" in *Time and Tide*

1 (8 October): 442–44. Reprinted in *New York American* as "Woman as I Have Seen Her" (14 November), 2.12:1–5, and as "Bernard Shaw Traces Woman's Evolution from Crying and Fainting to Swearing and Smoking" (21 November), 2.5:1–3. [C2301]

"The Womanly Woman." *The Quintessence of Ibsenism.* London: Constable, 1913: pp. 36–45 and passim. Reprinted in J. L. Wisenthal, ed., *Shaw and Ibsen: Bernard Shaw's The Quintessence of Ibsenism and Related Writings.* Toronto: University of Toronto Press, 1979, pp. 124–31 [A307], and in *Bernard Shaw: Major Critical Essays* (Harmondsworth: Penguin, 1986), pp. 54–63.

Women as Councillors (Fabian Tract No. 93). *Fabian Municipal Program* (Second Series), No. 4 (March 1900). [A38]

"Women and Friendship" (letter). *Clarion* (13 February 1897): 49:6, 50:1. [C1191]

"Women in Politics." *Leader Magazine* 2 (25 November 1944): 5–6. [C3556]

"Women in Politics" (letter). *Liverpool Echo* (2 March 1948): 4:4–5. [C3787]

"Women in the War" (interview). *Leader* 1049 (16 August 1941): 15. [C3427]

"Women Losing Voice Beauty?" (symposium). *Daily Mirror,* 16 October 1934, 2:4. [C3070]

"Women, Love and Marriage." *The Sayings of Bernard Shaw.* Ed. Joseph Spence. London: Duckworth, 1993, pp. 23–28.

"Women, Socialism and Love" (letter). *Hearst's Magazine* (New York) 43 (January 1923): 5, 131. [C2435]

"Women Suffrage" (letter). *The Times,* 31 October 1906, 8:4. Reprinted as "Shaw on Woman's Rights," in *New York Times,* 15 November, 7:4, and as "The Influence of Women in English Politics" in *New York American & Journal* (16 December): 20:1–4. [C1557]

"Women Typists' Salaries" (letter). *Daily Mail,* 26 November 1907, 6:6. [C1618]

"The Women's Vote." *Manchester Guardian,* 5 July 1945, 6:2. [C3596]

Section B: Works About Bernard Shaw

Adams, Elsie. "Feminism and Female Stereotypes in Shaw." *Shaw Review* 17.1 (January 1974): 17–22. Reprinted in Rodelle Weintraub, ed., *Fabian Feminist,* pp. 156–62.

———. "Shaw's Ladies." *Shaw Review* 23.3 (September 1980): 112–18.

Allett, John. "*Mrs Warren's Profession* and the Politics of Prostitution.": *The Annual of Bernard Shaw Studies 19*. University Park: Penn State University Press, 1999, pp. 23–39.

Barnicoat, Constance A. "Mr. Bernard Shaw's Counterfeit Presentment of Women." *Fortnightly Review* (New York) 85 (March 1906): 516–27. Reprinted in *Living Age* (14 April 1906).

Barzun, Jacques. "Eros, Priapos, and Shaw." *The Play and Its Critics: Essays for Eric Bentley.* Ed. Michael Bertin. New York and London: University Press of America, 1986, pp. 67–88.

Berst, Charles A. "Passion at Lake Maggiore: Shaw, Molly Tompkins, and Italy, 1921–1950." *SHAW: The Annual of Bernard Shaw Studies 5*. University Park: Penn State University Press, 1985, pp. 81–114.

Besant, Lloyd. "Shaw's Women Characters." Dissertation. University of Wisconsin, 1964.

Block, Toni. "Shaw's Women." *Modern Drama* 2 (September 1959): 133–38.

Bosch, Marianne. "Mother, Sister, and Wife in *The Millionairess*." *SHAW: The Annual of Bernard Shaw Studies 4.*University Park: Penn State University Press, 1984, pp. 113–27.

Burlin, Robert B. "Shaw, Women and Opera: Determining the Voice." *Cahiers Victoriens et Édouardiens* 45 (April 1997): 73–81.

Carpenter, Charles A. "Sex Play Shaw's Way: *Man and Superman*." *Shaw Review* 18.2 (May 1975): 70–74.

Carter, Patricia M. "'Until It Was Historical': A Letter and an Interview." *SHAW: The Annual of Bernard Shaw Studies 24*. University Park: Penn State University Press, 2004, pp. 11–37.

Conolly, L. W. "*Mrs Warren's Profession* and the Lord Chamberlain." *The Annual of Bernard Shaw Studies 24*. University Park: Penn State University Press, 2004, pp. 46–95.

Crane, Gladys M. "Shaw and Women's Lib." *Shaw Review* 17.1 (January 1974): 23–31. Reprinted in Rodelle Weintraub, ed., *Fabian Feminist*, pp. 174–84.

Doan, William J. "*The Doctor's Dilemma*: Adulterating a Muse." *SHAW: The Annual of Bernard Shaw Studies 21*. University Park: Penn State University Press, 2001, pp. 151–61.

Du Cann, C. G. L. *The Loves of George Bernard Shaw.* New York: Funk & Wagnalls, 1963; London: Barker, 1963. [K180]

Dukore, Bernard F. "The Fabian and the Freudian." *The Shavian* 2.4 (June 1961): 8–11.

———. "G.B.S. and S.E.X.: Sexuality and Sexual Equality." *Essays in Theatre* 6.2 (May 1988): 81–94.

———, ed. *Bernard Shaw: The Drama Observed,* 4 vols. University Park: Penn State University Press, 1993. [A326-S]

————. "Sex and Salvation." *SHAW: The Annual of Bernard Shaw Studies 24*. University Park: Penn State University Press, 2004, pp. 112–18.

Follain, John. "Shaw failed to persuade secret mistress to keep their love child." *London Times*, 13 June 2004. [Interview with Peter Tompkins about his mother's affair with Shaw. See also "Owen."]

Gahan, Peter. "*Jitta's Atonement:* The Birth of Psychoanalysis and 'The Fetters of the Feminine Psyche.'" *SHAW: The Annual of Bernard Shaw Studies 24*. University Park: Penn State University Press, 2004, pp. 128–65.

Gainor, J. Ellen. *Shaw's Daughters: Dramatic and Narrative Constructions of Gender*. Ann Arbor: University of Michigan Press, 1991. [K345-S; see "Shavian Androgyny," esp. pp. 67–94]

Gates, Joanna E. "The Theatrical Politics of Elizabeth Robins and Bernard Shaw." *SHAW: The Annual of Bernard Shaw Studies 14*. University Park: Penn State University Press, 1994, pp. 43–53.

"G. B. Shaw Condemns Sex Appeal in Movies." *New York Times*, 19 November 1927, 5. [see also "Shaw Chides the Movie Producer," *New York Times*, 4 December 1927, Part XI, p. 2]

Gerrard, Thomas J. "Marriage and George Bernard Shaw." *Catholic World* 94 (January 1912): 467–82.

Gill, Stephen. "Shaw, the Suffragist." *Literary Half Yearly* 14 (1973): 153–56.

Gilmartin, Andrina. "Mr. Shaw's Many Mothers." *Shaw Review* 8.3 (September 1965): 93–103. Reprinted in Rodelle Weintraub, ed., *Fabian Feminist*, pp. 143–55.

Goldman, Michael. "Shaw and the Marriage in Dionysus." *The Play and Its Critics: Essays for Eric Bentley*. Ed. Michael Bertin. New York and London: University Press of America, 1986, pp. 97–111.

Grecco, Stephen. "Vivie Warren's Profession: A New Look at *Mrs. Warren's Profession*." *Shaw Review* 10 (September 1967): 93–99.

Greer, Germaine. "A Whore in Every Home." In Rodelle Weintraub, ed. *Fabian Feminist*, pp. 163–66. [on *Mrs Warren's Profession*]

Greiner, Norbert. "Mill, Marx, and Bebel: Early Influences on Shaw's Characterization of Women." In Rodelle Weintraub, ed. *Fabian Feminist*, pp. 90–98.

Hanley, Tullah Innes. *The Strange Triangle of G.B.S.* Boston: Bruce Humphries, 1956. [fictionalized treatment of Shaw's relationship with Janet Achurch and her husband]

Harris, Frank. "Shaw's Sex Credo." *Bernard Shaw*. New York: Simon & Schuster, 1931, pp. 227–45; London: Victor Gollancz, 1931, pp. 223–38. [See "To Frank Harris on Sex in Biography" in Section A]

Henderson, Archibald. "Bernard Shaw on Women (My Friend Bernard Shaw: VI)." *Sunday Chronicle* (Manchester), 6 February 1927.

———. "G.B.S. on Women." *Encore* 10.23 (July 1946): 118.

Henderson, Lucile Kelling. "Shaw and Woman: A Bibliographical Check-list." *Shaw Review* 17.1 (January 1974): 60–66. Reprinted (and expanded) as "A Bibliographical Checklist." In Rodelle Weintraub, ed., *Fabian Feminist*, pp. 262–71.

Johnson, Josephine. *Florence Farr: Bernard Shaw's "New Woman."* Totowa, N.J.: Rowman and Littlefield, 1975.

———. "The Making of a Feminist: Shaw and Florence Farr." In Rodelle Weintraub, ed., *Fabian Feminist*, pp. 194–205.

Kakutani, Michiko. "G. B. Shaw and the Women in His Life and Art." *New York Times*, Sunday 27 September 1891.

Kelley, Katherine E. "Shaw on Woman Suffrage: A Minor Player on the Petticoat Platform." *SHAW: The Annual of Bernard Shaw Studies 14*. University Park: Penn State University Press, 1994, pp. 67–81.

Kester, Dolores. "The Legal Climate of Shaw's Problem Plays." In Rodelle Weintraub, ed., *Fabian Feminist*, pp. 68–83.

Khanna, Savitri. "Shaw's Image of Woman." *The Shavian* 4.7–8 (Summer 1973): 253–59.

Laurence, Dan H. "Katie Samuel: Shaw's Flameless 'Old Flame.'" *SHAW: The Annual of Bernard Shaw Studies 15*. University Park: Penn State University Press, 1995, pp. 3–19.

———. "Victorians Unveiled: Some Thoughts on Mrs Warren's Profession." *SHAW: The Annual of Bernard Shaw Studies 24*. University Park: Penn State University Press, 2004, pp. 38–45.

Leary, Daniel. "Don Juan, Freud and Shaw in Hell: A Freudian Reading of *Man and Superman*." *Shaw Review* 22.2 (May 1979): 58–78.

Le Mesurier, Lillian. *The Socialist Woman's Guide to Intelligence: A Reply to Mr. Shaw*. London: Benn, 1929.

Lorichs, Sonja. *The Unwomanly Woman in Bernard Shaw's Drama and Her Social and Political Background*. Uppsala: University of Uppsala Studies in English, 1973.

———. "The Unwomanly Woman." *The Shavian* 4.7–8 (Summer 1973): 250–52.

———. "The 'Unwomanly Woman' in Shaw's Drama." In Rodelle Weintraub, ed., *Fabian Feminist*, pp. 99–111.

MacCarthy, Desmond. "What Is Sauce for the Goose—G. B. Shaw on Woman's Emancipation." *New Statesman and Nation* 27 (15 April 1944): 255.

McCauley, Janie Caves. "Kipling on Women: A New Source for Shaw." *Shaw Review* 17.1 (January 1974): 40–44. Reprinted in Rodelle Weintraub, ed., *Fabian Feminist*, pp. 23–30.

Mackworth, Margaret Haig (Thomas) [2nd Viscountess Rhondda]. "Shaw on Sex." *Notes on the Way.* New York: Macmillan, 1937, pp. 71–75. Reprinted by Books for Libraries Press. Freeport, N.Y., 1968.

Molnar, Joseph. "Shaw's Four Kinds of Women." *Theatre Arts* 36 (December 1952): 18–21, 92. Adapted as "Shaw's Living Woman," *Shaw Society Bulletin* 49 (June 1953): 7–11.

Morgan, Margery M. "Shaw and the Sex Reformers." *SHAW: The Annual of Bernard Shaw Studies 24.* University Park: Penn State University Press, 2004, pp. 96–111.

"Mr. Bernard Shaw on Sex Instruction." *The Times,* 20 June 1914, 5. [Shaw at a London symposium]

"Mr. Shaw's Newest Woman." *New York Times,* 19 December 1920, part III: 21. [Shaw detects that women have ceased aping men and are now asserting their femininity]

Murrenus, Valerie. "Hostages of Heartbreak: The Women of *Heartbreak House.*" *SHAW: The Annual of Bernard Shaw Studies 23.* University Park: Penn State University Press, 2003, pp. 17–25.

Nathan, George Jean. "Shaw as a Lover." *American Mercury* 13 (February 1928): 246–48.

Nathan, Rhoda. "The Shavian Sphinx." *Shaw Review* 17.1 (January 1974): 45–52. Reprinted in Rodelle Weintraub, ed., *Fabian Feminist,* pp. 30–38.

———. "All About Eve: Testing the Miltonic Formula." *SHAW: The Annual of Bernard Shaw Studies 23.* University Park: Penn State University Press, 2003, pp. 65–74. ["Shaw's Eves come in a variety of guises."]

Nelson, Raymond S. "*Mrs. Warren's Profession*" and English Prostitution." *Journal of Modern Literature* 2 (1971–72): 357–66.

Nethercot, Arthur. "G.B.S. and Annie Besant." *Shaw Bulletin* 1.9 (September 1955): 1–14.

———. *Men and Supermen: The Shavian Portrait Gallery.* 1954. New York: Benjamin Blom, 1966, 2nd ed., corrected [K142; see "The Female of the Species," 77–126]

Owen, Richard. "Shaw's secret fair lady revealed at last." *London Times,* 14 June 2004. [Interview with Peter Tompkins about his mother's affair with Shaw. See also "Follain."]

Pagliaro, Harold. "Truncated Love in *Candida* and *Heartbreak House.*" *SHAW: The Annual of Bernard Shaw Studies 24.* University Park: Penn State University Press, 2004, pp. 204–14.

Pederson, Lise. "Shakespeare's *The Taming of the Shrew* vs. Shaw's *Pygmalion:* Male Chauvinism vs. Women's Lib." *Shaw Review* 17.1 (January 1974): 32–39. Reprinted in Rodelle Weintraub, ed., *Fabian Feminist,* pp. 14–22. [reprinted title reads "Lib?"]

Peters, Margot. *Bernard Shaw and the Actresses.* New York: Doubleday, 1980. [K295]

Peters, Sally. "Ann and Superman: Type and Archetype." In Rodelle Weintraub, ed., *Fabian Feminist,* pp. 46–65.

———. *Bernard Shaw: The Ascent of the Superman.* New Haven and London: Yale University Press, 1996. [K372-S; Shaw as crypto-homosexual]

———. "From Mystic Betrothal to *Ménage à Trois:* Bernard Shaw and May Morris. *The Independent Shavian* 28.1–2 (1990): 3–14.

———. "Shaw's Life: A Feminist in Spite of Himself." *Cambridge Companion to George Bernard Shaw.* Ed. Christopher Innes. Cambridge: Cambridge University Press, 1998, pp. 3–24.

Pharand, Michel W. "Introduction: Dionysian Shaw." *SHAW: The Annual of Bernard Shaw Studies 24.* University Park: Penn State University Press, 2004, pp. 1–10.

Powell, Kerry. "New Women, New Plays, and Shaw in the 1890s." *Cambridge Companion to George Bernard Shaw.* Ed. Christopher Innes. Cambridge: Cambridge University Press, 1998, pp. 76–100.

Rhondda, Lady. "Shaw's Women." *Time and Tide* 11 (7 March–11 April 1930): 300–301, 331–34, 364–66, 395–96, 436–38, 468–70. [for individual essay titles, see Wearing, nos. 3608 to 3613]

Roberts, R. Ellis. "The Inhibitions of Bernard Shaw." *Bookman* (London) 79 (October 1930): 4–7.

Sachs, Lisbeth J., and Bernard H. Stern. "Bernard Shaw and His Women." *British Journal of Medical Psychology* 37 (1964): 343–50. [Shaw as latent homosexual]

Sauer, David K. "'Only a Woman' in *Arms and the Man.*" *SHAW: The Annual of Bernard Shaw Studies 15.* University Park: Penn State University Press, 1995, pp. 151–66.

Shaw and Women. BBC-TV Production (U.S. Distributor: Peter M. Robeck and Company, Inc., 230 Park Avenue, New York, N.Y. 10017). 16 mm. black and white, 45 min. [no date; listed in Henderson, *Fabian Feminist,* p. 271]

"Shaw Favors Women on Censorship Staff." *New York Times,* 12 June 1926, 4. [Support of a proposal that a woman should assist the Lord Chamberlain in the censorship of plays]

Shields, Jean Louise. "Shaw's Women Characters: An Analysis and a Survey of Influences from Life." Dissertation. University of Indiana, 1958.

Silver, Arnold. *Bernard Shaw: The Darker Side.* Stanford: Stanford University Press, 1982.

Singer, Irving. *The Nature of Love 3: The Modern World.* Chicago: University of Chicago Press, 1987, pp. 239–53. [on sex, love, the Life Force, and Shaw's "vitalistic Puritanism"]

Sirlin, Lázaro. "La sexología en las comedias de Jorge Bernard Shaw"

(Sexology in the comedies of George Bernard Shaw). *Sagitario* (Argentina) 7 (October–November 1926): 50–58. [in Spanish]

Sterner, Mark H. "Shaw's Superwoman and the Borders of Feminism: One Step Over the Line?" *SHAW: The Annual of Bernard Shaw Studies 18.* University Park: Penn State University Press, 1998, pp. 147–60.

Stone, Susan C. "Whatever Happened to Shaw's Mother-Genius Portrait?" In Rodelle Weintraub, ed., *Fabian Feminist,* pp. 130–42.

Timmons, Ann. *Shaw's Women.* [stage play; publication data unavailable. See on-line at http://home.earthlink.net/~anntimmons/aet.htm]

Uttley, Diane. *Shaw's Women* and *Shaw, Women, and Feminism.* United Kingdom: The Bernard Shaw Information and Research Service, no date. ["Info Subject" pamphlets sold on-line]

Vesonder, Timothy G. "Eliza's Choice: Transformation Myth and the Ending of *Pygmalion.*" In Rodelle Weintraub, ed., *Fabian Feminist,* pp. 39–45.

Waltonen, Karma. "*Saint Joan:* From Renaissance Witch to New Woman." *SHAW: The Annual of Bernard Shaw Studies 24.* University Park: Penn State University Press, 2004, pp. 186–203.

Wasserman, Marlie Parker. "Vivie Warren: A Psychological Study." *Shaw Review* 15 (May 1972): 71–75. Reprinted in Rodelle Weintraub, ed., *Fabian Feminist,* pp. 168–73.

Watson, Barbara Bellow. *A Shavian Guide to the Intelligent Woman.* London: Chatto & Windus, 1964; New York: Norton, 1964. [K192]

———. "The New Woman and the New Comedy." *Shaw Review* 17.1 (January 1974): 2–16. Reprinted in Rodelle Weintraub, ed., *Fabian Feminist,* pp. 114–29.

Weimer, Michael. "*Press Cuttings:* G.B.S. and Women's Suffrage." In Rodelle Weintraub, ed., *Fabian Feminist,* pp. 84–89.

Weintraub, Rodelle, ed. *Fabian Feminist: Bernard Shaw and Woman.* University Park: Penn State University Press, 1977. [B437]

———. "Introduction: Fabian Feminist." *Fabian Feminist,* 1–12.

———. "The Gift of Imagination: An Interview with Clare Boothe Luce." *Shaw Review* 17.1 (January 1974): 53–60. Reprinted in *Fabian Feminist,* 206–13.

———. "The Center of Life: An Interview with Megan Terry." In *Fabian Feminist,* 214–25.

———. "The Irish Lady in Shaw's Plays." *Shaw Review* 23.2 (May 1980): 77–89.

———. "What Makes Johnny Run? Shaw's *Man and Superman* as a Pre-Freudian Dream Play." *SHAW: The Annual of Bernard Shaw Studies 24.* University Park: Penn State University Press, 2004, pp. 119–27.

Weintraub, Stanley. "Shaw's Lady Cicely and Mary Kingsley." In Rodelle Weintraub, ed., *Fabian Feminist,* pp. 185–92.

———. "Who's Afraid of Virginia Woolf? Virginia Woolf and G.B.S." *SHAW: The Annual of Bernard Shaw Studies 21*. University Park: Penn State University Press, 2001, pp. 41–62.

———. "Shaw's Sculptress, Kathleen Scott." *SHAW: The Annual of Bernard Shaw Studies 24*. University Park: Penn State University Press, 2004, pp. 166–85.

Wherly, Eric S. *Shaw for the Million*. Belfast: Gulliver Books, 1946. [see "Shaw on Sex" pp. 35–36, and "Shaw the Gay Lothario," pp. 37–39]

West, Rebecca. "Contesting Mr. Shaw's Will: An Analysis of G.B.S.'s Final Word on Women and Socialism." *Bookman* (New York) 67 (July 1928): 513–20.

REVIEWS

Shaw's Black Girl: Layers of Ideas

Leon Hugo. *Bernard Shaw's "The Black Girl in Search of God": The Story Behind the Story*. Gainesville: University Press of Florida, 2003. The Florida Bernard Shaw Series. xvi + 170 pp. Index. $55.00 (cloth).

In February of 2001, I received a communication from Leon Hugo. He was interested in getting involved in matters pertaining to Shaw, such as proofing articles for *SHAW* and writing reviews for future issues. In that same correspondence, he gave me an update of his project on *The Black Girl*. He indicated that he had to put it on hold in June/July last but that he was now getting back into it. He wrote, "Not a long text, can't be by its very nature, but I hope to be able to augment it with lots of black and white pictures—Farleigh's, Shaw's and those that appeared with the 're-buttals' that followed publication of the BG. My hope is to get it published as one of the Shaw Series of the University Press of Florida. Dick Dietrich seems keen to see it. My estimated submission date is mid-year." It is inter-esting to note that he did indeed finish his project as noted, that he not only gained the support of Dick Dietrich for the publication of the work in the Florida Bernard Shaw Series, but he also got Dick to write the Fore-word. Also of note is the reference that Hugo makes to the black-and-white pictures with which he hoped to augment the text. Between chapters 3 and 4 there are eleven pictures, four from the Farleigh woodcuts that appeared in the 1932 and later publications of *The Adventures of The Black Girl in Her Search for God*. These four woodcuts are paired with the sketches Shaw had made to illustrate his text. They clearly demonstrate that Shaw had the eye of an illustrator but needed the execution of an artist. Farleigh was indeed a great discovery, and according to Hugo his reputation soared after *The Black Girl* was published. He seems to have fallen into the Shavian playfulness when he includes the face of Shaw on the title-page woodcut that depicts the naked black girl in the jungle with African and Christian icons. What is surprising, however, is that Shaw allowed the Christian icon of Christ on the cross to stand, but he may have done so to emphasize his view that Christianity had become Crosstianity. Hugo includes three other illustrations taken from the cover designs or title pages of publications that were rejoinders to Shaw's work. One is from C. H. Maxwell's *Adventures of the White Girl in Her Search for God,* one from W. R. Matthews's *The Adventures of Gabriel in His Search for Mr. Shaw,* and the other from Marcus Hyman's *The Adventures of the White Girl in Her Search for Knowledge.* If you have seen the Farleigh woodcuts printed by R & R. Clark, Limited, Edinburgh, in *The Adventure of the Black Girl in Her Search for God,* you will acknowledge their superiority over all others as well as the power they evoke in illuminating the text. As Leon Hugo informs us, the woodcuts themselves added to the controversy that followed the book's publication. One critic did not want Farleigh's drawings to go unchallenged. This unidentified writer wrote: "I should be surprised if the illustrations have not done more harm than the text." It is a shame that this unnamed critic did not go into more detail so that we could understand the nature of the objections. Regretful as that may be, we do know that that critic wanted to harass both artist and author so that "they might enjoy a well deserved burning together."

Besides Dietrich's Foreword, there are six chapters, each devoted to varying aspects of the composition of *The Black Girl*, before and after publication. Dietrich narrates the immediate circumstance that led to the writing of *The Black Girl*. He also makes use of an extended metaphor on driving to illustrate one of the major concepts in the book, namely, the depiction of religious philosophies that from Shaw's perspective were running on automatic pilot instead of braking for more thoughtful, original thinking on matters religious. He, like Dan Laurence, chooses to classify Shaw's work as a fable, contrary to Hugo's choice of the term "allegory." Hugo's choice of terminology is made patently clear in his final chapter, of which I will deal later. At the end of his Foreword, we are told of Leon Hugo's death and that it was his children, especially Pippa, who oversaw the book's transformation from manuscript to page proof. The Shavian community of scholars is grateful for their efforts in bringing their father's work to publication.

In chapter 1, "Antecedents," Hugo reminds us of Shaw's usual practice of bringing work with him while on vacation. This trip to South Africa was no exception. He was working on "The Rationalization of Russia," producing some forty pages on the eighteen-day passage from Southampton to South Africa in January 1932. That work was superseded by *The Black Girl* when Shaw's driving accident landed his injured wife, Charlotte, in recuperative rest for a couple of weeks at a hotel in the small hamlet of Knysna, three hundred miles from Cape Town.

Hugo is right to point out here that *The Black Girl* is rather unique among Shaw's body of works; however, as an allegory about religious philosophies it has a resonance with an earlier work, *Androcles and the Lion* and its Preface. Hugo recognized this but chose to pass over it without extended commentary. His immediate concern here is to chart the classical antecedents for *The Black Girl*. He draws parallels between the black girl and the classical conception of the goddess Athena, sees the similarity of the black girl's quest for knowledge echoing that of John Bunyan's *Pilgrim's Progress*, and views Shaw's heroine as a black and female version of Voltaire's hero in *Candide*.

Chapter 2, "Foreshadowing," is really a kind of discovery chapter; it is truly the story behind the story, the source for much of Shaw's ideas that are the intellectual underpinnings of the fictional text. The first involves his association with a Mabel Shaw (no relation), a missionary in Africa. A Quaker friend, J. E. Whiting, shared with Shaw extracts from Mabel Shaw's letters about her past and her present mission to bring Christianity to the natives. Shaw corresponded with her in 1928 and invited her for lunch at 4 Whitehall Court in May 1930. He questioned her desire to bring black children to the white way of worshiping God and scorned her for focusing on the Crucifixion as the central emblem of Christianity. Moreover, he chided her for transferring such horrendous torture upon herself, describing it as "a craze for self-torture." These reprimands are all "foreshadowed" in the black girl's questioning of matters religious.

Another "foreshadowing" that Hugo develops in this chapter is the essential message that Shaw came to South Africa to deliver—that "all are equal in the sight of God." It is a central tenet of Shaw's belief and a major theme throughout *The Black Girl*. A very practical conclusion from his message of equality is his caveat: "If you let other people do everything for you, you will soon become incapable of doing anything for yourself." It was a forceful message to the South African whites in the 1930s and one that was carried over even more forcefully with the publication of *The Black Girl*.

Chapters 3 and 4 are short and deal for the most part with factual information. Chapter 3, "Accident," narrates the particulars of the accident itself, noting the various versions of the incident, Shaw's and the press's. Shaw and his driver, Newton, were unhurt, but Charlotte was shaken and badly bruised. Though she did not need to be hospitalized, she was confined to her bed in the Royal Hotel in Knysna. During her recuperation, Shaw dropped his plans of writing a play and instead began working on *The Black Girl*. He wrote most, if not all, of it in about eighteen days, hiring a local stenographer, Dorothy Smith, to assist him.

In chapter 4, "Publication," Hugo provides the reader with detailed information about its eventual publication in spite of Sister Laurentia, the Abbess of Stanbrook, who had threatened not to forgive Shaw if he published it. The most interesting part of this chapter is to learn of the role that William Maxwell, director of R. & R. Clark, played in its publication. Not only did he enable Shaw to override his scruples regarding Dame Laurentia McLachlan's stern admonition against publication, but he also was the one who recommended to Shaw the young wood engraver, John Farleigh, as illustrator. Shaw wrote to Farleigh on 13 November 1932, "At last the book has gone to press. It isn't half a bad job, is it? The girl makes a charming leitmotif running through all the pictures. Anyhow, it's been a bit of fun." *The Black Girl* was published on 5 December 1932. Charlotte had given a prepublication copy to T. E. Lawrence and 25,000 copies went out to bookstores. The book was in such demand that it was reprinted five times in December alone, bringing the total to 57,000 copies. Another 48,000 copies, or nine more printings between 1933 and 1936, were sold. In 1934, *The Adventures of the Black Girl in Her Search for God* was incorporated in *Short Stories, Scraps, and Shavings* in the Standard Edition (Constable). In 1946 the Penguin edition appeared with its shortened title, *The Black Girl in Search of God and Some Lesser Tales*. Other publications that Hugo mentions are the definitive text Penguin brought out under the editorial supervision of Dan H. Laurence in 1977 and the Viking edition of *The Portable Bernard Shaw*, compiled and edited by Stanley Weintraub.

In chapter 5, "Reaction, Censorship, Repudiation," Hugo traces the public response to *The Black Girl*. He notes that not only did Shaw come under public scrutiny, but so too did the printer and illustrator. A Mr. Olsson, writing for the *Printing Trades Journal*, opined that "the printer was a trifle more important than the author and translator." He went on to say that "the inspiration and direction behind this achievement was the printer, Mr. William Maxwell of R. & R. Clark of Edinburgh. How did he do it? He secured the illustrator Mr. John Farleigh." British and American reviews were a mixed bag of praise and denigration. Those that praised the work understood that Shaw's quarrel is not with the Bible itself but with people who misread and misapply it. On the other hand, religious zealots denigrated it as an attack on Christianity. What typically followed from such attacks was censorship. The Cambridge Town Council upheld the decision of its library committee to ban the book from the public library, and the education committee of the London County Council considered the requisition list of the teachers' library at County Hall from which the book had been pointedly excluded. Two other rejections are worthy of note: that of the Irish Censorship Board, which on 1 May 1933 prohibited the sale and circulation of the book. The other was, of course, from the Abbess of Stanbrook, Dame Laurentia McLachlan. Hugo treats these two rejections in detail, attempting to discover the reasons behind the rejections. It appears that the Irish Censorship Board had a strong clerical element that urged the suppression of the book because it was repulsed by Farleigh's depiction of a nude black girl. The second rejection, by Sister Laurentia, was of greater concern to Shaw because of his personal relationship with her. Shaw had sent her a copy of the book and she proved to be his most severe critic. No matter how Shaw defended himself, she was unforgiving. To her, Shaw had done dishonor to almighty God and, as Hugo concludes, "it was impossible for her to accommodate this iconoclastic Shaw in her heart and soul."

Hugo treats the next repudiations of *The Black Girl* in the form of rejoinders. In chapter 6, "Rejoinder," he views *The Black Girl* from the perspective of the controversy that followed its publication from 1933 to the late 1990s. One or two of the early publications or rejoinders were written to repudiate Shaw, one or two to further develop his message, and one to mock him. What these works reveal is that they affirm the continuing impact that Shaw's tale has on religious sensibilities.

The first of these rejoinders was Charles Herbert Maxwell's *Adventures of the White Girl in Her Search for God,* published in March 1933. As Hugo points out, this work is nothing but a conveyance of received doctrine. It was followed by Lawrence Durrell's *Bromo Bombastes* in 1933, a work written in jingling verse when the poet was twenty-one. Dr. W. R. Matthews's *The Adventures of Gabriel in His Search for Mr. Shaw* was published in August 1933. It is a humorous account of the Archangel Gabriel being sent to Earth by Saint Peter to investigate the strange noise coming from a man named Shaw. Another rejoinder, strictly a variation on Shaw's theme, by Mr. and Mrs. I. I. Kazi appeared in September 1933 entitled *The Adventures of the Brown Girl (Companion to the Black Girl of Mr. Bernard Shaw) in Her Search for God.* In the fall of 1934, *Four Men Seek God: A Reply to a Famous Author's Book* came out by C. Payne, followed by Marcus Hyman's *The Adventures of the White Girl in Her Search for Knowledge* in October.

Hugo's summaries of these rejoinders in this chapter had previously been seen in his article "The Black Girl and Some Lesser Quests: 1932–1934," published in *SHAW 9: Shaw Offstage: The Nondramatic Writings,* edited by Fred D. Crawford in 1989. In his book he adds to the list H. M. Singh's *The Adventures of the Black Man in His Search for God,* published in 1937, and C. E. M. Joad's *The Adventures of a Young Soldier in Search of the Better World,* published in 1943. The next work to be derived from *The Black Girl* was Brigid Brophy's *The Adventures of God in His Search for the Black Girl* in 1973. Then in the form of the literary pamphlet, Donald Sutherland published in 1999 his work, *Further Adventures of the Black Girl in Her Search for God.*

Recent adaptations of the tale for stage, radio, and television appeared sporadically. A production I saw at the Mark Taper Forum in 1996 was an adaptation of Christopher Isherwood. It ran from 20 February to 4 May and was, Hugo writes, a stageworthy play. I concur. Aubrey Hampton and his wife, Susan Hussey, produced a version of *The Black Girl* at the Gorilla Theater in Tampa, Florida. That production played to near-capacity houses on 9, 10, 16, and 17 March 1991 with a predominately black audience. Neither of these two stage adaptations has been repeated, but Dan H. Laurence presented his adaptation in a solo reading at the New York Public Library (22 September 1961) and a full cast reading at the Shaw Festival in Niagara-on-the-Lake on 16 July 1999. There were only a few radio broadcasts of *The Black Girl*. The BBC did one in 1941 and again in 1944. Dan H. Laurence's version, recorded in a reading performance at Niagara-on-the-Lake Shaw Festival, was broadcast by the Canadian Broadcasting Corporation Radio 1 in its Sunday Night Playhouse on 27 February 2000 and was repeated the following Monday.

The final chapter, and the most interesting, is "Champion." In this chapter the reader comes to realize why Hugo was insistent on labeling Shaw's tale an allegory. He systematically analyzes the tale from the perspective of its religious, feminist, and political/racial layers. Hugo sees these allegorical levels as causes and traces the black girl's emergence from them as a "champion." In confronting the religious, Shaw's black girl debunks not the Bible itself but the unquestioning veneration people have of it. Bible-educated humans have now become the ignoramuses. They refuse to think for themselves. The black girl will have nothing to do with them; she will not be an ignoramus; she is determined to find God for herself.

Visitors to Shaw's Corner in Ayot St. Lawrence will recall the proliferation of Bibles throughout the house, one most conspicuously on a small table beside his bed. Shaw was a voracious reader of the Bible and regarded it as a superb literary work. He takes the black girl on a journey through the Bible, where she rejects not only the false gods of the past but also the false gods of the present as represented by science, by Islam, by art. She then encounters Voltaire, tending his garden, and later she meets the Irishman, Shaw, working in the kitchen garden. These two encounters, disguised as Deism and Creative Evolution, constitute the summation of her quest, the resolution of the religious allegory.

"Shaw," says Hugo, "is the unsung feminist of the twentieth century." His black girl remains true to her feminist cause, naked and resolute in asserting her right of self-determination. When I read this portion of Hugo's book, I knew he was writing an apology of Shaw's feminism, and that his target, among many, was the strident and exclusive feminism voiced by J. Ellen Gainor in *Shaw's Daughters: Dramatic and Narrative Constructions of Gender*, published in 1991.

The third and final allegorical layer Hugo uncovers is that of the black girl as a political/racial icon. Shaw's own voice is cleverly muted and emerges as the voice of the black girl. Her forceful voice carries the message that the "inhumanity of white exploitation spares no soul." Shaw recognized the danger of a political policy of apartheid and through the black girl he voiced his concern about South Africa's future. The marriage between the black girl and the Irishman is a model for the survival of the whites and blacks of South Africa, the solution, if you will, to resolve racial strife.

Hugo's work is a clarion call that Bernard Shaw is still worth reading, that he speaks to all generations. It is a shame that both articulate voices—Hugo's and Shaw's—have been silenced, but their work will remain a constant reminder of the vital issues that confront all humanity throughout the ages, past, present, and future.

Gale K. Larson

Letters of Shaw and the Webbs Survive Editing

Selected Correspondence of Bernard Shaw. Bernard Shaw and the Webbs. Edited by Alex C. Michalos and Deborah C. Poff. Toronto: University of Toronto Press, 2002. xxxii + 312pp. Index. C$65.00

The idea of including a volume devoted to the letters between Shaw and Sidney and Beatrice Webb in the Shaw Correspondence series must have been self-recommending, so it is not surprising to discover that one was commissioned some time ago by the original editor of the series, the late Percy Smith. No political friendship was more important to Shaw than that with Sidney Webb. It is the equivalent in significance of his friendships with William Archer or Granville Barker. And, as the volume that has now emerged shows, this is a correspondence that lasted longer than any other in Shaw's long life, spanning more than sixty years. It begins with a letter from Sidney Webb three years after they met and ends with a 1946 letter also from Sidney just over a year before he died and four before Shaw's death.

Shaw and Webb first met in 1880. Webb and Sidney Olivier (Laurence Olivier's uncle), together with Graham Wallas, were, Shaw later said, "the Three Musketeers of Fabianism, with myself as D'Artagnan." The Fabian Society emerged from the left-wing sectarianism of the 1880s as a strong political force." The four musketeers were indispensable to the stature the Fabian Society established in its early years, particularly with the publication of *Fabian Essays* in 1889. The editor was Shaw and five of the eight essays were written by the four. Shaw also wrote the brief Preface, which ended with the words: "There are at present no authoritative teachers of Socialism. The essayists make no claim to be more than communicative learners." The *Essays* were reprinted in 1908 (new Preface by Shaw), 1920 (Introduction by Webb), 1931 (Preface by Shaw), and in a Jubilee edition in 1948, with a new Postscript by Shaw, entitled "Sixty Years of Fabianism." In addition to the five essays, between 1884 and 1892, more than seventy-five percent of the first forty-three Fabian Tracts, as they were called, were the work of the musketeers: Webb wrote twenty-four, Shaw seven, and Olivier and Wallas one each.

Both Webb and Olivier were civil servants, which somewhat inhibited their ability to participate in politics publicly, and may have encouraged the notion of educating and influencing whatever political party would listen to their ideas; hence the emphasis on pamphlets and tracts, which the Fabian Society published in abundance. When he married, Sidney Webb was persuaded by his wife to resign his civil-service position and devote himself to writing and politics. Olivier became a colonial governor—shades of Hector Hushabye and *Misalliance*'s Summerhays—and thus put himself at a greater distance from the local political fray. Webb and Shaw, on the other hand, both entered municipal politics in the 1890s and were elected in different London boroughs, Shaw to the St. Pancras Vestry and Borough Council, until he lost his run for re-election in 1902, Webb to the London County Council for Deptford until, in 1910, he decided not to re-offer. Wallas was also briefly a member of the L.C.C.

Beatrice Potter, whom Webb married in 1892, was one of a family of brilliant sisters. I once tried to ask Kitty Muggeridge, Beatrice's niece, about the Webbs. Speaking of Sidney, she said emphatically: "He was the devil, that man—*the Devil*." But what then, I pursued, attracted Beatrice to him. "Oh," she said, "it was power, sheer power." Alex Michalos and Deborah Poff[1] provide a more detailed, careful, and altogether more persuasive account of Beatrice's eventual agreement to marry Webb. No doubt, though, she was attracted by his powerful intellect. When one of the Webbs' secretaries retired, he was presented with a set of *Encyclopaedia Britannica;* Shaw quipped that this would compensate for the fact that he would no longer be working for Sidney. Above all, the marriage of Sidney and Beatrice was to be a working partnership. Beatrice Potter had already, she thought, found her life's work in participating as a researcher for what became a seventeen-volume work, her cousin Charles Booth's *Life and Labour of the People of London*. In his Foreword to Beatrice's *My Apprenticeship*, Shaw said that Booth "financed his great enquiry into poverty to prove that it did not exist and that Karl Marx's world-shaking description of it was a fable," but, as a result of Beatrice's research, "Karl Marx won hands down."[2] Shaw became increasingly attached to Beatrice as the years passed. Of the letters here from the end of World War I until her death, the vast majority are between Shaw and Beatrice, at least nominally.

Both the Webbs began by working on local government issues, but they came to see that local issues were always controlled by national and global governing and economic systems. Their work was descriptive before it was prescriptive, and when it became the latter, good Fabians that they were, they always concerned themselves with what was practically possible.

Much of the work that bound the three friends to one another involved writing books. Collaboration between Shaw and Sidney Webb was intense in their early Fabian days, and they continued to exchange work for criticism and correction. Beatrice's *Diaries* have much to say about this, and only a little of it is used by Michalos and Poff. Four letters from Shaw to Beatrice here discuss his *Intelligent Woman's Guide to Socialism and Capitalism*. In the notes, we are told that Ramsay MacDonald thought this "after the Bible . . . the world's most important book." The view of Michalos and Poff is that it is "not a particularly easy read . . . a strange stew of occasionally half-baked ideas sweetened with Shavian witticism," which "doesn't go down as well as one might have hoped." They then quote at some length from Susan Orkin, whom they describe as "the editor of its most recent edition." The only edition included in the list of references, however, is the first of 1928.[3]

Generally speaking, the editors prefer to repeat the judgments of others rather than work out their own. Thus, we are given A. J. P. Taylor's brisk dismissal of the Webbs' *Soviet Communism: A New Civilisation?* as "the most preposterous book ever written about Soviet Russia," while Shaw's review of the book has apparently escaped the editors' somewhat tattered net.[4]

The Introduction to this volume is fairly well managed, the editors' best work, marred only by some occasionally awkward expressions and a couple of careless mistakes. There are vivid portraits of the correspondents, their personalities confidently and sensibly assessed. However, the assertion that these 140 letters constitute "a fairly uninterrupted record" is untenable: there are several interruptions of more than a year. Furthermore, as Archibald Henderson remarked half a century ago: "Being Londoners and constantly thrown together, in the Fabian Society and through personal association, there was little reason for frequent exchange of letters."[5]

The list of books and articles provided as "References" contains items not referred to at all in the Introduction or in the notes to the Letters. At the same time, a number that one would have expected to see used are omitted.[6] The most important work that has been ignored, with significant consequences, is the third of Archibald Henderson's biographies of Shaw, *George Bernard Shaw: Man of the Century* (1956). Henderson devoted a

whole section of his book to Shaw and the Webbs, including two chapters—some thirty pages—to "Shaw's Letters to the Webbs." Henderson's
pages include not only some letters that Michalos and Poff say "have never
been published before," but also eight letters from Shaw to Sidney or Beatrice that do not appear here at all, as well as substantial material that is
missing from two letters that are here.[7] It is in one of the missing letters,
to Beatrice, nearing death, that Shaw wrote: "I have been reading some
of your stuff lately to remind me of some of the positions we conquered
on paper; and the contrast between you two at your best and Shaw at
eightysix is conspicuous. But so it was really when I was fortysix. In the
biographical dictionaries I shall figure as 'SHAW G.B. Twentieth century
playwright, remembered only as a friend of the Webbs.'"

As for the editing of the letters that are here, much is left to be desired.
Michalos and Poff tell us that "mere typos are silently corrected," though
this is not consistently so. The book's major failing, however, lies in the
annotation provided for the letters, or lack of it. Their "working assumption," the editors say, "was that everything worthy of mention by our authors was in principle worthy of explanation." This means that they
identify such well-known people as Marx, Lenin, Washington, Lincoln,
Napoleon, Stalin, Hitler, Voltaire, Rousseau, Beethoven, and Einstein,
though not Shakespeare, Milton, Martin Luther, or Ibsen. Surprisingly, in
view of this predilection for the familiar and famous, we are not told that
Lady Kennett was first married to Scott of the Antarctic, despite the clue
provided by Shaw's reference to "Scott's widow." The identifications the
editors do provide sometimes fail to explain the particular reason for the
invocation of the name in the correspondence, and they sometimes raise
an eyebrow. Einstein "taught physics" at various universities. Lincoln, we
are told, was "16th President of the United States" but not that he was
assassinated, which is the point of Shaw's reference to him.

As far as previously published letters are concerned, Michalos and Poff
have relied heavily on earlier editors, Dan Laurence in the case of Shaw
and Norman Mackenzie in the case of the Webbs. This generally saves
them from serious mistakes, and very occasionally they improve on, or
correct, their predecessor, as when they amend Laurence's (and Shaw's)
identification of David Hume from English to Scottish. Sometimes their
predecessors' notes are read too narrowly. For example, Shaw writing to
Beatrice refers to an Ibsen play she could have seen but had not. Dan
Laurence's note to this letter does not identify the play or the production,
so neither do Michalos and Poff. But the reason Laurence does not provide the information is that he has already done so in a previous note.
Necessary annotations provided by Mackenzie or Laurence are sometimes
ignored. In the headnote to the very first letter, Mackenzie's correct explanation that the Lambeth Parliament was "one of several such 'mock' as-

semblies which served as political debating clubs" is ignored, and the editors instead suggest, improbably, that it was "a precursor of the borough council created in 1888," as though it were an elected body rather than a club. They do not deem "Hankin's prodigal" worth annotating, although Laurence carefully explained the reference. Instead of correcting Mackenzie's failure to point out the error in Beatrice's recommendation that Shaw "read Aldous Huxley's *His Eminence Grise*"—she means *Grey Eminence*—there is a note on Huxley, implying that this is a novel, which it is not. Aldous's brother, Julian, mentioned by Shaw a couple of letters later, gets no note. The opportunity to correct Laurence's reading of Shaw's letter of 18 October 1898, "I would not trust a chicken's neck" for "I would not twist a chicken's neck" is also missed.

The previously unpublished letters are, however, much less well annotated. The editors sometimes have difficulty with Shaw's handwriting, a difficulty that would not arise if they had a better general knowledge. For example, the *Times* journalist referred to as "De Blowity[?]" is obviously Henri de Blowitz, the paper's sometime Paris correspondent, notorious for some sensational reporting about Franco-German relations. In a letter to Sidney of October 1916, Shaw is made to refer to a "Birrell Lady Bunald[?] Party." The reference to Augustine Birrell, who had resigned as Chief Secretary for Ireland following the Easter Rising earlier in the year, is clear, and we understand, though we are not told, that this might well have made the social encounter of interest to Shaw. But Lady Bunald is impossible. This should perhaps be Lady Cunard, a society hostess whom Shaw records having met at the opera a few months before. In a letter said to be in typescript, the unusual word "folkoonery" appears; Henderson, who published this letter previously, has "poltroonery," which certainly seems more likely and at least makes sense. The editors also make an elementary mistake with Sidney Webb's handwriting when they transcribe what is obviously "24th inst.", meaning 24th of this month, as "24th incl."

There is a serious error regarding Shaw's letter to Sidney telling him that "I am also a widower. Charlotte died this morning at 2:30." Instead of the correct date of 12 September 1943, the editors date this letter 12 November. In their headnote they quote from Shaw's letter to *The Times,* his "omnibus reply" to the many letters of condolence he had received, but this is also misdated as 20 November rather than 20 September. The result is that the letter is misplaced in sequence. It is made to follow a letter to Sidney in which Shaw discusses Charlotte's legacy to him, offering to arrange for it to be paid promptly if he is in financial need. Thus, the error should have been obvious not only to the editors but also to the several readers whose help is fulsomely acknowledged.

No one at the University of Toronto Press seems to have a knowledge of Latin and so the editors are allowed to make up words in that language previously unheard of. The word they inventively transcribe as "netia-nus[?]" in a 1904 letter is surely "retiarius." Shaw is employing the meta-phor of gladiatorial combat to urge Webb to see the strength of an opponent's position and his argumentative skill. He made use of this again when he came to write *Androcles and the Lion,* and introduced "a nearly naked man with a net and a trident," Retiarius, who successfully outmaneuvers Secutor, a man "in armor with a sword." There is more mistranscribed and erroneous Latin in this letter: "Inem Deus vulk per-dere &c &c &c," we read, which is gibberish. Not surprisingly, no English version of this is given. What Shaw no doubt wrote is "Quem Deus vult perdere &c &c &c." The usual translation is: "Whom God would destroy He first makes mad." (This is the Christian version; the Romans, and be-fore them the Greeks, would have understood "Whom a god . . .")

Headnotes and footnotes are all too often inadequate or irrelevant, even when they are not just plain wrong. To take a single example of the edi-tors' handiwork, the annotation provided for a letter from Shaw to the Webbs of 6 January 1919 is quite inadequate. This letter was written less than two months after the end of the Great War, and shortly after the results of the hastily called General Election had been declared. The elec-tion had produced an enormous majority for Lloyd George's Coalition government, but had also increased Labour representation, despite the loss of several senior figures. Shaw, as the editors tell us, had followed a punishing schedule for the two weeks leading up to the election, speaking for Labour candidates who were also Fabians. In this letter he reports to Sidney and Beatrice on an Albert Hall meeting called by the Labour Party in the aftermath of the election. The headnote completely misses the par-ticular circumstances of the meeting. Instead we are told that it was one of "the almost constant public fora in which the Fabians and, in particular, Shaw performed and presented opinions and positions," which begs more questions than it responds to. The purpose of this meeting was quite spe-cific. Partly a rallying of the party after the election aimed at consolidating its status as the official opposition and government-in-waiting, it was prin-cipally planned as a demonstration of the Labour Party's support for a League of Nations to prevent future wars. The Fabian Society had been in the forefront of this campaign ever since its Research Department had drawn up a detailed study of the idea, of which Leonard Woolf was the author; Shaw provided an introduction when it was published in 1916.[8] But the French government regarded the League with skepticism, arguing that the balance of power was a better guarantee of peace. "Mr. Shaw," *The Times* reported, "added to the gaiety of the evening by summarizing M. Clemenceau's attitude towards the League of Nations in the 'familiar quotation from Tennyson'—'Half a league! Half a league!'"

Shaw begins his letter to the Webbs by saying that he was "seized" after the meeting by "Kenworthy and a new MP airman Captain Malone." Our editors provide a note on J. M. Kenworthy, but not on Malone. Shaw says he was approached because these two wanted "to go to Lausanne" as experts and, he says, "they *are* authentic experts." Anyone wanting to know what the attraction of Lausanne was for them, or on what their claims to expertise were based, and why it is relevant, will search the notes in vain. The footnote on Kenworthy says he was "elected for Central Hull in 1918," and that "in 1918, he campaigned on the abolition of conscription, free trade, and negotiation with Russia." In fact he won a by-election in April 1919, five months after the Armistice, which casts his campaigning in an altogether different light. His victory took the seat away from the governing Coalition. Joseph Montague Kenworthy had served in the Navy, commanding various ships, and then as a member of the Admiralty War Staff, hence his expertise. In 1926 Kenworthy switched to the Labour Party, and Shaw sent a letter supporting his successful campaign for re-election. Malone is Cecil L'Estrange Malone, an interesting character who was a friend of Kenworthy's and a pioneer of naval aviation. He *had* been elected in the 1918 General Election, for Leyton East. Although he had run as a Coalition Liberal, his views were as radical as Kenworthy's. It is revealing that he was later convicted of provoking sedition at a "Hands Off Russia" meeting. The reason Kenworthy and Malone were interested in going to Lausanne was that there was a proposal to hold an International Labour and Socialist Congress there, including the Germans, as an alternative to the Paris Peace Conference.

Shaw turns from this to his plans to come up to London later in the week (he is writing from Ayot St. Lawrence) "to witness Michael Pease's debut." There is no note on this and what exactly it refers to remains unclear. Was Michael perhaps one of the two sons of the Fabian Society's founder, sometime secretary and historian, Edward Pease? Nor is it clear whether Shaw's comment that "the Labor Research Committee . . . neither knows or cares anything for the silly old Fabian" means that he will attend the committee meeting, or won't, that the L.R.C. and a Fabian meeting (at which Michael Pease would speak?) were in conflict, or indeed whether he means that fixing meetings for 6.30 on a Friday is inconvenient for an old Fabian like him. The Labour Research Department had evolved from the Fabian Research Department, which was a brainchild of Beatrice's; she saw it as a project comparable in importance with the London School of Economics and *The New Statesman*, also her idea. Shaw was chairman of the Labour Research Committee. Dan Laurence, in a note to another letter, says he was therefore obliged to attend the committee's meetings. None of this is mentioned anywhere.

Shaw reverts to the Albert Hall meeting, one of the other speakers at which was George Lansbury. He is identified, though the details about the *Daily Herald,* of which he was editor, are not quite correct. But the editors do not tell us whether Shaw's comment, that Lansbury "stood for the Communist Manifesto 'of 1871,'" is intended to point out a mistake or is a reference to some other manifesto than the 1848 one of Marx and Engels, or to the Paris Commune. Given the general tone of Shaw's discussion here, one suspects that Lansbury made a mistake and confused the dates of *The Communist Manifesto* and the Commune.

Finally, Shaw reports that he has been invited to speak at "the Bolshevist meeting" but has refused "on the ground that I am a parliamentarian." This meeting is not identified, but it was surely called to condemn British intervention against the Soviet Union, and to support the revolutionary movement in Germany and its potential spread elsewhere. The Soviet government had recently announced its intention to establish a Communist International (Comintern). Shaw goes on to say that "this is not a time to be sentimental about McLean, Liebknecht." Michalos and Poff think they have identified these two. McLean, they tell us, notwithstanding the different spelling, is Sir Donald Maclean, "a solicitor who was appointed by Asquith chairman of the non-coalition Liberals in Parliament 1919–22." The other man, they say, was Wilhelm Liebknecht, "a member of the Reichstag and co-founder of the German Social-Democratic Party." Both identifications are plainly mistaken. A wider political knowledge might have prevented the mistakes, but it is only necessary to look thoughtfully at the context in which Shaw makes this remark: his reference to Bolshevism and the link he makes between McLean and Liebknecht as political figures. Donald Maclean was not likely to be the object of maudlin enthusiasm at any communist meeting, and neither was Wilhelm Liebknecht (d. 1900). The McLean Shaw refers to is no doubt the Clydeside radical, John McLean, who had been sentenced to five years in jail for sedition during the war. A campaign for his release had succeeded and he had fought the 1918 General Election as a candidate in Glasgow. Although he lost, this had not inhibited his revolutionary agitation. As for Liebknecht, he is obviously not Wilhelm but his son, and Rosa Luxemburg's comrade, Karl, who was leading the violent Spartacist uprising in Berlin, and was soon to be killed. Shaw would have read that very morning a report from *The Times*'s correspondent in The Hague of Liebknecht's pronouncement: "We do not want a lemonade revolution, but will raise an iron fist against everyone who opposes the social revolution of the proletariat." Shaw was not the only one to link Liebknecht and McLean. Page Arnot, a member of the Labour Research Department, later wrote that "Lenin . . . regularly single[d] out McLean, 'the Scottish schoolteacher,' along with Karl Liebknecht and the Bolsheviks in Russia as those 'who remained faithful to socialism.'"

Obviously then, the Bolshevist meeting Shaw was not going to attend was designed to rally support for revolutionary action, and particularly for Liebknecht and McLean. At this stage neither Shaw nor the Webbs had fully worked out their attitude to the Bolsheviks or the attempts to spread revolution. They were by no means sure that this was helpful to the achievement of socialism; it seemed more likely to strengthen the resistance to it and make gradual progress more difficult to achieve. Fabianism of course had established itself as the evolutionary path to socialism, committed to gradualism, and against violent revolution. A despairing Beatrice expressed her reservations about the Bolshevik Revolution in her diary, wondering, "in the dark hours of sleepless nights," whether the struggle between political democracy and revolutionary dictatorship meant "the end of western civilization."[9] For the revolutionary Lenin, on the other hand, Shaw was "a good man fallen among Fabians." Thus, there is a much more important context for this letter than the editors' loose reference to "the almost constant public fora in which the Fabians and, in particular, Shaw performed," and their interesting but largely irrelevant footnote on the Webbs' meeting with Trotsky in 1929.

This is a singularly egregious example of editorial failure, but it indicates a significant weakness of the book, sufficiently pervasive to distract from, and undermine confidence in, otherwise interesting editorial work. Contexts are frequently wanting, and mistakes pop up everywhere. Ethel Smyth, the composer, for example, was certainly not "Smythe." Lord Alfred Douglas puts in an appearance in the Introduction as "Arthur Douglas," as does Ramsay MacDonald as "Ramsey." Grant Richards was not "Shaw's first publisher." Lord Randolph Churchill appears in the index as "Randolf." In a note to an already published letter from Shaw to Beatrice of 1901, the editors follow Dan Laurence's identification of the Halifax Shaw mentions as "a church leader," helpfully refining this to "a prominent Anglo-Catholic leader." Then, almost forty years later, just after the outbreak of World War II in 1939, Shaw, again in a letter to Beatrice, this one previously unpublished, comments in parentheses: "imagine Chamberlain and Halifax having aims, poor dears!" The editors recognize that this is not the Joseph Chamberlain, also mentioned in the 1901 letter, but his son Neville, the British Prime Minister of Munich fame, and so they provide a new note. But they assume that the Halifax *is* the same person (even though their note to the 1901 letter says that Halifax died in 1934); thus they see no need to provide a fresh note. That they think the Halifaxes are one and the same is confirmed by the index, which has a single entry for "Halifax, Viscount." The 1939 Halifax, however, was, like Neville Chamberlain, the son of the man referred to in 1901, and was Chamberlain's Foreign Secretary. (Strictly speaking, he was not a mere viscount, but an earl.)

Having read the text only once, I have detailed here only some of the errors and omissions; other readers may well find more. It is evident that the editors have not succeeded in carrying out their working assumption, to explain "everything worthy of mention by our authors." This does not destroy the value of this book, however. We can still observe in Bernard Shaw and Sidney and Beatrice Webb people of high intelligence thinking aloud, trying out their ideas on one another, arguing, and occasionally gossiping, or, with the passage of time, lamenting the ailments and vicissitudes of old age. We become aware of the practical issues that constantly present themselves to political thinkers who want results. We see through their eyes the development of projects for human betterment in the first half of the last century. All of this gives the dialogue of these participants a substantial interest, and even contemporary relevance. Their letters are very well worth reading and thinking about. Not a few readers will share the editors' hope "that this collection will bring them closer to a new generation entering a new millennium with a valuable agenda still largely unrealized." It is also to be hoped that those who share this enthusiasm will not be too far misled by the errors and omissions in the notes.

In a well-organized world, the University of Toronto Press would increase the value and usefulness of this book by withdrawing it and preparing a more reliable edition, but even distinguished academic publishers no longer see their responsibilities in this way. There is a possible alternative. Despite his unrivaled knowledge, Dan Laurence knew that some mistakes are inevitable in editorial work of this kind, and he made a point of seeking publication for corrections. Volumes II, III, and IV of the *Collected Letters* contain pages amending errors in previous volumes. For the fourth volume, the corrections were published in *SHAW* 20. Perhaps Alex Michalos and Deborah Poff could consider making amends in a similar way in a future volume of this annual.

Meanwhile, *caveat emptor.*

Alan Andrews

Notes

1. Alex Michalos is Director of the Institute for Social Research and Evaluation at the University of Northern British Columbia; Deborah Poff is Vice-President Academic and Provost there.

2. Beatrice Webb, *My Apprenticeship*, vol. 1 (Harmondsworth: Penguin Books, 1938), p. 10.

3. This is attributed to "London: Brentano's Inc."—which erroneously conflates the En-

glish edition, published by Constable, with the American, published in New York by Brentano's.

4. "The Webbs' Masterpiece," *Left News*, no. 16 (August 1937). Also missing from their frame of reference, apparently, are Shaw's review of the Webbs' *Constitution for a Socialist Commonwealth of Great Britain* ("The Webb Constitution," *The Observer*, 8 August 1920); his long preface to their *Prisons under Local Government* (London: Longmans, Green, 1922), published separately in the United States as *Imprisonment* (New York: Brentano's, 1925) and subsequently included as the first part of "Crude Criminology" in *The Works of Bernard Shaw* (London: Constable, 1931), vol. 22, pp. 173–240; and his foreword to the Pelican edition of Beatrice's *My Apprenticeship* (actually a reprint of an article, "Beatrice Webb, Octogenarian," *Spectator*, CLX, 21 January 1938).

5. Archibald Henderson, *George Bernard Shaw, Man of the Century* (New York: Appleton-Century-Crofts, 1956), p. 362.

6. These include, in addition to the items referred to already, the collections of Shaw's previously unpublished economic and political essays and lectures, collected and edited by Louis Crompton in *The Road to Equality* (Boston: Beacon Press, 1971) and by Lloyd J. Hubenka in *Practical Politics* (Lincoln: University of Nebraska Press, 1976); the anthology and symposium, *Shaw and Society*, ed. C. E. M. Joad (London: Odhams Press, 1953); Dan Laurence's collection of some of Shaw's speeches, *Platform and Pulpit* (New York: Hill & Wang, 1961); the selection of Shaw's letters to the press published by Laurence and James Rambeau in *Agitations* (New York: Frederick Ungar, 1985); Shaw's book reviews, published as *Bernard Shaw's Book Reviews*, edited by Brian Tyson, vol 2, 1884–1950 (University Park: Penn State University Press, 1996); his article about the Webbs, "Two Friends of the Soviet Union," *Picture Post*, XII (13 September 1941), reprinted in *Picture Post 1938–50*, ed. Tom Hopkinson (London: Penguin, 1970); "The History of a Happy Marriage" (Shaw's review of Margaret Cole's *Beatrice Webb*), *Times Literary Supplement*, 20 October 1945; Shaw's letters to *The Times* on Sidney's death in October 1947, urging that the Webbs be honored with burial in Westminster Abbey; Sydney Olivier's *Letters and Selected Writings* (London: George Allen & Unwin, 1948); and Kitty Muggeridge and Ruth Adam, *Beatrice Webb* (London: Secker & Warburg, 1967). Shaw's 1941 broadcast talk entitled "The Unapproachable Subject" is presented by Michalos and Poff as though this is its first publication; it can, in fact, be found in *Platform and Pulpit*.

7. The letters from Shaw that Henderson includes and that are missing from Michalos and Poff are those to Sidney dated 22 September 1914, 26 October 1924, and 8 October 1943; and to Beatrice dated 24 July 1901, 13 July 1924, 5 September 1929, 8 April 1941, and 2 July 1942. Henderson also includes a long letter to John Burns of 11 September 1903. This belongs in the Shaw-Webbs correspondence because Shaw sent a copy of it to Sidney and Beatrice with an added note; clearly he wanted them to know what he had written to Burns. The letter is in Laurence's *Collected Letters*, and he mentions the copy to the Webbs, but not the note; both letter and note are missing from Michalos and Poff. Of Shaw's letters of 7 May and 13 October 1898, Henderson includes substantial portions that are missing from both Laurence and Michalos and Poff. Also missing are several unpublished letters now in the British Library's Shaw archive.

8. L. S. Woolf, *International Government: Two Reports Prepared for the Fabian Research Department Together with a Project by a Fabian Committee for a Supernational Authority That Will Prevent War*, Foreword by Bernard Shaw (London: George Allen & Unwin, 1916).

9. Entry for 8 December 1914. *The Diary of Beatrice Webb, vol. III, "The Power to Alter Things," 1905–1924*, ed. Norman and Jeanne Mackenzie (Cambridge, Mass.: Harvard University Press, 1984), p. 326.

"From Little Acorns . . ."

Selected Correspondence of Bernard Shaw: Bernard Shaw and Barry Jackson. Edited by L. W. Conolly. Toronto: University of Toronto Press, 2002. xlii + 218 pp. Index. $60.

In the surprisingly mundane correspondence between Shaw and Barry Jackson (with occasional notes to Jackson from Charlotte Shaw and Shaw's secretary, Blanche Patch, interspersed), Shaw repeatedly offers acorns to Jackson from a superabundant oak tree in his domain, and Jackson's planting of a few of those at Blackhills, his home in Malvern, led to some mighty oaks. That is good enough as an objective correlative of their relationship, which was noteworthy for the way Shavian seeds in the form of both plays and advice significantly contributed to the growth of Jackson's two principal enterprises, the Birmingham Repertory Theatre (beginning in 1913) and the Malvern Festival (1929–37 of the Jackson years), where Shaw was treated like "the Wagner of Malvern."

But Shaw had more seeds to offer than Jackson could use, and sometimes he withheld seeds Jackson thought he needed; Jackson at least once turned down a golden seed in the form of the world première of *Saint Joan,* and seemed to collude in what Shaw saw as the blacklisting of his plays at Stratford, all of which lent some tension to a relationship that otherwise was ironically lacking in drama. Mutually respectful and admiring of each other's accomplishments and staunch spirit, mainly they provided solace for each other, a sympathetic ear to discouragements and frustrations, as they grew old together (though Jackson was thirteen years younger and did not die until 1961). Perhaps their two most frequently sounded notes were complaints about the sickness of the theater and the sickness of themselves and their partners (colds, flu, headaches, cholera, scarlatina, lumbago, appendicitis, cancer, heart attack, etc., almost always seeming to play a role), reminding us of how the English climate especially plagues the elderly even as the climate of the English theater plagues the playwright and producer who would attempt to cure the nation of what ails it.

Although the majority of the exchanges between Shaw and Jackson are businesslike and matter-of-fact, without the coruscating wit and playful spirit that characterizes so much of Shaw's correspondence with, say, females (and since Jackson was "gay," what can we make of this lack of sparkle here?), this correspondence is nevertheless very informative and in some respects more revelatory of the "human" Shaw than the more famous correspondences in its glimpses into how the Shaws lived from day to day, especially in the later years, with accounts of the war years and their bombings and other tribulations being most engaging. Shaw's income was taxed at 97.5 percent in those years! No wonder he described this as "confiscatory."

The general blandness of this correspondence is nevertheless flavored from time to time with bits of news and gossip and especially theater chat (about the casting of actors and actresses, the difficulties attendant upon certain productions, the programming of "seasons") and, from Blanche Patch, acerbic comments upon the "parasites" around Shaw in his last years. And we hear that Charlotte was often bored and restless in the country (Ayot St. Lawrence), and it is good that Shaw could work anywhere, because anywhere is where they spent a lot of time during the 1920s and 1930s. Many of these letters came from hotels, ships, or other people's houses, a surprising reason, in some cases, being that they gave long vacations to their staff and apparently could not live at home without them! Jackson was also often on the move, as he transferred successful productions at the Rep to London, and then took holidays on the Continent to recover from the stress.

The picture that comes out of this is of Shaw and Jackson, as celebrity playwright and deep-pockets producer (Jackson inherited a grocery store chain), doughtily battling the cultural inertia and lowbrowness of the theater, and scoring many artistic triumphs along the way in their attempt to make art trump commerce, while always fighting a losing financial battle in general and in the long run. Although Jackson's earliest theater company, the "Pilgrim Players," staged many Shaw plays between 1910 and 1923, the Shaw-Jackson friendship was not founded until the bold staging of *Back to Methuselah* in its British première at the Birmingham Rep in 1923 introduced Jackson to Shaw as a risk-taker extraordinaire and a likely patron. Their friendship and artistic relationship probably had its greatest flowering with the Malvern Festival, which followed up the experiment of the earlier Court Theatre in London of using Shaw as a flagship playwright and revived him as a playwright (would Shaw have written most of his late plays without the Malvern being there?), and had its darkest hours when the Malvern Festival collapsed and the Birmingham Rep wavered in the early days of World War II.

But at Malvern, Jackson and Shaw, with an assist from the featuring of the music of Edward Elgar, constructed a model of the Festival Theatre, of the summer festival of eclectic fare designed to attract the culturally starved, that has since well served other, similar ventures, such as the far-more-successful Shaw Festival Theatre at Niagara-on-the-Lake, Ontario, which so far has escaped the short-sighted "municipal parsimony" that helped to do in Jackson's Malvern Festival.

The story did not end with Malvern, however, for Jackson went on to attempt to revive the Shakespeare Memorial Theatre in Stratford-upon-

Avon, as director from 1946 through 1948, succeeding to some extent artistically, especially as a pioneer in modern-dress Shakespeare, but ultimately undermined by an interfering executive committee that used deficits as an excuse to replace him. Shaw, now in his nineties, girded his loins for battle and shot off missives replete with strategies for contesting the issue, but, as this collection's editor, Leonard Conolly, puts it, "Jackson preferred to keep his sense of grievance private, using Shaw, rather, as a friend who would listen sympathetically to his version of the events that led to his dismissal." Friend, yes, but Shaw also at times presented himself as Jackson's infallible "father." One letter from Shaw admonishes Jackson to "listen to your father," and in another letter Shaw explicitly alludes to how Jackson has replaced Harley Granville Barker as his "son" in the theater, which reminds us of the childless Shaws' proclivity for taking on younger people as surrogate children, which ultimately added up to an impressive brood, although Sir Barry may have been the only one knighted (in 1925, at Shaw's instigation).

This correspondence is prefaced by a well-researched, very informative Introduction and Afterword by Leonard Conolly, the book's editor and now the General Editor of the University of Toronto Press's Shaw correspondence series. This is the fourth volume in the series, which was conceived by Dan H. Laurence and begun under the general editorship of J. Percy Smith, now deceased. It is clear that the series is in good hands with Professor Conolly and will continue with impressive contributions to the growing collection of Shaw's correspondence. Not the least of Conolly's contributions here is his brief contextualizing where needed before the letter and detailed footnoting after, which seldom misses an allusion that needs glossing. This review can only hint at the wealth of knowledge and the richness of detail this collection provides of these crucial years and significant events in the life of the British theater and the British nation.

Richard F. Dietrich

Bernard Shaw: Realist, Reformer, Revolutionist

Stuart E. Baker. *Bernard Shaw's Remarkable Religion: A Faith That Fits the Facts.* Gainesville: University Press of Florida, 2002. xviii + 264 pp. Index. $55.

In *Bernard Shaw's Remarkable Religion*, the fifth volume in UPF's Florida Bernard Shaw Series, Stuart E. Baker has drawn upon Shaw's plays, prefaces, speeches, letters, and critical writings to weave an intricate carpet of

interconnecting threads—philosophical, political, social, and dramatic—in an effort to distill a Shavian worldview, one that embraces science, religion, ethics, economics, and government. Even given what Baker
terms the "astounding consistency" of Shaw's philosophy, this is no small
undertaking.

Baker begins by tracing Shaw's intellectual roots to Irish physicist John
Tyndall ("a major influence on the youthful Shaw") and George Eliot's
Middlemarch, concluding that Shaw "was blind to the spiritual promise in
Tyndall and the careful optimism of Eliot, and both could have been useful to him," although, like them, Shaw "believed in an orderly universe.
Theirs was materialistic and mechanistic; his was teleological." In short,
for Shaw, "The universe is orderly, human reason is capable of understanding it, and will can change it. Will is not caprice but the working out
of universal principles. All will is Divine Will." This, according to Baker, is
the crux of Shaw's "remarkable religion" and one of the central premises
of Baker's study.

Next, by way of Ibsen and Plato (for Shaw, Platonism is "a belief that
the universe is orderly and comprehensible"), and via Shaw's rejection of
idealism and espousal of the primacy of the will—which "not only determines values but governs, or at least guides, belief"—we arrive at "Shaw's
Religion: What It Is and Is Not." Here we are given an outline in six parts
of Shaw's "core ideas" (52–54), and as a lucid exposition of Shaw's belief
system, this short section deserves to be read attentively before proceeding to the next chapter, an analysis of the plays.

"Shaw's comic endings," writes Baker, are "happy (usually) in that they
show hope for the future; and they are open-ended in insisting on the
responsibility of the characters to realize that hope." Although many
works are discussed in "A Playwright's Progress"—*Widowers' Houses, Mrs
Warren's Profession, The Philanderer, Candida, The Man of Destiny, Man and
Superman,* and *John Bull's Other Island*—*Major Barbara* warrants a separate
chapter and the longest analysis (twenty-four pages), as Baker considers
the play "the single most complete statement of Shaw's philosophy and
the epitome of the dramatic method he developed to express that philosophy." Baker reads it as "a mosaic of altered and overturned expectations,"
a parable in which "Barbara stands for religion, spirit, and morality; her
father for matter, wealth, and destructive power." But he also notes the
numerous similarities between the two—among them, that each is an "ethical anarchist"—and points out that "the real conflict is not between father
and daughter, but between realism and idealism," one of the most important advocates of the idealist viewpoint being Cusins. *Major Barbara,* Baker
concludes, "does not deny the existence of evil, insisting emphatically that
it cannot be avoided; it only denies the possibility of isolating and destroying it."

In the next chapter, "Ethics, Economics, and Government," we learn that "Shavian ethics are frightening because they are relativistic and subjectivistic." But Baker is not loath to tackle some of Shaw's most controversial and even unpalatable views: his preference for (humane) execution over imprisonment for those who cannot be rehabilitated; his ideas on eugenics; his pronouncements on Stalin, Mussolini, and Hitler ("He insisted that, whatever their faults, they represented an advance on capitalist plutocracy"); and his reaction to the Holocaust ("He did not believe it because he could not believe that people could do such things"). In discussing these topics, Baker is careful to place Shaw's opinions—wrongheaded as many of them were—within the greater context of a personal worldview, one that considers mistakes as necessary stepping-stones to progress.

If the chapter on *Major Barbara* can be read as a separate essay—and rewardingly so—others can also, although "The Marriage of Science and Religion" is a heady, extended discussion (forty-six pages) requiring the reader's full powers of concentration, in particular during the technical but interesting section (under "Darwinism: The Linchpin of Materialism") entitled "Monkeys and Typewriters." One should note that this chapter also synthesizes the ideas of Karl Popper, Thomas Kuhn, René Descartes, Gilbert Ryle, George Berkeley, and Bertrand Russell, among others, but that Shaw makes only a few cameo appearances. The closing section entitled "What Is Mind?" is particularly challenging, and Baker concludes that "Teleological, purposeful, causation must exist. Don Juan was right."

Shaw resurfaces in earnest in the very short final section, "A Peroration," a summing-up that closes the book on an impassioned note: "The Holy Ghost, the Holy Will, is an undeniable fact. That is the central truth of Shaw's religion, his ethics, his socialism, his life, and his works. We still do not see it. . . . Shaw opened his realist's eyes and saw the Holy Ghost. When, and if, we acquire the courage to open our own eyes so far, Shaw will finally make his mark." Like many of Shaw's plays, Baker's book ends with "hope for the future."

"The realist is always a reformer, if not a revolutionist." Baker's aphorism might stand as the motto of his book, one that, in seeking to formulate and defend a Shavian "faith," paints a portrait of a realist whose attempts at reform were often criticized as revolutionary, when they were not condemned as impractical or heretical. As such, the book succeeds, but a few caveats are in order. Essays and lectures by John Tyndall—"Science and Man," "Scientific Materialism"—are referenced in the text but not listed in the Works Cited; and two books by Pierre Teilhard de Chardin are found in the Works Cited, but their author is not listed in the index. More seriously, the index is frustratingly (and for this type of book, unforgivably) short—barely three pages—and almost exclusively biographical. Thematic references are limited to Creative Evolution, Darwinism, Idealism, Life Force, Pan-psychism, Realism (metaphysical, Shavian), Solipsism, and a few others. Yet the index to a work so dense in discussions of ideologies deserves a far broader selection of rubrics (and subheadings) as evidence of the important role played in it—and frequently in Shaw's thinking—by concepts such as Consciousness, Democracy, Design, Determinism, Economics, Epiphenomenalism, Ethics, Faith, God, Imprisonment, Materialism (atheistic, scientific), Morality, Moral Equality, Politics, Realism (dramatic, scientific), Relativism, Subjectivism, Teleology, Truth, Vitalism, and Will (free, human, world-).

Bernard Shaw's Remarkable Religion: A Faith That Fits the Facts is a wide-ranging overview of Shaw's beliefs, their self-contradictions and practical applications, and the controversies they continue to generate. The rubrics listed above are merely signposts to a complex system of thought whose "astounding consistency" is nothing less than a tour de force, given Shaw's longevity and the sociopolitical upheavals he witnessed. Stuart E. Baker's book will reward those wishing to learn how Shaw's "faith" (his beliefs, ideology, philosophy, or worldview) "fits the facts," and not only the facts as Shaw perceived them, but the facts as science has reinterpreted them—for better or worse—during the half-century since his death.

Michel W. Pharand

Shaw Completely Dated

A. M. Gibbs. *A Bernard Shaw Chronology.* Houndmills, Basingstoke: Palgrave, 2001. xvi + 436 pp. Index. $59.95.

Over a career of writing about Shaw that began in the late 1960s, Arthur M. Gibbs has firmly established himself as one the most distinguished Shaw scholars in the world. I use the term "scholar" to emphasize his affinity for and mastery of grassroots scholarship, so marginalized in the present climate of literary academe and yet so vital to whatever publish-or-perish project anyone might choose. And I say "in the world" partly because his home base is far from the centers of Shavian research, Australia, yet he has apparently visited so many of them so often and with such great profit that he must be a remarkable world traveler indeed.

The book is his contribution to Palgrave's "Author Chronologies" series, which already numbers at least a dozen volumes on British and American authors. As Gibbs explains it, the chronology "aims at a record of significant events in Shaw's intellectual, emotional and creative life, and in the course of his relationships with other people, as well as occurrences which belong to the more public domain." Although the chronology form does not permit a sustained investigation of or reflection on these events, it can project "an almost uniquely graphic form of life-portrait" and "often reveal juxtapositions and patterns of events" in an individual's life. As a fact-respecting chronology-maker myself—on modern British, Irish, and American drama since 1865, and thus oriented not toward biography but literary cross-fertilization—I can vouch for the advantages he claims. Taken in short doses, detailed chronologies such as his, featuring a wealth of minor revelations and apt quotations, can also be downright enjoyable to read.

As one would expect with a subject whose activities reached out in so many directions and gained so much prominence during his life, the source materials that form the basis of this chronology are voluminous. Not only are there Shaw's writings of all sorts, including personal memoirs, private diaries, letters, interviews, film and radio recordings, and an unprecedented number of contributions to biographies of himself; there are also legal documents and local histories that pertain to him, theatrical and publication and speech-making records, letters written by a host of people both to him and about him, innumerable newspaper and magazine writeups, and discussions of him in memoirs by his friends (and enemies). Many of the biographies and critical studies on Shaw also yielded grist for Gibbs's mill. (He cites about eighty of the books he consulted most in his list of abbreviations, but these are by no means all of them.)

A very special source was the files and records of Dan H. Laurence, to whom the chronology is dedicated. Sprinkled liberally throughout the volume one encounters facts and details for which Gibbs found no other source than the Laurence collection at the University of Guelph Library or simply "DHL," indicating a private communication from the most formidable Shavian scholar of them all. In the Guelph collection Gibbs found Laurence's record of a 1912 motoring tour with Shaw and Granville Barker that Shaw's secretary at the time, Judy Gillmore, had told him about. It contains my choice for the human highlight of the book: "All through the journey the two men chatted and joked and giggled like schoolboys. Then Shaw suddenly threw a Shakespeare quotation at Barker, who threw one back, and they kept shouting quotations rhetorically back and forth, laughing uproariously all the while" (196). My vote for the most distinctive of the DHLs is a notation of the exact day (Christmas Eve, 1913) on which Madame Tussaud's Museum unveiled a wax figure of Shaw.

One of the most impressive features of this chronology is the number of obscure and elusive sources that Gibbs dipped into for revealing material about his multifaceted subject. He found an interview with Shaw in an 1896 issue of *The Young Man* in which the Fabian's chief spokesman insists that "a Fabian is a Socialist who is not a Socialist" (125). He gained permission from the University of Sheffield to quote relevant Shaw items in un-published letters from the political economist W. A. S. Hewin to Sidney Webb. He visited the Carlow County Library in Ireland to extract a sample of Shaw-as-landlord sentiment: a lady tenant in the Carlow Assembly Rooms which he reluctantly administered "apparently made up her mind from the first that she would never pay her rent in full" and now wants him to spruce up her digs. He tells his agent that if he were to grant such a request, "the lady will be asking us next year to pay for her clothes" (218).

Gibbs (perhaps with the help of research assistants, whom he acknowl-edges) found items of interest in Karachi and Auckland newspapers and, notably, news articles in the *Cape Times* (Cape Town) that added fascinat-ing sidelights to Shaw's visit there in 1932. The widely reported nation-wide broadcast in which he excoriated the results of apartheid in the country is of course noted, but so is his criticism of an all-male University Club and his comment in an interview that *Too True to Be Good* is about the "breakdown of morality" in World War I, followed by the pointed analogy: "You cannot turn morality upside down . . . and say, 'Evil, be thou my good'" (285). *The Western Mail* of Cardiff yielded a significant event that Gibbs apparently found nowhere else (or he would cite the source): in November 1936, Hitler sanctioned the arrest of a Danzig bookseller for selling books by Shaw, despite the qualified support the author of *Geneva* had given him; "In doing so Shaw is effectively banned by the Nazi re-gime," Gibbs concludes (304). One of the cutest Shavian items among this previously untapped treasure trove is a 1935 interview in *The Motor* enti-tled "George Bernard Shaw says—'They Shouldn't Allow Me to Drive'" (301).

Gibbs was able to milk these diverse and far-flung sources partly because as far back as 1990 he had already compiled and published a carefully researched set of interviews and recollections of Shaw. More significantly, his labors in fashioning this sumptuous, meticulously documented volume will all pay off in a "thematic biography" he has been working on, one that he hopes will prove more trustworthy than those presently available. That sweeping criticism embraces the older biographies of Henderson, Pear-son, Ervine, Rosset, and others, but he says flatly that the most imposing newer one, Michael Holroyd's, is often "unreliable as a work of reference" (5). And he supports this convincingly in "'Giant Brain . . . No Heart': Bernard Shaw's Reception in Criticism and Biography," *Irish University Review* 26, no. 1 (Spring–Summer 1996): 15–36, and in "Bernard Shaw's Family Skeletons: A New Look," *Bullán: An Irish Studies Journal* 3, no. 1 (Spring 1997): 57–74.

The principles of inclusion and elaboration that Gibbs followed in the book go well beyond mere usefulness. That indispensable requisite is cer-tainly fulfilled; it is not difficult, for instance, to scan the early pages of the chronology and nail down a useful array of "firsts" in Shaw's young life:

- *first accident* (9-8-57; age 1): Sitting on the kitchen table, Nurse took her eyes off him and he fell backwards, bashed a pane of glass and an iron bar. He wasn't even scratched.
- *first attended a stage play* (1-20, 21,or 22-64): Tom Taylor's *Plot and Passion* with the pantomime *Puss in Boots.*
- *first attended an opera* (10-19-67): Verdi's *Il Trovatore.* Taken by Vandeleur Lee.
- *first employment* (11-1-71): office boy for a land agent at 18 shillings a month.
- *first publication* (4-3-75): letter to a weekly news digest, *Public Opinion,* scorning revival meetings of the evangelists Moody and Sankey and declaring himself an atheist.
- *first finished a novel* (11-5-79): *Immaturity.*
- *first rejection of a novel:* a week later.
- *first quits a job* (7-5-80): resigns from the Edison Telegraph Company, but the company keeps him (for six more months) by increasing his salary.
- *first writes a theatre review* (4-7-80): on *The Merchant of Venice,* starring Henry Irving and Ellen Terry. It remained unpublished until 1993.
- *first disease* (5-25-81): smallpox.
- *first love affair* (2-?-82): with Alice Lockett. It lasts three years.
- *first address delivered* (2-8-82): at the Zetetical Society, on capital punishment.
- *first inspiration toward Socialism* (10-5-82): attends a speech by Henry George on Land Nationalisation and Single Tax.
- *first exposure to Marx* (2-?-83): begins reading *Das Kapital* in a French translation.
- *first novel published* (3- to 12-84): *An Unsocial Socialist,* serially, in the monthly magazine *To-Day.*
- *first exposure to Fabianism* (5-16-84): attends a meeting of the Fabian Society.
- *first begins writing a full-length play* (8-18-84): *The Way to a Woman's Heart,* based on William Archer's scenario.
- *first musical criticism published* (2-8-85): in *The Dramatic Review.*
- *first dramatic criticism published* (5-2-85): in the same magazine, on Browning's *A Blot on the 'Scutcheon* and Shakespeare's *Comedy of Errors.*
- *first radical clothes* (6-19-85): a Jaeger suit, designed to allow the body to "breathe" while adding distinction.
- *first sexual intercourse* (7-26-85): with Jenny Patterson, celebrating his 29th birthday.

I have omitted his first infatuation (with a dark-haired woman he refers to as "Calypso") (29) because it could not be dated more precisely than the year, 1871.

The extent to which Gibbs surpasses the minimum requirement of usefulness, and his procedures in doing so, can be illustrated by tracking *Widowers' Houses* through the book from its inception to its first performance and publication. Drawing mostly on Shaw's diaries but also noting verifications in other sources, Gibbs summarizes the entire course of events on the date Shaw began the play, then repeats each key event on the date it occurs so that it can be considered in the context of his other activities. (He passes over the insignificant continuation date of 1885—ironically the year to which the play's inception was assigned by many writers, even as late as Arthur Ganz in 1983—because they repeated what Shaw had misremembered.)

Thus, beginning on 18 August 1884, "Shaw worked intermittently on the first draft. . . . The plot materials, suggested to Shaw by William Archer, were derived from Émile Augier's play *La Ceinture Dorée*. The first working title . . . , *The Way to a Woman's Heart,* was changed to *Rheingold,* and subsequently to *Rhinegold.* After writing two acts and a substantial part of Act 3, Shaw temporarily abandoned the project on 18 November. He resumed work on it in 1885, 1887 and again in the Summer and Autumn of 1892 when he completed the play . . . as *Widowers' Houses* on 20 October" (53). A highly practical and welcome violation of the strict bounds of chronology, I would say. The relevant entries that follow are:

> September 3, 1887: "Shaw resumes work on *Rhinegold*" (77).
> October 6 (Gibbs quotes from the diary): "Shaw reads the first two acts of *Rhinegold* to William Archer who 'received it with great contempt.' Archer was 'utterly contemptuous of its construction' and during the reading of Act 2 'fell into a deep slumber,' whereupon Shaw 'softly put the manuscript away and let him have his sleep out'" (77–78).
> July 20–21, 1892: "Shaw alters the title of his play, *Rhinegold,* to *Widowers' Houses,* and finishes it by inserting a new scene near the end of the second act. J. T. Grein accepts the play for the Independent Theatre [no specific date is given for the acceptance]." This begins a series of entries on pp. 106 to 110, which I will compress when desirable:
> November 25: First rehearsal of the play with the full cast.
> December 5: "Shaw's close supervision (and continual interruption) of the rehearsals . . . annoys the director [Herman de Lange] and distracts the cast. Shaw agrees to stay away from rehearsals so that the cast can learn their lines."

December 9: The play opens at the Royalty Theatre, Soho, "with Florence Farr playing Blanche Sartorius and comic actor James Welch . . . playing Lickcheese. After the performance, Shaw addresses the audience on Socialism."

December 12: Shaw makes some alterations to the play for the next performance on December 13.

December 14: "William Archer's review of *Widowers' Houses* in *The World* draws a sharp response from Shaw in a postcard of the same date in which he calls Archer 'a sentimental sweet Lavendery recluse.'"

Christmas day!: "Shaw finishes four days of collecting and pasting into an album the 130 press cuttings, of reviews and notices, relating to *Widowers' Houses*" (Gibbs's punctuation).

January 5, 1893: Shaw spends all day working on the appendix to the impending published text of the play.

May ?, 1893: "Publication of *Widowers' Houses* by Henry and Co. in association with J. T. Grein of the Independent Theatre but, without effective marketing, the edition sold only 150 copies."

Subsequent entries referring to the play note the publication of *Plays Pleasant and Unpleasant* on 19 April 1898; the first American production on 7 March 1907; the first public production in England—at Manchester on 7 October 1907; and a London production at the Everyman Theatre to commemorate Shaw's seventieth birthday on 26 July 1926. If Gibbs had been unusually prescient, he would have recorded the stunning Shaw Festival revival in 2003.

We must excuse him for that, but (a negative note coming here, indispensable in an academic rave notice, especially near its finale) Gibbs either missed or ruled out for inclusion the London performances of the Manchester company beginning on 7 June 1909, at the Coronet Theatre, Notting Hill Gate, as documented in Raymond Mander and Joe Mitchenson's *Theatrical Companion to Shaw* and in reviews listed in J. P. Wearing's *G. B. Shaw: An Annotated Bibliography of Writings About Him, Volume I: 1871–1930*. I could also argue with the occasional mangling of commas, as in the sentence above marked "(Gibbs's punctuation)" or in "Sculptor, Lady Kennet, widow of Captain Scott, who was also present recalls . . ." (227), but perhaps Australian practice differs from American even more than English does. Otherwise the writing and editing seem as immaculate as an edition done by Dan Laurence, Stanley Weintraub, or Bernard Dukore. A useful bonus is a fifty-five-page "Shaw Who's Who," which will serve as a valuable aid to research on Shaw even for those who do not want a chronology.

Charles A. Carpenter

John R. Pfeiffer

A CONTINUING CHECKLIST OF SHAVIANA

I. Works by Shaw

Shaw, Bernard. "Ayot St Lawrence 17th October 1950: Notes Made by Judy Musters after Her Last Visit to Shaw." *The Independent Shavian* 41:1 (2003): 8–9. Musters, herself 53, a cousin of Shaw, had served for a time as Shaw's secretary. Shaw was home from the hospital and would die about two weeks later on 1 November. Musters engages Shaw with humorous and poignant effect. These notes from the Burgunder Collection are first printed here.

———. *Candida*. See *Man and Superman and Three Other Plays*, below.

———. *The Devil's Disciple*. Mclean, Virginia: IndyPublish.com, 2003. Not seen.

———. *The Devil's Disciple*. See *Man and Superman and Three Other Plays*, below.

———. *Doctor's Dilemma*. Boston, Massachusetts: IndyPublish.com, 2003. Not seen.

———. *Doctor's Dilemma*. See *Pygmalion and Three Other Plays*, below.

———. Excerpt from "Duse and Bernhardt" (1895). Helen Sheehy's *Eleonora Duse: A Biography*. New York: Alfred A. Knopf, 2003; pp. 143–45. "Considered one of the finest essays ever published about the art of the actor."

———. Excerpt of stage directions from *Pygmalion*, in "A Brief Introduction to the Modern Theatre." *Retellings: A Thematic Literature Anthology*. Edited by M. B. Clarke and A. G. Clarke. Boston: McGraw-Hill, 2003; pp. 571–72. Approximately 300-word text of direction for Eliza's returning home at the end of act one; is here meant to demonstrate how modern playwrights attempt to control the director's interpretation of their plays.

———. *George Bernard Shaw: Eight Interviews by Hayden Church*. Selected by Edward Connery Lathem. Peacham, Vermont: The Perpetua Press, 2002. These interviews, or excerpts from interviews, are selected from over 25 years worth of interviews of Shaw by Church. They are "G.B.S. Wants Women Rulers," *Sunday Express* (London), 28 December 1924; "Shaw May Come Here—in Movies," *The World* (New York), 5 December 1926; "Mr. Shaw Speaks of Hates Across the Sea," *Liberty* (Chicago), 5 January 1929; "Mr. Shaw Speaks out—On Diet, Prohibition, and America," *Liberty* (Chicago), 20 September 1930; "Why Old Men Don't Matter," *Sunday Express* (London) 1 March 1931; "Halt, Hitler!" *Sunday Dispatch* (London), 4 June 1933; "Bernard Shaw Tells Us All About:—My Plays, My Work, My Novels, My Money," *Sunday Graphic* (London), 17 December 1933; "The Prospect of Living 300 Years," *Leader* (London), 13 October 1945. At under 90 pages, a very economical representation of an always fascinating autobiographical, mature Shaw.

———. "George Bernard Shaw Scolds a Show Producer for Obtaining Rights for an Amateur Show for Use in a Professional Venue." Typed letter, signed, of 6 April 1911, to "Mrs. Dunningham." Excerpt: "If you have simply procured an authorization for an amateur performance and are availing yourself of it to give a professional one, you are committing the blackest crime possible in theatrical business." Scott J. Winslow Associates, Inc., mail and phone and email auction catalogue (closing 5 December 2003), item 134, $1,250–up. A readable picture of the one-page letter, along with a parallel printing of the letter's full text, is provided.

———. *Heartbreak House. The Longman Anthology of Modern and Contemporary Drama*. Edited by Michael Greenwald et al. New York: Longman Publishers, 2004. Not seen. Includes "Showcase: 'Notes for a Production of *Heartbreak House*'" by Robert Clurman."

———. *Heartbreak House*. Mineola, New York: Dover Publications, n.d. Not seen. Dover order #: 29291-6, $2.00. Mail: 31 E. 2nd Street, Mineola, NY 11501; fax: 516-294-9758; online: www.doverpublications.com.

———. *Heartbreak House*. See *Pygmalion and Three Other Plays*, below.

———. *Major Barbara*. Mineola, New York: Dover Publications, n.d. Not seen. Dover order #: 42126-0, $2.00. Order by mail: 31 E. 2nd Street, Mineola, NY 11501; fax: 516-294-9758; or online: www.doverpublications.com.

———. *Major Barbara*. See *Pygmalion and Three Other Plays*, below.

———. *Man and Superman and Three Other Plays*. New York: Barnes and Noble, 2004. "Introduction," Notes, and "For Further Reading" by John Bertolini. Also includes *Mrs Warren's Profession, Candida*, and *The Devil's Disciple*. At $7.95 U.S., a good teaching text at a bargain price.

———. *Misalliance*. McLean, Virginia: IndyPublish.com, 2003. Not seen.

———. *Mrs Warren's Profession*. See *Man and Superman and Three Other Plays*, above.

———. "On *A Doll House*." *Literature and Its Writers: A Compact Introduction to Fiction, Poetry, and Drama*. Third edition. Edited by Ann Charters and Samuel Charters. Boston and New York: Bedford/St. Martins, 2004. Not seen.

———. *Plays Pleasant*. Edited by Dan H. Laurence. New York: Penguin, 2003. Not seen. Introduction by W. J. McCormack. Uses the Bodley Head texts of *Arms*, *Candida*, *You Never Can Tell*, and *Man of Destiny*.

———. *Pygmalion*. Edited by Dan H. Laurence. Introduction by Nicholas Grene. London and New York: Penguin, 2003. Laurence's editions present the Bodley Head texts of Shaw's plays.

———. *Pygmalion*. Edited by Martin J. Walker. Harlow: Longman, 2003. Not seen.

———. *Pygmalion*. *The Longman Anthology of British Literature*. Volume B. Second edition. Edited by David Damrosch et al. New York: Longman Publishers, 2004. Not seen.

———. *Pygmalion*. Mineola, New York: Dover Publications, n.d. Not seen. Dover order #: 28222-8, $1.50. Mail: 31 E. 2nd Street, Mineola, NY 11501; fax: 516-294-9758; online: www.doverpublications.com.

———. *Pygmalion and Three Other Plays*. New York: Barnes and Noble, 2004. "Introduction," Notes, and "For Further Reading" by John Bertolini. Also includes *Major Barbara*, *The Doctor's Dilemma*, and *Heartbreak House*. At $7.95 U.S., a good teaching text at a bargain price.

———. *Saint Joan*. Edited by Dan H. Laurence. New York: Penguin, 2003. Not seen. Laurence's editions present the Bodley Head texts of Shaw's plays.

———. "Shaw, George Bernard (1856–1950)." Autograph manuscript of *The Table Talk of G.B.S.*, Shaw's answers to questions compiled by Archibald Henderson, 1925; the questions written in a different hand, and Shaw's answers, of varying length, written below them, 95 pages. Three examples of the questions and answers are in the advertisement. Christies.com/Lotfinder (sale ending 3 March 2004), item 301, The Halsted B. Vander Poel Collection of English Literature, £15,000–20,000.

———. "Shaw, George Bernard (1856–1950)." Typescript with autograph emendations of his essay "Beerbohm Tree from the Point of View of the Playwright," December 1919, annotated at head "proof to G. Bernard Shaw 10 Adelphi Terrace W.C.2" and "Please follow copy exactly," 20 pages; provenance: purchased from Scribners, New York, 6 November 1945, $23. Christie's.com/Lotfinder (sale ending 3

March 2004), item 300, The Halsted B. Vander Poel Collection of English Literature, £1,200–1,800.

———. *The Shewing Up of Blanco Posnet.* Edited by William-Alan Landes. Studio City, California: Players Press, 2003. Not seen.

———. "The Technical Novelty in Ibsen's Plays." *Stages of Drama: Classical to Contemporary Theater.* Fifth edition. Edited by Carl H. Klaus, Miriam Gilbert, and Bradford S. Field, Jr. Boston and New York: Bedford/St. Martins, 2003. Not seen

II. Books and Pamphlets

Albert, Sidney P. "G.B.S. in Hellas: A Resource for Classicists." *SHAW: The Annual of Bernard Shaw Studies.* Volume 23. University Park: Penn State University Press, 2003; pp. 167–80.

Allen, Nicholas. *George Russell (AE) and the New Ireland, 1905–30.* Dublin: Four Courts Press, 2003. Not seen. Roy Foster's *TLS* (16 May 2003): 9, review, notes "AE's writings are used very effectively, notably his surrealist novel about 1916, *The Interpreters* (1922), an amalgam of *roman-à-clef*, neo-socialist manifesto and political satire, which Allen relates to Shaw's" *Methuselah*.

Andrews, Alan. See *Misalliance*, below.

Baker, Stuart. "Is the Holy Ghost a Scientific Fact? Why Shaw's Creative Evolution Might Become the Scientific Religion of the Twenty-First Century." *SHAW: The Annual of Bernard Shaw Studies.* Volume 23. University Park: Penn State University Press, 2003; pp. 59-64.

Bamforth, Iain. *The Body in the Library: A Literary Anthology of Modern Medicine.* New York: Verso, 2003. Not seen. Reviewer Peter Porter, *TLS* (9 April 2004): 5, says *Doctor's Dilemma* is a "hard case," and is sorry it is missing from this collection.

Bauer, Susan Wise. *The Well-Educated Mind: A Guide to the Classical Education You Never Had.* New York and London: W.W. Norton & Company, 2003. A typical entry recommends *Saint Joan* with a one-page commentary—not a summary.

Beaton, Cecil. *Beaton in the Sixties: More Unexpurgated Diaries.* London: Weidenfeld and Nicolson, 2003. Not seen. Reviewed by Philip Hoare in *TLS* (6 February 2004): 25. Hoare: "Refusing to be outmoded by the age, Beaton's designs for *My Fair Lady*–in the Oscar-winning wake of which these entries are written—coincide stylistically with 1960s nostalgia."

Berg, A. Scott. *Kate Remembered.* New York: Putnam's Sons, 2003. No index. Hepburn's Epifania in the *Millionairess* film was successful in part because of her athleticism. Her knowledge of and liking for Shaw was from her very early years, introduced to her by her parents. This book is a eulogy biography appearing shortly after Hepburn's death in 2003.

Bhatta, Vinoda. *Vinodi, Jivanacitro: [Portraits of Anton Chekhov, Bernard Shaw, Charlie Chaplin, and Saadat Hasan Manto in humorous style].* Enlarged and "researched" edition. Mumbai [Bombay]: Navabharata Sahitya Mandira, 2003. Language: Gujarati (the language of Ghandi). Not seen.

Black, Martha F. *"Back to Methuselah*: A 'Grand Precurser' [*sic*] to *Finnigans Wake.*" *SHAW: The Annual of Bernard Shaw Studies.* Volume 23. University Park: Penn State University Press, 2003; pp. 7–16.

Bryden, Ronald. *Shaw and His Contemporaries: Theatre Essays.* Niagara-on-the-Lake: Mosaic Press, 2002. Includes thirteen articles on Shaw topics: *Mrs Warren, Arms, You Never Can Tell, Devil's Disciple, Caesar, Captain Brassbound, Major Barbara, Heartbreak, Apple Cart, Millionairess,* Shaw's letters, Sally Peters's *Bernard Shaw: The Ascent of the Superman,* and Shaw's diaries. Nineteen more are on "Shaw's Contemporaries." Eight are on non-Shavian subjects.

Chen, Wendi. "A Fabian Socialist in Socialist China." *SHAW: The Annual of Bernard Shaw Studies.* Volume 23. University Park: Penn State University Press, 2003; pp. 155–66.

Church, Hayden. *George Bernard Shaw: Eight Interviews by Hayden Church.* Selected by Edward Connery Lathem. Peacham, Vermont: The Perpetua Press, 2002. This selection is from many interviews with G.B.S. spanning more than 25 years. The *Saturday Review of Literature* in 1946 called Church, a well-known journalist, Shaw's "favorite interviewer." See also *George Bernard Shaw . . .* in I. Works by Shaw, above.

Conolly, L. W. "GBS and the BBC: In the Beginning (1923–1928)." *SHAW: The Annual of Bernard Shaw Studies.* Volume 23. University Park: Penn State University Press, 2003; pp.75–116.

Essaka, Joshua. "Nineteenth-Century Pygmalion Plays: The Context of Shaw's *Pygmalion.*" In Essaka's *Pygmalion and Galatea: The History of a Narrative in English Literature.* Hants, England: Ashgate Publishing Limited, 2001; pp. 97–134. "Gilbert's exploitation of a similar duality in his characterization of Galatea [in his *Pygmalion and Galatea*], a duality highlighted by its obvious suppression in performance (and in [Henry Pottinger] Stephen's burlesque *[Galatea; or Pygmalion Reversed]*), makes him a more relevant context for Shaw than Ovid. It is a feature that is also present in the Cinderella variants of the Victorian period. The popularity of the *Cinderella-déclassement* theme on the nineteenth-century stage, and Shaw's direct allusions to the tale, make it another likely context for understanding Shaw's development of Eliza. . . . In the ways in which the Pygmalion plays focus on the expanding role of Pygmalion as educator, and in the way in which

Galatea's innocence and inexperience are portrayed effectively as obstacles to their union, these plays are the precursors of Shaw." Reviewing at least eleven of the nineteenth-century plays and fictional treatments of the Pygmalion story, Essaka concludes Shaw's is not a dramatic departure from them but a genuine variant of the Ovidian myth. This book chapter is a substantial embodiment of Essaka's 1998 article (see III. Periodicals, below), but there are interesting differences between them that do not bear directly on Shaw topics.

Evans, Judith. *The Politics and Plays of Bernard Shaw.* Jefferson, North Carolina: McFarland, 2003. Not seen. From the publisher: "This work offers a readily accessible means of looking at the nature and the progression of Shaw's thinking. All the plays included in the major canon are reviewed, and, except for brief plays and playlets (which are grouped), they are presented in sequential order.

Gahan, Peter. "The Achievement of Shaw's Later Plays, 1920–1939." *SHAW: The Annual of Bernard Shaw Studies.* Volume 23. University Park: Penn State University Press, 2003; pp. 27–36.

Harding, Jason. *The Criterion: Cultural Politics and Periodical Networks in Inter-war Britain.* Oxford: Oxford University Press, 2003. Not seen. Reviewed with other books by Stephen Romer, *TLS* (14 November 2003): 6–7. As editor of *Criterion*, Eliot used Montgomery Belgion as a privately trained bulldog, to "snarl around the trouser-legs of favorite Eliot targets like Shaw, Gide, Freud and Bertrand Russell."

Hart, Jonathan. "T. E. Lawrence and the Shaws." In *The Waking Dream of T. E. Lawrence: Essays on His Life, Literature, and Legacy.* Edited by Charles Stang. New York: Palgrave, 2002; pp. 131–61. Not seen. Reviewed in *ELT* 47:2, the reviewer concluding that Hart does not shed much new light on Lawrence's relationship with the Shaws, and also ends up saying very little that cannot be gleaned from a reading of the letters themselves.

Hugo, Leon. *Bernard Shaw's The Black Girl in Search of God: The Story Behind the Story.* Gainesville: University Press of Florida, 2003. Hugo's terminal paragraph: "When leaving South Africa at the end of his second visit, only weeks before his 'interview' in the *Daily Telegraph*, [Shaw] recommended fusion and the abolition of legislative barriers between the races. Put your house in order and quickly, he said in effect, otherwise there would be 'a lot of bloodshed and the cutting of throats. . . . I can see you people in a pretty mess before you get everything cleared up.' It could be that his comments on the effect of the climate on white fertility were built on this uncompromising scenario; that he was pointing beyond population ratios to what he discerned as an inevitable process of history: the collapse of white hegemony and its policy of racial discrimination, the condign punishment that would fall on the godless ones, the fulfilling of the Black Girl's prophecy. Perhaps this unofficial Bishop of Everywhere was advocating miscegenation, as exemplified in the marriage of the Black Girl and the Irishman, as the solution to racial strife; perhaps it was his way of saying, 'Make love, not war—for God's sake.'"

Innes, Christopher, editor. *A Sourcebook on Naturalist Theatre*. London and New York: Routledge, 2000. See "6. Bernard Shaw: 1856–1950," a chapter consisting of sections on 1) Context, 2) Shaw's Naturalistic Drama, 3) *Mrs Warren's Profession* (a. The play, b. Chronology of major early performances, and c. Performance and reception), and 4) *Heartbreak House* (a. The play, b. Chronology of major early performances, and c. Performance and reception.) Reprints substantial texts and extracts from texts by Shaw, his contemporaries, and modern scholars, for both plays.

———. "Utopian Apocalypses: Shaw, War, and H. G. Wells." *SHAW: The Annual of Bernard Shaw Studies*. Volume 23. University Park: Penn State University Press, 2003; pp. 37–46.

Jahan, Rahmat. *The Ibsen-Shaw Kinship*. Calcutta: Writers Workshop, 2002. From the "Forword" by Jahan's teacher, Alo Sircar: "In [this book] convergences and divergences between Ibsen and Shaw have received due emphasis. That Shaw was indebted to Ibsen in several ways is nothing unknown or even radically novel. But the exact areas where the debts were operative were none too well defined or consistently brought out. It is this function that the book performs in a clear, concerted and disarmingly forthright manner. As Shaw is almost omnipresent on English literature syllabi in India and abroad and the Ibsenite strands of his dramaturgy are essential to a complete comprehension of Shaw, the thinker, and Shaw, the artist, both students and teachers of the subject are likely to benefit from having the book within ready reach." From Jahan's "Conclusion": "Shaw, in a sense, fails to note that there is much more to Ibsen's plays than their naturalist and anti-idealist stance. The emotionally surcharged, and intensely poetical idioms of most of Ibsen's plays seem to have escaped Shaw's attention. He gives an account of Nora's rebellion against marriage and Mrs. Alving's protest against the family life but does not take notice of Oswald Alving who is enamoured [sic] of the glorious freedom of the beautiful life. Hedvig's inexplicable love for the wild duck has also been lost sight of. We cannot but conclude, therefore, that his thematic concerns apart, there are tell-tale affinities between Ibsen's and Shaw' s dramatic craft. Not only has Shaw inherited from Ibsen a naturalist idiom, the art of making a play debate social issues and his anti-idealistic perspective, he has, like Ibsen, put both the common man and his actual problems on the stage. He has abstained from creating characters who are either all-white or all-black and has brought us face to face with a world of topsy-turvy values. But we cannot also fail to observe that Shaw's Ibsen is not all there is to Ibsen. One can hardly help suspecting that Shaw has deliberately turned a deaf ear to Ibsen's essential romanticism, his emotion-drenched symbolism and his poetic idioms, which come to the doorsteps of modern expressionism. One can hardly help feeling that Shaw's Ibsen is not necessarily the essential Ibsen."

Lambert, Gavin. *Natalie Wood: A Life*. New York: Knopf, 2004. One reference: In 1958 Wood finally turned down an offer to appear in a "relatively slight role . . . in [in a film of *Devil's Disciple*] in the company of Laurence Olivier, Burt Lancaster, Kirk Douglas, and Eva Le Gallienne." "Although it was not modern, it was 'prestige.'"

Larson, Gale K. "General Introduction: Shaw's Brave New World Conference, Marquette University Milwaukee, Wisconsin, 19–21 April 2001." *SHAW: The Annual of Bernard Shaw Studies*. Volume 23. University Park: Penn State University Press, 2003; pp. 1–6.

Lawrence, T. E. *Seven Pillars of Wisdom: The Complete 1922 "Oxford" Text*. Woodgreen Common near Fordingbridge, Hants SP2 2BD: J. and N. Wilson, Castle Hill Press, 2004. Not seen. Reviewed by Robert Irwin in *TLS* (2 April 2004): 3. One reference to Shaw, who advised Lawrence to suppress the opening chapter, "How and Why I Write," which appeared in the *Oxford Times* printing in 1922 but was deleted in the 1924 subscribers' edition.

Lenker, Lagretta T. "Why? Versus Why Not? Potentialities of Aging in Shaw's *Back to Methuselah*." In *Aging and Identity: A Humanities Perspective*. Edited by Sara M. Deats and Lenker. Westport, Connecticut: Praeger, 1999; pp. 47–59. Referring to *Heartbreak* and *Caesar* as well as *Methuselah*, Lenker concludes, "First, Shaw understood that society's ideas about aging . . . are a product of our imagination. . . . Second, like today's humanistic gerontologists . . . , Shaw also intuited that many disciplines have valid insights into the study of the aging process. Finally, Shaw realized that society must search beyond providing the practical accommodations for the aged such as pensions and affordable housing if humankind is to reach its potential."

Lillie, Sophie. *Handbuch der enteigneten Kunstsammlungen Wiens* [Handbook of the expropriated art collections of Vienna]. Vienna: Czernin, 2003. Not seen. Leo A. Lensing's review, *TLS* (27 February 2004): 8, says the inventories from various sources are virtual archives. In the case of Shaw's translator, Siegried Trebitsch, the inventory includes a partial listing of the owner's library. Trebitsch owned *Die Grundlagen of neunzehnten Jahrhunderts* (1899) by Houston Stewart Chamberlain, whose anti-Semitism strongly influenced Hitler.

London, John. "Non-German Drama in the Third Reich." *Theatre Under the Nazis*. Edited by John London. Manchester and New York: Manchester University Press, 2000; pp. 222–61. London's essay has a section, "The Exceptional Case of George Bernard Shaw," which gives about four pages to explaining how "Shaw ended up being the most successful non-German dramatist alive under Nazism and productions of his plays actually increased as the war broke out. In academic circles he was given an Irish, anti-English gloss and associated with healthy 'non-Jewish' drama. Schlösser thought Shaw had reached the status of a 'semi-classic of the Third Reich.' He was considered a pupil of Schopenhauer, Wagner, Ibsen and Nietzsche, while Goebbels and Hitler were in agreement in wanting to protect Shaw from censorship." Especially successful were *Apple Cart*, *Pygmalion*, *Superman*, *Caesar*, *Mrs Warren*, *Doctor's Dilemma*, *On the Rocks*, and *Saint Joan*.

Loon, Seong Yun, Robin. "Rewriting Shakespeare and Englishmen: George Bernard Shaw's *Caesar and Cleopatra*. In *Postcolonial Cultures and Literatures: Modernity and the (Un)Commonwealth*. Edited by Andrew Benjamin, Tony Davies, and Robbie B. H. Goh. New York: Lang, 2002; pp. 227–43. In his "rewrite, Shaw challenges conventions of dramatic historiography established by Shakespeare in his two Roman plays. . . . [it] actively addresses received notions of greatness, historicity and celebrates the greatness of the human spirit. . . . [It] is a negotiation across discourse, ethics, convention, artistry and history . . . a generic transformation, importing certain Shavian ideas on theatre, morality, Englishness and pragmatism in the rewriting process. . . . Shaw's Caesar is what the Englishman should be—a paragon of imperfect virtues characterized by self-awareness and self-irony. Shaw humbles Caesar by humbling Shakespeare—humanizing this historical figure as the quintessential Englishman by re-writing the play."

Manista, Frank C. "'The Gulf of Dislike' Between Reality and Resemblance in Bernard Shaw's 'The Black Girl in Search of God.'" *SHAW: The Annual of Bernard Shaw Studies*. Volume 23. University Park: Penn State University Press, 2003; pp. 117–36.

McDiarmid, Lucy. "The Abbey and the Theatrics of Controversy, 1909–1915." *A Century of Irish Drama: Widening the Stage*. Edited by Stephen Watt, Eileen Morgan, and Shakir Mustafa. Bloomington and Indianapolis: Indiana University Press, 2000; pp. 57–71. McDiarmid revisits the political determination of Lady Gregory and Bernard Shaw, revealing how theater controversies function as both discursive sites and alternative theater. Three controversies constitute a little sequence of causes and effects: the controversy over Shaw's *Blanco Posnet*, banned in England for blasphemy and obscenity, but performed in Ireland in 1909; the controversy over the Philadelphia production

of Synge's *Playboy* in January 1912; and the 1915 debate over whether
Shaw's *O'Flaherty* should be produced at the Abbey. "Controversies
are large forces in a small site. The great drama of social revolution
that historians see in wars, or political demonstrations, or in voting
patterns, in the Magna Carta," is also present in controversies, the
micro-units of social change.

McDougall, Kathleen. "Bernard Shaw and the Economy of the Male Self."
Mapping Male Sexuality: Nineteenth-Century England. Edited by Jay
Losey and William D. Brewer. Cranbury, New Jersey: Associated University Presses, 2000; pp. 324–42. The editors apologize for including a piece on Shaw among other essays that concentrate on male
homosexuality, not aware apparently of Sally Peters's provocative
treatment of G.B.S. in *Bernard Shaw: The Ascent of the Superman* (1996).
"As a competitor on the marketplace of cultural criticism, Shaw had
to lend his works value by making himself the guarantor of their relevance and authority. This meant presenting a self that was energy-
efficient and collectivity-minded, as opposed to a marginalized other
that was parasitical, wasteful of energy, and selfish. . . . Shaw's prevalent strategy was to construct a sublimated self, the workings of which
were often couched in scientific terms. In doing so he was met halfway
by bourgeois ideology, which reserved a space for art that tran-
scended scientific truths and their quotidian usefulness." "Shaw defines inferiority primarily in terms of economy of self (rather than
gender, social class, and so on). The less one is able to quell selfish,
atavistic impulses (in particular sexual ones), the lower one's place in
his hierarchy." "Believing that 'the health of society as an organic
whole' can only be as sound as the individual organisms composing
it, Shaw thought that reproduction should be regulated in such a way
as to create a race of unselfish, work-oriented, intellect-driven people.
To realize this project he and fellow socialists of the Fabian variety
advocated 'a highly scientific social organization' and put forward a
roster of scientific tools: eugenics, statistics, sociology, political economy, and so on. [new paragraph] According to Shaw there are two
ways to serve the Life Force: The physical production of human beings, and the production of ideas for them to inherit. These evolutionary roles correspond (most of the time) to femininity and
masculinity. . . . They also correspond to two options between which
Shaw hesitated in his presentation of self: practicality at the socio-
organic level, compatible with an ordinary economy of self; and practicality in the spiritual realm. The latter option is a bid for a position
of authority 'as a vessel of the Zeitgeist or will,' a 'genius . . . selected
by Nature to . . . build up an intellectual consciousness of her own
instinctive purpose.'" "In *The Perfect Wagnerite* (1898) Shaw describes

four possible economies of self. There are 'instinctive' people who give free rein to impulse and lay the world to waste, and 'stupid, respectful, money-worshipping people' who quell all their instincts. Neither of these kinds of people makes any contribution to humanity. Then there are 'the intellectual, moral, talented, people who devise and administer States and Churches,' members of an aristocracy/meritocracy who are characterized by a healthy equilibrium, spending themselves in a measured way. Lastly, there is the yet unrealized possibility of the hero, prefigured in Wagner's Siegfried. . . . The hero's economy of self can be defined as a healthy disequilibrium: he does not withhold or misspend his energy (he embraces neither thrift nor deferral), but rather releases all of it because he is certain that it will serve a worthy purpose. He embodies a kind of joyful entropy at the service of evolution. Shaw's hero is free of inner tension because convention has no hold on him—he is completely a child of nature."

Misalliance: Shaw Festival 2003 (Shaw Festival production program). Includes "Director's Notes" by Neil Munro, and "Misalliances" by Alan Andrews, which among other things explains references to H. G. Wells in the play and concludes, "The ideas that the play debates—sexual attraction, family relationships, revolutionary socialism—were those which Wells had urged the Fabian Society to take up. An unsuitable marriage was traditionally known as a misalliance. Shaw also wants to point out that the mismatches occur between parents and children. And there had been another misalliance of a different kind: H. G. Wells's relationship with the Fabian Society."

Murrenus, Valerie. "Hostages of Heartbreak: The Women in *Heartbreak House*." *SHAW: The Annual of Bernard Shaw Studies*. Volume 23. University Park: Penn State University Press, 2003; pp. 17–26.

Nathan, Rhoda. "All About Eve: Testing the Miltonic Formula." *SHAW: The Annual of Bernard Shaw Studies*. Volume 23. University Park: Penn State University Press, 2003; pp. 65–74.

O'Flaherty, Gearóid. "George Bernard Shaw and Ireland." *The Cambridge Companion to Twentieth-Century Irish Drama*. Edited by Shaun Richards. Cambridge: Cambridge University Press, 2004; 122–35. Not seen. The contents include pieces on Yeats, Lady Gregory, Synge, Wilde, O'Casey, Teresa Deevy and Marina Carr, Beckett, Brian Friel, and Tom Murphy.

O'Hara, Maureen (with John Nicoletti). *'Tis Herself: A Memoir*. New York and London: Simon & Schuster, 2004. One reference: At 14, in 1934, O'Hara was accepted at the Abbey Theatre. "W. B. Yeats and George Bernard Shaw were two of the greats who helped found it."

Orlans, Harold. *T. E. Lawrence: Biography of a Broken Hero*. Jefferson, North Carolina: McFarland, 2003. Not seen. From the publisher: "Study . . .

based on a review of virtually every published and unpublished English source in British and U.S. libraries and archives, including the important archive of Lawrence's letters and papers in the Bodleian Library."

Peters, Margo. *Design for Living: Alfred Lunt and Lynn Fontanne: A Biography*. New York: Knopf, 2003. Not seen. Reviewed by John Simon in *New York Times Book Review* (14 December 2003): 13–14. "Over the years they had marvelous times—and successes—with *Arms and the Man* [and] *Pygmalion* ('Alfred was not satisfied with his Henry Higgins 'until, one night, he sat up in bed and realized that Higgins must carry a green umbrella')."

Peters, Sally. "Outwitting Destiny: The Artist as Superman." *SHAW: The Annual of Bernard Shaw Studies*. Volume 23. University Park: Penn State University Press, 2003; pp. 137–48.

Schrank, Bernice. "Staging John Bull: British Identity and Irish Drama." *Postcolonial Cultures and Literatures: Modernity and the (Un)Commonwealth*. Edited by Andrew Benjamin et al. New York: Peter Lang, 2002; pp. 128–60. The article examines "four popular and representative plays by Irish playwrights," Shaw's *John Bull*, Sean O'Casey's *Plough*, Brendan Behan's *Hostage*, and Frank McGuinness's *Someone Who'll Watch Over Me*, "each of which undermines some aspect of either the colonial or the nationalist construction of Irish and English identity. Shaw and O'Casey replace what they regard as the narrow and repressive aspect of the discourses of colonial domination and national liberation with the totalization of Marxism; Behan and McGuinness substitute for what they perceive as the imprisoning ideology of nationalism a transnational and transsexual humanism."

Sheehy, Helen. *Eleonara Duse: A Biography*. New York: Alfred A. Knopf, 2003. Shaw admired Duse greatly. Sheehy quotes at length from Shaw's "Duse and Bernhardt' (1895), in full sympathy with G.B.S. See Works by Shaw, above.

Shimizu, Yoshikazu. *Dorama [drama] no sekai banado sho [Bernard Shaw]: shekusupia kara waguna made*. Tokyo: Bunkashobohakubunsha, 2002. Language: Japanese. Not seen. ISBN 4830109718.

———. *Dorama [drama] no tanjo banado shoo [Bernard Shaw]*. Tokyo: Bunkashobohakubunsha, 2003. Language: Japanese. Not seen. ISBN 4830109963.

Strait, Daniel H. "'Fighting Friends': The Chesterton-Shaw Debates." *SHAW: The Annual of Bernard Shaw Studies*. Volume 23. University Park: Penn State University Press, 2003; pp. 47–58.

Thurber, James. *The Thurber Letters: The Wit, Wisdom, and Surprising Life of James Thurber*. Edited by Harrison Kinney, with Rosemary A. Thurber. New York and London: Simon & Schuster, 2003. Includes two mentions of G.B.S., both in letters to E. B. White: 18 July 1952: "If you missed Joseph Wood Krutch's dialogue between Thoreau and G. B. Shaw in the *Saturday Review* of May 24, you better get one. . . ." 19 June 1961: "If the United States had you and G.B. Shaw working together, would the country have the EBGB's? If so, it would have been good for us."

Truss, Lynne. *Eats, Shoots & Leaves: The Zero Tolerance Approach to Punctuation.* New York: Gotham Books, 2004. Not seen. Edmund Morris in his *New York Times Book Review* (25 April 2004): 7, transmits a Shaw reference: "When George Bernard Shaw saw the manuscript of T. E. Lawrence's *Seven Pillars of Wisdom*, he submitted it to a polite form of colonic irrigation."

Tunney, Jay. "The Playwright and the Prizefighter: Bernard Shaw and Gene Tunney." *SHAW: The Annual of Bernard Shaw Studies.* Volume 23. University Park: Penn State University Press, 2003; pp. 149–54.

Widowers' Houses: Shaw Festival 2003 (Shaw Festival production program, 2003). Includes "Director's Notes" by Joseph Ziegler, and "How to Make an Audience Uncomfortable" by J. L. Wisenthal. Excerpts: "The "necessity for us to confront unpalatable and embarrassing economic realities is one of the ways in which *Widowers' Houses* deliberately makes its audience uncomfortable." "Although the play offers a radical critique of contemporary society, it does not provide—or even suggest—any solutions." "*Widowers' Houses* leaves us with the uncomfortable feeling that there is something more to be done, that the theatre is not a sealed-off refuge for pleasant entertainment, and that the artificial neatness of a conventional play is a dishonest falsification of the unpleasant realities in which we find ourselves."

Wisenthal, J. L. See *Widowers' Houses*, above.

III. Periodicals*

Barzun, Jacques. "The Artist as Prophet and Jester." *American Scholar* 69:1 (2000): 15–33. Barzun gives a long paragraph to *Heartbreak House*, interpreting it as an allegory that embodies the experience of World War I "by showing former codes of conduct and belief as obsolete and society in decay." "The West has brought on itself the housecleaning

*In his talk at the International Shaw Society conference, Sarasota, Florida, 17–21 March 2004, "How Do You Find Out What's Written on Shaw?" Charles A. Carpenter names an array of online reference tools, the use of which in the period covered by this 2004 Checklist would list some 500 newspaper reviews of performances of Shaw works. The principle of selection of those very few included below is intended to be illustrative, guided by serendipity and the nominations of Shaw scholars who sent them in. Reviews of performances and publications are not annotated in the Checklist.

its foul habits deserved; whoever looks about him and reflects should welcome it."

"Bernard Shaw." *InfoTrac Custom 150 Full Text Newspapers* 5 May 2004. These are English-language newspapers. Search "in entire article content" returned mentions in "Arts and Entertainment" 206, "Lifestyle" 123, "Opinion and Editorial" 44, "Sports" 14, "Business News" 17, "News" 403, and "Regional News" 84. A number of these refer to the journalist Bernard Shaw. Most are to G.B.S., quoting Shaw or reviews of Shaw plays. "George Bernard Shaw" in this reference tool returns about ten percent fewer listings.

Bertolini, John. "Shaw's Vision" (review of Stuart E. Baker's *Bernard Shaw's Remarkable Religion*). *ELT* 47:2 (2004): 225–27.

Birchall, Paul. "*Mrs Warren's Profession* at the Court Theatre [Los Angeles]" (review). *Back Stage West* 11:7 (12 February 2004): 17.

Blanchard, Jayne. "Dull *Heartbreak* Houses Shaw's Steel; Battis, Anderson Still Stand Out" (review of the Round House, Washington, D.C., production). *The Washington Times* (21 November 2003): D4.

Brock, H. I. "A Drama of the Drama Comes to Light: The Charming Actress, Bewitched Playwright, and Stage Monarch Who Figure in the Shaw-Terry Letters." *New York Times Magazine* 4 February 1931. *The Family Records Centre*. Download of "reprint," 13 February 2004: www .ellenterry.org/shawterrynytimes.htm

Brustein, Robert. "Robert Brustein on Theater: Shotover's Apocalypse." *New Republic* (17 November 2003). Not seen. Teaser abstract on *New Republic* website suggests that *Omnium Gatherum* by Theresa Rebeck and Alexandra Gersten-Vassilaros, which played at the Variety Arts Theatre, New York, between October and November, "seems to have been deeply influenced by *Heartbreak House*."

Cardullo, Bert. See Kauffmann, below.

Chung, Kwangsook. "Reading War, History, and Historicity in Shaw's *Arms and the Man*." *Journal of Modern British and American Drama* 16:1 (April 2003): 55-76. In *Arms* "Shaw uses not only historical events, but also presents anachronistic elements to enable the reader and audience to see beyond incidents that occurred in the past."

Cole, David. "Shaw's *Heartbreak House*." *Explicator* 62:1 (2003): 22-23. The play's last words are not spoken but performed by Randall on his flute—the bars of "There's a silver lining / Through the dark clouds shining. / Turn the dark cloud inside out"—the refrain of "Keep the Home Fire Burning."

"Dame Wendy Hiller: G. B. Shaw's Eliza, Barbara: Obituaries." *Variety* (26 May–1 June 2003): 64. Hiller died on 14 May 2003. The obituary reports that Hiller's appearances in film renditions of Shaw's plays brought her enduring fame. She also starred in the staged *Saint Joan*.

Day, Crosby. "*Caesar and Cleopatra*" (review of Gabriel Pascal's 1945 film). *Orlando Sentinel* [Florida] (15 November 2003): www.orlandosentinel.com

Einsohn, H. I. Review of Leon Hugo's *Bernard Shaw's Black Girl in Search of God. Choice* (January 2004): 908.

————. Review of Alex C. Michalos and Deborah G. Poff's edition of *Bernard Shaw and the Webbs. Choice* (June 2003): 1743–44.

Elkins, Dennis R. Review of L. W. Conolly's edition of *Bernard Shaw and Barry Jackson*, and Alex C. Michalos and Deborah G. Poff's edition of *Bernard Shaw and the Webbs. Theatre Journal* 56:1 (March 2004): 138–39.

Eshelman, D. J. Review of Michel Pharand's *Bernard Shaw and the French. Theatre History Studies* 23 (2003): 124–25.

Essaka, Joshua. "The Mythographic Context of Shaw's *Pygmalion.*" *Nineteenth Century Theatre* 26:2 (Winter 1998): 112–37. See Essaka in II. Books and Pamphlets, above.

Evans, Lloyd. "I Was Wrong" (review in part of Tricycle Theatre [London] production of *John Bull*). *Spectator* 293 (4 October 2003): 62–63.

Fenedon, P. J. "Bernard Shaw and Grants of Arms to Villages." *The Coat of Arms: An Heraldic Quaterly Magazine Published by the Heraldry Society* N.S. 12:183 (Autumn 1998): 279–80. "The editorial in the Spring 1996 issue of this magazine on the subject of grants of arms to village . . . calls to mind some comments on the subject made by Bernard Shaw in January 1897." Summarized, Shaw noted that "of late years" an extraordinary number of local bodies had been created, each wanting a coat of arms or devices for seals. But where were they to get them? He noted that these might come from local artists, or the Herald's College (in whose competence he had little confidence), which charged £76.10s—and would the College consider reducing its fee for public bodies to £2.10s to £5.00? An example of impish Shaw, considering his perfect restraint in not referring to the absurdity of coats of arms and seals, which mean antiquity and elevated reputation, supplied to brand-new public bureaucracies.

Froese, Rainer. "Ghoti: Ghoti Papers." *Fish and Fisheries* 5:1 (2004): 86. This magazine's title for a section to "publish succinct commentary and opinion that addresses important areas in fish and fisheries science," headed by Shaw's famous clever spelling of "fish," i.e., "ghoti."

Gates, Eugene. "The Music Criticism and Aesthetics of George Bernard Shaw." *Journal of Aesthetic Education* 35:3 (Fall 2001): 63–71. "Shaw was a radical voice in late nineteenth-century music criticism. By example, he changed the course of music journalism in the English-speaking world, making it comprehensible to even the general reader."

Gussow, Mel. "The Actress Who Became the Original 'Doozy'" (review of Helen Sheehy's *Eleonora Duse: A Biography). New York Times* (22 August 2003): Books 22.

Handleman, Jay. "Students Present Disarming Shaw" (review of the Asolo Conservatory [Sarasota, Florida] production of *Arms and the Man). Sarasota Herald Tribune* (16 April 2004): 28.

Horton, Merrill. "Bergsonian Laughter in Bernard Shaw's *Back to Methuselah." Analecta Husserliana* 56 (1998): 71–76. "In *Methuselah*, Bergson's two theories, Creative Evolution and Laughter, complement one another; laughter aids life in its struggle against mechanism; it 'softens down whatever the surface of the social body may retain of mechanical inelasticity,' and becomes an expression of both knowledge and will."

Horwitz, Simi. "A Veteran Actor Tackles Shotover (Face to Face: George Morfogen)" (review of the Pearl Theatre, New York, production of *Heartbreak House). Back Stage* 44:13 (28 March 2003): 7–8.

"How Shaw was Duped by Stalin." *Europe Intelligence Wire* (26 June 2003). Downloaded 25 April 2004. List: "Bernard Shaw." *InfoTrac OneFile, Europe Intelligence Wire* 26 June 2003. "How committed [Shaw] was to Stalin has been shockingly revealed in a new collection of papers about to come up for auction at Sotheby's."

Hughes, Frances. "Noel Coward and Shaw: An Aide-Memoir." *The Shavian* 9.4 (2002–03): 16–18. Notes two meeting points between the two authors, and Coward's connection to *Pygmalion, Apple Cart, You Never Can Tell*, and *Androcles*.

Huisking, Charlie. "*Arms and the Man* Forces Self-Examination" (review of the Asolo Conservatory [Sarasota, Florida] production). *Sarasota Herald Tribune* (9 April 2004): 37.

———. "A Rich Role for Asolo's Carolyn Michel" (review of Asolo Conservatory [Sarasota, Florida] production of *The Millionairess). Sarasota Herald Tribune* (9 November 2003): G3.

Hurwitt, Robert. "Shaw's 'Trifle' Rises to a New 'Destiny'" (review of Aurora Theatre [Berkeley, California] production of *Man of Destiny). San Francisco Chronicle* (7 February 2004): D1.

———. "This *Pygmalion* a bit too Perfunctory" (review of Center Repertory [Walnut Creek, California] production). *San Francisco Chronicle* (6 June 2003): D3.

"J.C." "NB." *TLS* (11 July 2003): 16. Reprints some of the poem illustrating Shaw's desire for alphabet reform from Barbara Smoker's *Shavian* (9.4 2002-03) article, along with an advertisement for Shaw Society membership.

Jefferson, Margo. "I Wish I Had Said That, and I Will." *New York Times Book Review* (11 April 2004): 23. From her notebook of quotations:

Shaw: "If I were God I should try to create something higher than myself. I do not wish to be uncomplimentary, but just think about yourselves, ladies and gentlemen: can you conceive God deliberately creating you if he could have created anything better?"

Kantha, S.S. "Nobel Prize Winners for Literature as Palliative for Scientific English." *Croatian Medical Journal* 44 (20–23 February 2003). Not seen. From ISI Web of Science abstract: "I suggest the writings of three literati—Bernard Shaw, Bertrand Russell, and Ernest Hemingway—as palliatives for autotrophic plagiarism in scientific publishing."

Kapelke, Randy. "Preventing Censorship: The Audience's Role in *Sapho* (1900) and *Mrs Warren's Profession* (1905)." *Theatre History Studies* 18 (June 1998): 117–33. Government censorship of both of these plays was not in the end enforced. "This essay argues that traits and behaviors of the audience abetted the defendants, including: its enthusiasm for the plays and suggestive content, its social composition, its gender and finally its symbolic value for the performers."

Kauffmann, Stanley, and Bert Cardullo. "Stanley Kauffmann Interview: On Shaw's *Pygmalion*: Play and Film." *Literature and Film Quarterly* 31:4 (2003): 242–47. No major original material, but it is buoying to read Kauffmann's expression of great admiration for G.B.S. and *Pygmalion* in the English-language 1938 film version.

Kosok, Heinz. "'No War is Right': Shaw's *O'Flaherty V.C.*" *The Shavian* 9.6 (Winter 2003-04): 3–8. "The Victoria Cross was, of course, the highest military distinction a soldier could achieve . . . ; it comes, therefore, close to an act of sacrilege to question its significance or joke about it, as Shaw does here. Moreover, it should be noted that Shaw was careful to place this speech in a strategic position where O'Flaherty . . . had already been established as a charming and sensible son . . . so that his words . . . carry the full weight of a summing-up of the author's purpose. 'No war is right,' coming as it does from a soldier decorated by the King for his bravery, must at the time have been both shocking and disturbing."

Kuchwara, Michael. "Uta Hagen (1919–2004). Obituary." *Back Stage West*. Hagen died 14 January. One of her roles was as Joan in *Saint Joan*.

Leary, Daniel. "A Note on Borges and Shaw." *Independent Shavian* 41:1 (2003): 5–7. Notices two Borges remarks about G.B.S., and an instance of indirect connection in that both authors appreciated Bunyan's *Pilgrim's Progress*.

———. "Why Didn't Shaw Write Tragedy?" *The Independent Shavian* 41:2–3 (2003): 45–53. A charming and smart dramatic interlude featuring two CCNY professors emeriti (with real names). Samplings: "Dan[iel Leary]: . . . The best of his [Shaw's] drama deals with heartbreak, disbelief, the shattering of old certainties—Joan realizes the world is not ready for its saints, Caesar realizes the same for the world's heros, Barbara the same for its liberals, Ellie and Shotover the same for its dreamers." "Den[nis DeNitto]: . . . Shaw was temperamentally too practical and enjoyed too much the play of the intellect to write poetry in its tragic form, or any other form: Shaw could not depict 'a terrible beauty' emerging from a hero's clash with physical or moral corruption. For Shaw tragedy is a waste of time, a futile self indulgence. He was a child of the Enlightenment and believed in—or tried to believe in—the Life Force which he saw manifesting itself in the evolution of man through social progress. For him, drama was a pedagogical device, a witty, ironic, gloriously verbal device it's true, but, at best, an edifying screen on which to project man's evolution."

Levitas, Ben. "Plumbing the Depths: Irish Realism and the Working Class from Shaw to O'Casey." *Irish University Review: A Journal of Irish Studies* 33:1 (Spring–Summer 2003): 133–51. "The potential for a drama that would respond to the social polemics available in Ibsen and Shaw and become capable of staging the radical agendas of the Irish left would develop into a wiry thread of theatre practice running through the fabric of the Revival. [new paragraph] Consideration of that tradition is crucial to a re-evaluation of realism's impact on Ireland. . . . Irish mimesis . . . was only occasionally allowed to fit into the narrow band of properly deterministic naturalism. The Irish school was more typically realist . . . [;] an array of realisms was available in Ireland, refracting a range of politics." In Shaw's *Widower's Houses*, Levitas finds an example of Shaw's adaptation of his familiarity with socialist circles in the 1880s, influenced also by Ibsen, and contrasts it with George Moore's *The Strike at Arlingford*. "While Moore's excursion into social conflict imparts a naturalist fatalism to its subject, Shaw's acted to persuade in specific battles: Fabian pamphleteering over housing issues and finally politicking of the new London County Council elections." This discussion of Shaw foregrounds the article, after which it discusses later ones without substantial reference to Shaw.

Lorenz, Paul. "The Shavian Gospel as Revealed in *The Adventures of the Black Girl in Her Search for God*. *Publication of the Mississippi Philological Association* (2001): 15–25. In his afterword to *Black Girl*, "Shaw chose to talk about how the Bible documents the fact that the human perception of God has evolved over time. Shaw's concern is that the tradition of accepting the King James version of the Bible as the word of God, despite some of its obvious errors in translation (errors which Madame Blavatsky pointed out in *The Secret Doctrine*), has led to the institutionalization of harsh Old Testament attitudes that conflict with many of the teachings of Jesus in the New Testament. He also argues, like Lawrence, that the teachings of the modern church represent a pseudo-Christianity, which combined with technology, contemporary events, and modern skepticism, has made the Bible appear to be irrelevant to many people. . . . Shaw ends by calling for a reasoned reevaluation of religious beliefs."

Mannion, Kristina. "*Mr. Shaw Goes to Hollywood* at Laguna [Laguna Beach, California] Playhouse" (review). *Back Stage West* 10:15 (10 April 2003): 16.

Mason, Nicholas. "Bernard Shaw, Journalist: An Insider's View of a Master of the Art." *The Shavian* 9.5 (Summer 2003): 7–12. Shaw rose from "office boy (except that he did not work in the office) to Columnist of the Decade (except that such egregious accolades mercifully did not exist in those days) in barely a dozen years. Any journalist since would have been more than happy to do it in forty."

Miller, C. Brook. "Exporting the Garden City: Imperial Development and the English Character in *John Bull's Other Island*. *Xchanges* 2:2 (May 2003) (www.americanstudies.wayne.edu/xchanges/2.2/miller.html) In *John Bull*, "Shaw combines an interrogation of English and Irish national stereotypes with a discussion of land development policies in Ireland. . . . Here, and elsewhere in Shaw's work, national characteristics are reinscribed even as they are deconstructed, while alternative visions of land development provide no certain route to Irish independence. These twin dilemmas are not only incidentally left unresolved—they are more intimately linked through their articulation in the linguistic garb of turn-of-the-century English Liberalism. Finally, the play critiques contemporary Liberal bromides for investment capital projects which foster Irish dependency. At the same time, he points to the colonial psychology which legitimates Liberalism even while it has been thoroughly discredited. . . . Shaw's "selection of 'foreigners' masquerading as Englishman-Americans, Italians, and Jews—indites [sic] monopoly capital and syndicalism as the forces of modern economic transformation. The xenophobic nature of Shaw's claim was not unusual in commentary of this period; what is particularly interesting about it is the manner in which it is embedded in a deconstructive argument about nationality itself. In a sense this connection completes the analysis begun within the pages of *John Bull's Other Island*: We see English illusions as a reaction formation to the corporatization and rationalization of the modern world economy."

Morrow, Laurie P. "The Playwright in Spite of Himself: George Bernard Shaw: Man, Superman, and Socialism." *The World and I* 18:5 (2003): 242–53. Morrow is identified in an author note as "the host of 'True North with Laurie Morrow,' heard weekdays on WKDR 1390 AM, in

Burlington, Vermont." Her piece rushes through a summary of
Shaw's life and works that contends, "With the passion of a Puritan
minister dispensing hellfire sermons, Shaw preached through his
plays his vision of How Things Ought to Be. This included, at various
times, such harmless beliefs as vegetarianism and abstention from alcohol, but they also included such vile beliefs as the endorsement of
fascism and a blind devotion to Stalinism. All had a cynical edge to
them, of disdain for lesser folk." Clearly Shaw remains threatening
enough to elicit the energy of this fulmination.

Murray, David. "Shaw Festival Niagara-on-the-Lake, Ontario" (review of
a "reading" of *Blanco Posnet* for later CBC broadcast, *Widowers' Houses*,
and *Misalliance*). *The Financial Times* (24 July 2003): 10.

Nash, Charles C. Review of Allen Brooke's *Twentieth Century Attitudes: Literary Powers in Uncertain Times* (which treats GBS). *Library Journal* (August 2003): 81.

Nickson, Richard. "Nomenclature in the Shavian Epoch." *The Independent
Shavian* 41:2–3 (2003): 39–42. A digression on Shaw's lifelong negotiation of his "Anglo-Irish"ness.

Parsons, Melinda Boyd, and Gary Joseph Pascuzzo. "Bernard Shaw: 'Un-
mechanical' Photography and Unconventional Science." *History of
Photography* 26:3 (Autumn 2002): 170–77. "For Shaw, truth was defined by his socialism as well as by relations among art, science, and
religion. These ideas merge in his provocative essay of 1902, 'The
Unmechanicalness of Photography. . . .'" "Ironically, while photography's mimetic truthfulness led most critics to call the camera mindless
and 'mechanical,' Shaw sees it as the essence of photography's 'unmechanicalness.' The reference points for this theme are both aesthetic
and scientific." "At the end of 'Unmechanicalness,' Shaw criticizes academic conventions in art: 'The Academic enthusiasm is a wonderful
and beautiful thing when young; but it leads to a dull and decrepit
age. . . .'" In [Herman von] Helmholtz, [Armand] Trousseau, and
[John] Tyndall, Shaw found unconventional scientists with unconventional ideas that he would use throughout his life. In Tyndall, especially, he found a future-oriented creative force to fight against a dull
and decrepit age."

Perteghella, Manuela. "Language and Politics on Stage: Strategies for
Translating Dialect and Slang with References to Shaw's *Pygmalion*
and Bond's *Saved*. *Translation Review* 8 (2002): 45–54. "This article
identifies the possible strategies and methods used in the stage translation of vernaculars and nonstandard language, with specific examples from a German translation of the cockney dialogues in Edward
Bond's *Saved* and an Italian translation of Bernard Shaw's *Pygmalion*.
I analyze the decision-making process, positioning the translations

within different acting traditions and theatrical conventions, while looking at possible reception 'effects' of each of these strategies on monolingual and monocultural audiences abroad." Saba Sardi, "the Italian translator attempted to re-create Shaw's cockney by fashioning what he calls a 'horrible linguistic mixture.' He uses a fusion of dialects from across Northern Italy, the agricultural Po Valley area, and from the urban areas of Milan, because of their Latin-Celtic matrix, which makes them closer to the sonority of cockney."

Peters, Margot. "Alfred, Lynn, and GBS." *The Independent Shavian* 41:2–3 (2003): 31–38. A gathering of information on Alfred Lunt's and Lynn Fontane's performance in a number of Shaw plays, and their relationship with G.B.S. himself. Peters has written *Design for Living: A Biography of Alfred Lunt and Lynn Fontanne*.

Peters, Sally. "Bernard Shaw's Dilemma: Marked by Mortality." *International Journal of Epidemiology* 32 (December 2003): 918–19. "On the subject of doctors and medicine Shaw put forth a dazzling display of partial truths, the clear prose giving a seeming lucidity to his arguments. The incessant repetition declares what he needed to believe. In extolling the purifying properties of sunshine and fresh air, he moved the theatre of action from a dark crawling world of unseen organisms upward to a brightly lit, clean, incorporeal world, the only world his psyche could tolerate." Peters's source is principally the long Preface to *Doctor' Dilemma*, but she mentions also *Philanderer* and *Blanco Posnet*.

Pharand, Michel W. "Saint Joan on the Continent: Jeanne in Paris and Giovanna in Rome." *The Shavian* 9.4 (2002–03): 8–15. Provides a comparison of "how Shaw's work was treated in France and Italy at the outset, with particular attention to *Saint Joan* (1923), and [compares] the reception of the 1925 Paris premiere, with Ludmilla Pitoëff as Joan [to rave reviews], to the first production in Rome the following year, starring Emma Gramatica [to mixed reviews]."

Phillips, Robert. "1. George Bernard Shaw to H.G. Wells." *Prairie Schooner* 7:1 (Spring 2003): 54. "Charlotte died this morning at 2:30," is the first line of a first-person voice poem of two nine-line stanzas. Charlotte appears to grow younger as she dies and lies dead. Shaw is moved much beyond his expectations. Shaw himself wrote poetry only rarely.

Pomata, G. "Reply to Pygmalion: The Origins of Women's History at the London School of Economics." *Quaderni Storici* 37 (August 2002): 505–44. Not seen. From the ISI Web of Science abstract: "Reconstructs the history of the Shaw scholarship, set up at the LSE in 1904 by Charlotte Payne Townshend Shaw (1857–1943), a leading member of the Fabian Women's Group and the wife of George Bernard Shaw." Draws on materials from the London School of Economics archives.

Reddy, K. Srinath. "Commentary: Shaw's Critique of Health Care is Still Valid." *International Journal of Epidemiology* 32 (2003): 919–21. "The preface provided by George Bernard Shaw to *The Doctor's Dilemma* is a profoundly insightful and deliberately provocative essay on the shortcomings of health care. . . . Most of the ideas developed in the preface are of great contemporary importance."

Robertson, MaryAnn. "Oldest Profession Takes Back Seat to Mother-Daughter Complexity" (review of Players' Ring Theatre [Portsmouth, New Hampshire] production of *Mrs Warren*). *Spotlight/Seacoastonline* [hard copy] (12 February 2004): 7.

Salama, Mohammad R. "The Aesthetics of *Pygmalion* in G. B. Shaw and Tawfiq Al-Hakim: A Study of Transcendence and Decadence." *Journal of Arabic Literature* 31:3 (2000): 222–37. "It would indeed be unjust to think of *Pygmalion* as a play about the possible marriage between Eliza and her maker, Higgins. Although most criticism tends to go in that direction, the play transcends this sentimental individual level of a personal relationship to a higher lever of linguistic aestheticization. Shaw's *Pygmalion* is a play on the society, in which both Eliza and Higgins are types of two unequal social classes, whose gap could only be bridged through the beauty of language. To think of it in the sentimental terms of the possible growth of love between teacher and pupil, or creator and his creation, is to misconceive its aesthetic value. Eliza acquires independence and freedom through the aesthetics of language, through the beauty of her new linguistic identity."

Seaman, Donna. Review of Allen Brooke's *Twentieth Century Attitudes: Literary Powers in Uncertain Times* (which treats G.B.S.). *Booklist* (15 September 2003): 193.

Sparks, Julie A. Review of Michel Pharand's *Bernard Shaw and the French*. *Comparative Literature Studies* 40:4 (2003): 452–56.

Sterner, Mark H. "Shaw's *Devil's Disciple*: The Subversion of Melodrama/ The Melodrama of Subversion." *Modern Drama* 42 (Fall 1999): 338–45. In *Devil*, "Shaw interpolated an ethical house of mirrors in which respected matriarchs are empty-hearted skinflints, Presbyterian clergymen become military heroes, and devil-worshiping outcasts are revealed as saints. . . . The real subject of the play becomes the developmental struggle of its characters, their need to discover the inner truth beneath the tawdry façade of their environment. The audience is invited to join this struggle, to gaze beneath the status quo of the action on the play's surface."

Stokes, John. "Talk About a Menace to Society" (review of the Tricycle

Theatre [London] production of *John Bull*). *TLS* (26 September 2003): 18–19.

Taglienti, Paolina. Review of Judith Evans's *The Politics and Plays of Bernard Shaw*. *Library Journal* (1 October 2003): 75.

Waterman, David. "The Human Body as a Text of Resistance: Madness as a Social/Individual Wound in Wilfred Owen, George Bernard Shaw and Virginia Woolf." *Sprachkunst* 30:1 (1999): 67–96. "The 'strategic occupation' of madness/hysteria/shell shock becomes a way to resist ideological 'education' when such education clearly contradicts the subjects' critical experience. Resistance in the form of madness must then be segregated and reoriented by the dominant power, both through cultural sanctions of those who resist and, when necessary, the (ab)use of the institution of psychiatry to reinscribe the body/text. The body becomes the representation of the social system; control of the body means control of society, through ideological/repressive apparatus and regulatory regimes designed to place subjects in their proper place(s), thus preventing madness 'from speaking for itself, in a language of its own. . . . Bernard Shaw's *Heartbreak House* challenges the notion of uncritical acceptance of ideological dogma, thus creating an environment which allows for the critical examination of society's cooperation in its own self-destruction; the lack of familiar points of reference becomes a potential experience of liberation and growth."

Woodward, Joe, and Michael Holroyd. "The Chesterton-Shaw Debates." *The Chesterton Review* 24:4 (1998): 531–41. Reprints excerpts from 27 June 1998 *Alberta Report* (Woodward), and volume 2 of Holroyd's biography of Shaw.

Wormald, Patrick. "The Proper Study: The Importance of the Humanities Cannot be Measured in Pounds, or even Euros." *TLS* (16 January 2004): 12–13. Wormald taps the Olivier film of *The Devil's Disciple* for the reassurance, "History, Sir. History will tell lies, as usual."

The Independent Shavian 41.1 (2003). Journal of the Bernard Shaw Society. Includes "Jacques Barzun Weighs Dissimilar Views of a Mozart Passage," "Shavian Indignation," "On Being Didactic," "Prescient Shaw," "A Note on Borges and Shaw" by Daniel Leary, "Ayot St Lawrence 17 October 1950: Notes Made" by Judy Musters, "A Great Number of Bernard Shaws" by James Stephens, "As They Liked It" by Dan H. Laurence, "Theatre Review: *Heartbreak House* at the Pearl Theatre" by John P. Koontz, "Theatre Review: *Mr. Shaw Goes to Hollywood*" by Arthur Horowitz, "Floridian Shaw," "Authentic Bentley" by Eric Bentley, "Book Note" by Richard Nickson: *George Bernard Shaw: Eight Interviews by Hayden Church*, "Letter from England" by T. F. Evans, "Ray Bradbury is Reading Plays of Shaw," "Our Cover," "Recent Commendations," "Society Activities," "Obituaries," "News About Our Members," and " 2002 Index." See also Leary, Daniel, and Musters, Judy, above, and "Ayot St Lawrence . . ." in I. Works by Shaw, above.

The Independent Shavian 41:2–3 (2003). Journal of the Bernard Shaw Society. Includes "Alfred, Lynn, and GBS" by Margot Peters, "The Impatient Patient," "Nomenclature in the Shavian Epoch" by Richard Nickson, "Chess," "Mr. Bernard Shaw's 'Galvanizing Methods'" by James Agate, "'Why Didn't Shaw Write Tragedy?' An Improvisation" by Daniel Leary, "Tax Accountant Shaw," "Bernard Shaw's Dilemma: Marked by Mortality" by Sally Peters, "Letter From England, January 2004" by T. F. Evans, "Theatre Review: *Pygmalion*" by John P. Koontz, "Theatre Review" *Arms and the Man*" by Isidor Saslav, "Obituary: Uta Hagen, 1919–2004," "Katherine Hepburn and *The Millionairess* by Douglas Laurie, "News About Our Members," and "Society Activities." See also Leary, Daniel ("Why"), Nickson, Richard, and Peters, Margot, above.

The Shavian 9.4 (Winter 2002–03). The Journal of the Shaw Society. Includes "Editorial," "Obituary," "Some Last Thoughts" by Christopher Newton, "Sir Oracle 1924," "Saint Joan on the Continent" by Michel W. Pharand, "Noel Coward and Shaw" by Frances Hughes, "GBS and the ABC" by Barbara Smoker, "Onwards to Conquer" by Derek Wellman, "Our Theatres Today" ("Shaw Festival, Niagara" by Robert Tanitch, "*Pygmalion* in Manchester" by Chris Honer, *Mrs Warren's Profession*" by Anthony Ellis, and "Other Theatres at Home" by Adolphus Bastable), "Book Reviews" (Mary Leach's review of the Shaw-Barry Jackson correspondence, University of Toronto Press, edited by L.W. Conolly; David Francis' review of Simon Callow's *Laughton*; T. F. Evans's review of Barbara Smoker's *Freethoughts*; and Barbara Smoker's review of Stuart E. Baker's *Bernard Shaw's Remarkable Religion*), "Scraps and Shavings," and "Contributors." See also entries for Hughes, Frances, and Pharand, Michel W., above.

The Shavian 9.5 (Summer 2003). Journal of the Shaw Society. Includes "Editorial," "Obituary," "Bernard Shaw, Journalist" by Nicholas Mason, "William Hazlitt," "From the (Very) *New Statesman*, "Shaw on Musical Criticism," "From the Archives," "Programme Notes" by A Player, "Agate Revisited," "Our Theatres" by Bastable and Others, "Book Reviews" (T. F. Evans's review of Stanley Weintraub's *Charlotte and Lionel*, Hayward Morse's review of Judith Evans's *The Politics and Plays of Bernard Shaw*, and "*Captain Brassbound's Conversion*" by Tom Miller). See also Mason, Nicholas, above.

The Shavian 9.6 (Winter 2003–04). Journal of the Shaw Society. Includes "Editorial," "'No War is Right'" by Heinz Kosok, "To the Editor," "Obituary," "A New Critic," "Our Theatres 2003" by R. Tanitch,

"More Theatres," "A Return," "Brand," "An Enemy of the People," "Shorter Notices," "Book Reviews" (Robert Tanitch's review of L. W. Conolly's edition of the Shaw–Barry Jackson correspondence; unsigned reviews of Ronald Bryden's *Theatre Essays: Shaw and His Contemporaries*, and Leslie Yeo's *A Thousand and One First Nights*), and "Autumn Meetings." See also Kosok, Heinz, above.

IV. Dissertations

Bailey, Sharon Marie. "The Dream of a Better Way to Live: The New Man in English, German and Russian Literature of the Early Twentieth Century (George Bernard Shaw, Georg Kaiser, Bertolt Brecht, Mikhail Afanas'evich Bulgakov, Yury Olesha)." The Pennsylvania State University, 2002. *Dissertation Abstracts International: UMI ProQuest Digital Dissertations* 63-09A: 3179. "Whereas utopian literature posits that people will be happier when society is well ordered, New Man literature starts with the assumption that mankind is the cause of disorder in society. To achieve a better society, we must first improve human nature." The study examines "how five European authors . . . use the character of the New Man to criticize contemporary social issues." Criticizing the middle class in England, "the change which George Bernard Shaw proposes in *Man and Superman* is that humans increase their potential for contemplation and self-awareness by means of a quasi-Lamarckian program of eugenics."

Dailey, Jeff S. "The Successful Failure: Arthur Sullivan's *Ivanhoe* (England)." New York University, 2002. *Dissertation Abstracts International: UMI ProQuest Digital Dissertations* 63-07A: 2417. "After twelve successful comic operas, written in collaboration with W.S. Gilbert, Arthur Sullivan wrote a grand opera, *Ivanhoe*, that was performed 166 times in 1891 in a theatre especially constructed for it. In spite of this impressive record, some critics, both at the time of its premiere and in recent years, have described it as a failure. This dissertation explores the opera and its place in Sullivan's career and in the context of the musical theatre of the 1890s. . . . Special emphasis is placed on the music criticism of George Bernard Shaw, whose witty but scathing review of *Ivanhoe* has been frequently reprinted and quoted."

Fenn-Smith, Jeremy. "Staging Intersubjectivity: Queer Theory, Queer Theatre, Tony Kushner and *Angels in America*." New York University, 2003. *Dissertation Abstracts International: UMI ProQuest Digital Dissertations* 63-11A: 3793. "Although subtitled 'A Gay Fantasia on National Themes,' the first performances in 1992 of Tony Kushner's play *Angels in America* coincided with the beginning of the academic movement known as 'queer theory.' Use of Jessica Benjamin's model of recognition from object-relational psychoanalysis illustrates how Kushner puts an intersubjectivity on stage. . . ." Kushner's plays have been described as a theater of dialectics, and Finn-Smith's chapter 3 analyzes two theaters of dialectics—Shaw's and Brecht's—that have strong resonances in *Angels*.

Herstad, Heide-Marie. "Laughter: Structure and Paradox in Drama Variations (Paul von Schoenthan, Franz von Schoenthan, George Bernard Shaw, Tove Jansson, Germany, England, Sweden)." Jyvaskylan Yliopisto (Finland), 2001. *Dissertation Abstracts International: UMI ProQuest Digital Dissertations* 63-04A:623. "The focus of the study is the underlying question: How do I create knowledge of the world through laughter?" "My hypothesis is that laughter is always ambivalent; it is a manipulation of the people and at the same time a paradox. Laughter can be structural, calculated, but people seldom really know why they are laughing. The theory is interdisciplinary based on pragmatic and on transcendental cognitive philosophies." Herstad's second of four models is "Transformation processes of satire. Satire is paradigmatically discussed with . . . Shaw's *Arms and the Man*. Satire is an intention to change society, people, and social conditions. Satire has no special structure of its own but can adopt any structure as drama, fable, story, and so on. Satire is a contract between the intentions of the work as a challenge and the recipient. Satire exists only as long as the recipient accepts the challenge. Otherwise it transforms into something different that is not a satire."

Lufkin, Patricia Ellen. "An Analysis of the Plays of Margaret Macnamara." Louisana State University and Agricultural and Mechanical College, 2002. *Dissertation Abstracts International: UMI ProQuest Digital Dissertations* 63-11A: 3794. Presents Macnamara's career as a playwright and dramaturge while exploring the cultural and political contexts of her work, and the influence of the Fabian Society on her work, and places her among such playwrights as Shaw, Barker, and Nugent Monck. Her play *Mrs. Hodges* (1920) is compared with *Widowers' Houses*. The dissertation attempts to resurrect Macnamara's work as information and a source of insight for theater and women's studies scholars.

V. Recordings

Arms and the Man. (1985/2002; in audiobook of 10 CDs; Shaw introduced and play put in context with appropriate music. Playtext is abridged and adapted. One of seven classic plays. Full cast. 13 hours for seven plays.) #0-7861-9639-4, $80.00. Blackstone Audio. Reviewed by Maureen K. Griffin in *Kliatt* 37:3 (May 2003): 53–54.

Berkman, Ted. *The Lady and the Law: The Remarkable Life of Fanny Holtz-*

mann. (2003; CD; offered as the true story of Fanny Holtzmann (1903–1980), a shy high school dropout from Brooklyn who battled her way into Fordham Law School and emerged as the most accomplished woman lawyer of her time. Shaw was among her friends. Originally published, Carpinteria, California: Manifest Publications, 1999). LCCN 99-65183. Not seen. *Major Barbara* (2003; on a CD of *The Wadsworth Anthology of Drama*, edited by William B. Worthen). OCLC: 53217784. Not seen. Lists also *Major Barbara* (2003; on a CD of *The Broadview Anthology of Drama*, Plays for the Western Theatre, Volume 2, The Nineteenth and Twentieth Centuries, edited by Jennifer Wise and Craig Stewart Walker). OCLC: 54977992. Not seen. *Pygmalion* (2003; on a CD of *The Longman Anthology of British Literature*, Volume 2C, The Twentieth Century, edited by David Damrosch). LCCN: 2002-66148. Not seen. Princeton, New Jersey: Recording for the Blind and Dyslexic, 2003. Distribution is restricted to RFB&D members who have a documented print disability.

Irish Writers. ([2004]; videocassette/DVD; Ireland through the eyes of its greatest writers from Shaw to Joyce, Wilde, and Yeats. "The rugged beauty of the wild island inspired some of modern history's most eloquent literary voices." Approx. 60 minutes). VHS IRWR801 or DVD IRWR401, $19.95. PBS Home Video catalogue, February 2004. Order: 1-800-645-4727; mail Catalog Mail Order Center, P.O. Box 609, Melbourne, FL 32902-0609; online: www.shopPBS.com; fax: 1-866-274-9038. Not seen.

Living Doll: Background to Shaw's "Pygmalion. (2002; videocassette/DVD: "Photos and footage from a number of productions, including the 1938 film adaptation, along with commentary from many experts, provide a detailed context in which to more fully appreciate Shaw's first dramatic success." 30 minutes). VHS: #JBA29866, $149.95; DVD, $174.95. Not seen. Lists also *Michael Holroyd on George Bernard Shaw*. (n.d.; "Questions the extent to which Shaw's life and art fed upon each other. . . . A second theme deals with the reciprocal relationship between biographer and subject." 53 minutes). VHS: #JBA10342, $149.95; DVD, $174.95. Not seen. Films for the Humanities and Sciences, P.O. Box 2053, Princeton, NJ 08543-2053; phone: 1-800-257-5126; online: www.films.com.

Major Barbara. See Berkman, Ted, above.

Michael Holroyd on George Bernard Shaw. See *Living Doll*, above.

My Fair Lady. (2004, 1964; DVD, region 1, 2 videodiscs special edition; English or dubbed French dialogue; French or Spanish subtitles; stars Rex Harrison and Audrey Hepburn. 172 mins.). Burbank: Warner Home Video. ISBN: 079078534X.

The Philanderer. (12 April 2003; archival performance 2 VHS cassettes;

featuring Kathleen Coons, Jason Stiles, Tricia McCAuley, Bill Hamlin, Conrad Feininger, Cody Lindquist, Steven Carpenter, C.L. Greenleaf; directed by John MacDonald. Not loanable; viewing restricted to library. 149 minutes). OCLC: 54360243. [Washington D.C.]: Washington Stage Guild, Washington Area Performing Arts Video Archive (WAPAVA). Not seen.

Pygmalion. See Berkman, Ted, above.

Shaw, Bernard. A "Historic Recording . . . ." (2003; "cassette tape 1 sound disc"; *The Spoken Word: Historic Recordings of Writers Born in the 19th Century/ Writers*, among 22 writers, including Beerbohm, Chesterton, Maugham, Barker, and Woolf. 72 minutes). ISBN: 0712305165, London: British Library Sound Archive, 2003. Not seen.

Shaw vs. Shakespeare: The Character of Caesar. (1970; videocassette of Shaw played by Donald Moffatt, analyzes Shakespeare's *Julius Caesar* and compares it with his own treatment in *Caesar and Cleopatra*. Called a "best seller" by Insight Media. 33 minutes) #68AG1709, $109.00, World Literature Catalogue, Insight Media, 2162 Broadway, New York, NY; phone: 800-233-9910 or 212-721-6316; email: cs@insight-media.com; online: www.insight-media.com. Not seen.

The Wit and World of GBS (1972; film; Harry Rasky, director. 90 minutes). Leonard Conolly's information: Original broadcast by CBC TV. It has Christopher Plummer, Barry Morse in *Man and Superman*, John Colicos in *Major Barbara*, Paxton Whitehead in *Doctor's Dilemma*, and Genevieve Bujold as Joan (she is terrific). Includes lots of clips of G.B.S.: at the Einstein dinner, at Malvern, at Ayot, etc. (The Japanese *My Fair Lady* is a hoot. Well worth seeing.) For information on how to acquire this film, contact Sarasota Film Society @ Burns Court Cinemas, 506 Burns Lane, Sarasota, Florida; phone: 941-364-8662; email: Mail@filmsociety.org. Not seen.

VI. Bernard Shaw on the World Wide Web*

On 10 May 2004, the search term "George Bernard Shaw" on the *Google* search engine produced 275,000 listings (336,000 in 2003), and 452,000 on the *Yahoo* search engine. Without quotations, for George Bernard Shaw, in 2004, *Google* returned 549,000, and *Yahoo* returned 927,000 hits. The items include many for the U.S. television journalist Bernard Shaw and some other maverick ones. Many of the important G.B.S. items produce on-line material that is dated, incomplete, simplifying, or factually inaccurate. Nevertheless, searching for Shaw on the Web will yield much important information. Even so, only a

---

*World Wide Web articles may be listed in III. Periodicals, above.

tenth of a percent of the hits will be relevantly informative or new. Meanwhile, this section of the Checklist is not generally about Shaw-related articles on the Web; nor is it about the special on-line reference search tools proliferated from or imitating the early *InfoTrac*. It is most importantly about certain websites that have information of both current and significant importance to Shaw studies. For cumulative information about Shaw on the Web, users of this Checklist should consult the corresponding sections in the Checklists beginning with *SHAW 22*.

By far the most important website, directed and managed by Professor Richard Dietrich (dietrich@chuma.cas.usf.edu), is *Shaw Bizness: Links to the Life, Times, and Work of Irish Playwright George Bernard Shaw*. It is a clearinghouse for matters Shavian. It links to the website for the International Shaw Society, which, through Dietrich's Herculean efforts, achieved nonprofit status in 2004, in time for the first International Shaw Society conference in Sarasota, Florida, 17–21 March 2004. Web searchers are advised that the *Shaw Bizness* site is listed as entry #28 for both *Google* and *Yahoo* search engines—confounding the organizing principle of Web search engines to list the most important sites first. Professor Charles A. Carpenter's *Modern British, Irish, and American Drama: A Descriptive Chronology 1865–1965*, initiated in 2003, has a section on Shaw for one of its nine major playwright listings. Carpenter is the dean of those who do research in Shaw secondary bibliography. Visit: http://bingweb.binghamton.edu/~ccarpen. "George Bernard Shaw" on the IMDb (Internet Movie Database Incorporated, 1990–2004) (http://us.imdb.com/name?Shaw%2c+George +Bernard) website accesses a substantial list of more than 70 items in the media, of Shaw works, pastiches, and newsreel appearances preserved among relatively accessible archived material. Bibliographic/filmographic location information for many pieces is scant.

CONTRIBUTORS

Alan Andrews is Professor of Theater at Dalhousie University. He edited Allan Wade's *Memories of the London Theatre, 1900–1914* (1983) and the *Dalhousie Review* for ten years. He has written and lectured frequently for the Shaw Festival in Ontario, on Shaw, Granville Barker, and St. John Hankin. He is currently working on Barker's uncollected essays, articles, introductions, reviews, and lectures, and on a collection of Shaw's correspondence with musicians for the Selected Correspondence of Bernard Shaw series.

Charles A. Carpenter is Professor Emeritus of English at Binghamton University. He is the author of *Bernard Shaw & the Art of Destroying Ideals: The Early Plays, Modern Drama Scholarship and Criticism, 1966–1990: An International Bibliography* (2 vols.), *Dramatists and the Bomb: American and British Playwrights Confront the Nuclear Age, 1945–1964,* and two other reference books. His website, entitled "Modern British, Irish, and American Drama, 1865–1965: A Descriptive Chronology," can be found at bingweb.binghamton.edu/~ccarpen.

Patricia Carter, a published poet, was an adjunct faculty member at Catholic, George Washington, American, and Georgetown universities. She wrote her dissertation for George Washington University on *Back to Methuselah,* entitled "The Gospel of the Biologist Shaw." She has also published two novellas and continues to write fiction and drama.

L. W. Conolly is Professor of English at Trent University and Adjunct Professor of Drama at the University of Guelph, as well as a Corresponding Scholar of the Shaw Festival, Ontario. He is editor of *Bernard Shaw and Barry Jackson,* the fourth volume in the Selected Correspondence of Bernard Shaw series (University of Toronto Press), of which he is the General Editor.

MaryAnn K. Crawford, Associate Editor of *SHAW,* is an Associate Professor of English at Central Michigan University, where she directs the Basic Writing/Writing Center programs and teaches linguistics and composition. She researches, writes, and publishes on a variety of literary, linguistic/ESL, and literacy issues, and she is working on a biography of Lowell Thomas, the late radio broadcaster and newsreel personality.

R. F. Dietrich, Professor Emeritus at the University of South Florida, is the author of *Bernard Shaw's Novels: Portrait of the Artist as Man and Superman, British Drama 1890 to 1950: A Critical History* and many articles on Shaw and other modern authors. He is the Series Editor of the Florida Shaw Series published by the University Press of Florida (http://www.upf.com/se-shaw.shtml). As president of the International Shaw Society, he invites prospective members to visit the ISS website (http://chuma.cas.usf.edu/~dietrich/iss.htm) or to contact him at dietrich @chuma1.cas.usf.edu.

Bernard F. Dukore, University Distinguished Professor Emeritus of Theater Arts and Humanities at Virginia Tech, has directed plays and written numerous books and articles on modern drama and theater. His most recent books are *Shaw's Theater* and *Sam Peckinpah's Feature Films*.

Peter Gahan, a graduate in Philosophy from Trinity College, Dublin, worked for some years as a documentary film editor in Ireland before relocating to Los Angeles. He has published several articles in *SHAW* and has just completed a book-length study of Shaw's writing in the context of poststructuralism.

Gale K. Larson, General Editor of *SHAW*, has been teaching for the last thirty-seven years at California State University, Northridge, where he has held various administrative positions. He has edited an edition of *Caesar and Cleopatra* and has written articles on that play as well as on *"In Good King Charles's Golden Days"* and has reviewed works on Shaw in various journals. He is the Chief Reader for Advanced Placement in Literature.

Dan H. Laurence, author of *Bernard Shaw: A Bibliography,* editor of Shaw's *Collected Letters* and *Shaw's Music,* and Editorial Supervisor of *Bernard Shaw: Collected Plays with Their Prefaces,* was Literary and Dramatic Advisor to the Shaw Estate from 1973 to 1990 and is an Associate Director of the Shaw Festival, Ontario.

Margery M. Morgan, Emeritus Reader in English at the University of Lancaster, is the author of *The Shavian Playground* and *File on Wilde*. She has published books and articles on Shaw and on Granville Barker over many years. She has also written an unpublished biography of Granville Barker and is currently completing a study of his collaboration with Shaw to create a theater "for the public good."

Harold Pagliaro, Provost Emeritus and Alexander Griswold Cummins Professor Emeritus at Swarthmore College, is the author of numerous articles on eighteenth-century English literature. Among his books are *Henry Fielding: A Literary Life* and *Selfhood and Redemption in Blake's Songs.*

John R. Pfeiffer is Professor of English at Central Michigan University and bibliographer of *SHAW.* He has published articles on Richard Francis Burton, Octavia Butler, John Christopher, John Brunner, Aldous Huxley, Ray Bradbury, and on collective bargaining in U.S. universities.

Michel W. Pharand, author of *Bernard Shaw and the French,* is currently editing *Bernard Shaw and His Publishers* for the Selected Correspondence of Bernard Shaw series. He has also written on Robert Graves, Richard Aldington, Lawrence Durrell, and Rohinton Mistry.

Peter Tompkins is the author of *A Spy in Rome, Italy Betrayed, Secrets of the Great Pyramid, The Secret Life of Plants, Secrets of the Soil, Mysteries of the Mexican Pyramids,* and *The Magic of Obelisks,* among many other books.

Karma Waltonen is a doctoral student at the University of California, Davis, and teaches at Sacramento City College and American River College. Her article on Margaret Atwood is forthcoming in *Identity and Alterity in Canadian Literature.* Her research interests, although varied in time period and genre, always seem to be about "bad girls."

Rodelle Weintraub, former assistant editor of *SHAW,* has edited *Fabian Feminist: Bernard Shaw and Woman, SHAW 5: Shaw Abroad,* and the Garland *Captain Brassbound's Conversion.* She has also co-edited, with Stanley Weintraub, two Bantam volumes of Shaw's plays: *Arms and the Man & John Bull's Other Island* and *Heartbreak House & Misalliance.*

Stanley Weintraub is Evan Pugh Professor Emeritus of Arts and Humanities at Penn State University and Adjunct Professor at the University of Delaware. A member of the *SHAW* editorial board, he edited the *Shaw Review* and *SHAW* from 1956 to 1990. He has written or edited more than twenty volumes about or by Shaw.